'*Document and Eyewitness* is an essen
involved in or influenced by the punk maelstrom of 1976, a riveting evocation
of a period in musical history that becomes more important the further we
get away from it … Taylor's book is a joy … If you read one music book
this summer, make it this one'   Dylan Jones, *Independent*

'*Document and Eyewitness*'s treatment of its main players is affectionate-
going-hagiographical, but the implication of that end-point is inescapable.
The journey from the mid-70s to now denotes the arrival of an altogether
duller world: music that tends to be reverential rather than iconoclastic'
Guardian

'Taylor knows his stuff, painting a picture of a chaotic organisation with a
good heart … a story that's fascinating and entertaining in equal measure'
Big Issue

'The Fall and The Smiths – even if these were the only bands Rough Trade
had signed it would be worth a 400-plus page book like this'
Manchester Evening News

'Long overdue … The type of reader who buys rock biographies will crave
the detailed information that spans the late 70s to 1991 – and they will not
be disappointed'   ****, *Record Collector*

Neil Taylor was born in Sutton Coldfield and now lives in Winchester. Once an NME journalist, for some time he has worked as a publisher and literary agent and, more recently, he founded the digital publishing company Ink Monkey.

DOCUMENT AND EYEWITNESS:

AN INTIMATE HISTORY OF
ROUGH TRADE

NEIL TAYLOR

An Orion paperback

First published in Great Britain in 2010
by Orion
This paperback edition published in 2012
by Orion Books Ltd,
Orion House, 5 Upper St Martin's Lane,
London WC2H 9EA

An Hachette UK company

1 3 5 7 9 10 8 6 4 2

ISBN 978-1-4091-3558-6

Typeset by Input Data Services Ltd, Bridgwater, Somerset

Printed and bound by CPI Group (UK) Ltd, Croydon, CRO 4YY

The Orion Publishing Group's policy is to use papers that
are natural, renewable and recyclable products and
made from wood grown in sustainable forests. The logging
and manufacturing processes are expected to conform to
the environmental regulations of the country of origin.

www.orionbooks.co.uk

To Frankie Freddie Tilly Ivo

'And these images – what do they deal with? I do not claim that they represent truth – they are too varied, even contradictory, for that. But they represent human experience ...'

Humphrey Jennings,
Pandaemonium: The Coming of the Machine As Seen by Contemporary Observers

'One of the feelings was that you were part of a very special elite group that was outside and downtrodden. You felt like you were part of a different community, a more secretive one ... I know in my mind I am still a member of the secret community. I might be the only one ...'

Bob Dylan

CONTENTS

AUTHOR'S NOTE

This is a work of collective remembering. It draws upon the testimonies and recollections and in some cases personal artefacts of many of the principal characters who together help make up the Rough Trade story. It is a work told largely in the words of the participants and entirely from their viewpoint. The formidable soundtrack that this extraordinary group of people helped to create is also the story, but one that has been more comprehensively dealt with elsewhere.

For nearly thirty-five years, Rough Trade has been at the vanguard of contemporary music and a settled historical view of it has emerged: that of an ethically minded, idealistic, radical record business that set out to redefine the market on its own terms – and did so spectacularly successfully – only to be knocked back by a combination of overly rapid growth and naïve business management, to then once more rise up again in an altered form and have even more success than first time around.

Many of the best independent artists found their start or did their best work, and often both, on Rough Trade – Cabaret Voltaire, Subway Sect, The Fall, Scritti Politti, The Pop Group, This Heat, Essential Logic, The Raincoats, Swell Maps, Robert Wyatt, Young Marble Giants, The Smiths, The Sundays, The Strokes, British Sea Power, The Libertines, Sufjan Stevens, Eddi Reader, Antony & The Johnsons, Emilíana Torrini, and Micachu & The Shapes, to name but a few. An equally impressive and even larger number of artists were beneficiaries of Rough Trade Distribution, which, prior to its collapse in 1991, handled, among thousands of others, releases by Rough Trade's own acts as well as those by Joy Division, Crass, Depeche Mode, The Specials, Pigbag, Orange Juice, Throbbing Gristle, the Cocteau Twins, Yazz, and The KLF, whose collective record sales number in the many tens of millions. Although an echo of the music of those artists resonates through *Document and Eyewitness*, the book aims primarily to be a work of social history, one that tells the (often-overlooked) stories of the people who, in helping the musicians to create the music, lovingly created something different and every bit as enduring.

The book retells the Rough Trade phenomenon in a largely critique-free way – *Mass Observation*-style. Part One, which briefly stretches back to the mid-1960s and ends at the time of the move to Blenheim Crescent in winter 1980, is an entirely eyewitness account. Parts Two and Three use documents and eyewitness accounts and take the story from Blenheim Crescent, through Rough Trade's time at Collier Street and Seven Sisters Road, up until the company's collapse in 1991. In these sections I have made use of an extensive if somewhat incomplete and random archive of original documentation, which Richard Scott rescued on leaving the company in 1988. Infuriatingly, the archive material relates largely to the years 1981 to 1989, with a few useful exceptions. Information from the documents is used in footnotes to illustrate/confirm/contradict the accounts of the main text. Very occasionally I have used other footnotes to explain some event that may now have been forgotten or have occurred too long ago for certain readers to recall, such as the inner city riots of 1981 and the nurses strike of the following year. Prior to Part Four, which reverts to eyewitness and is an account of contemporary Rough Trade, there is an interlude that deals with the inbetween years.

There are, as in any book of this kind, absences and omissions, which are largely arbitrary and accidental. There were a small number of musicians with whom I tried, and failed, to engage. There were also a number of Rough Trade employees – the real heroes of the story – who I didn't reach or who declined to be interviewed: their absence I regret more.

History is – as they say – a lie agreed upon. Everybody I interviewed for *Document and Eyewitness* had a different view of what represented *the* Rough Trade story: yet none of them can deny the lasting contribution they collectively made and continue to make to the culture they helped to create.

Neil Taylor, spring 2010

CAST (AS THEY APPEAR)

Geoff Travis – founder, Rough Trade; Jackie Rafferty – sister of Geoff Travis; Alan Travis – brother of Geoff Travis; Vivien Goldman – journalist; Jo Slee – housemate of Geoff Travis, Rough Trade Custom Leather employee; Jon Savage – Rough Trade customer; Carolyn Holder – textile designer and partner of Geoff Travis; Peter Travis – father of Geoff Travis; Steve Montgomery – Rough Trade employee; Pete Flanagan – Harlequin Records employee; Savage Pencil – Rough Trade customer; Sandy Robertson – Rough Trade customer; Richard Boon – founder, New Hormones; Peter Walmsley – Rough Trade employee; Richard Scott – Rough Trade employee; Robert Christgau – journalist; Daniel Miller – musician, founder Mute Records; Richard H. Kirk – musician; Green Gartside – musician; Mayo Thompson – musician, Rough Trade employee; Simon Edwards – Rough Trade employee; Gina Birch – musician; Ana Da Silva – musician; Patrick Keiller – musician; Shirley O'Loughlin – Rough Trade employee; Pete Donne – Rough Trade employee; Tom Vague – Rough Trade customer; Joly MacFie – proprietor, Better Badges; Slim Smith – designer; Robert Wyatt – musician; Steve Jameson – Rough Trade employee; Dick O'Dell – proprietor, Y Records; Gareth Sager – musician; Mike Hinc – Rough Trade employee; Chris Williams – Rough Trade employee; Charles Hayward – musician; Chris Cutler – proprietor, Recommended Records; Doug Kierdorf – Rough Trade employee; Jim Moir – Rough Trade customer; Patrick Moore – Rough Trade employee; Tony K – founder, Red Rhino Records; Lloyd Harris – employee, Revolver Records; Bob Last – founder, Fast Product; Johnny Appel – founder, Backs Records; Geoff Davis – founder, Probe Records; Johnny Marr – musician; Robin Hurley – founder, Red Rhino Midlands (Nine Mile); Sandy McLean – founder, Fast Forward; Tony English – lawyer; John Duguid – musician; Marek Kohn – journalist; Jeannette Lee – Rough Trade employee; Don Letts – manager, Acme Attractions; David Whitehead – Rough Trade employee; Jeremy Boyce – Rough Trade employee; Duncan Cameron – Mute Records employee; George Kimpton-Howe – Rough Trade employee; David

Murrell – employee, KPMG Peat Marwick; Martin Mills – founder, Beggars Banquet Records; Eddi Reader – musician; Jarvis Cocker – musician; Clare Britt – Rough Trade employee; Patsy Winkelman – Rough Trade employee; Bernard Butler – musician; Cathi Gibson – Rough Trade employee; Dai Davies – employee, Sanctuary; Joe Cokell – employee, Sanctuary; Jeffrey Lewis – musician; Ben Ayres – Rough Trade employee; Martin Noble – musician; Stuart Murdoch – musician

BEFORE

PART ONE:

202 KENSINGTON PARK ROAD

ROCK 'N' ROLL MECHANICS

'We figured we could change the world, or at least our little corner of it, and in so doing we would take one step forward for everybody.'

Steve Montgomery

Rough Trade emerged out of that marvellous, miasmic, and – in terms of pop culture – largely unexplored, period of the mid-1970s. It was in this age of inbetweenism that the early Rough Trade pioneers honed their ideals – which were anti-establishment, collectivist, communal-influenced, pro-feminist, egalitarian. The ideas of the late 1960s underground, which influenced Rough Trade (and came before), were in remission, and the attitudes and postures of punk, which altered it (and came after), had yet to be developed.

Geoff Travis returned from travelling in America in the late autumn of 1975 and, after a false start in Kensal Rise, opened the Rough Trade shop at 202 Kensington Park Road in West London in February 1976, almost to the day that the Sex Pistols first appeared in the national music press.[1] Punk changed Rough Trade in much the same way that it changed the rest of the music business and it is likely that had punk not emerged, the shop would not have survived. The economy was in a lamentable state as Prime Minister Harold Wilson slipped out of office in March and handed over control of the failing state to Jim Callaghan. Unemployment had reached the unprecedented and then staggering figure of one million and not long after, fuelled by the rigours of living through one of the hottest summers on record, the frustrations of certain sections of the community, particularly those in the inner cities, manifested itself in a series of disturbances. The most prominent of these was the riot at the Notting Hill Carnival, the direct result of confrontational policing and a subject later immortalised in the Clash song 'White Riot'.

Almost three and a half decades later, it is that early, frustrating, combustive and ultimately creative period which for some most defines Rough Trade. Indeed, as early as the start of the 1980s, Rough Trade already evoked a *notion*, an aspect of the late 1970s that was and remains instantly

1. *NME*, 20/02/76.

recognisable. In any decade, only a handful of enterprises will go on to become such ciphers – in the 1970s, it was Rough Trade, *Sniffin' Glue*, Sex, Acme Attractions and Compendium which mirrored the status afforded Middle Earth, *International Times*, *Oz*, Granny Takes A Trip, Indica Books and the Arts Lab from the decade before.

Geoff Travis tribally describes himself as being 'between the cracks'. He wasn't a punk, he wasn't a hippy. And when Rough Trade opened, it could certainly not count itself amongst the tiny handful of originators for whom punk was already a living reality. The shop self-consciously resembled an end of the hippie-era emporium. There was a wagon wheel adorning the building, which allegedly drew Geoff Travis to the premises, and in the window hung the original swirly Rough Trade sign that had been designed and stencilled on plywood and hand cut using a fret saw by Geoff's original business partner Ken Davison, modelled somewhat on the work of Roger Dean.

There were some lugubrious potted plants and a table and chairs. There were new records and second-hand records. (Leftfield singer-songwriters such as Jackson Browne and Kevin Coyne shared space with arty mainstream bands like 10cc and Steely Dan and the usual heavyweights, a smattering of bootlegs and a lot of reggae. Crucially, there were also the early manifestations of both Geoff's taste and his trip to America in the form of a reasonably large amount of garage rock 'n' roll.) For a time, according to both Jo Slee and Steve Montgomery, two very early Rough Traders, they even had a rental section, hoping to capitalise on the fact that recordable tapes had recently become commercially available.

Reggae was the first type of music to distinguish Rough Trade and 1976 was a vintage year with extraordinary albums released by, amongst many others, The Abyssinians (*Satta Massagana*), Bunny Wailer (*Blackheart Man*), Augustus Pablo (*King Tubby Meets Rockers Uptown*) and The Mighty

Diamonds (*Right Time*), all of which Rough Trade stocked. Reggae was particularly important for a shop keen not to be seen as a cultural interloper in an area dominated by a West Indian community.

Initially – at least after a month or two – there were two businesses operating from the premises. Front of house was the principal concern of the Rough Trade record shop but in the back there was the lesser-known Rough Trade Custom Leather (with its own post-hippie swirly sign designed by Jo). John Kemp had been Geoff's best friend at Cambridge University and ran the leather workshop in the shed out of the back of the shop along with his partner Jo Slee. They sold leather boxes and belts, hand-made shoes and sandals and clothing, which they had taught themselves to make the previous year in Amsterdam. John had salvaged materials for the shed from across the road when a row of Victorian dwellings – once the election offices of Fascist sympathiser Oswald Mosley – had been demolished.[2] It was rudimentary, exposed to the elements and lacked heating.

*

Geoff Travis had gone up to Churchill College, Cambridge, in 1971 and met John Kemp, the son of an English nuclear physicist, on his first day. By their second year, they shared part of a sprawling rented house in Huntingdon Road and had met Jo Slee, who had answered an ad for a spare place in the house which she'd seen on the Grad Soc noticeboard. She was staying at Girton College with a friend, having run away from her husband in Cornwall. Although not a student – for a brief period she gained implausible employment measuring grass for the National Institute of Agricultural Botany – Jo Slee fell into the student life and went to concerts with Geoff and John.

After graduation in the summer of 1974, John and Jo went travelling, first to Amsterdam. By November they ended up in a house in the draft-dodgers region of downtown Toronto. Back in England, Geoff meanwhile had gone off to teacher-training college and was about to undergo a famous *Dice Man* moment when he decided, while waiting for the bus to take him to college, that if the bus didn't arrive in the next five minutes he would throw it all in and go and do something else. The bus duly failed to arrive.

Geoff Travis eventually wound up in Toronto at the house where John

2. Richard Scott, the creator of the Cartel, has said that his socialist aunt, Molly Empson, was responsible for the building of the old people's housing that now stands opposite 202 in her role as a senior civil servant in what was then the Ministry of Housing.

and Jo were living and it was there that he met Ken Davison. Ken was a music man, a guitarist and lover of photography, a wanderer who had spent large periods of time away from his native Newcastle and had acquired a worldy-wise air – he was that bit older – that settled easily on the other three. His great claim to fame was that he once knew, or had met or had played in a group with, Hilton Valentine from The Animals. This impressed Geoff.

Ken Davison (left), co-founder of Rough Trade, with Jo Slee and friends, Niagara Falls, 1975.

It was Geoff's plan to end up in San Francisco where he was to visit an old school friend, 'Big Al' Newman. 'Big Al' had been Geoff's school buddy and they often went together to see bands at venues such as the Marquee. Ken and Geoff got on well enough for Ken to decide to travel with Geoff at least part of the way to San Francisco before heading off there himself directly, and it was while on the road that Geoff started to plunder thrift shops for vinyl. As ever with Geoff, he acquired far more vinyl than he would ever be able to listen to, and so Ken suggested that the simplest solution would be to ship the stuff home and open a record shop. In a period when music was cooling its heels, there would be ample opportunity to listen to the records, relatively undisturbed by customers.

By the time Geoff and Ken returned to Toronto in the summer of 1975, the germ of the Rough Trade idea was starting to infect, but it was still not certain that it would be a record shop that would be opened. The four of them – Geoff, Ken, John and Jo – knew that they would do *something* together and they discussed the various options. Jo recalls the idea of a café/bookshop. This appealed to Geoff, who had been to visit Lawrence Ferlinghetti's City Lights bookstore while in San Francisco and had admired the customer-friendly vibe, a vibe he would seek to emulate at Rough Trade, where the table and chairs would encourage people to hang out without feeling pressured into buying. Back in Toronto, they went out to watch Carol Pope's rock band Rough Trade, a name that certainly stuck. At the end of the summer, with John's and Jo's visas long expired, they returned home.

Back in England, the first problem was where to live. In time-honoured fashion, the immediate solution that presented itself was squatting. By the mid-1970s, many tens of thousands of people squatted across Britain and – for most of them – squatting had largely become an exercise of necessity, due to unaffordable rents. In the 1960s, squatting had been radicalised, motivated by any number of causes and concerns: Gay Liberation, Black Power, Women's Lib, assorted political movements (Anarchist, Marxist, etc), Claimants Unions, and even the desire to set up radical community newspapers or food co-ops. The folk-devilic and romantic notion of Hell's Angels upturning their helmets at the Hyde Park Free Festivals to collect money for the squatters at the famous 144 Piccadilly squat, as had happened, had been supplanted by a grim reality.

Aside from some very detailed and site-specific accounts in underground magazines such as *International Times, Oz* and *Friends/Frendz*, and later in publications including the radical photography magazine *Camerawork* and the anti-racist fanzine *Temporary Hoarding*, information on squatting during the late 1960s and early 1970s is disjointed and there is only one, somewhat academic, unified account.[3] One of the few really good – albeit brief – portraits of squatting at this time was created by Twickenham Council, who were prescient enough to realise that the relatively large number of squatters in the borough had concerns that merited investigating.[4]

They found that people often squatted with the passive approval of the buildings' owners – as was the case with large building firms, who turned a blind eye (while it suited them) in the knowledge that property was less likely to fall into disrepair occupied than unoccupied. Squatters were victimised[5] yet they could be exemplary occupants, often paying their general and water rates. Squatters in the much-squatted Grosvenor Road in Twickenham in 1973, for instance, as well as tending vegetables and flowers and generally keeping their gardens neat, held a 'scrap art' exhibition, took

3. *The Squatters*, Ron Bailey (Penguin, 1973).
4. *Squatting in Central Twickenham – A Survey*, ed, Chris Whitehouse, 1973.
5. One of the more ruthless NIMBYs who pestered squatters in Twickenham was the Tory councillor George Tremlett, whose other occupation was writing pot-boiler biographies of rock stars.

communal meals and took an annual communal holiday at one of the major rock festivals. They set up a summer gala offering 'acoustic and electric music, video, Punch & Judy, a jumble sale, film, fringe theatre, free balloons, clowns and an art exhibition'. They even had their own postcard printed.

Geoff first squatted in Mile End with his girlfriend from Cambridge, Miriam. John and Jo found space in an enormous squat in Cornwall Terrace on Regent's Park, which was being run by Piers Corbyn, the self-styled 'king of the squats'. 'Always cold, always dark, always homeless, utterly grim,' is how Jo Slee describes her existence at this time. After the squat was broken into, while Jo was inside and John was away in Manchester, they moved quickly to another squat in Archway, which had the advantage of being near the flat where Geoff's sister, Jackie Rafferty, lived. They visited Jackie for the use of basic amenities, such as hot baths when they could stand the cold no longer, and often fell asleep on the rugs in the front room through exhaustion, but more usually gratefully accepted the free dinner she laid on for them and passed the night playing board games.

Geoff and Ken scoured West London for premises for a record shop, which Geoff had announced would be called Rough Trade, and initially thought they had found what they were looking for in Duddenhill Road, W10. John and Jo set about the back-breaking job of 'stripping ten layers of crap off the walls with a blowtorch'. They had barely finished their labours when a passing Polydor Records rep pointed out the hopelessness of the shop's position, which would attract virtually no 'passing trade'. After the meaning of the term was explained to them, they set about looking elsewhere.

When they discovered it, 202 Kensington Park Road was in so many ways ideal. Like much of what Rough Trade would come to represent, it was off-centre but not too off-centre, in the scene but detached from it, unassuming and self-sufficient.

*

The topographic fabric of London, W11, in late spring 1976, in places resembled a bomb site. The second issue of Jon Savage's *London's Outrage* fanzine, published ten months or so after, is a photographic record of the author having walked the area at the time to record its decay, and it brings home the bleakness and desperation – but also the beauty and the charm – of the area's desolation. Corrugated iron proliferated, spread like weed around the dilapidated housing stock, which was perfectly habitable save for the fact that years of council neglect had left it too expensive to repair. Pubs were boarded up and derelict. A rag-and-bone man,[6] thought to be the inspiration for *Steptoe & Son* – the BBC studios at White City were close by – still had a yard in nearby Frestonia, which was itself subject to a marvellous *Passport to Pimlico* moment when it declared itself an independent free state.[7] Children roamed abandoned, flattened sites where the occasional unexploded bomb from World War II lurked. The locals were a mix of Jamaicans, working-class whites (many of whose families had suffered in the previous decades at the hands of notorious slum landlord Peter Rachman), bohemians, artists and musicians.

A 1977 guidebook to the area lays claim to the fact that 202 Kensington Park Road was 'the country's first Head shop' but this is so unlikely as to be arbitrarily dismissed, although a Head shop of sorts had occupied the premises at one time.[8] Ten years earlier the epicentre of the underground had shifted west from the King's Road to Portobello Road and when Rough Trade opened, hippie vibes still lingered. Local hipster outlets, such as I Was

6. Said to be Arthur Arnold, whose scrap-yard was on Latimer Road.
7. The Republic of Frestonia occupied about eight acres of West London. Cleared artisans' dwellings were occupied by squatters for a couple of years and on 30 October 1977 they held a plebiscite and unilaterally declared themselves independent from Britain. They asked the United Nations for a peace-keeping force 'in the event that the GLC should invade'.
8. Among the more colourful local characters were Ron and Gloria, who ran the Wavy Lane provisions shop a couple of doors down from Rough Trade. Gloria, a formidable woman whose 'medicine chest' of uppers and downers she frequently dispensed to Rough Trade staff in need, had told Steve Montgomery that the arrival of Rough Trade had been a welcome improvement on previous tenants who sold 'drug paraphernalia'.

Lord Kitchener's Valet and the equally marvellously named record shop The Magic Phonograph, had disappeared. However, the underground news-paper *International Times* still had a presence at 2 Blenheim Crescent (above what had once been the old Family Dog shop and which up until recently remained the longest-running counter-culture premises in England), and also at 286 Portobello Road, where space was shared with Joly MacFie's badge-producing emporium Better Badges. Better Badges had serviced the hippie community and would go on to mass-produce punk badges and set up a punk fanzine printing service.

On the first day of trading, one of the first people through the Rough Trade doors, according to Jo Slee, was Steve Montgomery, who was squat-ting locally and filled in his days roaming the market. Steve would be the first in a long line of key people who, hanging around for a sufficiently long period, would eventually be offered a job at Rough Trade. There was an immediate rapport between him and Ken Davison (formed while Geoff was often out on buying sprees), whose insane passion for music (although allegedly not work) Steve could relate to. Ken's broadly left-wing politics, as well, chimed with Steve's, which were far more full-throttle. When, after a couple of months, Ken decided to pursue photography, he put Steve up as his replacement and Steve formally joined the fold.

Steve Montgomery is one of the most influential people to have worked at Rough Trade. His indefatigable spirit, relentless enthusiasm and dedi-cation – not just to the music but also the way in which the music would be sold, in terms of ethics and politics – defined Rough Trade and remains part of the basis upon which 'Rough Trade' has been perceived ever since. He was the first and loudest to vocalise the politics he shared with Geoff (who was every bit as politically committed, probably even more so – but perhaps not as *loud*) and which gave Rough Trade a distinct persona. He was also self-effacing and committed to the cause, and later became a celebrity in the shop (if such a thing could be said to have existed) through authoring very wittily the mail order catalogues, prompting droves of bedroom-bound souls to venture to 202 Kensington Park Road in search of the anonymous person they were sure was their soul mate.

For a long time, Rough Trade was just Geoff and Steve (with Jo occa-sionally helping out). Geoff would take care of the music: Steve would organise the shop. Steve had notepaper printed up – dubbing them 'rock 'n' roll mechanics' – and took care of postal enquiries that started to grow as the stock mutated. Geoff had been writing to like-minded souls further afield and as a result they were starting to receive the prototype examples of the coming singles explosion – records from Pere Ubu's David Thomas (who was sending over Hearthan label releases from Cleveland), from Greg Shaw (who was supplying stock from his Who Put The Bomp? label), and from Terry Ork (who was shipping over copies of the Television single he had released on Ork, 'Little Johnny Jewel'). Legendary distributor Larry Debay, who had set up Bizarre Records in Praed Street – probably the UK's first independent record distributor – and made deliveries out of the voluminous boot of his Mercedes coupé, was supplying material from the avant-garde French label Skydog, who had issued the two early Flamin' Groovies EPs, *Grease* and *More Grease*, both big shop sellers, as well as more 'legally vague' releases by Iggy Pop and the Velvet Underground.

In the very early months of the shop, Geoff trawled the pub rock scene – back to basics, *inbetweenism* – going on his own to supersize pubs such as the Hope & Anchor in Islington, the George Robey at Finsbury Park, the Red Bull at the Angel, the Bull and Gate at Kentish Town and the Dublin Castle in Camden, to see bands including Ducks Deluxe, Eggs Over Easy, Brinsley Schwarz (a particular pre-punk favourite), Chilli Willi and Kilburn & The High Roads.

What happened next is a well-told story. The Sex Pistols played the 100 Club for the first time in March: they appeared at the Screen on the Green (with The Clash and Buzzcocks) in August. In between these two dates, the pop-cultural world somehow got turned upside down. Patti Smith played the Roundhouse in May. The Ramones played the Roundhouse in June. Issue one of *Sniffin' Glue* appeared in July when the Damned also played the 100 Club, supporting the Sex Pistols. In September, Stiff Records released their first single, 'So It Goes' by Nick Lowe (although a couple of notable independent labels – Raw in Cambridge and Chiswick in West London – were well under way by then). It took some time for the consequences and effects of all of this to register and before it did Rough Trade ushered in the new by giving prominent space to the nascent but burgeoning fanzine scene.

*

Rough Trade was the first shop in London to stock *Punk* magazine, which they bought direct from its publisher John Holmstrom in New York and sold from its first issue (which came out one month before the shop opened in February 1976). But it was the home-grown literature of the revolution that they helped make famous. Between July 1976 and June 1983, when, to their eternal shame, the Rough Trade organisation officially stopped taking fanzines, they handled almost every fanzine produced in Britain (and many from abroad).

Fanzines were 'bulletins from the front line', a 'call to arms', written 'from inside the musical movement', that didn't seek to critique the moment. Although the early examples tended to be London-based, as fanzines proliferated they enabled Rough Trade to engage in the politics of decentralisation – something it would dramatically develop with the realisation of the Cartel, the independent distribution network tentatively begun in 1980 and formalised in 1982 – and enable people to hear voices (or, even better, rants) that would otherwise have gone unheard. They also furthered Rough Trade's love of community spirit.

Rough Trade would even help in the assembling of them – what Jon Savage calls the 'let's make a revolution out of loo roll' aspect. They encouraged potential buyers to sit at the table and chairs in 202 Kensington Park Road and browse the wares; and they encouraged fanzine editors to assemble their fanzines around the table as well.

Prior to the advent of the UK punk fanzine in July 1976, Britain hadn't lacked an alternative media in which discourses flowed unfettered by the restraints of establishment ownership. But by 1973, the more grand voices of the alternative press – *Oz* magazine, *International Times*, *Friends/Frendz* – were either obsolete or had gone missing. *Zigzag* marched cheerfully and obliviously on after that point but wouldn't offer much of a viable alternative voice until a staff mutiny forced it to take the punk line in 1977.

A number of thriving fanzines that existed between 1973 and 1977 (some went on longer and started earlier) fulfilled some of the services – they tended to lack the public-spiritedness and largely toeed the music-business line – that the best punk fanzines would later provide. *Supersnazz, Bam Balaam, Fat Angel, Hot Wacks* and *Dark Star* all variously provided an alternative medium if not always an alternative voice. West Coast, prog and Krautrock, troubadour solo artists in the Tim Buckley mould, or maverick singer/songwriters such as Tom Waits and almost anything post-Velvets, were their favoured editorial subjects: but some looked back to snapshot periods, covering mods, freakbeat and other hard pop areas. These fanzines looked the same and they were assembled in the same way as those that came after.[9]

Because fanzines were free voices, uncensored, there was initially a variety of both voice and style. The earliest punk fanzines the shop stocked were Mark Perry's *Sniffin' Glue*, Tony D's *Ripped & Torn*, Sandy Robertson's *White Stuff*, Adrian Thrills's *48 Thrills* and Jon Savage's *London's Outrage*, which was the first fanzine to print the Rough Trade address as a point of contact on its cover.[10] Pretty soon the net was cast beyond these largely London-centric examples and trawled in regional fanzines such as the exceptional *Gun Rubber* from Sheffield. Other fanzines that sold well enough to be included in the early mail order catalogues included Shane MacGowan's *Bondage, Shews, Jolt, Situation Three,* and *Flicks*.

Being, as they initially were, largely a response to the live scene, early fanzines tended to lack any kind of political content. This infuriated Steve Montgomery, who detected a vehicle through which suppressed views might be expressed. He came close, allegedly, to being allowed to guest-edit 'a Maoist issue' of *Sniffin' Glue*, but it didn't go anywhere: later he

9. Richard Boon, who set up New Hormones and worked for eight years at Rough Trade, first in production and then as editor of *The Catalogue*, produced, along with his friend Howard Trafford (later Devoto), the 'proto fanzine' *Bullsheet* while still at Leeds Grammar School. As well as boasting 'ten pages of news and info, rock n roll, black power, art, life and laughter', the first issue also extracted – for the first time in the UK – Bob Dylan's *Tarantula* and, for some reason, noted not just upcoming concerts but also events at Leeds Model Railway Club: '... a private joke', according to Richard.

10. Very important. Fanzine editors and later record DIY-ers invariably printed the Rough Trade address on their wares, actively encouraging what former journalist Vivien Goldman has called *les marginals* to do Rough Trade's A&Ring for it. After Daniel Miller had released his Normal single he claims to have become a record label by default. Having printed his address on the sleeve of the record, he was immediately swamped with demo tapes.

would issue an edict saying that all fanzines to be featured in the mail order catalogues would be scrutinised for content and only those considered most suitable would make it onto the mail order list, although the terms weren't defined.

By the end of 1976, the effect of the so-called punk explosion was manifesting itself as more and more seven-inch singles were finding their way into Rough Trade, and the legendary Rough Trade wall was starting to take shape. Records released by Stiff, Chiswick, Raw, Private Stock, Sire and those sourced worldwide by Geoff, filled up this wall. Two independent records only available on import bookended Christmas 1976 and New Year 1977. 'X Offender' by Blondie and 'Love Goes → Building on Fire' by Talking Heads sold in their hundreds over the festive period at Rough Trade and signalled that the major-label dam really had well and truly been breached.

*

In January 1977, when Buzzcocks released their DIY *Spiral Scratch* EP, a record primarily distributed by Rough Trade, it was the start of an era that would transform the Rough Trade shop from being merely a well-stocked provider into something far beyond that: it would become a nexus point for information. Like the record itself – full-spirited, ambitious, revolutionary and fiercely independent – Rough Trade would become impossible to ignore.

During the first half of 1977, the fruits of the revolution were abundant and the shop filled up with both records and, more importantly, customers. By late spring it became clear that Geoff Travis and Steve Montgomery couldn't cope with the demand. As well as the records sold through the shop, they had started a mail order business and were constantly fielding calls from other record shops looking to buy any overstocks.

Richard Scott joined Rough Trade in June 1977, brought in ostensibly to help develop reggae. In fact, he put himself to work on mail order. The former co-manager of reggae band Third World, Richard would go on to be the architect of the Cartel. One of the earliest things he is also responsible for was redesigning the Rough Trade letterhead. A previous logo had been created by Steve Montgomery as a rubber stamp for the shop's brown bags. Richard recreated the image at his kitchen table using his son's John Bull Number 3 printing kit for use on the letterheads. In its various distressed (or otherwise) states it remains today the most enduring symbol of the Rough Trade 'brand'.

Prototype version taken from Richard Scott's notebook.

An architect by training, Richard Scott had taught at the North East London Polytechnic, and prior to that had also spent time in Canada, at the height of the first summer of love, the psychedelic manifestations of which he cheerfully admits passed him by. He, too, had returned from his travels with armfuls of vinyl: in his case, classical recordings on the Nonesuch label and field recordings collated and released by Alan Lomax.

He had collected seven-inches since the mid-1950s and when he moved to London from Oxford, with his wife and two children in 1971, he discovered reggae by record-collecting in junk shops and playing his finds on a Wurlitzer jukebox bought many years before.

When he set about putting his architectural training into practice, he formed, along with a couple of fellow graduates, the Electric Gypsy Road-show in 1971. This 'energy exploration' project looked into the future of cities, using Bristol as a model, with the intention of staging a festival – the Bristol Urban Microcosmic Propaganda Festival (BUMPF) – arranging a catalogue of 'comprehensive resources to help people', and 'an alternative control agency ... to provide the possible mechanics whereby user require-ment and choice become the major elements in environmental design'. Detailed in a spread in the underground newspaper *Frendz* in 1971, all of this echoes with his later work on the Cartel with Rough Trade.[11] A short time later, he set up the Last Museum, 'a museum of environments' in Allen Road, Hackney, before going off to manage Third World.

In some respects, 1977 became a year of expansion *and* consolidation for Rough Trade – expansion in the sense that the exponential growth in the singles market meant that every day, seemingly, there was a new band, a new future legend, a new box of singles (often arriving unsolicited) to deal with, and consolidation in as much as they had to start learning how to deal

11. Anyone wishing to explore this further should look at the November 1971 issue of *Archigram* magazine, which has a brilliant and extensive essay on rock festivals as moving cities, including the IOW, Bath – 'the Hippie Ascot' – and Mick Farren's Phun City.

more professionally with what they were increasingly co-responsible for creating. By the end of 1977, staff numbers had doubled and by the end of 1978 they would have not just a shop but also a booking agency, a record label and a nascent distribution company.

Rough Trade released twelve singles in 1978 and they remain an extraordinary testimony to the A&R skills of both Geoff Travis and other Rough Trade staff. The records are deliciously eclectic, from the inaugural, metallic French punk of Métal Urbain's 'Paris Maquis' through to the suburban experimentalism of Swell Maps' 'Dresden Style'. Field recordings allegedly made at Heathrow (by File Under Pop) found a home among the dub reggae of Augustus Pablo, the Dada-esque interpolations of Cabaret Voltaire and the oddly normal eccentricity of the Monochrome Set. There were also at least three unequivocally classic releases in Subway Sect's 'Ambition', Electric Eels' 'Agitated' and Swell Maps' 'Read About Seymour'. There were two defining singles as well from Stiff Little Fingers, who would go on to provide Rough Trade, and the independent industry, with its first mainstream Top Twenty chart success in the following year.

By 1978, 202 Kensington Park Road had started to fill up in a way that Geoff Travis could probably never have imagined in spring 1976. The customers were only one contributing element – there was also a steady stream of major-label A&R men, surreptitiously sniffing around for a hint of the future or else blatantly begging to be guided in its direction; there was a constant flow of people picking up records and dropping them off, people bringing and taking away fanzines, and there were musicians, many of whom looked to Rough Trade for the most basic guidance. The shop, in conjunction with Scritti Politti, who would go on to be one of their major artists, produced a stapled aid in the form of *Making Your Own Record – A Temporary Guide*,[12] which they sold over the counter and included in packages to other shops, distributing hundreds in the process and disseminating valuable information country-wide.

Back in 1977, the mainstream music press, like the mainstream record labels, had been slow to spot a trend and even slower to let go of it once it no longer merited attention. The endless 'punk round-up' articles would continue well into the start of the next decade,[13] long after those with their fingers on the pulse-beat had lost interest. Staff at *Sounds* had nearly mutinied in November 1977 when asked by their editor to yet again come up with a new punk music round-up. Instead, what they produced was a two-issue special on electronic music, which jumped the gun on their competitors and brought to the attention of their reading public a whole gamut of seemingly punk-contrary music: Disco, The Residents, Throbbing Gristle, Devo, Kraftwerk, Siouxsie & The Banshees and much else.

12. Why it was 'temporary' isn't apparent.
13. The *NME* in 1983 had even come up with a variant, when the punk moniker was well and truly looking beyond revival, and ran a cover story on a 'genre' it effectively and – for a short period successfully – created, 'positive punk'. In essence, the 'movement' was later co-opted into goth.

If Rough Trade as an organisation became for a period the barometer – the dead weight for independent music – then 1978 was arguably its most important year. Alongside its own releases, Rough Trade distributed and/or sold an extraordinarily inventive range of music that could scarcely have been contemplated less than a year before. Music by The Residents, The Normal, Thomas Leer, Robert Rental, Throbbing Gristle and a number of other non-label proponents, as well as Rough Trade's own Cabaret Voltaire, was potentially more radical than anything created by the punk movement that had in a lot of cases inspired it. The future was whatever you imagined it to be. Progress took the shape of believing in something previously unbelievable.

The 4th May 1979 changed, of course, a lot of things. For some, the election of Margaret Thatcher, and the concomitant, vigorously encouraged age of selfishness it ushered in, marked the real end to the 1960s, to the values and ideologies upon which Rough Trade had largely been based. It is no accident that punk purists cite 1979 as the year when many of the ideas and aspirations that inspired independent music got emasculated in the muscular beliefs of some key players who recognised that here was a market ripe for exploitation. Marginal became marginalised.

Ironically, and with no such motivations, Rough Trade became that year the first independent label to have a Top Twenty record when it released its debut album, *Inflammable Material* by Stiff Little Fingers. This reached Number Fourteen in the charts (one place above Barry Manilow's *Greatest Hits*), and in the process sold 115,000 copies. The first of two Rough Trade package tours was arranged on the back of it and such was the impact of Rough Trade at the time that the *South Bank Show* filmed a programme about them.

Broadcast in March 1979, the Rough Trade *South Bank Show* remains a wonderfully fresh document, an almost innocent depiction of a scene that would shortly become over-analysed and hackneyed. The very fact that the programme was made indicated that Rough Trade had reached a crossroads. Over the next few years it would go on to have what some see as its most enduring creative success. In so doing, it would also set itself some formidable challenges.

CHAPTER ONE:

PRE-1976

'It poured down with rain and a
Rolls-Royce pulled up'

Big Jeff/Little Geoff – Rock 'n' roll and other early influences – Beatles at
Poll Winners' show – Venues – Record stores – America – Festivals –
Cambridge – Canada – Ken Davison – John Kemp – Squatting – Duddenhill
Road – Rough Trade

Geoff Travis: I was about seven or eight when my cousin Jeff came over
from Canada with his father to stay with us for a while after his mother
died. At first I didn't realise that he had effectively come to live with us and
wasn't aware of the family trauma: I thought he'd just come to visit. He
was about ten years older than me. Jeff had a record player and a box of
records which he'd brought with him. We sat and played those records for
hours and hours. I remember he had records by Buddy Holly, the Everly
Brothers, Freddie Cannon, The Crickets, other rock 'n' roll stuff. I can
vividly picture the scene now. They were the first records I heard and in the

end I played them more than Jeff did. I fell in love with them. That was the earliest influence, 1959, 1960.

My older sister Jackie was into music and had quite cool taste for the time, and that would have influenced me. Most people were into Cliff and Elvis but Jackie had records by Muddy Waters, Chuck Berry and Bo Diddley as well. And obviously I heard those getting played. Jackie would later chaperone me to some amazing concerts.

Jackie Rafferty: Jeff was about ten years older than Geoff and so they became Big Jeff and Little Geoff: we also had a neighbour called Alan and our brother Alan, who was younger, so they became Big Alan and Little Alan, very funny. Because of the circumstances, it was quite a strange time and I'm not sure that there was much of a connection between Jeff and Geoff, apart from the records, which had a real effect on Geoff. I do remember, though, Jeff teaching me to jive.

Geoff Travis: We grew up in Finchley in a normal, pretty middle-class Jewish family. Although we weren't Orthodox – we were far too dysfunctional for that – my religious upbringing for a while was quite intense and I would go to Hebrew School on Sundays, and on Monday night and Wednesday night. I ate separately from the non-Jewish children and used to have to go to the synagogue for school dinner. I remember that on High Holy Days – just on High Holy Days, as I recall – Frankie Vaughan would come to the synagogue and that would cause a frisson of excitement to go round the place. The family name, which was anglicised to Travis, was actually Tuchinsky (some people later mistook it for Tchaikovsky) and my grandfather's family had come to England from Russia in the 1930s to escape the pogroms.

Jackie Rafferty: My mother helped out in my grandparents' shoe shop in Hackney on Saturdays and my father, who was a loss adjustor, would often have to work that day. So, sometimes, I would be in left in charge of taking Geoff and Alan over to the shop to meet up with them. I was twelve, Geoff was nine, Alan was six and I would take them on three separate buses from Finchley to Hackney. Geoff liked being in the shop and he liked going to the market, which was near the shop. There was a stall he went to where he could exchange comic books and we would all go to the local park, which had swing-boats and a real parky with a peaked cap. My grandfather liked to bet on the horses and occasionally, if the shop was busy, Geoff would be the one sent in to put the bet on.

Geoff Travis: After primary school I went to Dame Alice Owen's School, which was then still in Islington. It was a grammar school that also took some local kids so it was an interesting mix of suburbanites and ruffians. My younger brother Alan also went there. Viv Berger was at our school and he later went on to be one of the guest editors of the notorious school kids issue of *Oz* magazine, but my best friend was called Al Newman. Al was a great character, very funny and with a forceful personality, a giant who was up for anything: a bad influence on me in the best possible way. Al lived on a council estate between Highbury Corner and Old Street and I'd quite often spend time around there. We weren't the obvious match – he was working class, I was middle class; he was inner city, I was suburban. He was Catholic, I was Jewish. But it was good for me to have that broad experience. When we were seventeen we went on holiday together to Spain and drove there in a tiny Hillman Imp, which was quite cramped considering that I am over six foot and Al is at least six foot six. A Catholic organisation paid us to sell newspapers on the beach – I pretended to be Catholic – and we lived in a kind of commune. They wanted the locals and tourists to mix more and they thought this would help bring it about.

I used to go to a Jewish youth club in Woodside Park and one of the earliest concerts I remember seeing took place there, late spring 1965, when I went to see Unit 4 + 2, who had a hit with 'Concrete and Clay'. Just after that, in early June, Jackie took me to that year's *NME* Poll Winners' Concert at the Empire Pool, Wembley. Loads of people played – The Searchers, Moody Blues, Them, The Animals, Freddie and The Dreamers. The Rolling Stones played, The Beatles received their award and played and then The Kinks played, I think. We were in the third row from the back and could barely see anything, really, but when The Beatles came on there was this tidal wave of screaming that gradually came towards us. It was very exciting.

I'd already started buying records by then and at first I used to get them from the local electrical shop in Finchley. You'd have to walk through a shop full of cookers and fridges, washing machines, vacuum cleaners and televisions to the record booth at the back where, for a few shillings, you could pick up the latest Stones or Beatles singles. I bought everything by The Kinks, everything by The Yardbirds, everything by Jimi Hendrix, everything by The Who. And that was just for starters. Later I sought out all the new things I was reading about and my favourite record shops became Music Land in Dean Street and One Stop in South Molton Street, both of which, by about 1967, were starting to get in US imports. I used to visit them in my school lunch break, if I could. I also went to Oasis, which was in the basement of a tiny shop on Newport Court in Soho, and I loved the John Lewis sale: you could always turn up something unexpected. I started very quickly to also get an interest in music beyond rock – jazz, folk, which Al and I would go and see at Les Cousins, country, et cetera. I was never into a scene, I just liked the stuff that appealed to me. I was never a mod. I was never a rocker. I was never a punk. I've always been in between the cracks, really.

I used to work for the milkman in the mornings to get some money for records and I had a paper round – both short-lived; I was terrorised by dogs – but I never had enough money to buy all the records I wanted or to pay to go to all the gigs I wanted to go to. I remember one day, though, someone at school saying to me did I want to go and see 'Queen' and just because it was a concert, naturally, I said yes. I didn't care who it was. It turned out to be Cream and they were playing at the Saville Theatre with the Bonzo Dog Doo-Dah Band and The Action. It was a fabulous show, which John Peel compèred.

Jackie Rafferty: By his mid-teens Geoff was already a music nut. And it wasn't just records. We would sit down and avidly watch *Juke Box Jury* and *Ready Steady Go!* and the *Six-Five Special*, which was on at Saturday teatime. We listened to Radio Luxembourg and later to John Peel's *Perfumed Garden*. I know very early on he started buying alternative papers. As well as concerts, I took him to a few festivals. We saw Led Zeppelin in Bath in 1969, and in the same year we went to the Isle of Wight for that festival. We were hitching and planned to camp, but we didn't have much luck getting a ride until it poured down with rain and a Rolls-Royce pulled up and gave us a lift. They were going to the festival too and I remember we stayed with them on the ferry and they drove us all the way to the site in the Rolls. Geoff was obsessed with music. Later, when he went up to Cambridge, the joke about Geoff was that at night, just as he was falling into unconsciousness, his arm would come over and lift the needle off the record, and that in the morning, just as he was coming back into consciousness, it would lift it back on again.

Geoff Travis: I was doing reasonably well at school by the time I started sixth-form in 1968. I've never been a great socialiser and at school I was never that outrageous but in the sixth-form I took to wearing a green velvet jacket all the time. I thought it was the latest style but looking back it probably was ridiculous. I was doing my A levels and the headmaster was keen that I try for a place at Churchill College, Cambridge. They'd had one boy previously get in. I was sent with another boy called John Kotcher to study for the Cambridge entrance exam at the LSE library. I'd pelt off after to Soho to get in the queue for something maybe going on at the Marquee. I remember seeing The Who there in April 1968 and it was one of the best nights of my life. That was the first time I saw The Who. Real Who fans would have been seeing them every night they played in London. I wasn't one of the 'in' crowd. I was a suburban kid. But I felt lucky to be seeing them at all since the queue to get in was incredible.

I had started to be aware also of the counter-culture and had worked as part of the medical volunteer team at the anti-Vietnam march on Grosvenor Square a couple of weeks before. I remember we were given these armbands to wear and we tended the people who got trampled on or were caught up or were overwhelmed by it all. I was a great joiner of any political movement … I must have started buying *Oz* magazine and *International Times* and from then on I bought all of the alternative press stuff. Thinking back, it wasn't until the early 1970s that I really started taking an interest in the mainstream music press. When I went for my Cambridge interview (I had decided to study philosophy) they asked me what I had been reading on the train on the way up – they were probably expecting me to say something like Plato or Wittgenstein – but I decided to play it straight and said *Melody Maker*. I think, on reflection, it was the right decision to have been so disarmingly honest.

Nineteen sixty-nine was the year that I first went to America – I don't know how I found the money – on one of the more bizarre trips of my life, as it turned out. I had a good school friend who worked at the Co-op in Wood Green, selling records. He was as fanatical as I was and we used to share records and swap them. We decided to fly to New York. I remember phoning my parents just before we took off because I was expecting my exam results. We had absolutely no plans and didn't have a clue what we would do when we landed. But at that age, of course, you have an innate sense that you can go anywhere and find some like-minded people. We got off the plane and got talking to this guy who invited us to stay with him and his family in Queens. We thought Queens must be the centre of New York. We caught a bus and hung out with this guy and his Italian family who were just incredibly welcoming and hospitable. In the day we'd be in the basement of their house listening to Creedence Clearwater Revival and American rock radio, which was fantastic. Or we'd be out buying records from the local record store. That was a big musical trip. At night we'd wander around the old site of the World's Fair. We never even made it into Manhattan.

Nineteen sixty-nine was also a good year for going out and seeing bands. I went with Jackie to see Led Zeppelin at the Bath Festival and to the Isle of Wight to see Bob Dylan, but I remember a real highlight of the year also was when I went to see Soft Machine play at the Country Club on Haverstock Hill. Ten years later I would go on to work with Robert Wyatt, who is a truly remarkable individual. They were a thrilling live band. I also saw the Rolling Stones in Hyde Park in July, two days after the death of Brian Jones. I saw all of those free concerts in Hyde Park.

Just at the end of being at Owen's, I remember I went with my girlfriend Joy, who was at the Dame Alice Owen's Girls' School, to see Free, who I loved. Joy was a fantastic person who had a great, original perspective on things. She was totally unimpressed and thought they were a complete bunch of posers. I thought about it and realised, much as I loved their music and could put up with their posturing, she had a point and it taught me a lesson. Later, I went to a lecture Mick Farren gave at the London School of Economics when he was involved with the White Panthers and, apropos of nothing to do with the lecture, he took out a gun and started waving it around and said to us, in true revolutionary fashion, 'Before we start, I want to teach you how to clean your piece.' He proceeded to lecture us on how to keep the gun in good shape. It was really funny. It was totally absurd – everyone in the audience just found it absurd. I loved the Deviants but he just took himself *so* seriously. That was a moment left out of his autobiography. Another lesson.

If anyone wants to know what London was like in that period for me then I suggest they try to get a copy of the film *Bronco Bullfrog*, which Barney Platt-Mills made in 1969. It's an absolute classic. It's kind of a mod film, what went on to be called suedehead, about a couple of council estate kids who go off for a day out to the Wimpy in the West End and drift into a bit of petty crime. To me it was exactly what being young in London was like back then. There's no glamour in the film, no romance, it's quite inarticulate, but completely fascinating. And it sums up for me an element of what I was experiencing at exactly that time.

I finished at Owen's in the summer of 1970 and took a gap year before going to Cambridge. I had my interview for Churchill College: they wanted me to do an 'S'-level in English, a sort of extra hurdle, and I had to redo French. I had interviews at York, and Sussex too. Only a couple of boys from school got into university that year so it was a big thing. I was still studying but that was a period when I went travelling a bit. I met a Dutch girl called Ellen and went with her to Amsterdam and Utrecht, just hanging out really. I went out to see lots of bands and I did a lot of reading. I was a voracious reader and as a teenager I read a lot of political stuff – Marx and Trotsky. I tried to read Hegel but I didn't understand a word of it. I read some of the books that were around at the time: I remember Michael Horovitz's anthology of poetry, *Children of Albion*, which was a kind of English answer to the American Beat poets and had Alexander Trocchi,

Pete Brown and Michael X in it. I read Germaine Greer's *The Female Eunuch*, which had just come out, William Burroughs's *The Soft Machine* and *Junky*, George Jackson's prison letters, *Soledad Brother*, with the introduction by Jean Genet, whose stuff I also read. I read Balzac, Dostoyevsky, Céline, stuff by Nelson Algren, John Fante, Robbe-Grillet and Vladimir Nabokov. I loved *Ada* by Nabokov – thrilling! I remember Valerie Solanas's *S.C.U.M. Manifesto*, which had not long come out and was causing a fuss. Then, obviously, there was all the music mags and alternative press stuff. I played a *lot* of records.

Alan Travis: Nobody in the Travis family could play a musical instrument so it is quite a paradox that Geoff should have gone on to do what he did do. The family joke was that he was 'tone dumb'. In fact, I think we all were. I remember being taken by Geoff to see my first rock concert, when I was thirteen, when we went to see a band called Battersea Power Station. And I think I went with him and Jackie to see the Cream farewell show.

Jackie Rafferty: The point about the three of us was that we could only ever sing with each other because we *all* sang a half note out.

Geoff Travis: During my gap year, I went up to see Al a lot. He had started at Warwick University by then. It was while I was up visiting Al that I first met Vivien Goldman, who was also at Warwick and who had become a friend of Al's.

Vivien Goldman: 'Big' Al Newman was a friend of mine and he was also a friend of Geoff's. He'd invited Geoff up on one occasion and had asked me whether I would let Geoff crash on my floor in the hall of residence I was in. I was as interested in music as Geoff and we just rabbited on for hours and hours and a friendship was born. What were my first impressions? Tall and gangling. And he had that famous Afro. A piercing gaze. Very softly spoken. One of those intelligent people who know they don't have to shout about their intelligence. As we began to talk, I realised he was very fair and very committed, very obviously *socially* committed. Idealistic. He told me he had spent time on a kibbutz. I think that experience had given him a template, a way of behaving towards other people that would set up a blueprint for Rough Trade. Funnily enough, after that first meeting, I didn't really see Geoff much until after I left Warwick, when I ran into him in the street and he got me some tickets to see The Who. We got our friendship back on track and eventually he moved into my flat at 83a Cambridge Gardens and then came with me when I moved to 145a Ladbroke Grove, but that was much later.

Geoff Travis: I'd been to a kibbutz at quite an early age, about nine or ten. An uncle and aunt had emigrated from Leeds to Israel and got involved with a kibbutz in Haifa. This was very early on in the movement. So my parents sent me out and I loved it. I loved the communal experience. We ate breakfast communally, we sorted out a rota for what we would be doing. Some people might be working in the fields, riding the tractors, others inside cleaning up, doing the washing-up, or the laundry. We arranged fun things, too – sports events, that kind of thing. I gained quickly the romantic notion that here was equality; everyone pitched in to create this sort of utopian community. I liked that idea, I really did, and it made a big impression on me. I was made to feel really welcome there – everybody embraced me. I came away and the experience stayed with me as a kind of way of living. I know later the whole kibbutz dream went sour and became commercialised and was used for political purposes. But what was good about it stayed with me and I am sure it became part of my wanting to set up Rough Trade as a cooperative.

*

Geoff Travis: University is parallel living: there's always the safety of home to run back to. My parents were very happy that I had got into Cambridge, and a bit bemused. The whole Oxbridge snobbery thing didn't occur to me. I went off to read philosophy but struggled after the first term. I found logic too difficult and that was a big part of the course. Eventually, I asked if I could switch and I was able to transfer over to English. Lucky. I had absolutely no career path in mind and I'm not sure that my parents had any burning ambitions for me either.

On the first day at Churchill College I met John Kemp, who went on to be one of the three really good friends I had at Cambridge. The other two were Miriam, who became my girlfriend for a while, and Jo Slee, who we all met later when she came to live in our house. John had been at Manchester Grammar School and was doing a course in sociology and social psychology. John's father was a nuclear physicist and had worked at Windscale, I think. I instantly got on well with John and loved his personality. Very warm, friendly, very funny. We immediately started spending a lot of time together. I remember part of John's course involved him having access to certain museums at nights and we used to go in and handle skulls and priceless treasures that ordinarily weren't to be touched. John was very sporty and we played football together, but whereas he would make the college first team I'd struggle to limp into the second eleven.

John Kemp, c.1972.

We spent the first year in halls, as you were required to do, but in the second year we moved out to a big house in Huntingdon Road, which had four or five bedrooms. Jo Slee came to live with us – I think we'd advertised a vacancy and she turned up one day and more or less moved in on the spot.

Jo Slee: I was twenty in 1972 when I first met John and Geoff. I had split up with my husband and run away from Cornwall. I hitched to Cambridge to visit an old school friend who was at Girton College. I wasn't going back. I slept on the floor at my friend's place for a while and then started to look around for somewhere more permanent. I saw this advert on the Grad Soc noticeboard for a shared house in Huntingdon Road. It was a 1930s council house – a lovely building.

John answered the door and we had a chat about the vacancy. He said that I should come back at dinner time when I could meet the rest of them and I asked if I should bring a bottle of wine. 'No,' he said, 'we might not like you.' I went back round and virtually moved in straight away. The other people in the house were Miriam, a woman called Helen and a guy called Dave. Every square inch of the house was put to use. I ended up having one of the rooms downstairs: Geoff and John in true student fashion shared a room upstairs. I remember – it may even have been on that first night – Geoff playing me *Exile on Main Street*, which he was very excited about. They had all these books in the room and it made me immediately conscious of the fact that I hadn't gone to university but Geoff put me at ease by saying that they hadn't actually read any of them. It turned out they never bought books, either; they tended to steal them from the main bookshop in town. It was apparent immediately that Geoff had a very generous spirit, was very gentle, and very nice. It was clear as well that he and John were well attuned.

Right from the start, John and I became soul mates. I loved his smile. I loved his high-pitched, slightly girlish laugh. He was incredibly funny and very opinionated in a sort of left-wing way. We were well matched and quickly got together. He told me everything about what it was like to be a bloke and I told him everything about what it was like to be a girl. I have suffered from depression and I remember early on having to teach him what moods were. He didn't understand why if he invited me out one night I wouldn't just come out.

Jackie Rafferty: Around about this time I went up to stay with Geoff in Cambridge for a while and moved in briefly. My first impression of John was that he was really very good-looking. I got the impression that either he put women on a pedestal or he just didn't really bother with them. I think his relationship with Geoff was interesting. Geoff was very reserved and I think I ended up talking to John more than Geoff the time I was there.

Jo Slee: We set up systems in the house. We had house meetings, a cooking rota, that kind of stuff. We tried to buy only from the food co-op: a sack of carrots, a sack of potatoes. Generally, the cooking would be something with brown rice, or lentils, classic hippie fare, but when it was Geoff's turn to cook, it was invariably the same thing: a fried egg each and a packet of crisps. Geoff would not touch any food that was green.

It was a happy house to live in. The only time we had a problem was when we let a traveller called Big John come and live with us. For a while he had been living in the disused bomb shelter at the bottom of the garden and I think we took pity on his plight and offered him a place in the house. But he started stealing food out of the kitchen and taking things like our bikes without asking and just dumping them wherever he was out. It took about sixty-three house meetings but we finally agreed to ask him to leave.

Geoff – even back then – wasn't too interested in the meetings and preferred to disappear up to his room where the thump of the Rolling Stones would start coming through the ceiling, letting us know that all was well.

Geoff Travis: I had always assumed that there would be a happening music scene in Cambridge: I thought Henry Cow would be playing somewhere every night. I quickly learned that you don't go to Cambridge for the rock 'n' roll! In fact, we more often than not would have to go back down to London for gigs. I had a moped and it took me about five hours to get back there – crazy. I remember, though, we saw a late incarnation of the Velvet Underground at St Margaret's Hall in Cambridge, where we also saw Captain Beefheart. That was good. I also loved Andy's Records stall in the market square. I spent a fortune there. And at Red House Records, another great shop.

Jon Savage: I went up to Cambridge in 1972 and I went to that same Captain Beefheart show. I was a sort of passing acquaintance of Geoff's really – he was pretty unmistakable with his hair – but we never really got to know each other till later. Red House Records was a rather small but beautiful record shop, which I went to all the time. I have a distinct memory of buying Neu! records there. I would see Geoff because there really weren't that many people in Cambridge who were as fanatically interested in music as we were.

Jo Slee: Geoff and John were also fanatical about film and I remember them trying to teach me all about American film noir, which they adored and knew everything about. Two of their favourite films – films of that moment really – were *Two-Lane Blacktop*, which had James Taylor and Dennis Wilson from the Beach Boys in it, and *Electra Glide in Blue*, the cops-on-bikes movie. They also got into college am-dram.

Jackie Rafferty: Churchill College put on a Neruda play and John, Jo and I got involved and it was one hell of a commitment. For some reason, I remember John played a cowboy in it.

Jo Slee: John and I went to watch Geoff in a performance of *As You Like It*. He appeared to be moving twice as fast as anybody else in the production. It was all rather wonderful and rather funny.

Geoff Travis: I went on tour with the Cambridge Players and we took a van to Ireland and performed a Yeats play and a play by Wole Soyinka. I had a small part in both of them. We went to visit Samuel Beckett's school in Enniskillen and performed *Dreaming of the Bones* there. It was tremendous fun. I mean, absolutely ludicrous, of course, a bunch of English people going to Ireland to perform Yeats ...

Jo Slee: Performance art – it was all happening then. John and Geoff had a friend, a rather well-off student, who refused to go back to college one term. Instead of talking him through it, the boy's father called the police and had him arrested! I never knew his real name – we came to know him as Dolmen – but he was part of an avant-garde theatre group who were in the process of changing their name from Transmedia Explorations to the more grandiose-sounding World Theatre. Six of them would travel the country in an old army ambulance performing *Finnegans Wake* in public. Dolmen would come and stay with us at Huntingdon Road when they were in Cambridge and when he did he slept in one of our trees. It all seemed part of the integral weirdness of Cambridge at the time. The leader was an Irishman, steeped in Joyce, whose cult name – and they were a cult – was Agoshaman. Agoshaman had for a short time been employed as artist-in-residence at Churchill College until it was discovered that he hadn't got a home and was, in fact, sleeping on top of the Art Department cupboards, at which point he was booted out. Other members included someone called Walter Sollywobble, who was so-called because, having a liking for LSD, he had gone out for some sugar one day and had not returned for a year. Agoshaman's girlfriend Umiak the Bear had thigh-length hair, which was never washed but regularly anointed with bay rum. She wasn't allowed to manage the money as she had allegedly once left £800 in a phone box. They had their own language and they made their own clothes. They were wonderful, marvellous, fascinating. John and I went to live with them later on for a short and slightly hair-raising time in King's Cross, where they had a squat.

*

Geoff Travis: I have always been more interested in the dissenting rather than the joining tradition, and at Cambridge I did get involved in what turned out to be the tail-end of the student protest movement. I took part in a few sit-ins and I deejayed one time when we had a protest at the Senate

House. I remember we protested about the Greek Colonels. We were always protesting about the university laws. And there would always be some guest speaker like Daniel Cohn Bendit or Tariq Ali turn up to lecture us.

Alan Travis: Being that bit younger, I kind of got to know the Cambridge people a little bit later. Now, I think that people like John Kemp, and Geoff's girlfriend Miriam, were key and had quite a significant effect on Geoff in terms of politics and how he brought it into play with Rough Trade. Geoff forged concepts like the collective working idea out of a kind of inter-pretation of the counter-culture ethos that was around Cambridge at the time he was there. Living in Cambridge in a large house with a large group of people, he was already living a collective lifestyle, anyway. University, as it often is, was like an experiment for what was to come later.

There were a lot of people around Geoff living their life in that communal way and there was a lot of Communist Party and broadly left affiliation – I mean Miriam came from a strong CP background. John was very political. Connected to their circle was Steve Hart, the son of the Labour minister Judith Hart, who resigned under Jim Callaghan, and he had very strong CP links. But whereas for some of them the politics was the only thing, for Geoff what was important was taking some of these ideas and using them to escape – to live his life how he wanted to live it.

I think this all showed Geoff that he could live his life the way he wanted to live it without necessarily having to go off and become a teacher, which was what was sort of attracting him at the time. He could make a difference *and* make it work for him.

Jo Slee: The era of student protest was largely over by then and anyway Geoff has always been more interested in music. Everything led back to that point. If you bought Geoff a birthday present, he'd accept it appre-ciatively, very politely ask you for the receipt, take it back to the shop and get the money back, and then spend the money on records. He generally only ever wore check or tartan shirts and it was a standing joke that he did once actually keep a tartan shirt John bought him for his birthday. Generally, Geoff was completely incapable of doing anything normal.

I lived a kind of suspended existence because although I shared their student life, I wasn't actually a student. I went on the dole for a while. I didn't realise it but I was clinically depressed at the time; the dole was the worst possible thing for me. Eventually, I got a job measuring grass for the National

Institute of Agricultural Botany – my first and possibly only real job.

At the end of that academic year I moved out of the house and went travelling for a bit with John. Afterwards, John and Geoff moved to the other side of Cambridge and, although I slept under their kitchen table for a while, I eventually got my own place. I think they had to put a lot more work into that third year and when the time finally came to leave, I don't think anyone had really thought about what they might do. To some extent we all came from dysfunctional backgrounds and John particularly seemed terrified of commitment. We had some tough moments. It could be really hard being with him. At the end of the final term I told him I had decided to move to Amsterdam and was fed up of the are-we-or-aren't-we-together bullshit that had been going on. To my surprise he just turned around and said, 'Can I come too?' That was it – off we went to Amsterdam and six months later we were in Canada.

But just after Cambridge and before Amsterdam we reacquainted ourselves with World Theatre. They were based in a collection of squats in Calthorpe Street near King's Cross. It was all very Dickensian, a group of townhouses linked together by runways that went over garden walls. They had their own blacksmith and a welding shop. It was like fantasy, but slightly sinister. It was a completely closed order and I think had it not been benign it would have been quite difficult to get away. When you arrived you were given a new name and encouraged to cut all ties with your past (except for any savings that might be lying around). My name was Coloroforme Brune, John's was Carthorse (they said he snorted and stamped his foot). A source of much inspiration and culture was *Finnegans Wake*. I thoroughly enjoyed the language (Islington was 'Isn't-linked-on' and the British Museum the 'Bruitish MuseeRoom', Calthorpe Street 'Cowthump Street', et cetera), and the adventure. But after three weeks the novelty of reinventing oneself from scratch rather wore off. John walked out, and I followed under cover of darkness two days later.

Some time earlier, Genesis P-Orridge, who would later find fame with Throbbing Gristle, was part of their clan but was thrown out for driving their ex-army ambulance up and down Oxford Street late at night and ringing the bell, attracting unwanted police attention. He was then called Otto, or Lemon, as he had shaved his hair into the shape of a lemon.

Geoff Travis: At the end of my time at Cambridge I really didn't know what I wanted to do. Some big things had happened to me there and when I look back now I think my relationship with Miriam was very important, because she later went on and had a difficult time, a terrible time and I think what we had was special. The first thing I did was to panic. I had no idea what I should do. I'd got a 2:1 overall – a first in my Modern paper – and it did cross my mind that I might become an academic or go into some research work or other. But I worried that there would be hideous politics in the world of academia and it also struck me as a slightly lonely life to be leading, which, given my own natural inclinations to be pretty non-sociable, probably wasn't a good idea. If I wanted to be anything at that point it was a writer, but I knew I wasn't going to turn into some sort of Black Mountain poet: I wasn't William Carlos Williams and was never going to be.

At that time, one of the big issues was feminism, something I was enormously sympathetic to and something which had a great effect on me. I enjoyed doing drama at college as well. It struck me that I might be able to do something that would combine my English and Drama experience with something positive, something more practical. Women's theatre groups at the time were often educative and informative, as well as being entertaining, and would give out information – say things on sexual health, personal politics – designed to help the audience. I thought I might be able to do something similar from a male perspective. I think it was on the spur of the moment then that I applied for and was accepted by Maria Grey Teacher Training College in Twickenham, where I started a teacher-training course.

I moved into a squat in Crouch End with Miriam and we later moved to one in Mile End and then to one in Camden. I didn't want to go back home after Cambridge and back then living in a squat was the natural thing to do. But not a lot of my contemporaries at college were doing it and so I seemed to be living this double life. It was an odd time for me. I wasn't taking drugs, didn't really smoke dope or anything and didn't have a lot of interest other than in the need to get money to buy records. I remember for a very short period having a job in a jam factory, but I really have no idea how I got the money to go to college.

Jackie Rafferty: I remember that when Geoff graduated he refused to go to the official graduation ceremony at the college and instead went to an unofficial one in Granchester Meadows, where a load of rock bands performed. I don't think he really knew what he would do when he left and for a while it was just him and Miriam together. I think Geoff got very close to

Miriam. I don't think Geoff has ever been close in that way to many people.

Geoff Travis: I started, as part of my training, going into schools to learn to teach and I loved that, standing up in the classroom and talking to the kids. But I hated the staff-rooms. I was just a misfit in them really. People would just look at my hair and single me out as not normal. For the most part, the teachers were small-minded Conservatives who just didn't give the kids enough respect. I saw myself as a classic left-of-centre radical and would encourage the kids to talk about whatever they wanted to talk about. I think the other teachers got a bit freaked out by me.

I was teaching at a girls' school in Mill Hill at the time I had my famous *Dice Man* moment. I walked out to the bus stop and waited for the bus to come to take me to work. When it hadn't arrived after a while I thought, I don't know if I really want to keep doing this. I decided to wait five minutes and if the bus came in that time I'd get on it and go to work and carry on with the course and maybe my life. If it didn't arrive, I'd chuck everything in. It didn't arrive.

*

Geoff Travis: I formed a loose plan to go travelling. The next day I caught a plane to Montreal to see a woman called Barbara Mackay. Barbara was the mother of an old girlfriend and had been a drama teacher at my school and was now working for a children's theatre in the city. I watched her give drama classes during the day and, since I had nowhere to stay, she let me stay overnight in the theatre. She would leave and lock me in. I didn't stay in Montreal for very long before moving on to Toronto, where I met up with Jo and John.

Jo Slee: In November 1974, John and I had moved to Toronto on tourist visas and ended up staying there about nine months. While we'd been in Amsterdam, John and I had learned how to make leather clothes and shoes. Geoff's friend Big Al Newman had come to visit us in Amsterdam – a lovely man, if a bit of a wild card – and we adored him. He was a great cook and used to rustle up fantastic vegetarian food. I remember he had absolutely huge feet and used to wear a kind of Mary Jane shoes for men, which you could buy in Holland at that time. When Geoff came to see us in Toronto he was on his way to visit Al, who by then was living in San Francisco.

Jo Slee and typewriter, Toronto, 1974.

The amount of money we had with us when he had moved to Toronto lasted us about a month and John and I had had to come up with a plan as to what we might do to get by. We used our last $60 to buy some tools and some leather and we began making simple things, boxes and belts and set up a little table on Yonge Street to sell them. We sat in the snow and eventually sold everything we made and doubled our money. We never made a fortune but from then on until we left that was how we supported ourselves. For me, this was a huge breakthrough for my confidence – I realised that as someone who couldn't face the idea of a 'normal' job, from now on, if all else failed I would be able to support myself by making these leather goods. I felt free – brave almost.

Geoff arrived in the summer of 1975. We were living in the draft-dodgers' region down on Sullivan Street and I remember Geoff sitting in our idyllic little back garden and reading Virginia Woolf to us. It was magic. In the house we shared, there was also a Geordie called Ken Davison, who was a bit of a wanderer. Ken was slightly older than us and had spent quite a lot of time travelling. I don't think he'd been home to his family in a long time. It felt to me that Ken didn't have any firm roots and maybe as a result of that, fairly quickly he fitted in with our little community.

Geoff Travis: I met Ken for the first time at John and Jo's and we got on well. He was a music man who played guitar and told me that back in the day he knew or had played in a band with Hilton Valentine from The Animals at home in his native Newcastle.

Jo Slee: Geoff and Ken certainly hit it off because when Geoff carried on travelling, at least for part of the way Ken went with him. And they met up again of course on the West Coast. Geoff set off for the States with a girl called Penny Riegle, who he'd met while he was staying with us. First of all they headed for Chicago.

Geoff Travis: The plan was to arrive in San Francisco and hook up with Big Al. We went to Chicago and visited the Biograph, the great rep cinema in which Al Capone had been shot, and we went to some of the legendary blues clubs where we saw nobody famous but where lots of guys tried to hit on Penny. I started buying thrift-shop records – they were just so incredibly cheap: a quarter, 50 cents, a dollar. After that, we hitchhiked all the way from Chicago to San Francisco to see Big Al and to meet up with Ken, who had gone on ahead there. Al was in San Francisco selling jewellery and leather goods.

San Francisco, for me, was this legendary city of Lenny Bruce, of Jefferson Airplane, of the City Lights bookstore. I was so excited about going there. But in fact when we arrived, there was this massive air of desolation about it. There were the dregs of the Haight Ashbury scene and, although the park was a great place to visit, the highlight turned out to be a free concert by Hot Tuna. I did get to visit City Lights and see Lawrence Ferlinghetti in there, but I didn't speak to him.

I met up with Al and with Ken and I was carrying on buying up the records. Ken asked me what I was going to do with all the records, although in truth there weren't *that* many, and he suggested that I open a record shop. Thinking about it now, although it was a suggestion of something *I* might do, he very clearly included himself in it as well.

Penny and I got a drive away back and delivered it to someone in Detroit. Then we hitched back to Toronto. People today might think it mad to have hitched but it was a more innocent age and the best bits always were being dropped in the middle of nowhere.

Jo Slee: They arrived back and we all sat around in the garden talking about what we might do. John's and my tourist visa had expired and all of us knew we would be going back to England. We all – Ken, John, Geoff and I – talked about what we might do. We thought we might work together and came up with a few ideas: a bookshop/café was one of them. But by then Ken had sowed the seed and Geoff only ever wanted the one thing and he won.

*

Jo Slee: So we all came back. Geoff went back to his parents briefly before starting squatting again. I think Ken squatted, too. I figured out that I would last no more than two days back at my parents', so John and I also looked for a squat. John was really good at squatting – for a nice middle-class boy he had nerves of steel. He was completely fearless about it and totally activist in the sense that he saw occupation as his right. This for me was the most depressing of times. It was winter when we arrived back so of course it was pretty miserable. There was a period when it seemed it was always dark, we were always cold and we were always homeless. It was utterly grim.

The Squatters' Handbook *had first been printed in 1973 and this, the third edition, came out just at the time when Geoff, John and Jo began squatting in London. Something rough was clearly in the West London air around this time. Inside are listings for the 'Rough, Tough, Cream Puff Estate Agency (founded 1281 by Wat Tyler) 217A Westbourne Park Road W11', and for the 'Rough Theatre, 32, Bravington Road W9'. Two 'squatters bands' are listed – The Derelicts, described as 'Non-sexist squatters rock band available for benefits in or out of London', and The 101ers, listed as 'squatters rock band c/o that tea room, 37, Great Western Rd'.*

John heard about a squat in Cornwall Terrace on Regent's Park which was being run by Piers Corbyn, the self-styled 'King of the Squats'. It was in a mansion block. We went over and were shown into a room which was the size of a ballroom. We had one mattress and two carrier bags' worth of belongings between us. It was a bit bizarre. In fact, our time there lasted less than a week and ended horribly.

John went to Manchester to visit his parents and I was in the squat on my own when a guy who was drunk tried to break in. I was absolutely terrified. He tried to kick the door in. I grabbed my purse, quietly unbolted the door, and stood behind it as this guy stumbled in, ranting. I ran outside and starting knocking on doors but no one answered. It was the middle of the night. Eventually, a black guy called Buddha, who was squatting in the basement next door, came out with a large African blade and went to investigate. About twenty minutes later he came back with the knife all covered in blood. He decided that as payment for rescuing me he ought to be given the reward of sleeping with me.

The other guy was eventually taken off for some stitches – someone had heard the altercation and had called an ambulance – and I had to just spend the next four hours using all my wiles to keep Buddha at bay until he fell asleep, which he did. I ran out without shoes, which I didn't bother to retrieve from the squat, and got the first tube over to Mile End, and woke Geoff, who came back to Regent's Park with me and helped me move my stuff. Years later I learned that Buddha, by trade a kindly nightclub bouncer, had been in Vietnam and had a metal plate in his head. John and I then found another squat in Archway.

Jackie Rafferty: I was living not far from Archway with my boyfriend in a flat we rented, one which therefore had heating and hot water and luxuries like that. Geoff used to come over and so did John and Jo and they would have lots of discussions about the future there.

Jo Slee: Archway for me was cold, full of traffic and ghastly. But Geoff's sister Jackie lived just the other side of the big roundabout and we used to go over there when we couldn't stand the cold any more. It had central heating – what heaven! We used to curl up on the rugs in the front room and often we'd fall asleep there, or we'd play endless games of Monopoly. Jackie would feed us dinner – she was so good to us. This was a time when my depression was very bad. Since returning from Canada, I'd been on the dole and because we were living in a squat it wasn't deemed a 'safe' address and so no cheques could be sent out there. On more than one occasion I stood in a phone box with 12p in my pocket, all the money I owned, waiting on hold for someone at the dole office to tell me when I could pick up my money. It put stress on our relationship and John and I had some melodramatic fights – throwing china and all that. I like to think we were acting it all out, but it was hard.

On one occasion we were at dinner at Jackie's when Geoff announced that the record shop would be opening and that he had thought of a name. In Toronto, we'd been out a lot to see Carole Pope's funk-rock band Rough Trade and I'm pretty sure that Geoff took the name from them, although he hadn't mentioned it before. He told us the shop would be called Rough Trade. He said that he and Ken were looking for premises. This would be around Christmas 1975.

Carolyn Holder: At the end of 1975 I was sharing a flat with Stuart Joseph, who had been up at Cambridge at the same time as Geoff and knew him from there. Geoff was just about to open the shop in Duddenhill Road, or had just done so – they may have got as far as decorating it, although I doubt Geoff would have done much of that. Geoff came and slept on Stuart's floor for a while. I was going out with somebody else and we didn't properly get together until probably a year or so after that first meeting. I remember going and seeing the shop they finally settled on and thinking how run-down it was.

Jo Slee: The first place they found was in Duddenhill Road, up near Kensal Rise, and they took over a lease and started to prepare the shop for business. John and I spent the whole of one night through to the morning stripping ten layers of crap off the wood-panelled walls with blowtorches. Ken got his saw out and started making some bins. And Geoff – I'm not sure what Geoff would have done, as he wasn't safe with a blowtorch – something useful in the background to do with records. We'd barely got the place in some sort of shape when a Polydor Records rep came in and asked us why we were opening there since there was no passing trade as such. After he'd explained what passing trade was, we abandoned the idea and jumped in a car and started looking for better premises.

Geoff Travis: John, Jo and I drove around and ended up in the Ladbroke

Grove area. We knew we couldn't afford a shop on Portobello Road – that would be too expensive – so we started looking around the roads near Portobello. We came down Kensington Park Road and the first thing we saw was the wagon wheel hanging outside 202. It really drew us in. By chance, the old occupants were on the point of moving out. So, fatefully, this was going to be Rough Trade.

CHAPTER TWO:

1976

'They were like four soft toys commandeered by
the Wicked Witch of the West'

Kensington Park Road – Paternal loan – Ken Davison – Steve Montgomery –
Leatherworks – Pub rock – Patti Smith at the Roundhouse – Ramones in-
store – Fanzines – Punk

Geoff Travis: 202 Kensington Park Road didn't need doing up too much
and after Duddenhill Road that was a good thing. It had been used as a
printing business and we were told that it had, in fact, been a Head shop.
It was much bigger and needed more stock. Ken and I had put in the
equivalent of about £2,000 each to cover the lease and stuff and I then got
a further loan from my father and bought some more records to fill up the
extra space. I'd heard that Red House Records was closing down, and I was
able to buy some stock. We had the records that I had brought back from
America, but when Rough Trade opened, most of the stock came from Red
House. They were the records they had been unable to sell. And we were
able to get those because my father lent me the money.

My parents were wonderfully non-judgemental about my career choice and never put pressure on me to do anything. All my heroes were counter-culture ones so, thinking about it, I was unlikely to be looking to go out and get a proper job. You could read that as an absence of parental care, or as the best possible encouragement that could be given.

Peter Travis: All in, I think I probably ended up over a period lending him about £7,000 for the rental of the property, stock, fitting it out. I'd supported them when they wanted to open at Duddenhill Road but when I saw the place I knew that wasn't really good enough for what they wanted. It was too small.

Geoff had left Cambridge with a 2:1 and wanted to pursue a career in music. It was an unconventional career path as we saw it but we were very supportive, as we tried to be with all our children. Right from the start, I helped Rough Trade with sorting out their finances, taking care of the VAT, and in fact I was friendly with their bank manager, who wasn't, I have to say, the typical kind of person you'd find visiting 202 Kensington Park Road. Consequently, I made it my mission to go there and pass back to him any relevant information I thought he should have. So, at least for the first couple of years, I spent a lot of time going in and out of the shop. Geoff was always more interested in promoting the music than promoting the business, so I tried to help out.

Jackie Rafferty: When the punk thing started to happen and the shop really took off, Dad must have been the hippest fifty-year-old on the planet. He really took an interest. He'd go in there and read the *NME*, cover to cover; he'd read *Melody Maker* and *Sounds* and he knew quite a lot about the bands that they were dealing with. And this was at a time when you weren't really allowed to be older and into rock music.

Peter Travis: I was a loss adjuster and I used to go into the shop straight from work, so I'd be wearing a business suit. Sometimes I'd get jeered and shouted at by punks but I always used to say to them: 'I don't object to the way you dress, why should you object to the way I dress?' That was a bit later. When it started I remember John and Jo doing their leatherwork in the back and Ken was the person in the shop.

Geoff Travis: The shop couldn't have got going without the support of my father. Or if we had got it going, it would have had a lot less records in it. Though I do remember him being concerned that at first records might not be a winner, and that we should have something more commercially sensible to fall back on, like luggage. He wanted us to have a line of luggage because it was his view that people always needed luggage.

Jackie Rafferty: I think Dad had an in to somebody pretty high up at Samsonite, it may even have been a relative of ours.

Geoff Travis: So when the shop opened, it was just me and Ken. Jo and John moved in later, maybe after about a month. They were in the shop anyway most of the time even before they moved in. I liked Ken. I got on well with him. He was a sweet soul. The problem was that when it was time to work he wasn't always that interested. After a couple of hours he'd say, 'Well, I'm off to play tennis now,' or something similar, and I'd say, 'All right, Ken, but it's not the weekend yet.' I think Ken secretly wanted to be an artist. He wasn't as committed to the records as I was; there wasn't the same burning passion. I mean, I wasn't thinking, 'Well, we'll try this for a month and see . . .' It was always the only thing I ever wanted to do.

Jo Slee: Photography was Ken's overriding passion. He also liked playing the guitar and he loved American guitar music – Steely Dan, Little Feat, that kind of thing. When we squatted the Trafalgar pub – the so-called 'Rough Trade Hotel' – he played those albums *every* single day he was there. And when Steve Montgomery turned up, they would spend hours in the shop talking about records. There certainly weren't many customers interrupting their conversations at that point. Steve Montgomery came into the shop on the first day, one of the first customers.

Steve Montgomery: I was living in a squat in Powis Square with my partner Annie and our baby daughter. We'd moved to Dorset originally because I figured that it would be better for the kid out of London but of course as soon as we had got there we realised there was nothing to do and not much chance of employment. So we wound up back in London. I used to spend my days out wandering around the market with my daughter and one day, after I'd done the shopping and was pushing the buggy up Kensington Park Road, I noticed a record shop which I didn't recall being there the day before. I went into the shop. Matting on the floor. A table and chairs. And this scruffy guy with curly hair sitting in this little box-like booth. Behind him there were loads of albums. I thought it was a bit weird. I started going through the sleeves in the racks and Ken said to me, 'Don't worry if you can't afford it, you can rent it and bring it back tomorrow.' I think Ken saw it as renting culture out. Commercially available blank tapes had only been available about a year and taping was the new thing. I think they were trying to tap into a potential market.

From that point on I went in every day. My first impression – a mistaken one – was that these guys were music snobs. They had a fantastically diverse range of stock from rock to garage to jazz to country to reggae. They even had a classical music section. I mistook diversity for exclusivity. No, they weren't snobs. Initially, I mistakenly thought Geoff was aloof, whereas Ken was much more grounded. We could spend three hours talking about the guitar solo on a particular record. Geoff's problem was that he acquired far more vinyl than he could ever hope to consume. He sucked vinyl the way the rest of us suck air. He'd rave about a particular album and a week later Ken and I would be playing it and Geoff would come in and say, 'This is good. What is it?'

I think there was a sort of mutual convenience to the relationship between Geoff and Ken. Ken's input enabled Geoff to realise his dream, and I think Geoff realised that Ken's ambitions, were they to come to fruition, were more likely to be visually rather than musically realised. Ken had a touch of the radical spirit in him and I think he recognised that in me. And since Geoff's role in the structure was, as it always would be, to source the stuff, he was often out and Ken and I were left together for quite long periods and we developed quite a friendship. We weren't troubled much by customers. I loved Ken. He was straightforward and equitable with everyone. Music wasn't about the country of origin, or the colour of the musicians, but about what it actually *did* to him.

Jo Slee: Ken had an enormously artistic side – he was very gifted. We forced him to design the first Rough Trade logo, which he cut out of a big sheet of plywood using a fret saw. It hung in the window for years.

Steve Montgomery: I didn't realise how unhappy Ken was. He was away from his girlfriend Vera, who was in Holland, and really wanted to do his photography but had set this thing up with Geoff, thinking it was a good idea, but then realised it probably wasn't what he was looking for. Ken lived in the pub and going into his room was like going into an Arabian tent. He had fabrics billowing down from the ceiling, cushions on the floor, red lighting, joss sticks burning. It was fantasy. It was leaving reality and stepping into make-believe. I found that weird. My room was like, 'This is where I sleep when I'm not spending fourteen hours a day at Rough Trade,' which later I would go on to do.

It was early summer when Ken decided to leave and he put me up to Geoff to replace him. What Geoff didn't know was that I'd already been sort of working there anyway. Geoff would be out looking for records and I would be hanging around talking to Ken, bringing him coffee, that kind of thing, and gradually I started asking him if he wanted to pop out for some lunch. And he'd go out and for long periods I was the only one behind the counter. I kind of replaced him before I replaced him.

Steve Montgomery, in a rare moment of repose.

By May 1976, the shop really didn't look that different from any other similarly minded record shop of the time. We had albums by all the obvious classic bands and artist – Rolling Stones, Dylan, Velvet Underground, Doors, Beatles, Bowie – but there was also a lot of garage stuff that Geoff had picked up in America – things like original Stooges albums, records by The Fugs, 13th Floor Elevators, Chocolate Watchband – and that made it kind of different.

Geoff Travis: We had some more obscure things we stocked: Garland Jeffreys's absolutely wonderful first solo album, *Garland Jeffreys*, and Jesse

Winchester's first album, which The Band played on, which is an absolute classic. Bobby Charles, *Small Town Talk*, one of the best albums ever made, we sold that. A beautiful record, one we would almost certainly have heard on Charlie Gillett's fabulous *Honky Tonk* radio show at the time.

What we didn't have, really, were customers.

Steve Montgomery: At times, we were the only people in the shop. Often – for long periods. And since Geoff spent time going out sourcing stock, it was sometimes just me in the shop, and Jo and John, who were doing their leatherwork, in the shed out the back.

Jo Slee: John built the first Rough Trade 'shed'. There were some perfectly sound but unmodernised Victorian buildings opposite the shop, which were being demolished, and John went and salvaged materials to put together this place for us to work. We put in two workbenches. It had a tin roof and absolutely no heating whatsoever. We had our tools from Canada, which John augmented with new ones from cobblers' shops: he seemed to have a knack of stumbling upon shoe-repair shops that were about to close. I used to cycle over to warehouses in South London and buy rolls of leather and leather dyes.

We used to boil up fantastic potions – leather moisturiser made from beeswax, neatsfoot oil, linseed oil and other stuff – and store it in old paint tins. All of the sole leather would be properly pre-oiled.

The first Rough Trade Shed, complete with Rough Trade Custom Leather swirly sign courtesy of Jo.

John was very creative and very inventive, and always prepared to take it that extra step. We made sandals, but John went on to learn how to make proper shoes. He'd walk around with notebooks, studying the shoes of everybody he would come across, and making notes on them. Later he went to Cordwainers College, the famous saddlery college. I was content making decorated boxes and camera cases but John learned how to make clothes. I found a Japanese colouring book with amazing line drawings in – of golden carp and ancient Japanese heroes – and copied them onto my boxes. We worked incredibly hard for seven days and made about £8 a week, which was what we would have got if we'd signed on the dole. It was really satisfying. I mean, we were squatting so we only really needed money for food.

Steve Montgomery: This was all before punk took off and so the shop walls certainly weren't filled with seven-inch singles, as they would be a few months later. Mainly, John and Jo's leather goods were hanging around the walls – so it was a bizarre-looking record shop if you happened to stumble in off the street. The photographer Mick Rock – either to encourage us, or possibly taking pity on us – gave us some framed photographs of his to put on the wall. Of course, over a period they all got nicked, but that was later when it got so crowded that you couldn't even think straight let alone keep an eye on what was happening.

Geoff Travis: Change was in the air. Gigs had already long moved into that pre-punk period when pub rock was happening. I'd been going out and seeing a lot of those bands, like Kilburn & The High Roads, Ducks Deluxe, and a little earlier Brinsley Schwarz, who were one of my favourites, at venues like the Hope & Anchor, the Sir George Robey, the Dublin Castle and the Nashville Rooms. The records in the shop started to change as well. The Red House stock was starting to run down and I was replacing it with more records by garage bands. The Standells, The Chocolate Watchband, stuff like that. I discovered a whole stash of original New York Dolls albums in a warehouse in Manchester. It was a company dealing in deletions and I spent the whole day in this dark room, nearly going blind, looking at thousands upon thousands of rubbish records and then finally hit gold with a couple of hundred Dolls albums, which they sold to me for about 30p each.

I was getting a lot of records from Lightning up on the Harlesden Road and had heard also about Larry Debay who worked from a tiny office over in Praed Street, Paddington, not far from where The Clash would later rehearse. Larry was involved with Skydog, a French reissue label, and had set up Bizarre, which was a shop and went on to become one of the earliest independent distribution companies. We were getting things like the Flamin' Groovies' EPs, *Grease* and *More Grease*, and the ten-inch *Sneakers*, and the Iggy Pop bootleg *Metallic KO* from them.

Pete Flanagan: I was working in Harlequin mid-1976, which had gone from being a One Stop in, I think, 1975. Larry Debay was this legendary figure who used to deliver the records in his beaten-up, super-size Mercedes coupé, back in the day when there weren't traffic wardens, or yellow lines, or congestion charges. He'd pull up, flip the boot and he'd have box after box of goodies. He was importing stuff from America as well. He was a larger-than-life guy. Mike Georgiou, who worked with me at Harlequin, was walking down Wardour Street one day with Larry when they saw Roy Wood coming the other way. Larry had long ginger hair, a bright green beard at the time, and looked not dissimilar to Roy, who was sporting long ginger hair and a bright red beard. It was like a stand-off in a spaghetti western while they each sized up the unexpected vision of the other. They muscled around each other and then went on their way.

We had a pretty good set-up at Harlequin, plenty of import records, unusual things, and we heard quickly about Rough Trade. People talk about the in-store events – The Ramones, and so on – but we'd been putting on events for a while by 1976. The 101ers did an in-store in July 1975, and we put on Rat Bites (From Hell) an early, pre-incarnation of the Only Ones.

The good record shops in the West End at that time, apart from us, were Musicland, who were in Berwick Street, Oasis, who had a basement in Newport Court quite close to the market where Ted Carroll's West End Rock On stall was, which was run by Roger Armstrong and sold a lot of revivalist stuff. Ted also had his stall in Golborne Road, I think that was the first. Cheapo Cheapo was at the bottom of Berwick Street. Keith Stone ran Daddy Cool, which was also in Dean Street and was very important for reggae. And then there were some other specialist but really rather good shops, like Harold Moore's, which was a classical shop, and Ray's Jazz.

The Sex Pistols had played the 100 Club in March and the Glitterbest offices were round the corner in Dryden Chambers, so they were in Harlequin all the time, as was Jamie Reid, who I remember haggling with over whether or not to swap a couple of T-shirts with American country acts on that he wanted for some Sex Pistols shirts which he was offering me.

I couldn't work out if it was a good deal or not! But I think more than anything, it was after Patti Smith played the Roundhouse in May that we really started to notice the change; that we really started to feel something was in the air.

Savage Pencil: I queued up all afternoon to get into the Patti Smith concert at the Roundhouse and when they opened the doors I shot in and got right down the front. It was worth it, even if I did have to sit through a dreary Stranglers set before Patti came on. Although I wasn't aware of them at the time, a lot of people who were quite influential, or went on to do something, told me they were at that show and that it changed them in some way.

Sandy Robertson: I moved to London at the end of the year, 1976, but I did come down for things before that, and the Patti Smith concert was one of them. I'd been into Patti Smith before she'd made any records, even before 'Piss Factory'. I was a big Blue Öyster Cult fan and she'd written lyrics for some of their songs and occasionally sang with them. She'd done a poem called 'Band Aid', which was given away with a Todd Rundgren album printed on the image of a Band-Aid. So, even before I thought about starting my fanzine *White Stuff* I was very interested in her. Traditionally, pop stars got knickers thrown at them on stage but I'd heard that at Patti Smith concerts people threw books on stage, so that's what I did; I threw on to the Roundhouse stage a book of my poems, which I'd self-published, and also a copy of Colin Wilson's *The Outsider*. About twenty years later some journalist fingered me for it.

Steve Montgomery: In July, we were all back at the Roundhouse for The Ramones and The Flamin' Groovies. Geoff had somehow talked Seymour Stein, who ran Sire, into letting us have The Ramones in to 202 Kensington Park Road for a signing. We'd had Patti Smith, Lenny Kaye and Ivan Kral in before that, but that had been more informal. For The Ramones, the kids mobbed the place out. Shane MacGowan was there, Mark Perry with Harry Murlowski, Sandy Robertson and I think Tony D – possibly only Mark had done a fanzine at this point. Jane Suck was also there. It was a strange event.

The Ramones in-store event at Rough Trade. Steve Montgomery in the background, to the immediate left of Joey, Jane Suck, bottom right foreground.

Seymour came with his wife Linda – a whiney, screechy woman who clearly had grand management intentions towards the band. Seymour owned the label, and therefore the purse strings, but Linda saw the band as *her* boys. They were like four soft toys commandeered by the Wicked Witch of the West and didn't seem to be that connected to anything that was going on. At one point it was noticed that Joey had gone missing and so I went to try to find him. The bemused fruit and veg lads in Portobello Road market soon pointed me in the right direction.

Geoff had insisted that The Ramones should be given any records they wanted, gratis, but I figured – we pay for your records so you should pay for ours – and I told them so, and I think I might have done a cost deal on anything they took. The evening was rounded off by Captain Sensible head-butting a framed picture on the wall of some other members of The Damned and me chasing him up Kensington Park Road.

Jon Savage: I believe I first went into Rough Trade in late summer 1976 and I was struck straight away by the fact that there was a lot of reggae, which was unusual, and they had copies of *Punk* magazine, including issue one. They were the only record shop in London stocking *Punk* at that time. Prior to coming across Rough Trade, I had to buy my reggae at places like the stalls in Shepherd's Bush market, which could be quite heavy. So it was nice to find a place where I could get the stuff without being glared at. I recognised Geoff from Cambridge but I got on more with Steve Montgomery, who was the one behind the counter. It always seems to me that Steve has either been written out of history, or has chosen to write himself out of history, but he was a very key figure in the early days of the shop.

Geoff could be reserved at times, but Steve would always come over and chat. He was a very outgoing man who loved his reggae. In keeping with the times, he loved his drugs as well, but then this was the late 1970s and everywhere was sort of awash with drugs; after all it was rock 'n' roll and the whole idea was that you walked on the wild side.

Geoff Travis: There was a big Jamaican community around Ladbroke Grove and it was important to me that we weren't just seen as tourists. The Grove was an interesting place: there were still the slums and the Rachman-ite landlords, so you had plenty of musicians because it was cheap to live; there were working-class enclaves like the flats where Mick Jones lived, and you had the Jamaicans. Some of the finest records ever made came out in that early period after the shop opened when we were selling records by Culture, The Wailers, The Heptones, The Mighty Diamonds, The Abyssinians.

I'd go up to Jet Star, the wholesalers, every weekend and come back with a lot of pre-s. The point about the pre-s was that there weren't that many around so they became highly sought after. Soon enough, the local dreads found out about the stuff and they'd come in and you'd be spinning for them. A lot of musicians have always had an interest in reggae so we had a lot of white customers for the stuff, and as punk took off they were buying that, too. So you had the crossover. Of course, generally, the Rastas – some of whom knew a hell of a lot about all kinds of music – were less likely to be buying punk.

Steve Montgomery: In the late 1960s there had been this underground stream of reggae and ska releases either put out in or shipped over to England. But it wasn't Jamaicans who were buying this stuff but disenfranchised white kids who couldn't really work out if they were mods or rockers. They soon became the much-derided skinheads. The alliance between reggae and western rebel music has always been strong. And, of course, it was very working class. It was only when the album-buying culture emerged in the early to mid-1970s that rock music became trenchantly middle class. It took punk to reverse that and get it back to working-class kids spending their pocket money.

Geoff was a terrific buyer of reggae for the shop and would get a fantastic cross-section of stuff but there was always the problem of getting enough of it. Pretty soon people started coming into the shop with suitcases full of pre-s, which they'd brought back from a trip to Jamaica the week before, and you'd give it the thirty-second burn to see if you thought it would be a winner. All the while, the dread is standing over you. Really, these guys were doing no different to what Chris Blackwell did when he started Island, albeit on a smaller scale. They'd sell the records to us for a pound and we'd put them out at £1.25 – it was important, not just in reggae, to keep the records affordable.

A little bit later, about 1980, they set up a sound system outside the shop for the carnival and, unlike other shops, we never had to board up our windows and never once had them smashed in. We were respected. Though we didn't really engage with the carnival until the street we were on became almost derelict.

Jo Slee: That first carnival for us in 1976 – well, we could see trouble coming a mile away and we all left town. John and I went up to a craft festival in Norwich and when we drove back down Ladbroke Grove on the Monday the place was awash with broken glass and burnt-out cars. It was quite impressive, really. There was some really bad confrontational policing at the time and the police were largely right wing and very provocative.

Geoff Travis: The Mangrove, which was not far away, had famously been the source of much racial tension. We had a dreadful local council, a really bad Tory council in 1976, and of course the police were always trying to bust that place. When they weren't doing that they would be harassing everyone with the Suss laws, which back then gave them enormous powers to stop and search people.

I'm proud of the fact we never boarded up at carnival. I think had we done so, and got a brick through the window afterwards for doing so, then that would have been fair enough in a strange way.

Savage Pencil: Steve had this love of dub, which I shared, and I can only describe his love as going deep: really, really deep. He'd listen to the stuff as if his life depended on it. I think Geoff loved his reggae in a different way, or at least so it always seemed to me. That summer was the summer of the Punk Rock Festival and the Sex Pistols had a residency at the 100 Club. Roger Armstrong from the Rock On stall had told me about the Pistols and I ended up duly trooping along every Tuesday night, as I think it was. Most nights there'd be about fifteen people in the audience watching them do these incredible sets, which were minimalist, powerful,

threatening and weird. You always came out thinking that the night had
been amazing. But, jump forward a few months to when 'Anarchy in the
UK' came out and it was hopeless; all that energy had gone. I just laughed
when I heard it – I thought it was pathetic.

The point being that after the reggae, for me, it was the American stuff
that started appearing that was exciting. English punks to me were just like
The Beatles but dirtier. Whereas a band like Television, whose Ork single
'Little Johnny Jewel' I'd bought off Roger's stall, well, they were like gods.
John Holmstrom's *Punk* magazine – an immediate and visually beautiful
thing – had all these bands in it like The Ramones, Patti Smith, Richard
Hell, Television – as if they were family. To us, they were high Olympians:
we couldn't get anywhere near them. I loved Television. I loved them before
I even heard their records. I had a T-shirt made in the King's Road with
'Television' on it in iron-on letters before I even heard what they sounded
like, and wore it at the next Royal College of Art disco. People came up to
me and said, 'Wow, what a great T-shirt. What does it mean?' Even the
word had the power to set the imagination racing. Whatever it was, you
wanted to be part of it.

Steve Montgomery: By now Geoff had started writing to like-minded souls and
we started receiving boxes of things unannounced, at least to me, in the post.
All the deals he did, he did COD – cash on delivery. So I used to have to make
sure I had enough money in the till in case the postman popped up with some
goodies and needed paying. In the autumn and winter of 1976 the trickle
started to steadily increase – Television's 'Little Johnny Jewel' from Terry Ork
in New York, early Pere Ubu singles on Hearthan from David Thomas in
Cleveland, '(I'm) Stranded' on Fatal from The Saints in Australia, things
Greg Shaw from Who Put The Bomp? was sending over from Detroit. It
seemed as if every day there would be a new box.

Geoff Travis: Stiff Records was going by September and we took and sold a
lot of their records. Nick Lowe, Roogalator, Richard Hell, The Damned –
I used to go and pick them up at the Stiff offices in Alexander Street. It
wasn't until 1977 that we had any major label accounts, so just about
everything had to be bought with cash. Chiswick – some great records came
in from them – the 101ers' 'Keys to Your Heart', issued and then reissued
when The Clash took off. Vince Taylor's 'Brand New Cadillac', a fantastic
record.

Steve Montgomery: We quickly got a reputation both for the stock we carried and the lengths we would go to find records for people. Because pretty soon the kids were ahead of the game and they would be coming in and asking us to find stuff for them whereas originally it was us getting the stuff and them being attracted to it. I saw it as my responsibility to give people what they wanted. If we didn't have a particular record, I asked for information and promised to source out the record and have it in stock as soon as I could. In some ways for me this was an attempt to live my life the best way I could. My stance was partly utopian, partly standing up for the working classes as I saw them, and partly providing a voice for people who weren't heard. It pretty quickly became apparent that we could help change things.

Geoff Travis: I'd been to the City Lights bookstore in San Francisco and for me that was a bit of a model for how I wanted Rough Trade to be. You could sit in the basement of that shop and read poetry and drink coffee and nobody would throw you out. I wanted Rough Trade to be a place where you could come in and look around and not feel hassled. I thought it could be some sort of community focal point. It was important that we had the table and chairs, and when the fanzines started coming out people would sit there and read them and that was fine. They'd sit there and put them together and that was fine.

Steve Montgomery: In the summer, Mark Perry put together issue one of *Sniffin' Glue* and brought it in to show us. He was so enthusiastic about it. He had either given up or was about to give up his job in a bank. He didn't want any money, he just wanted to know that if we sold any we would pay him for them. I think he told me that he lost about £50 on the first three, then after that it became the most popular fanzine on the planet.

Geoff Travis: We took *Punk* magazine virtually from day one and we sold some of the magazines that predated the punk fanzines, things like *Hot Wacks*, *Dark Star* and *Zigzag*. After *Sniffin' Glue*, we very quickly started to get in others and the main ones were Tony D's *Ripped & Torn*, Sandy Robertson's *White Stuff*, Adrian Thrills's *48 Thrills*, Shane MacGowan's *Bondage* and Jon Savage's *London's Outrage*. All the fanzine writers were constant visitors to the shop.

What I liked about the fanzines was the fact that they were written from inside the musical movement. The fanzine writers were advocates of the music, they weren't just trying to critique it. They weren't in any way detached or academic. They were a call to arms and they gave people the ammunition to do their own thing.

To me, they were an indication of that specific mindset that there was a revolution in music and that this was the only thing that mattered. They were proselytising in a way that was really quite pure and they drew the battle lines of what really was and was not allowed. So they had the energy of early manifestos of art movements even though they were more amateur in design and perhaps not as intellectual or sophisticated. The energy was terrifically exciting. And of course, their amateurishness was part of their appeal.

I mean the idea that one day Mark P. is working in a bank and the next on the front line of punk is terrifically appealing . . .

Jon Savage: I used to buy a lot of those pre-punk fanzines at the time, like *Bam Balaam*, *Fat Angel*, publications coming out at that forgotten moment, that whole forgotten era of music publishing when it wasn't just *Zigzag*. For me, it wasn't so much the hippie stuff that was being covered that was interesting but rather the way people would go fanatically into sixties music like The Kinks, Creation and other hard mod pop that has had a much bigger influence on punk than has ever been recognised.

I realised pretty much straight away that I wanted to do my own fanzine. In 1976, my day job was training to be a solicitor working in the City of

London and I was feeling alienated and hated to a rather severe degree that I would not recommend. At the time, I was not in a good state psychologically. Punk presented me with an opportunity to write, something I had always wanted to do, and it presented the opportunity by virtue of the fact that it allowed me to go to gigs and feel plugged into something that I could see unfolding in front of my very eyes.

Sandy Robertson: By the time I came around to do my fanzine *White Stuff*, a couple of the early ones were already out. I didn't bother to look at them. I just figured that they would all be more or less the same thing and that I had to do something different. So I thought I'd write a fanzine about Patti Smith – and about the kind of things that I thought would be of interest to her. That was the reasoning. Jon Savage did a piece on Wilhelm Reich in one issue. I did stuff on Surrealism, Harry Crosby. Somebody wrote to me and asked me if I had heard of Austin Osman Spare, an English artist who was born in the 1890s and had been into automatic writing, drawing and sigilisation. The guy sent me a pasted-up article he'd written and I just put it in an issue – all I did was biro on the page numbers.

Sandy Robertson's White Stuff, *along with one or two others, looked beyond the accepted parameters of the genre. It was variously described (by itself) as 'a rock'n'roll magazine for the modern world', 'a rock'n'roll magazine for teen aesthetes', 'a rock'n'roll magazine for young existentialists' and 'a rock'n'roll magazine for the new romanticism'.*

I'd travelled down to London with Alex Fergusson, who later joined Mark P. in ATV after Mark gave up *Sniffin' Glue*. Alex and I were the only two weird guys – I mean *really weird* guys – in Renfrew just outside Glasgow. Our friends had been into Bob Dylan and Neil Young but Alex was the only other person I knew who had bought The Stooges' album *Funhouse* on the day it came out in 1970. We'd had a bedroom band called The Nobodies but I realised at some point that I wasn't going to make it as a singer and that we were getting older. Punk started to happen and it sort of discombobulated me. I read about the Sex Pistols – I hadn't heard them at this point – and they sounded horrible, just horrible, and I thought I'm going to prefer Eddie & The Hot Rods to this lot. They sounded like a skinhead band. But then I heard 'Anarchy in the UK' and I got it straight away. I thought it was brilliant. And I also thought that punk would create so much confusion in the music business that there would be a window of opportunity for Alex and me if we went to London at that moment. We could get our foot in the door, Alex as a musician, me as a writer. I started on *White Stuff* as soon as I arrived just before Christmas 1976. It felt so exciting. It felt like we were stamping out the future. Now, you look back and it just seems nostalgic . . .

Savage Pencil: Fanzines were great – they were like bulletins from the front line. I loved self-publishing and it was fanzines that really forced me to start doing *Corpse Meat Comics* and that ultimately, through the enormous support of Vivien Goldman – who was absolutely brilliant to anybody she saw with a good idea at the time – got me working for *Sounds* on my *Rock 'n' Roll Zoo* column.

I did once sketchily put together a template for a fanzine based on The Ramones called *Pinhead*. It was going to have no dialogue and no narrative, just images and collages inspired by The Ramones. I had insane ideas about how I would take words like 'Gabba Gabba Hey', which I knew had their origins in Tod Browning's *Freaks*, and stretch them to their limit. Anything I thought was Gabba Gabba Hey could go into *Pinhead*. I wanted it to confuse people. I wanted it to be about an inch thick, so thick you'd need nuts and bolts to put it together.

Jon Savage: The whole point about fanzines – indeed, the whole point about punk, it seemed to me, and I always bang on about this – was that you could do whatever you wanted to do. And so therefore you did not need to rely on established formats. Everything was supposed to be new. It wasn't supposed to be old hat. As a polemic, 'No Beatles, no Rolling Stones, etc' was a very good one, if one that was ultimately unsustainable. It was all so far under the radar that nobody gave a shit and really you could do whatever you wanted to. This was what was wonderful about early fanzines before they descended into that sub-music press rant that it all became. It was a wonderful opportunity to use your imagination in whatever way you wanted.

I got some money at Christmas 1976 and I started work on the first *London's Outrage*. It was a sort of existential blurting out, and looking back now it seems to me it is a strange mixture of some really great stuff and some really shit stuff. It was all done in a frenzy, the direct result of seeing the Sex Pistols and The Clash. It is important to recognise the desperation in it. That was very important.

The Xerox machine had really not long come on stream and there was a place in Waterloo where they had a colour Xerox. This was one of only two of these machines in London at the time. If you went down there to photocopy your fanzine you'd invariably be met with an ever-growing line of punks coming and going with their masterworks. It was all very *Blue Peter*, all very 'Let's-make-a-revolution-out-of-loo-roll'.

I photocopied *London's Outrage* surreptitiously at work and went around selling it where I could. I was approached by Shane MacGowan, who talked me into photocopying his fanzine *Bondage* for him. I had a few hairy days at work trying to avoid people while I was photocopying this thing with chains and razorblades on it.

I went into Rough Trade and had a chat with them about them selling my fanzine. I asked them whether I could use their postal address on the back of the fanzine and they allowed me to and so *London's Outrage* was the first fanzine to carry the Rough Trade address. There was a little community of fanzine writers that would all meet at 202 Kensington Park Road. It became a real focal point, not just a place where you went to buy records.

In January 1977, I went around the area – W10 and W11 – and took a whole bunch of photos that formed the basis of the second issue of *London's Outrage*. It was a kind of urbanism. I remember being fascinated at the time by the Westway. I was reading J. G. Ballard's *High Rise*, as were quite a few others at that time, as I recall. I think I was trying to get across this idea that we were simultaneously depressed about the fact that we lived in

this miserable shithole but we also took energy from it, because this was our playground. We were young and stupid and didn't really care because here was this big empty space that we could claim and traverse, which of course is now impossible in London.

Sandy Robertson: I used to get *White Stuff* printed up at a Prontaprint just off Regent's Street. They had a stapler in the corner and a table and chairs where I could sit and put the issue together. But pretty quickly Tony D, who started *Ripped & Torn*, told me about a guy in Cambridge who was dirt cheap. It really *was* worth getting on the bloody train for. This guy ran a small print works but his big passion was punk rock. He'd spend all day doing greetings cards, letterheads, business cards and crap like that and hated it. So he gave us the best deal you could possibly get. And as his equipment got better, so too did the way the fanzines looked. I think that by the time I did the last issue of *White Stuff* he'd got a scanner and a folding machine. The fanzines were very nearly looking like real magazines.

Jo Slee: Patti Smith came over in October to play the Hammersmith Odeon and her label Arista set up a press conference just for fanzine writers, which was great. A bunch of us went along from Rough Trade and we all sat on the floor in a cold room and everyone asked her questions. Many years later I was telling Morrissey about this and it turned out that he had been there as well.

Steve Montgomery: My ultimate gripe with the fanzines was that they never had enough social comment in them for my liking. I'd bend anybody's ear about this who would listen to me. I had some run-ins with Jon about it. I nearly convinced Mark Perry to let me guest-edit an issue of *Sniffin' Glue* – what others have called my legendary, mythical 'Maoist issue' – but at the end I think he got cold feet and it never happened. I think he just told me to fuck off.

Sandy Robertson: People criticised me and some of the other fanzine writers for going off and joining the established music press, but in my case I never made a secret of the fact that was what I wanted to do and, thanks to Vivien Goldman, I wound up on *Sounds*. I didn't put out *White Stuff* to become part of some Socialist revolution. I wasn't left wing and I wasn't right wing: I believed in what my great hero Colin Wilson called individualism.

*

Jo Slee: Back in the summer we had heard about this squatted pub in Bramley Road called the Trafalgar. We left the squat in Archway and moved in and so did Ken, although he left when he quit Rough Trade and headed back to Amsterdam. The squat was run by a couple of Granola Fascists, people Steve referred to as the 'Hitler hippies', who had some serious problems with aggression.

Since it was a squat and they were the first to move in, they kind of assumed rights and we had to try to move more and more people in to outnumber them. Sue Allegra from The Derelicts moved in with her boyfriend Mike and a two-week-old baby called Charlie, who had been delivered in Holloway because Sue had been done for Thai sticks at the airport. They introduced us to Peter Walmsley, a friend of theirs who had flown in from Australia and come straight to the pub. Eventually, not long before Ken went, the hippies had had enough and moved on. We repainted the place from top to bottom in forty-eight hours.

I spent a lot of that winter depressed, playing the piano at the pub and not really going out much. I'd pretty much given up on the leatherwork because without heating the shed was completely miserable. We had seventeen empty glue tins on the dirt floor under the leaks in the roof, and were working in hats and gloves and scarves, and I kept cutting my fingers because I couldn't feel anything but the cold. At that point I naturally gravitated towards the shop, where I started to help out and where it was warmer, though John carried on with the leatherwork until the spring of 1977, when he took a 'real job' in market research.

Geoff seemed pleased, though. 'It could be the start of a whole new career,' he told me. At the time, I thought, 'Yeah, right', then proceeded to work there for another thirteen years on and off.

CHAPTER THREE:

1977

'Having a customer walk in was an event. You had
to pretend not to get too excited'

Grundy fallout – *Spiral Scratch* – Moonlighting – Mail order – Rough Trade
Hotel – DIY – Arrival of Richard Scott – Logo – Bootlegs – The New
Sound

Steve Montgomery: At the start of 1977, the fallout from the Sex Pistols
appearance on the *Bill Grundy Show* in December was still filtering down,
and, pretty soon after, Janet Street Porter wanted to come and film in the
shop to get the 'kids' reaction' to this so-called infamous moment. I was a
little bit rude and I think she was taken aback by my appearance – green
boiler suit, Doc Martens, henna'd hair and earring. I certainly insisted on
keeping the shop open for business while they filmed. Shortly after that,
we heard about the Buzzcocks record.

Geoff Travis: We heard about *Spiral Scratch* at the start of 1977 and it was a
lovely way to start the year. It was easily the best of those early DIY records
and it was certainly our favourite one.

Richard Boon: Someone rang up from Rough Trade. Could they have two hundred copies? The following week I got a phone call from Geoff Travis saying could they have some more and it just went on from there.

We'd pressed up one thousand copies at a cost of £600 and didn't really know what to do with them. We'd kind of only done it to document a period of activity on the back of being enthused by the Sex Pistols. We sold two hundred to John Webster, who was managing the Virgin record shop in Manchester. We were selling the rest by mail order until Rough Trade contacted us. After they'd taken a second batch and then a third batch we seemed to have the rudiments of a distributor. They took thousands after that and in three months we went on to sell sixteen thousand copies, some through them, some through the French guys at Bizarre up in Praed Street, some mail order and some through the distributor Pinnacle.

I'd read about the shop because *Melody Maker* had run a piece on Patti Smith going in there and buying an Abyssinians album. I started to go in there and I got a warm welcome. Geoff and Steve were very enthusiastic. Geoff would be in the back, more reserved. All Steve would say when he saw me was – 'Great, more of them.' Steve was very obviously politically aware and could be fantastically engaging. He was amusingly hard-line. I had him pegged for a closet Maoist and, in fact, when I heard about his proposed Maoist version of *Sniffin' Glue* I thought it was great. I doubt whether Mark P. could understand or be bothered with it, but it would certainly have been something to play around with.

The way I saw it was that we had done this independent thing with no structures in place. The idea was then enthusiastically taken on by other people who had no structures in place. And from that moment, structures could start to emerge. And I think Rough Trade started to think about this.

I think *Spiral Scratch* kick-started them into thinking beyond the fledgling mail order they had set up to something that could become a focus for this kind of activity. It started to become a place for people to go with their fanzines and their records and it became a clearing house for *information* in its broader sense, a nexus.

Geoff Travis: *Spiral Scratch* was a record where we were able to sell not just hundreds in the shop but thousands to other shops and that is really the point where distribution started to come about.

Richard Boon: If the infrastructure had been in place already, we would have carried on, I think, and made another independent record. We had a three-track EP, *Love Bites*, ready and would have been happy to do that in the same piecemeal way, but our schoolboy drummer's dad came and saw us and said that his son was leaving school and was going to work in an insurance office – probably next to Mark E. Smith and Ian Curtis – and we realised we had to work out a way of getting income for the band.

The thing about Rough Trade was that although there were other small shops doing a similar kind of thing, all over the country, many of them just weren't as galvanised as Rough Trade. Rough Trade was open to new stuff. And in spite of everybody's best efforts to encourage regionalism, the reality was that the music business was still in London, and Rough Trade was in London, and journalists went there, which was very important. 202 Kensington Park Road was therefore a focal point. It was all about communication. When we started Buzzcocks I was living in a part of Salford where very few people had phones, but the landlord was an academic and had to have one. None of what happened subsequently with *Spiral Scratch* could have happened for us without that phone.

Steve Montgomery: More and more records were coming out and more and more customers were coming into the shop. And the amount of letters that we started to get went up dramatically. It pretty soon was close on a hundred letters a week asking for stuff, looking for stuff. It set us a challenge. Geoff had this rule that we must always answer individually each letter sent to us. That meant effectively that I would have to answer them because as anyone who has seen Geoff's handwriting can testify, you need to have spent fifteen years in a university studying it to decipher it. It's minuscule

and illegible. Many of the letters we would receive would be from abroad –
we got a lot from America – and it was in response to those that I first
started sending out a single sheet with releases on. I'd put it in with the
response to the letters, and that was the start of mail order. Enquiries
increased as did the number of people coming through the shop, to such
an extent that paperwork had to be relegated to the back office eventually
so I could cope with the customers.

Another indicator of how well we were doing was the stamping of the
brown bags. We had brown bags which we rubber-stamped 'Rough Trade'
at the start of each week. Pretty soon we had to do this every other day to
keep up. We started our chart as well – we'd pin up on the wall a chart of
records either our customers liked or we liked or we were trying to flog.

Carolyn Holder: They had these lists of records that were pinned up on the
wall, and I remember on one occasion, my boyfriend stole a list put up by
Jane Suck, the journalist. Jane's lists were legendary and my boyfriend
thought they were works of art. The next week, in place of Jane's list was a
notice from her demanding to know 'WHO IS THE FUCKER WHO
STOLE MY LIST?' Robin had a friend called Andrew, who Geoff had
promised to take out for fish and chips. When they got to the restaurant,
Geoff refused to sit down to eat because it cost more money. He stood at
the door, counting the people going in and out and working out the turnover
of the place. Geoff is incredibly generous now but back then he was a bit
mean. They bought the take-away meal and Andrew went home. He got a
bit stoned and late in the night went to Rough Trade with a can of spray
paint. There was some building work being done opposite the shop and the
site was fenced in with corrugated iron panels. Andrew sprayed in enormous letters on the corrugated iron the words: 'GEOFF TRAVIS
BOUGHT ME A FISH'. I went into the shop the next day and saw it and
thought it was absolutely hilarious, but Geoff was furious – furious and
embarrassed. 'Did you do this?' he asked me. I didn't eat fish at the time.
As the building work went on, the panels got moved so the words got
rearranged all the way around the site – upside down, transposed. This
went on for months and people always came in and would ask, 'What's all
this about Geoff buying a fish?'

Jackie Rafferty: I stopped going into the shop around about the time of
punk, because that whole punk thing really wasn't me. Some of the

people who started to hang around the shop made me feel a little bit uncomfortable and I'd never felt that before. I'd grown up just on the edge of the hippie era and for me punk was quite alienating and aggressive. Geoff's take on it always surprised me – aggressive would be the last word used to describe Geoff, and I think that much of what punk stood for was opposed to much of what Geoff stood for: it seemed a mismatch. There was the shared anti-establishment attitude, I suppose. I never knew whether for Geoff it was the political stance or the music – it always seemed to me, anyway, that the music was the most important thing about punk.

Alan Travis: DIY was a common thread that ran through from the hippies to punk, and DIY had been very much what was going on at Cambridge for Geoff and his group. The shared grass-roots DIY basis would have been clear to Geoff. It's important to remember, as well, Geoff's experience at the school we went to, which was actually pretty much a working-class school with a kind of middle-class import from various bits of North London. We saw kids walking around with knackered knives and kids from the school would be in gangs going up Tottenham Royal looking for Pakistanis to beat up on a Saturday, so the aggression of punk culture when it came along really wasn't that unusual.

Jackie Rafferty: Dad used to say to Geoff, 'How much did you take this week?' and Geoff would say, '£100', and Dad would say, 'Come back and see me when you've taken £200.' Well, pretty quickly it was £200, then £400, and then much more that they were taking. Dad was a solid Labour supporter but I am not sure he could understand why Geoff had set the thing up whereby everyone got equal wages. He saw the shop as a commercial proposition: Geoff saw it as a way of living . . .

Steve Montgomery: Everything was still being done with cash. So much stuff was starting to arrive at the shop that I was always paranoid that I wouldn't have enough cash and if necessary I used to dip into my own pockets. It wasn't until the Clash album came out in May that we were able to get major label accounts. That was the first one. When that album came out we may have sold as many as one hundred on the first day. We certainly were pushing towards sales of about one thousand in the first month and I think that was when the music business really sat up and took notice of punk and of us as a force. That was when they all worked out that maybe this music would last more than a couple of weeks.

I never took any wages for working at Rough Trade. The way it worked was that every Thursday I signed on and the dole money went more or less to Annie. So that meant every Thursday Geoff would have to open up the store. I then got by on very little – you didn't need much, just vinyl – and I am not ashamed to say that for a while I dealt some pot out of the shop to make that little bit extra to get by.

Jo Slee: What Steve did was incredible, really. He took no money and ultimately it was very sad because his experience with Rough Trade ended badly both here and when he went off to America for them. He was hopelessly generous, too. I remember a journalist coming in – a pre-eminent rock journalist of the time – and bumming a fiver off Steve to score drugs.

Geoff Travis: We paid ourselves no money and then a very small amount of money – maybe five pounds a week. But I only needed money to buy records, really. I'd moved into Vivien Goldman's flat at 145a Ladbroke Grove, above the betting shop and next to the chip shop. Dave 'Boss' Goodman had lived there, or maybe was still there. I remember looking in the fridge and all it had in it was a bottle of whisky and a bag of acid. Anyway, Boss worked at Dingwalls and he put me up to DJ there and I had an audition with Barry Myers, who later went on to be the Clash DJ. That went well, so I started doing that. It was great because I would be listening to bands like Talking Heads and The Ramones all day and then three nights a week I'd be playing black music at Dingwalls. So it was a good balance. I was also doing some journalism for *Record Mirror* and I once reviewed the singles for *Black Echoes*, which was a big thing to have done, at least in my mind: it was taken very seriously.

Jo Slee: Steve really cared about the music – you can see that from the love he put into the mail order catalogues – and he cared about the people who cared about the music. What he put into those catalogues reached somewhere no music paper could reach, no record shop could reach, no record label could reach. The mail order sheets, and later catalogues, would go out to kids and the kids thought they'd found a kindred spirit and increasingly started coming on pilgrimage to find this Steve Montgomery.

He really became a hero. This used to embarrass him. People would come in and ask him who Steve Montgomery was and if Geoff was on his way out and couldn't be caught Steve would point to him and say, 'There he is, but you just missed him.' Steve was the one always in the shop and he drove all of it. He got on incredibly well with the Jamaican community, because reggae was his favourite music. Plus, he used to smoke dope and deal dope. He was the perfect pillar of the community, in every possible way.

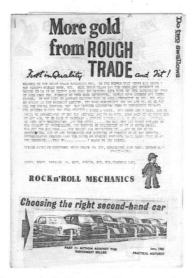

Early mail order catalogue, compiled by Steve Montgomery, late 1977/early 1978. Note, the Homepride Man 'rock 'n' roll mechanic' logo.

*

Steve Montgomery: I moved to the Trafalgar before Mr and Mrs Hitler left, sometime during 1976 after my relationship with Annie broke down, and it didn't seem too long after that the Scottish plague – Sandy Robertson, Alex Fergusson, Tony D and Tony's friend Skid Kid – moved in. On and off over the next year or so, the pub would provide accommodation for all sorts of Rough Trade waifs and strays, anyone who need putting up for the night really.

A rare photograph of the demolished Trafalgar pub at 2 Bramley Road – otherwise known as the 'Rough Trade Hotel' – prior to its being squatted. The rag-and-bone man in the picture is almost certainly Arthur Arnold.

The pub was in a shitty area – the local housing estate was more like a military bunker and there was always a fair amount of neighbourhood violence, alcohol and drug abuse. It really was a terrifying place. Lawless. Make no mistake, some members of the front line dished out violence to the community on a regular basis. We were as close to that as a bunch of mindless, naïve revolutionaries ever could be.

Jo Slee: The pub had four bedrooms, a public bar and a private bar, which early on I think Ken took. We got armfuls of posters from places like Virgin – Pistols posters – and put them on the walls. I had a piano in there.

Peter Walmsley: Essentially, I met everybody at Rough Trade and ended up working there through the pub, which I'd moved into in August 1976. I'd met Sue Allegra's boyfriend Mike while I'd been travelling in India and that was how I came to go to the squat. For a long time the pub was great, when there was a core of people looking after it. It was manageable mayhem, but it got messy when a lot of people started coming and going. Lots of bands had access to the basement – Métal Urbain rehearsed there and so did The Derelicts and prag VEC.

Sandy Robertson: I moved in because I basically couldn't get on with Fergusson. Then somehow he followed me in there. Fergusson might have ended up there on his own and the place made him nervous because he took to carrying a hatchet round with him everywhere he went in the pub.

Tony D and his mate the Skid Kid were also in there and Tony had this idea, this fantasy that Aleister Crowley had once lived in the pub. Where he got the idea from I have absolutely no clue. Tony one time brought in this coffin that he'd found in the street and propped it up against the wall. It looked like one of those temporary coffins used for shifting bodies to the mortuary. It wasn't finished in any way and had no handles. It gave off this terrific, ingrained and really quite unpleasant smell.

'The Scottish Plague' – Sandy Robertson, Tony D, and 'the Skid Kid' at the Trafalgar pub. Skid could occasionally be found in pyjamas at the kitchen table, immersed in a comic with a sign taped to his chest that read: 'Don't speak to me, I'm concentrating'.

Carolyn Holder: I used to go to see them at the Trafalgar quite a lot and it really was the most frightening and unpleasant place. The first time I went to visit I asked Jo where the loo was and she told me and warned me to be careful as the floorboards were up and there were some live electrical wires. There was a big, cavernous basement. It was not nice at all.

Jo Slee: At one stage water from a burst pipe had leaked into the wiring, so the metal bath became live. You had to jump with both feet from the floor onto the side of the bath to get into it without getting a shock. A friend of Steve's, Chris Ward – 'Sparks' as he was known – came in and fixed the problem, and also bypassed the electricity meter so that we could run electric fires. Before that we used to break up furniture from the dump across the road and burn it in open grates to keep warm. Even so, to get the water sufficiently warm for a bath from the tiny electric heater, you had to run the tiniest of trickles at almost boiling. It took about two hours, by which time it was still just about warm enough.

When the drains became blocked we ran a hosepipe from the bathroom window to the alley below, and you had to go down and suck the hose so the bathwater would siphon out.

The pub really was unsafe and for many years I had nightmares about it. I'd ride my bike to work at full speed in the middle of the road because there always seemed to be somebody following you, or somebody watching you. Or it was a ten-minute walk to Rough Trade through the flats – the ghetto – which I hated, especially after dark. Even Steve got mugged one time – pretty badly: he was hit over the head with a whisky bottle. I remember having a fit at Rough Trade and forcing them to pay for some new glasses for Steve. I figured that for somebody not even drawing a wage, the least they could do was buy him some new glasses.

Sandy Robertson: One time Peter Walmsley went outside down into the main sewer to try to unblock the drain. The police arrived, checked out that it was a squat and gave him a hard time. They told us that the rota brought them back around in one hour and that we would have to have it done by then. There were gypsy kids jeering us on.

We got burgled at the pub. Steve had a nice new second-hand stereo and these guys got in but were disturbed by John, who was coming up the stairs. He thought they were just visiting one of us but then he realised that there was a guy hiding in the toilet. The guy ran out and John started chasing them. We could see that in Steve's room the stereo was gone so we trooped up to Rough Trade to tell Steve the bad news. He was mortified. Then we got back and found the stereo in a carrier bag hidden behind the door of the toilet. We'd disturbed them just in time. So back we went to Rough Trade to tell Steve the good news.

Jo Slee: The fanzines that were coming out, the records, all of this was coming to the pub via Steve. John and I finally gave up the leather workshop and for three months in early 1977 went to work for a market-research company, so we were a little bit out of the loop for a while. John got in first and then got me in by telling them I had a degree in economics. There was a guy there who pestered John at the drinks machine for information on punk. He was incredibly posh and faintly irritating. He wanted to be told about punk. What did John think of it? What was happening? What did it mean? He told John his name was Peter York.

*

Jon Savage: There was quite a gap between *Spiral Scratch* and the Desperate Bicycles, which came out in the summer, so really it took a while for the whole DIY thing to get going. Of course, there were really lots of DIY bands, it's just that *Spiral Scratch*, the Desperate Bicycles and Scritti Politti are the most famous ones. Industrial Records were going early on and Genesis was always in the Rough Trade shop. That was good because it showed that Rough Trade weren't just into left-wing stuff but had a broader spectrum.

Early TG sticker.

Geoff Travis: Two of the Desperate Bicycles came in the shop and played us their record, 'Smokescreen'. What excited us about the Desperate Bicycles was that they'd done it themselves. It wasn't like it was the best record we'd ever heard – it didn't have an effect on us in the way that *Spiral Scratch* had – but the whole process was interesting. It had character and it had the message. We thought that they had a fantastic, surrealist sense of humour. 'It was easy, it was cheap, go and do it' – I think they were the first of the bands to demystify the process by explaining to you how it was done and how much it cost.

Steve Montgomery: Throbbing Gristle told us that we weren't going to be allowed to stock or sell on mail order or in any way distribute any of their product unless we gave them a window display for *Second Annual Report*, which came out later in the autumn. It was the first time Rough Trade had ever done anything like that – a window display. Apart from feeling manipulated, I didn't really have a problem with it! I thought they were thinking ahead. They had their marketing concept all worked out and were still taking advantage of the publicity from the previous year's infamous Prostitution event at the ICA.

They brought in a giant logo, one of those with TG lettering and the flash on, and we stapled up some covers in the window. It obviously worked – I think we sold quite a lot of the 785 copies they pressed up through 202 Kensington Park Road by the end of the year.

We were selling so many copies of records at that time that we needed some help. We were blessed in the shop with having some enormously talented customers. And they loved to do nothing more than hang out. I consider it a privilege to have been able to have spent time with people like Jon Savage, Vivien Goldman, Savage Pencil, Sandy Robertson, Jane Suck and Daniel Miller. There were lots of others. We had a few record company people in as well, people like Andrew Lauder from United Artists and Jumbo Vanrennan from Virgin, both of whom were enormously supportive and helpful. They were incredibly creative people, and of course many of them – in particular Vivien – never lost the opportunity to push Rough Trade. Many of them ended up working at *Sounds* in one capacity or another and, well, we got pretty good press in that paper. We tried to get one or two of them working for us, but that invariably never worked out. I think Jon Savage may have done a stint, and Savage Pencil certainly did a stint, for about a nanosecond.

Geoff Travis: It seemed as if the shop had quickly gone from not having any customers in it to being packed out, and we were stretched. When the shop first opened, having a customer walk in was an event. You had to pretend to not get too excited.

Steve Montgomery: It wasn't too long before there might be seventy-five kids packed in the shop on a Saturday. You could barely move. Over a period, they all started to look the same, dress the same, and ask for the same records. And that was the point where we'd either lost the battle or won the battle – I could never work out which. I did ultimately stick with the philosophy that if you wish to make change, then you have to keep changing. I think before too long we reached a point where we settled.

Geoff Travis: Vivien Goldman recommended Richard Scott to us. Vivien had been a press officer at Island Records and had met Richard when

Richard had been managing Third World. He came over to see us and eventually started working with us.

Richard Scott: The original plan was that I would be going in to help expand the reggae section. They were very interested in my experiences in Jamaica, where I'd spent time working with Third World and Island and had visited all the local reggae studios. So, I went to see Geoff one afternoon – and got spat out the other end thirteen or so years later.

Richard Scott (third from left, back row) and Third World, Boston, 1976. Allan Sturdy, who would later work for Rough Trade Inc. in America is first left, front row.

Steve Montgomery: Geoff approached me and said that he had met somebody he wanted to bring into the organisation and would I meet him. Richard stopped by the shop and told us all about his time with Third World. I was very reluctant to have Richard join, and I told Geoff so. I felt Richard had big ideas which weren't in keeping with how Rough Trade was at that time. Geoff said he'd think about what I said but a week later told me that Richard would be joining the company. Geoff's father and his sister came that day to meet Richard and they all had a big powwow out the back. The whole thing certainly undermined my position.

They had ideas about how we could develop Rough Trade and it felt like within a short time we were all going to be millionaires, just like the advert said on the back of *Sniffin' Glue*. I had this unsettling feeling. It all sounded like pipe-dream stuff. I believe that Mark Perry's negative comments about

Rough Trade came about because he actually could see what was coming down the line, in much the same way that he'd seen what was coming when The Clash signed to a major. I think he saw that we were transitioned between being your friendly community record shop and being like one of the majors who were the enemy.

Jo Slee: Richard came in as a father figure, quite paternalistic right from the start, and I think Geoff found some comfort in that and felt that Richard was probably somebody who would be able to hold an entire area – say mail order – without Geoff having to worry. He would then be able to get on with what he should have been doing, which was finding new music. I think he saw Richard's background and involvement in the music business as bringing something very valuable to the embryonic, near non-existent structure that Rough Trade was at the time. But I think Richard had the effect of seducing Geoff away from what he had got set up with Steve, and that was unsettling for Steve.

Richard Scott: One of the first things Geoff did when I joined was play me a record by the Sex Pistols. I'd been on the road in America and all of this stuff had passed me by. Geoff felt very strongly about bands like The Clash and the Sex Pistols. I'd never heard anything like it. There was an added edge. I was very impressed, and very impressed with Geoff.

Although I had come in to do the reggae, the first thing I turned my attention to were sacks of letters from people trying to buy records and fanzines that nobody had found the time to deal with. There was a company called Rough Trade Promotions, started by one of Geoff's friends from Cambridge, which I don't believe was anything to do with Rough Trade, which had been set up to sort of muscle in on the Rough Trade action and these letters were all addressed to them. I think they had a view to taking care of the mail order. The whole thing was just a complete mess and I told Geoff to just get rid of Rough Trade Promotions which, thankfully, he did.

One of the earliest, official Rough Trade missives was the one I sent out in response to the unopened mail which had piled up. I apologised for sending out what was effectively a flyer – there was no time to write personal letters – and assured them that we hadn't copped out and joined big business. I also told them not to deal with Rough Trade Promotions: 'We are not connected and if you have ordered anything from them (RT Proms) and haven't received it yet it would be a good idea to start hassling – then when you've got what you wanted you would be advised to deal direct with us.'

The interesting thing about the letter is that it was the first time that the Rough Trade logo most people recognise was used. Steve had done a design for the bags, which I messed around with at the kitchen table at home with a notepad and a John Bull Number 3 printing kit (which belonged to my son) and came up with something we could use on a letterhead. In the end, of course, it has been used on the Rough Trade shops as well.

The customer base really started to grow and a lot of it was through word of mouth. Somebody who would know about us would tell their friend, and their friend would write to us. We had some extraordinary early customers, including a shepherd in the Orkneys and a man who worked in air traffic control at Schiphol airport in Amsterdam. By complete chance, I once met the air traffic controller on a trip to Amsterdam to see Pere Ubu. He told me he bought a copy of nearly every record we put out.

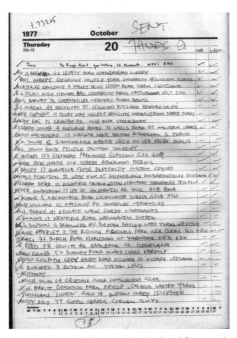

A 1977 mail order customer list includes David Whitehead from Rotherham, who would later be in charge of distribution.

It was pretty soon after I arrived that we started to get requests from shops looking to buy up any extra stock we had of records they couldn't get enough of or who were looking to get records they just couldn't find through their normal sources. At first, it was a few records at a time – and fanzines, there was always a big trade in fanzines. But it quickly started to grow.

Jon Savage: After Richard Scott's arrival, Rough Trade started to change. I was very friendly with Steve. I liked him. I liked it that he liked having fun. Richard's arrival, it seemed to me, was the start of the edging out of Steve. I didn't particularly have much to do with Richard but I could see that he was very different from the other two.

Jo Slee: At that point you could start to detect the first stirrings of trouble in paradise.

*

Jo Slee: I left the market research company and decided to come back to Rough Trade in the autumn. I did briefly move to premises over the road where I started to make feather jewellery, but that didn't come to anything. When I got back, one of the first things I did was go on strike. We had no structures, no systems to operate within any structure, and we led insane lives. I wrote a rather embarrassing manifesto about it. Steve said he supported my action but was too busy to join me. Richard said he'd go slow but that he couldn't work any slower than he already was. Geoff was just mightily pissed off about it all. No one really took a blind bit of notice, true to form. Many years later, having driven the writer Michael Bracewell to Morrissey's flat in Manchester and having told him expressly that smoking was forbidden in the flat, I found Morrissey wandering around looking for an ashtray for him. 'Doesn't anyone ever listen to anything I say?' I asked him in exasperation. 'No,' Morrissey replied, without missing a beat, 'but they're *very* impressed by the way you say it.'

Peter Walmsley: I had got a job through the Job Centre, working at a record-pressing plant called Unity Records some time I guess in the autumn of 1976, and the contract was for one year. I think they were receiving funding and the funding lasted a year. Unity made overtly political records which they seemed to think no one else would be interested in handling – they were very committed Marxists – and we used to mix the vinyl and hand-press it in the basement.

Throughout that year I was in and out of Rough Trade all the time and when Unity ran out of money, I suggested to them that I go to work for Rough Trade and help Unity out for free when I had spare time. I started first doing the Red Star deliveries – Wednesdays and Fridays – and then at the end of 1977, as they were moving towards becoming a record label, I started helping out with production because of course I had learned all that from my time with Unity.

Steve Montgomery: The Sex Pistols' album came out in October and we sold about one thousand copies of those every month over the next few months. That really capped 1977. We were doing so much business that bands would come in and talk to us about a repress and we would end up offering to take the entire repress and so they'd go away and double their order. We had done that first time round with the Eater single 'Thinking of the USA', and Throbbing Gristle pressed up another five hundred copies of *Second Annual Report* for us on the side, as I recall.

All the business at this time was being run on a cash basis. We really didn't go legitimate until 1978 kicked off, although we had always had someone doing the bookkeeping. In a funny way, Geoff was the biggest liability. *Receipts? What are they?* I used to have to keep a very strict eye on what went in and out of the till and I would force him to account, wherever I could. He just couldn't be bothered to deal with it. On more than one occasion I had to go through his coat pockets to find out what he'd paid for records so that I could work out what to charge for them. I regularly demanded he empty his pockets for me.

One of the more lucrative areas that we had started to explore was that of bootlegs. We really didn't start stocking them until demand just got too great to not have them. In 1977, there was a big desire, for instance, for Patti Smith bootlegs and a lot of our customers were coming in and asking us to get them. Geoff had a phone number for 'the bootleg man' – it was all very shady – and periodically the guy would come in with boxes of the stuff for us to pick out what we wanted. At that time, Springsteen, Dylan, Bowie, the Rolling Stones – there was huge interest in getting hold of bootleg material by them – and we got it and sold it. Legitimate shops like HMV and Virgin would sell the stuff – a lot more expensively than we did, mind – so there was a lot of hypocrisy over them. We very nearly got into serious trouble a couple of times.

A few weeks before *Never Mind the Bollocks* came out we were given the word that an alternative take of the album was going to be available on bootleg and were asked how many we would want. This was, of course, the legendary *Spunk* bootleg. Well, I think we may have taken as many as a thousand. I have some vague recollection that whatever the print run was, about half of them found their way to Kensington Park Road. The timing was to say the least fortuitous and of course many speculated on the real source of the record, many believing it to bear the stamp of Malcolm McLaren.

That wouldn't surprise me. We were on very cordial terms with certain members of the Virgin label – they were just around the corner in Vernon Yard and would come in all the time. And we would go to them. We were picking up records from them – Motors singles, Pistols, X-Ray Spex, stuff like that. In fact, they gave us armfuls of what would now be priceless Sex Pistols posters which we plastered all over the pub walls. I'd been to see Jumbo at Virgin over Christmas 1976, and saw on his desk an itinerary for the proposed Anarchy Tour. There were the dates for the tour and by the sides of some of them there was the word 'Cancelled' in brackets. When I picked him up on this, the sheet was hastily put away and I was told that I wasn't supposed to have seen it and that in fact I hadn't.

We'd sold a fairly colossal amount of *Spunk* when Virgin sent in the dogs. Luckily, some kind soul at Virgin – probably Jumbo – tipped us the wink and told us what to do. Virgin had sent in some staff who had surreptitiously bought copies of the album and now they were sending in the big boys to deal with us. We were told to say – it's ludicrous, I know – that we didn't realise that the records were unofficial and that we were sorry. We'd seen similar records in HMV and therefore thought they were legitimate. Could we give back to Virgin the copies we had left? We must have taken about twenty so there must be about five left, we told them.

I handed over about five copies of the album back to them, keeping about another fifty under the counter, which were sold very discreetly after that. Virgin went away and we heard no more about it.

Jo Slee: Geoff had himself got into trouble over selling copies of a David Bowie bootleg – *Bowie at Earls Court*, I think it was. He was seriously reprimanded. He was quite pissed off about it at the time and rightly so – bootleg records were more or less available over the counter everywhere and often being sold in record shops owned by the record labels who were complaining. Carolyn and I laughed our heads off, though: in Geoff's acceptance of the charge he made the comment: 'I don't *feel* guilty.'

Steve Montgomery: We had started to receive tapes from kids who wanted to know how they could get their record released, a trickle that turned into a deluge. The idea that we would start a record label pretty immediately was there as soon as the tapes came in. I believe we would have started the label earlier, but we didn't have enough finance. We were selling lots of records, we'd started distributing them, but there really wasn't that much spare cash around. We had pretty high overheads, largely courtesy of Mr Deverill, the landlord.

We were getting tapes in but Geoff would put them in his pocket to take away and listen to and we had no system for registering them. I used to get irate phone calls from people – I remember the Monochrome Set ringing up – demanding to know what we thought of their tape. What tape? I would ask. So they'd send another one in, and the process would begin all over again. I remember very early on receiving a tape from Cabaret Voltaire, possibly even before Jon did his piece in *Sounds*, which was really what led Cabaret Voltaire to Rough Trade.

Jon Savage: Alan Lewis, our editor at *Sounds*, called us in to plan yet another punk round-up issue for the paper. Vivien Goldman, Jane Suck, Sandy Robertson and myself were charged with this task in November and we rebelled. We told Alan that punk was long over for us. By now The Stranglers and The Jam were successful and all these old pub rock bands had come out of the woodwork with bleached hair and speeded-up Ramonic songs and it was all a bore. So instead, we decided to do a new music round-up about electronic music. We did a two-part special on Throbbing Gristle, The Residents, Devo, Kraftwerk, Disco and Siouxsie & The Banshees, all of which was rather impressive and annoyed the hell out of *NME*, who were way behind at the time.

I'd been on a mission since that punk summer to seek out the new. After the electronic music piece, I got a tape from Cabaret Voltaire and went up to Sheffield to interview them. I then put them in touch with Rough Trade.

Steve Montgomery: We had so many people from so many record companies coming in that I think it would have been impossible for us not to become a label. The point is that bands had started name-checking us on their sleeves. The sleeves would often make reference to the fact that the record could be obtained from Rough Trade. Consequently, lots of boring A&R guys from the majors used to come in and surreptitiously and sometimes not so surreptitiously fish for information. They'd pretend to be buying some records and gradually turn the conversation to the subject of what was new. They'd ask us what we were listening to, what had we heard that was still underground.

Sometimes it worked against us. EMI swiped The Saints from us and Virgin did the same with Devo. We'd got a tape from Devo and loved it and were trying to get in touch with them when Jumbo walked in and said 'Have you heard of this band Devo?' That was the end of Devo for us.

CHAPTER FOUR:

1978

Rock 'n' Roll Zoo column from Sounds, June 1978, based on Rough Trade and annotated in biro by Carolyn Holder who 'must have learnt every word of this by heart'.

'These were people I considered to be at the height of cool'

Robbery – First Rough Trade Records releases – Electronic music – Mail order catalogues – First contract – 'Skank Bloc Bologna' – Expansion – Synagogue

Steve Montgomery: The shop was so obviously doing well that sooner or later we were bound to be a target.

Jo Slee: We didn't have a real till – it was just a cash drawer – and on Saturdays when the shop was jammed full, it would be overflowing with money and would need to be emptied on a pretty regular basis through the day. This was at a time when we still had pound notes.

More staff had arrived. Sue Donne had joined and taken over some of the mail order from Steve so that his enormous workload could at least be reduced. On this particular Saturday there were three of us in the shop working. At the end of the day, when it was time to close up, Jon Savage was hanging around, as often he was, and also a guy called Johnny G who I didn't know but who had come to meet Sue. We had been unusually busy and had just locked the shop door to cash up. It was dark outside.

Steve Montgomery: These guys banged on the door and Jon came back to tell me that they said they knew what they wanted and weren't going to browse. When I opened the door, I suddenly had a gun thrust in my face.

Jo Slee: Steve decided to open the door, and three black guys burst in. They dropped the catch on the door: one of them was waving a gun around. His eyes were rolling and I instinctively tried to hide myself behind a record rack. A bearded guy in a trench coat was in charge.

As soon as they saw me move towards the record rack, one of them started screaming, 'No alarms! No alarms!' We hadn't even got a real till, let alone an alarm system. They rather melodramatically ripped the phone wires out of the wall. I was looking at the guy with the gun and thinking, 'One of us has been watching too much TV and I hope it's not him.'

Jon Savage: As soon as I realised what was happening I started yelling at the black guys to fuck off. I was absolutely furious. At the same time, Steve was yelling at me to shut up. It was insanity and really a quite dangerous situation. But the idiocy of youth was driving me on. At least until Steve managed to calm me down and got me to be quiet again.

Jo Slee: They took us out the back and made us lie down on the floor in the side office. I couldn't stop myself having a go at them – we were all cross. I asked them why they were doing it. One of the guys just said to me, 'It's a living, y'know?' So there we were – Sue, Johnny and me lying on the floor when one of those absurd moments occurred. I suddenly became aware for the first time that Johnny G was there and I blurted out, '*Who the bloody hell are you?*' It was all such an unreal blur – everything seemed to have slowed down and stopped and I couldn't focus. I'll never forget the look on his face. He may have wanted to strangle me at that moment.

Two of the guys took Steve into the office to get the shop takings and they made him empty his own wallet, though they let him keep a speed wrap he had in there. There was about £1,200 in cash and Steve had the foresight to take out the cheques and tell them that they wouldn't be any use, which was remarkably clever.

They kept us on the ground while they edged to the door and ran out and then it was over. And the first reaction of all of us was to be incredibly pissed off at what had been done to us. We had no phone line so we had to go round to Ron and Gloria, who ran the Wavy Line grocery shop a couple of doors down from us, to call the police. Ron and Gloria gave us brandy and shortly afterwards the police arrived, sirens, flashing lights, big drama.

Steve Montgomery: They wanted me to go around in the police car and try and find them. I was very uncomfortable about this, to put it mildly. They gave me a police helmet to cover myself up. We drove round to the Mangrove and somewhere along the way I saw them. They didn't need to go any distance before splitting up the spoils. There was no way I was going to point them out.

Jo Slee: Steve wasn't going to get a reputation for grassing people up to the police.

Steve Montgomery: We went over to Carolyn's after. Geoff wasn't there – he was out at a gig. Carolyn really looked after us. Then it all struck home and I broke down. Carolyn was really sweet and gave me a badge, which I've kept to this day. It reads 'I & I SURVIVE'.

There was a lot of bad feeling in the community over what had happened. The robbers came back in the following week, nonchalant, and I threw them straight out. *Irie,* man. From that moment on I got the respect of the Rasta community. I was no longer the fluffy boy in green dungarees with spiky orange hair.

*

Geoff Travis: We started offering to help bands with manufacturing and distribution and we started the label almost simultaneously. The Television Personalities' '14th Floor' single had come out at the start of 1978, a terrific record, which everybody in the shop loved. I went to see Dan Treacy from the band – this was my first home visit to an artist – in his mum's council flat off the King's Road, which was on the fourteenth floor. He played me some tracks from what would become the EP *Where's Bill Grundy Now?*. And I remember hearing 'Part-Time Punks' and being very impressed; to be able to have that caustic, witty parody of the whole scene down at such an early stage was quite an incredible thing: he saw through the whole plastic punk/weekend punk thing and of course he had the perfect vantage point from just off the King's Road on the fourteenth floor. So we took over the manufacturing of the EP and of course later released 'Part-Time Punks' as a Rough Trade single in its own right. We ended up selling 25,000 copies of the record.

We had already done a similar thing with Swell Maps, who became one of the most important Rough Trade bands. They'd put out 'Read About Seymour' on their own Rather Records label and Epic Soundtracks had sent it to me with a letter asking if we could help. Again, we funded it and then took it over as a Rough Trade record in its own right.

I went to see them play at the Railway Hotel in West Hampstead; they were one of the most exciting bands of that period and it was one of the best gigs of my life. With them, as with other bands, it was a case of they'd got so far on their own and then we offered to come in and see how much further we could take it.

When I got to know them – and of course both Epic and Nikki came and worked part-time in the shop – I realised how extraordinarily well versed in music they were. For me they were the quintessentially independent group. And they were very eccentric in the tradition of the great British amateur, tinkering in the shed. They had their pseudonyms and they created their own little magical world, all of which was quite unusual that early on – now everybody does it. One of the tragedies of Swell Maps, aside from the terrible loss of Epic and Nikki, is that not many people got to see them: I think Biggles Books was still studying at the time and it was always quite hard for the band to get together.

The second Rough Trade album we released, which was their first, *A Trip to Marineville*, had that marvellous cover with the picture of the burning suburban house, which always reminded me of a kind of more vicious version of Fairport Convention's *Unhalfbricking* cover. We released that album the same week as Joy Division's *Unknown Pleasures* came out on Factory and I remember bantering with Tony Wilson and saying my record is going to sell more than your record – and it *did*, for about five seconds.

A Trip to Marineville – *suburban tinkering complete with* Unhalfbricking *cover for the post-punk generation. The image was taken from an advert created by an insurance company who were thrilled to receive a free album in return for the rights to use the shot.*

Steve Montgomery: The strange thing about the Rough Trade label is that Geoff, for various reasons, wasn't around for the release of either of the first two singles. It was happening but in fact he went to New York at the time of the first record and was ill during the making of the second.

Métal Urbain had sent us their first single, 'Panik', which we played in the shop all the time and loved. They came over to England and wandered into the shop one Wednesday. I remember the day because they had gigs on the Thursday and the Friday. They played me a demo tape of 'Paris Maquis'. Geoff was in New York, hunting out new music and also he was supposed to be having the first real break he'd had since the start of Rough Trade, which he deserved, and I just thought it would be nice if we presented him with our first record on his return. So, after the gig on Friday we rushed off to a studio in Sussex, recorded the track over the weekend, got it all ready, and somehow I was on the station at King's Cross, Sunday night, waiting to take a train to the boat to Dublin, where it was cheaper to have the records pressed.

Jo Slee: I met Steve at the station café, where I drew a circle on a sheet of A4 using a café plate and did the 'artwork' for the record label. I was still finishing it off about three minutes before the train was due to leave. On the record label outer edge there's a circle with a jagged rip in it. That was my little joke about Rough Trade being a vicious circle (working ourselves into the ground while trying to change the world).

Steve Montgomery: I took all the money for the record out of the till. We were still a wholly cash organisation. I went the cheapest route and had ten thousand copies pressed up, when perhaps two thousand might have been enough. I think unsold boxes of that record provided foot support under desks for most of the workers up until the company went bust in 1991.

Richard Scott: Everton da Silva was a friend of Augustus Pablo and he walked into the shop one day and asked if we wanted to put out *Pablo Meets Mr Bassie*. I have a vivid memory of going to cut the record. When we arrived, the cutting man was finishing off his last job – cutting an album of that year's FA Cup final. When he wasn't looking, Everton unplugged all the VU meters on the machine, turned everything up full tilt and then switched everything back on. The engineer freaked out – but Everton was right. Played on a good machine that track sounds fantastic.

I'm not sure we expected the record to do terribly well, for some reason, and I think that is why we gave the record sleeve a sticker rather than a proper cover.

Peter Walmsley: George Peckham often used to cut the records – they were Porky's Prime Cuts – and I think he sometimes couldn't believe what we asked him to do. I remember turning up with a cassette tape of the Electric Eels single – that was all we had got to work from. I think he used to find it amusing.

Robert Christgau: I'd come to England at the end of 1977 to do an article on punk and somebody had told me that I needed to check out Rough Trade. So I went into the shop and on that first occasion I remember meeting Geoff Travis and Jon Savage, who was in the shop at the time. The shop was wonderful, wonderful because of the moment it was – more wonderful than it could ever be again. That was the start of a friendship with Geoff that has continued. After that he visited us in New York and was our house-guest for a while and one of the best we have ever had – he always folded up his daybed and always did the dishes.

I remember on that trip to London, Geoff turning me on to Culture's album, *Two Sevens Clash*, and I also remember Jon Savage telling me to go and see Wire when I couldn't decide whether to go and see them or Sham 69. As it happened, I believe I saw both during that trip.

Geoff had got the label going or was well advanced with it by the time of my visit. You got the feeling that if Geoff didn't feel a spiritual affinity with an artist, then he wasn't interested. Then and now he has always liked smart people – that is one of his virtues – and that isn't always a virtue in pop.

Steve Montgomery: It is funny: when 202 opened the only thing the postman brought through the door were bills. Now he was staggering in every day under the weight of tapes being sent to us. They were all screaming, *release me, release me* . . .

In the summer we had a visit from Tony Wilson, who came in to the shop for the first time and brought with him Joy Division, who had just released their *An Ideal for Living* seven-inch. I remember, he came in and walked up to the counter and said, 'Who's in charge?' After that was established, I listened to a tape of the single – it may even have been before they got the single out – and he said they wanted to release it as a twelve-inch; would we take some? Whatever we agreed to take, we never quite got them, because by the time the record was pressed, word was out and all that was left for us, I think, was about a couple of hundred copies.

I had difficulty coping around this time. Although we had started to employ more people – Ross and Judith Crichton came from Australia and started working with us, and we sneaked Peter Walmsley, one of the great unsung heroes of the enterprise, into the operation to do the Red Star, and Ana from the Raincoats was helping out part-time – I started to have doubts about my ability to cope with all the pressure. Gradually, I took to

ROUGH TRADE 202 KENSINGTON PARK RD. LONDON W.11

01 727 4312

VAT No. 241 7725 65   7th. AUGUST 1978.

FLAT
     CHATFIELD RD.,
CHORLTON,
MANCHESTER 21.

DEAR ROB,

        Regarding the distribution arrangement for the "Joy Division" 12" you
plan to release.

        This is what we will do: Upon receipt of the records we will pay half of
the sum outstanding the rest when we have sold them. The price agreed per u
unit between yourselves and us is: 65p. We understand from you that you are
intending to press 2,000 copies this means that we will pay you in total
after all the records have been sold a total of £1300.00p.

        I hope this letter is sufficient between us as an agreement. And
that we can work together for future projects.

                              Yours sincerely,

STEVE. for ROUGH TRADE.

ROCK n'ROLL MECHANICS

taking the odd bit of speed during the day to help me cope and buckets full of ganja at night to help me sleep.

Jo Slee: Steve could be pretty volatile and we were all under stress from the sheer amount of work. I think it is hard enough in those circumstances to get along with people when they don't take drugs, so when they do, it's doubly difficult. Back then, Steve was also capable of creating a problem without anybody else's involvement and sometimes his mood depended on what he was taking. Smoking spliffs was probably the best thing for him: but when he was doing speed and other stuff, well, his behaviour could change.

We all were under extraordinary pressure and, in fact, John and I made the decision to emigrate to Toronto. That 1977/78 winter, I often went with Peter Walmsley in the Rough Trade van to the Red Star offices around London to avoid freezing my arse off at the pub. It was warm in the van. I had a provisional licence and while Peter was dealing with the paperwork for getting the boxes of records sent off, I used to tootle around the goods yards. That was essentially how I learned to drive. Then one Friday, Peter cunningly made me drive back to the pub via Hyde Park Corner – there were no traffic lights in those days, it was more like one big dodgems circuit – and when that went all right, I knew I'd cracked it.

John and I were gone by May.

Daniel Miller: I loved electronic music and I loved punk and in my mind I saw them as totally linked and I suppose that was one of the ideas I was trying to express through my single. I'd not been a Rough Trade punter – my work as an assistant film editor for ATV kept me in Borehamwood most of the time. But I knew about the shop.

In fact, I phoned them up to get some advice on how many copies of 'T.V.O.D.' I ought to be looking to press. I spoke to Steve Montgomery, who said they didn't really deal with anything less than ten thousand, which took me aback a bit. It was only later that I found out that they'd massively over-pressed the Métal Urbain single.

I picked up some test pressings from the pressing plant and dropped in at Small Wonder, which was close by, and they played it and seemed to quite like it and said they'd take fifty. Then I went up to Lightning, the distributors, and they took some but didn't seem that interested. I had no record company experience and hadn't got a clue what distribution was. I had a test pressing of the single I had made in my bedroom; it was something physical, and that was all I really ever wanted. I was very excited.

I thought I might as well drop into Rough Trade, but I was very nervous. The way I saw it, Rough Trade had this aura of cool and I was just some bloke off the street coming in with a record. I talked to Steve and he sent me to the back of the shop to talk to Geoff and Richard. These were people

I considered to be the height of cool. They weren't cool, they were just enormously friendly, as was everybody who worked in the shop. They suggested we go and listen to the record on the shop stereo, and I panicked: the first time they heard the record, it was going to be a public airing. But they seemed to like it a lot and asked me what I intended to do. I said I'd press five hundred and hope for the best. They said that they would distribute it but that I'd have to press two thousand.

Jane Suck made it 'Single of the Century' in *Sounds* and the record got such good reviews that were way beyond my expectations. I really didn't think anyone would like it at all. But pretty soon there were masses of export orders and we were repressing all the time and before too long I was more or less based at Rough Trade. This was like a fantasy to me. I was twenty-six years old, a hopeless musician who only ever wanted to be involved, and suddenly here was a dream come true.

I never planned to start a record label – I didn't know what I wanted to do, really. After putting out the single I went to help at Rough Trade, doing some PR. But the weird thing about the success of the single was that the sleeve had my address printed on the back, and within days I started to receive demos. It sort of freaked me out. Having a record out didn't make me a record label. But I kind of became one by accident.

Geoff Travis: 'T.V.O.D.' and *Warm Leatherette* sum up that period brilliantly and I think if that record was rereleased today it would have a huge impact all over again, it still sounds so fresh.

Steve Montgomery: Daniel Miller was such a fantastically sweet man – but he was really quite shy. If other people came in and started talking to you while you were having a conversation with him he'd quietly slip away. He was so embarrassed when we played his test pressing in the shop. And at first, he didn't want to leave a copy, but after he did we had it on auto-play for about a week. So many people asked about it when they heard it played in the shop. A&R guys would fish for information – who are The Normal? Have they done any other tracks? How many are in the band? When I told people that it was recorded by one man in his bedroom, and that he still lived with his mum, they backed off as fast as they could. Daniel was keen to remain anonymous and we abided by that.

It was an important record, and a very well-loved record, but at first it wasn't that easy to distribute if people hadn't heard it because of course it was in a category all of its own. 'Electronic pop music – what's that?' people would ask. That soon changed.

Daniel Miller: I realised after I'd made my own single that there were other people doing a similar thing and in fact so many records around spring 1978 seem to relate to each other. 'Being Boiled' by Human League came out around then and so did the Cabaret Voltaire EP. There were records by The Residents and Tuxedomoon.

Geoff Travis: Those records became huge in the shop. The Normal, the first Cabs record, the Human League, and later Thomas Leer and Robert Rental. They were very pioneering records and they created a whole scene. I remember David Bowie coming in to 202 Kensington Park Road and buying all of those records, while we looked on, aloof. It wouldn't have been our style to pamper him.

*

Steve Montgomery: The mail order catalogues had gone from being single-sheet inserts to being a proper, albeit photocopied, affair. I used to write the material inside and then Savage Pencil would do the artwork. We did one where Jon Savage did the cover and wrote some of the copy as well, but that was a one-off. We did a mail order catalogue and a wholesale catalogue. Of course, in typical Rough Trade fashion, we never kept the lists and I'd have to re-Letraset the thing each time we redid it. There wasn't any word-processing back then. I'd put in my little word from the sponsor – the message to the kids – and occasionally the odd joke: Skrewdriver – *All Screwed Up* might become Shrewdriver – *All Shrewed Up*; that kind of thing.

Jo Slee: They were works of love and things of great beauty.

Savage Pencil: I based all the artwork on that mentality that US underground comic artists had – people like S. Clay Wilson, Robert Crumb and Gilbert Shelton. I was a great admirer of Cal Schenkel, who had done the Mothers of Invention artwork on *Ruben & the Jets*. I was obsessed with that and that is where I got this idea of portraying animals as people, which ultimately led to my *Rock 'n' Roll Zoo* column in *Sounds*. Instead of the

Two early mail order catalogues and one wholesale catalogue. 'We're a much more musical family since the Rough Trade mail order catalogue came into our lives,' opines a mail order catalogue designed by Jon Savage, who also provides the front cover copy; Savage Pencil's wholesale catalogue features the Rough Trade 'microvan' and various Rough Trade humanimals. Steve Montgomery's mail order catalogue is 'back with a bang'.

Mothers, the Sex Pistols or The Clash could be animals. What sparked the idea off was the fact that people all more or less look the same but there are millions of species of animals. I'd just adapt an animal to whatever idea I was trying to express. I did one drawing of an anteater with a big nose and nose ring and chain – a punk anteater.

I'd mess around with different covers for the catalogues – I put the Rough Trade microvan on one issue – and then keep to a template inside for the headings.

Steve Montgomery, Richard Scott, Geoff Travis, Jo Slee.

Inside it would be the team – Steve, Richard, Geoff and Jo. This borrows heavily from Cal Schenkel. Alex Fergusson always claimed that Geoff looked like a giant mouse. I don't know whether I took some of that in.

Then I had the Rough Trade dog, which was very obviously a send-up of the HMV dog. Ours had a safety pin through his ear. He was a punk dog.

The Rough Trade dog – HMV, eat your heart out.

The reggae heading would today be seen as being fabulously un-PC. It is a mad Rasta walking around like one of the nutty characters in a Robert Crumb comic. The butt of the joke isn't the black guy but the white guy who is listening to Althea & Donna and thinks it's fantastic because it's on his radio. The Rasta is just dissing him: *Crazy Bal Head.*

The last page had this spaced-out hippie freak and a punk who can't work it out and an alien who's just landed on Earth and likes what he hears, I suppose ...

Although I was giving them artwork, I have to say that one of my favourite things was the original Rough Trade logo, which Ken had done. I was fascinated by it. I was in awe of it. It seemed to tip perfectly into end-of-era hippie and early punk. It looked really cheap, but it was actually brilliant. I could never work out how he had done it. It drew you in. Mind you, the first time I went in the shop and saw the booth where the counter was, I thought I'd walked into a mini-cab office with records in the window.

Cabaret Voltaire photographed outside the Rough Trade shop.

Steve Montgomery: It seemed at the time that every single day something new was moving it along. It might be a box of some band's brilliant record arriving in the shop unsolicited, or a tape that we were excited about, or some band that suddenly you just had to go and see. But one of the most important bands to Rough Trade was Cabaret Voltaire, whose record we put out after Pablo's.

Richard H. Kirk: We'd formed in 1974 and done our first concert as Cabaret Voltaire in May 1975, but at the time of working with Rough Trade we hadn't actually officially released anything. We did a lot of recordings, often in Chris Watson's loft using basic equipment. We had released a limited-edition tape – very limited: I think we only did twenty-five. We'd sent Throbbing Gristle a copy after hearing *Second Annual Report* and were in touch with them and we'd sent a copy to Richard Boon at New Hormones. It was through him that we kind of made the Manchester connection. In fact, we played on the second night after they'd opened the original Factory club on Moss Side. We'd also sent the tape to Jon Savage and he'd been up and interviewed us and done a reasonably large piece in *Sounds* and another in the American magazine *Search & Destroy*.

　　Both Throbbing Gristle and Tony Wilson wanted to release something, but as I remember Throbbing Gristle didn't have the money and loosely suggested Rough Trade and although Tony Wilson did release a couple of tracks on the *Factory Sample*, we'd already gone to Rough Trade by then. In retrospect, it was the right choice. I liked the fact that Rough Trade let us do all our own artwork. If we'd gone to Factory, we'd have had Peter Saville foisted on us and been moulded into the Factory brand.

Jon Savage ultimately put the connections together to make the Rough Trade deal happen.

Jon Savage: After the *Sounds* round-up at the end of the last year, Cabaret Voltaire had contacted me and sent me their tape and I'd been up to interview them and written about them. I told Geoff that he should go and see them since they were supporting Buzzcocks at the Lyceum.

Geoff Travis: I saw Jon's piece and I went to see them at the Lyceum, where I met them, and shortly after that we put out the EP.

Richard Boon: Although lack of funds meant I wasn't able to do anything with the Cabaret Voltaire tape, I was able to help by putting them on the bill with Buzzcocks at the Lyceum.

Richard H. Kirk: An absolute nightmare of a gig. There were loads of bands on the bill and apart from us it was a full-on punk night. We didn't get an adequate soundcheck and the feedback was horrendous and when we came off stage we were covered in spit. Punks weren't really ready for Cabaret Voltaire at that point. It was a bit like when Suicide supported The Clash. I think we lasted about twenty minutes before we were forced off but it could have been worse. I think Buzzcocks had an iron bar thrown at them.

We didn't get any money for signing with Rough Trade – in fact, I'm not sure we ever actually signed with them; every record was done on a one-off basis, as I recall, although I think there were written agreements later – but what swung it was the fact that they offered us money for a four-track recorder. We'd been recording everything two-track up until then. We had the material for the EP but decided, having got the new equipment, to rerecord it. It was all very basic. We did the tracks almost live. We recorded it in mono. It was quite a long record and they cut it at thirty-three rpm but forgot to mention that on the actual record. An awful lot of people played it at the wrong speed, but they still enjoyed it.

Richard Scott: I got a phone call from Geoff, who was deejaying at Dingwalls, to say that he had this band called Cabaret Voltaire coming down from

Sheffield later that day and could I come up with some sort of contract. I just wrote something out in biro on an old notepad and that became the basis for all of the future fifty/fifty deals. It was barely two paragraphs long. It basically agreed to split everything after costs equally and to agree to work together until one or other of us could find a reasonable reason not to do so. I like to think that the contract still stands today as a fair deal.

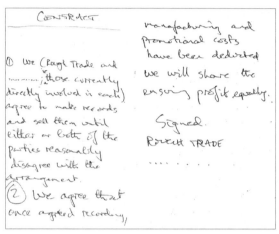

The original handwritten 'fifty/fifty' Rough Trade contract.

Richard H. Kirk: Geoff came up and saw us in Sheffield and we came down and met everybody at Rough Trade at 202 Kensington Park Road. I remember that there was this collective vibe around the place and they often seemed to have a band working in the shop. We'd have told them where to go, I think, if they'd asked us to work in the shop, although, of course, based in Sheffield that wasn't going to happen. When they opened up the offices above the shop, we often slept in there if we had a gig on – that's how glamorous it all was. Some of us didn't need that much sleep, of course, because some of us were taking speed. We definitely preferred to not get involved in that whole Ladbroke Grove scene.

We didn't really like much of the stuff that Rough Trade went on to put out. I remember we stayed with Stiff Little Fingers occasionally: they had a flat in Shepherd's Bush they let us crash at. They were nice lads, but their music wasn't our cup of tea. We liked The Pop Group and we liked The Fall, but that was about it. We got on well with Mark E. Smith – maybe it was because we were fellow Northerners and he could see we had a slightly different take on things. The Fall came up to Western Works and recorded four tracks. It was fantastic fun watching Mark tell the rest of the band what to do.

Mark used to say to me that Rough Trade were a bunch of lazy hippies. He was convinced that they were never there selling his records when they ought to have been. He said he wanted to hire a bus inspector's outfit, like Blakey wears in *On the Buses*, and hang around at 202 Kensington Park Road at nine o'clock one morning to see if the bastards did actually turn up for work.

I think Rough Trade gave us the ideal scenario to develop as a band. They never put any pressure on us, which was great, priceless really. They just let us get on with it.

Richard Scott: It must have astounded Cabaret Voltaire that we would just release the stuff exactly as it came in. It would arrive in a package and go straight off to be manufactured. It was brilliant but it used to make me laugh.

*

Richard Scott: When other people started joining the organisation – and by the end of 1978 we were up to approaching ten staff – politics, of a kind, became important. Very early on we decided that it would be an equal pay/equal say structure. We wanted a non-management structure where consensus was important. Decisions were made unanimously so consequently there were a lot of meetings even early on, often after we had closed the shop. Punk had been a very political movement and a lot of that political feeling was still hanging around by the time that Rough Trade started to grow. We had some broad rules in terms of what we would and wouldn't sell. Naturally, there was no place for anything sexist or pro-violence or that didn't fit in with a general political position, which was broadly left wing.

Jo Slee: Geoff once did an interview in which he said that Rough Trade was the only socialist record company. Carolyn and I laughed unkindly. It seemed a grandiose claim. Where the idea came from that Rough Trade was party-political, I'll never know. As individuals we each took a particular line, but I don't remember being out to make a political stand – except perhaps to change a little bit of how the record business was run. Personally, I had an entirely utopian dream of an open-minded, egalitarian workplace in which both individuality and community could flourish ... a functional family.

Equality was in some ways taken to ludicrous lengths – we would never have cleaners, for instance. In fact, because Geoff used to come in at the crack of dawn, he would often be found sweeping the warehouse at eight-thirty in the morning with a giant broom. He hated mess.

At the time, most things were judged as left or right wing. Having cleaners was viewed as demeaning to the cleaner and therefore elitist.

Peter Walmsley: That the company was run as a cooperative seemed natural to me, certainly the reality of how people worked overrode any legal reality. The commitment from Geoff and Richard was always that the company would be handed over to the staff and that made sense. I always thought Richard was the more philosophical in the approach to the cooperative idea, whereas for Geoff I felt it was instinctive for him to act that way.

When I first went there, it seemed to me Richard was very instrumental in getting the company running properly. Through his Island contacts, he'd set up a manufacturing arrangement and I think it was Richard who turned it into a structure. Along with Sue Johnson, our bookkeeper, he was the one organising things like PAYE and all that kind of stuff. They turned it into a proper company. Originally people weren't being paid and then, almost suddenly, six or so people were being paid a notional sum, and I think Richard was very forceful in making sure the equal pay structure was in place. Richard was someone who, more than anyone, I think, I felt I could go to for advice or depend on for help in trying to get my bit of Rough Trade working. I always saw him as someone I could lean on if I needed to.

Geoff loved the music but I think at times he could be as much of a nightmare to organise as he could be brilliantly creative in bringing the material in. Geoff became the record label because it was Geoff's role to arbitrate. If a tape came in, he decided whether it would be a Rough Trade release or a P&D deal, and of course that had different consequences in terms of cost allocation. We were forever wrangling with bands who had any kind of professional management because they would want to go through the contract working out how exactly costs would be allocated, and they probably knew more than we did early on about how the contracts should have worked.

Steve Montgomery: Everything emanated from Geoff, ultimately – the music we sold, the politics surrounding the way in which we sold that music, and the attitudes we adopted. Anything we brought to it needed the catalyst that was Geoff. I'll never forget that or deny him the credit he is due. When I came, I was able to more vocally express some of those views and take things really to the next stage politically.

Geoff Travis: I think that the most important thing that Rough Trade ever did was conceive of the idea that if you were an artist and you produced a record then what happened to that record after that point was very significant. What we wanted to achieve was a situation where we controlled the means of distribution and we decided the criterion by which a record would or would not enter the distribution system. And that was a theory of politics and a theory of supply.

Richard Scott: It seemed very important to me from very early on that anyone who wanted to be involved in the music business should be allowed access and that it was part of our job to enable them. It started out with us being able to sell someone's record in the shop, then being able to distribute it to other shops, then being able to put it out ourselves if we liked it. And when the Cartel was up and running, not only could we do that but we could help other people – people living in the regions – work in the music business as well, because they would then help distribute those records. Right from the start, getting rid of the London-centric attitude to the music business was important.

Jon Savage: The ideological side to early Rough Trade really appealed to me, because there was a lot about music that I didn't like, in particular the sexism. They had ideas there about community action, about decentralisation, primitive ideas about feminism, which appealed. I think fanzines and the dialogue that was created in the shop through them were an important part of helping develop it all: and 202 Kensington Park Road became a meeting place where ideas could be exchanged. Having the table and chairs in there was very important. It was more like a Head shop: it had that vibe.

Richard Boon: The shop wasn't just looking to make a quick buck. It was a nexus of information. It certainly took up the old trope that information is power – the idea of putting twenty copies of some fifteen-year-old's badly photocopied fanzine on the counter was fantastic. The shop became a public space where all sorts of information could be found. This was not Google – this was social networking before social networking became a multi-million-pound business.

Jon Savage: Famously, there was the time when Steve Montgomery refused to sell The Raped EP, *Pretty Paedophiles*, and burned it in front of their manager in the back of the shop. Everybody went yuck when they saw the thing, but I think Steve's rage was as much to do with how terrible the record was.

*

In true Scritti Politti fashion, months were spent deliberating the image on the first Scritti badge, before Joly MacFie, tired of waiting, created his own design and had them pressed up.

Green Gartside: Towards the end of my fine arts degree course at Leeds I'd stopped painting, the significance of which I'd started to question, and the polytechnic, for all sorts of reasons, wanted to kick me out. One of my tutors was Jeff Nuttall, who was wonderfully entertaining, rude and often very drunk. For my Final Show, I showed no paintings but stuck up writing in my studio space, and Jeff and another lecturer had to get one of the university lecturers in to decide if it was any good or not. They eventually awarded me a 2:1. It would have been a First but they penalised me for not attending lectures, which I'd more or less given up on.

One of the problems, as they saw it, had been that I'd invited undesirables, like the conceptual group Art & Language, up to the polytechnic. I was starting to get more into philosophy and even before leaving Leeds had begun reading French critical theory, stuff like Derrida and Lacan that would inform the work of Scritti. I'd also invited Henry Cow up and put gigs on in Leeds for them. I adored them. I remember hearing the Sex Pistols for the first time whilst with Henry Cow. Chris Cutler, the drummer, was spitting feathers at the whole thing, which he thought of as very bourgeois. We had a big falling out about it, and when our single came out one of the first letters I ever received was from Chris, saying, 'You stick to what you know and leave the music-making to people who know how to do it properly.'

So, it would be summer 1977 that we moved into a squat in Carol Street, and the game plan was – be in a band, make a record. There was myself, Nial Jinks, Tom Morley, my then girlfriend Lynne Hutchinson, and Dennis Cullum, who went on to become a film-maker.

Some friends of ours had left Leeds the year before and already squatted in another house in Carol Street. There was an old lady and her mother living in the house we wanted to move into but we knew they were being rehoused and so we contacted her and said we wanted to move in when she moved out and could she leave the back door open. As I recall, she went out the front door as we came in the back.

Carol Street squat.

There is a picture of Carol Street on one of the records, which shows how basic the place was. There was no bathroom and for a while no electricity, since the electric box took these big old ceramic fuses which the council had removed just before we sneaked in. You couldn't buy the fuses any more in hardware shops. We used to go to the public baths at Kentish Town, where you could rent out a bath for a specified amount of time. One day while I was doing this, I looked up and saw a fuse box with fuses similar to ours in it. I nicked one and took it back and tried it in Carol Street and it worked. It wasn't too long before we had the electricity back on.

The first time I came into contact with Rough Trade was when I was doing some work for the Young Communist League. I worked on a paper called *Challenge*, occasionally writing some journalism, and helping putting on gigs. There was a big gig at Alexander Palace with Subway Sect, Slits and Aswad, and another one I remember at Holloway with Sham 69 and Aswad. Geoff let me take some boxes of records to sell and fanzines to help support the YCL. He was enormously helpful. We didn't have any particular discussions about theory but there was an understanding that this was part of some broader joint project. I certainly felt it was important to him to enable us, to facilitate us.

When we'd been up in Leeds we had squatted in an old hotel in the Hyde Park area and it was there that we met Barney Boatman, Matthew Kaye, who became our manager, and Bob Scotland. They were some of the people who went on to form the St Pancras League of Young Communists. All would be part of the wider Scritti church and some of them went on to work for Rough Trade.

Steve Montgomery: I remember Green coming in for the records and fanzines for the YCL gigs and Tom Morley used to come in the shop a lot on his own. They came in one time and asked for Geoff and all trooped through to the back. About a month later they returned with boxes of records and told me that Geoff had agreed to distribute their record.

Green Gartside: We'd seen what the Desperate Bicycles had done and we regarded them very much as pioneers. We didn't know that you could just go out and make your own record until they showed us how. We got in touch with them and invited them over to the squat. At this point the squat was becoming a very lively place. It had got a reputation and people would just turn up and knock on the door. We had people from all over Europe arriving.

Fissures and ruptures are often exaggerated but I think post the Sex Pistols Anarchy Tour of the year before, there had been genuine change and one was aware of a new topography. I was certainly punk enough to be an early admirer of The Clash. I had been fascinated by that first album: it bewitched me. In fact, I knew a woman who worked with Jasper Conran and I asked her to get me some clothes made exactly the same as Mick and Joe's. Tailored trousers with red, gold and green stripes and a shirt with the Westway stencil.

So when we started to make music, I didn't see myself as doing anything in opposition to punk. It was just my take on it. Although given what we'd been through at Leeds, it was impossible that we would sound like, say, The Clash or The Cortinas.

It was important to us that we do everything ourselves when it came to making the record. We took our tape into Geoff and played it for him and told him that we wanted to do the record on our own label. We were keen to keep it on St Pancras because that was where the base of our Young Communist League was, and we were proud of that. We particularly liked the statue of St Pancras at the top of Parkway in Camden, the bas-relief of him being eaten by dogs, which we put on the sleeve.

Geoff Travis: They came in and played 'Skank Bloc Bologna' and I thought it was absolutely wonderful. I think they were looking for validation and sort of asking us if we would distribute it. I made the fatal mistake of asking somebody who worked at Rough Trade what they thought of it and they said that they thought it was a bit long in the middle. They thought it was a bit indulgent. So instead of it being a Rough Trade/St Pancras collaboration, it became a St Pancras record. I still regret that. I didn't ask for opinions after that.

Green Gartside: We were in the back garden of the Engineer pub in Camden one night listening to the John Peel show on a tinny little radio when he played 'Skank Bloc Bologna' for the first time. The Engineer was one of the few pubs in Camden we weren't banned from. Peel was really complimentary and said he'd love to meet the band. We downed our pints and ran through Regent's Park and down to Portland Place and waited for him outside. When he came out, he had a T-shirt on with what I took to be a food stain, around which someone had drawn a circle and written the word 'Food', which I took to be a reference to Lee Perry's *Return of the Super Eight* album, which has a similar design. We went for a pint with Peel and he asked us to do a session.

*

Steve Montgomery: Rigid Digits in Belfast had put out Stiff Little Fingers' 'Suspect Device' and we had offered to distribute it, which we went on to do. We then put out 'Alternative Ulster' on the Rough Trade label and then rereleased on Rough Trade 'Suspect Device'. I thought that Jake Burns had great onstage presence and I think if they had stayed with Rough Trade they might have had a career as big as The Smiths'. They were great kids, but they clearly had aspirations. They saw themselves as the archetypal Northern Irish punk band.

Geoff Travis: Steve Montgomery and I mixed 'Alternative Ulster' at Olympic Studios, our first experience as producers. They were great – all great. Henry Cluney was just a genius, one of the best rhythm guitarists ever. The media were suspicious of their manager Gordon, as I recall. He co-wrote the songs and there were allegations later that he operated a bit like a Svengali.

Richard Boon: I offered to put Subway Sect on a big tour supporting Buzzcocks and Bernie Rhodes, who was managing them, phoned me up and asked if it was a buy-on. This was the scurrilous practice of charging a band for the privilege of doing the support slot for you. So I told Bernie that it wasn't a buy-on but that the band needed to have a record out. The record was 'Ambition'. Bernie rang me again and said: 'You'll never guess, I've only gone and done a deal with Rough Trade, with Geoff Travis.' He made it sound like he'd done something absolutely ridiculous.

Steve Montgomery: Bernie Rhodes never foresaw what was going to happen after punk and it puzzled him, I suspect, a bunch of hippie types up in West London making strides with the kids. I always felt he wanted West London for himself.

Geoff Travis: I don't think Bernie, or Malcolm McLaren, for that matter, had any interest in any kind of alternative structures – I think both of them just felt that alternative meant inferior. They had a very selfish vision, which sort of blurred the status of the artists in their minds and which in the end was the downfall of both of them. They were classic Tin Pan Alley operators, manipulators, the fastest thinkers on the block who were always going to come out on top regardless of who might suffer. Rough Trade ran on a different philosophy – we were trying to put power back into the system. We weren't trying to recreate *Expresso Bongo*.

Richard Boon: 'Ambition' was Single of the Week in three different music papers, three successive weeks in a row – *NME* first, then *Melody Maker* and then *Sounds*. It couldn't have been better for the tour.

*

Steve Montgomery: Richard Scott's arrival disjointed me. I tried to get on with Richard but I think our approaches were very different. Richard had come in and picked up on the mail order, which Sue Donne then started helping with, and had taken on the job of developing distribution. I felt under-appreciated. I didn't, surprisingly, stand on the rooftops and hurl abuse as I usually did and instead threw myself into as many jobs as possible. But there were times when my behaviour was erratic – I'd walk from the back of the shop to the front and I'd have no idea why I'd gone there, so I'd return to the back of the shop and ask somebody what I'd gone for, a single, a fanzine order. So, I'd go back to the front of the shop again and when I got there I couldn't remember why I was there. Twenty-five paces – all it took for me to lose it.

By the end of the summer, I really didn't know what I did every day: I was a wreck, physically and emotionally. I would make decisions and it seemed Richard would go to Geoff and Geoff would undo them.

Peter Walmsley: Steve and Richard wrangled all the time. Steve didn't help his cause because he could be fairly truculent at times and I think that had the unfortunate effect of marginalising him.

Steve Montgomery: It all came to a head one evening when I had organised a meeting at a restaurant. We were all so flat-out busy that we had no time to discuss things properly and so I arranged the first of what would go on to be the legendary Rough Trade meetings. It was a horrible night, pouring with rain. No one turned up on time. Then they couldn't agree on what to eat. I was in such a state anyway that I just stood up and said I was quitting. I walked back to the pub with tears streaming down my face.

I felt that I had failed Geoff. I felt that I had failed Ken. And I felt that I'd failed myself.

I went into the shop the next day to clear my stuff. Geoff asked me if

I was really going. I told him that I felt I was spinning wheels and felt continually undermined. He didn't really say anything. It was over.

Two months later I came out of what must have been a clinical depression and got a job sorting letters with the post office at Paddington. I was told by the union rep to slow down and when that didn't happen I was put on collection, but I just used to whizz round and collect the letters from each box as fast as I could. I'd have all the boxes emptied well before their scheduled emptying time, so that didn't work either. I tried a stint streetcleaning for the council but that came to nothing.

A year or so after all that work ended, towards the end of 1980, I wound up in Los Angeles visiting a friend. I noticed a flyer for a Cabaret Voltaire show at the Sokel Club and persuaded the man in the ticket booth to pass on my phone number to the Cabs. Later that afternoon the Cabs called and to all intents and purposes, I was back on board.

*

Richard Scott: By late 1978 we were selling and distributing huge quantities of records, relatively unimaginable quantities by today's scale. A good single might sell ten thousand copies easily, an excellent one twenty-five thousand copies. In September, we took the entire first pressing of 'Teenage Kicks' by The Undertones. We were deluged with records and we needed more space. I brought in some builders I knew from my architecture days and they built a bigger shed in the back yard. I'd been an admirer of how Chris Blackwell organised Island and he arranged meetings around a large table where all his departmental heads would work. All bits of the company were constantly informed of what was going on. I decided to adopt the same approach for Rough Trade and we had a big table around which essentially everything got done. I built all the work surfaces and furniture. We hadn't bothered with planning permission and at some point the synagogue, a very near neighbour, came to see us to say that we had blocked off their fire escape. Geoff had shelves of records and tapes running across our side of the fire door. The synagogue wasn't busy and they didn't seem that concerned. They said that if we agreed to open the synagogue for them on certain mornings then they would turn a blind eye. They sometimes came in, though, and grabbed Geoff to make up the numbers for a minyan when they were short.

CHAPTER FIVE:

1979

'What we were trying to achieve could not be
achieved short of driving the machines mad'

Inflammable Material – Rough Trade Tour – *South Bank Show* – Politics –
The 'legendary' Scott Piering – Scritpop – Distribution – Rough Trade
Inc. – Blenheim Crescent

Peter Walmsley: There was so much production work by the start of 1979
that I was working full-time. There was the mastering, the pressing, the
label-printing, the cover-printing, and before that – the worst part – the
designing of the sleeves, usually using Letraset. We were forever using
Letraset, hours spent trying to make sure everything was level. I remember,
towards the end of 1978 we'd finished the production on the Stiff Little
Fingers album and it was Mayo Thompson who finally came up with a
design for the sleeve – using Letraset.

Mayo Thompson: I'd played in the Red Crayola in the mid-1960s and later
worked for Robert Rauschenberg and then I'd got involved with Art &

Language. By 1978, things with Art & Language weren't working out and I'd come to England unsure what I was doing. I'd read about Rough Trade in *Sounds* and went in one time and asked to hear 'Thirty Seconds Over Tokyo', the Pere Ubu single, because I'd read about that also and it seemed like something I might understand. That was my first visit. I came back a while later and took twenty-five copies of *Corrected Slogans*, an album I had made with Art & Language, in to see if they would buy them. Geoff said that he could sell them all, a claim that later turned out not to be true, but gradually more copies found their way into the system: more importantly, I found *my* way into the system.

Geoff and I hit it off, and I think part of the reason why we hit it off was because I was from the outside. I had a history of having made music and a reputation but I was also a neutral figure who came from nowhere.

I liked Geoff, I admired his candour and the fact that he was very sure about what he would and wouldn't take when people came in with stuff.

Initially, I hung around a while doing odd jobs – boxing up records, sorting out tapes – and I designed a poster for them based on an image in an old Italian comic book. Richard Scott had experience of the music business. Geoff had done some deejaying. Rough Trade was a confluence of competences – or a collision of incompetences – that compelled us to make things up as we went along. Once that energy got going, people came forward and embraced us, wanting to help out, wanting to get something out of it all. In a marketplace of goods and ideas, it was mutual exploitation.

Geoff entrusted the A&R desk to me. The job was basically one of saying no to people in a constructive way. Rough Trade was not a record company where you could necessarily send in your hit record and we would put it out. Geoff had to like it. His taste was everything. I was rejecting about twenty-five tapes a day and I went to Richard Scott and asked to help, and that was when the guide to making a record was put together.

Then, in 1978, the manager of the Monochrome Set approached me and asked me to produce a record. I told Geoff about this and he said he'd been approached by Stiff Little Fingers to produce their record. So, we decided to work together and that was how the producing got going.

Geoff Travis: We recorded the Stiff Little Fingers album in Spaceward in Cambridge, partly because the Mekons had used it and partly because it was cheap to independents.

Mayo Thompson: Stiff Little Fingers were basically a bar band who made it. I was told that Henry Cluney, their guitarist, was a Protestant and Jake Burns, the singer, was a Catholic, and their lyrics were written by their manager Gordon, who was a very smart guy, so it was all interesting. The thing about Rough Trade is that it could accommodate all kinds of variety, Jamaican, African American, working-class English, Northern Irish. It wasn't trying to produce *functional* music.

Geoff Travis: We did the album in one week and I think we did a good job; in fact, it rankles a bit that Mayo and I never got a credit on *Inflammable Material* when it was reissued. It doesn't matter; it's a great record and it was fun to do.

Richard Scott: I used to get the tube into work from Stockwell and in those days you were allowed to smoke in the carriages that were the ones before the front and back carriages. So I always sat in one of those. I remember getting on and lighting up and opening my copy of the *Daily Mirror* and seeing *Inflammable Material* in the Top Twenty. I couldn't believe it. I thought it was fantastic.[14]

Peter Walmsley: That record really took the roof off. The success of it was a kind of combined effort – they were getting to be enormously popular and we were ready for it in the sense that we could see what was going to happen. We'd had meetings where we had discussed Stiff Little Fingers and whether or not we could afford to take the gamble – because it was clear that they were getting big and that we would need to press and sell a lot of records. It is true that the music papers did have messenger bikes lined up to take the album back to the offices to get out a quick review. Stiff Little Fingers were really the first of those Rough Trade bands where the dilemma was whether or not they would go off to a major.

Richard Scott: As I recall, we parted ways with Stiff Little Fingers over a disagreement about advertising. We had a big meeting with them and flatly refused to do ads, which was in line with our policy at the time. Adverts were all that the band ever wanted. Chris Blackwell had once said to me

14. The record went into the charts the day before Jake Burns's twenty-first birthday and he has said that it remains his 'best birthday present ever'.

that the worst thing that could happen to a successful independent record label was if it had a big hit. There was a bit of that in my thinking, I believe. Ultimately, the disagreement led to Stiff Little Fingers leaving Rough Trade.

Peter Walmsley: Stiff Little Fingers wanted to do a tour, but they couldn't get a booking agent, so Sue Johnson and I went to see one and came away with a great long list of costs and demands required for the tour to go ahead. It was all nonsense, really. We knew they were popular so we decided to just get on the phone and book our own tour. It ended up thirty-six dates and some of them were booked through Richard Scott's customer connections.

Richard Scott: Probe helped out in Liverpool. Red Rhino did York and a fabulous man called Roly Reed booked a hall at Doncaster. He used to come and buy records off us and sell them at truck stop cafés. Wonderful. Factory, the club, put the show on in Manchester and on the poster it read 'STIFF LITTLE SINGERS'. Simon Edwards booked Birmingham. Simon eventually came to work for us but at the time of the tour he was working in a shop in Handsworth in Birmingham called Inferno. They were very important. Big reggae suppliers. They, along with other shops, used to provide Chris Tarrant's *Tiswas* with their weekly mainstream pop chart, which would then get read out on the show, and I remember later on one occasion when Simon arbitrarily put The Prefects' single 'Going Through the Motions' at Number One. A Wham! record was at Number Two. I really liked him for that.

The London gig was at the Electric Ballroom. Austin Palmer, one of our van drivers, set up his Mighty Observer Sound System and played between bands. It was fantastic.

Simon Edwards: Our relationship with Rough Trade came about through reggae. Two white guys ran Inferno and they used to go over to Jamaica and buy up masses of pre-s and bring them back and sell them to shops. This was quite a radical thing to be doing back then. We had a van driver called Ray who would take a Transit van full of pre-s down to London and go round the shops delivering them. Ray did all the deliveries with his Alsatian dog in the front seat. Rough Trade would hand over £3,000/£4,000 in cash in a brown paper bag each time he made a delivery.

Richard Scott: Every record we got from Inferno we had already sold and we could quite easily have used more, but they weren't that easy to get.

Geoff Travis: We must have decided that we needed to be like Stiff Records and have a package tour – Stiff Little Fingers, Essential Logic and Robert Rental and The Normal. They were marvellously well-attended shows and the whole thing was a great success. Simon Frith, who is now an esteemed professor of music and music connoisseur, and who worked on the Rough Trade *South Bank Show*, says to me that the show he saw in Leicester was one of the best gigs of his life.

Peter Walmsley: The tour was incredible, if occasionally scary. I remember being paid in Liverpool in soggy pound notes and walking around in the middle of the night in what would now probably be regarded as quite a dangerous part of the city with thousands of pounds in cash on me. I think we rarely slept in hotels and probably didn't need to since we were doing things to keep us awake anyway.

I had experience of being on the road and in fact the first gig I had done had ended badly. Métal Urbain had played the Nag's Head in Aylesbury and needed a driver at the last minute. I saw it as part of my job to go and collect the money after the show and when I did the promoter refused to pay and pulled a knife on me. I was dumbfounded, but I thought, they are due their money and it is part of my job to get it for them. In the end the band pulled me off a fight I was almost certainly going to lose.

Daniel Miller: The Stiff Little Fingers album wasn't out when the tour started and it was all supposed to be very egalitarian, but it quickly took on the classic structure of a rock 'n' roll tour. The album came out and went Top Twenty while we were on tour and it was incredibly exciting. Stiff Little Fingers became huge at that point and went down incredibly well. Robert and I were put up in the Rough Trade van, which had no windows and had a door that didn't close properly. It was the middle of a very cold winter. It wasn't miserable: it just wasn't how it was supposed to be.

And we used to go down really badly on stage, in a violent way. People would throw things at us and jeer. We had some extreme reactions to our music, and I suppose in a way that was what we hoped for, and, anyway, the more abusive the audience got, the more musically noisy and difficult we became.

The tour was incredibly badly routed because it had started out as a small tour and then, as it became successful and the Stiff Little Fingers album charted, new dates were added all over the place. It was very arduous. At Eric's in Liverpool, the backing tape hadn't been rewound from the night before so it played backwards for the entire gig; no one seemed to notice and it was all in the spirit of the time. John Peel came to the Nottingham show and gave us a great write-up. I used to have conversations with Robert during the set about when we would flee the stage but we never actually did. Since we used a backing tape the set had to last the same amount of time each night, anyway.

Mayo Thompson: Daniel Miller was brilliant on stage. He could twist a knob with a grimace on the face similar to the grimace I wore playing a Telecaster.

Peter Walmsley: Before the tour started I had a screaming match with Daniel Miller outside 202 Kensington Park Road. He was having a panic attack and refused to go on tour.

Geoff Travis: *Inflammable Material* was the first independent record to break the Top Twenty and it sold over 115,000 copies very quickly. It was what enabled us financially to develop Rough Trade Records. It was a big success for us at the time and meant we could move forward in a much more secure way.

Richard Scott: Around about the time of the tour, there was a *South Bank Show* devoted to Rough Trade. There was half an hour on Rough Trade and half an hour on the sculptor who made tables out of nude figures. For some reason, although Melvin Bragg introduced the show, he didn't present it; it was all done by Simon Frith. During the filming, Geoff said something about how after their first work an artist is never as interesting, because of how they are treated, and the production guy or the camera man turned round and said to me very confidently, 'Melvyn will *love* that.' I'll always remember that.

Carolyn Holder: Around about the time of the *South Bank Show*, I remember the *Sunday Times* ran a profile on Geoff. It was the first mainstream piece on him – there had been the stuff in fanzines – and on the day it was published I remember we drove up and down Ladbroke Grove in Geoff's clapped-out car while he decided whether or not to buy the newspaper. For

all sorts of political reasons, we wouldn't be *Sunday Times* readers but there
was also the issue of Geoff embracing or not the idea that there might be
publicity about him. It was a little bit like the bands who wouldn't go on
Top of the Pops at the time – you didn't do it.

*

Gina Birch: Before moving to London, I'd been at Trent Poly doing a
Foundation Course and while I was there I got involved with what you
might call a conceptual art tribe, people involved in Art & Language. It was
very political because there were always lots of factions, but it was also very
exciting. When I moved to London, though, and started studying at Hornsey
Art College, although the course I was on was interesting, and it had some
interesting fellow students – like Elizabeth Taylor's daughter, who painted
horses, and Anish Kapoor – there was no core to it, no tribe like there had
been in Nottingham, so I became lonely. I was living with a bunch of drug
dealers in Islington when Neil from the Tesco Bombers said I could move
into his squat in West London. This was a squat within a group of squats
and this became my new tribe. Richard Dudanski, who played drums in
The 101ers, was there with his partner Esperanta, whose sister Palmolive
played in The Slits.

There was this great community of punks and hippies and everyone
joined in. We all used the Tea Room, which was a kind of local café and
food co-op in a squat where for 20p you could get brown rice and vegetables,
a pudding and a glass of sarsaparilla. The punks and the hippies really
joined at this point and in some ways the DIY ethic chimed with many of
the hippie ideals. I suppose that's what we were, really – middle-class punk
hippies.

Even by the time I'd left Nottingham in 1976, I already had a kind of
proto-punk look. Fine artists had then been going for a look loosely based
on Abstract Expressionists and Conceptualists, drainpipe trousers, jumpers
with holes in, a look which, when I trawled the charity shops of London,
was augmented with mohair, spotty dresses gathered up with old ties for a
belt, funny old boots, in fact anything that looked peculiar. We had lots of
discussion about punk, heated arguments: Neil and Richard were ambiva-
lent at first, but Palmolive was into it straight away.

Ana Da Silva: I knew Gina from college and she hung out in the house
I lived in with my cousin Manuel. I'd been to the Patti Smith gig at the

Roundhouse and as a result of that I had cut my hair like hers but it was a long while before we thought about forming a band. By 1978, there were a few all-female bands and we put The Slits on at our college but it wasn't until we were sitting in the pub one day that we just decided to form a band. At the beginning, there wasn't a conscious desire to make it all-women, in fact I felt initially it would be better to have a mix of the sexes.

Gina Birch: It was after I'd seen The Slits at Harlesden that I became aware of what I wanted to do for the first time. Previously, I'd been a consumer of music, a supporter, without really feeling I could be involved. But after I saw The Slits, I thought, 'Why aren't I doing this?'

I went out and bought a bass guitar – a bass because it had four strings and I thought it would be easier to play – and two spray cans of bright blue paint. I took all the knobs off the guitar and spray-painted it. Nick Turner came to play drums and Ross Crighton, who was working at Rough Trade, came and played guitar. Tymon Dogg gave us a support slot. Within three weeks, somewhat bizarrely, we did a tour in Poland. All the posters used the words 'punk rock' and the locals would tear out those words and pin them to their clothes. People threw eggs and tomatoes at us, whether through love or disgust I don't know. The reviews described us as 'whores escaped from prison'.

After Ross left, Jeremie Frank joined. She had these wonderful green high-heel snakeskin boots and it all gave us a bit of a Runaways feel, but it wasn't going to last, fun though it was. Then Patrick Keiller briefly joined and that was when Geoff gave us some demo time.

Patrick Keiller: I was teaching an afternoon a week up at North East London Polytechnic, where Richard Scott had taught, and had a friend who introduced me to Gina and Ana. I think Gina might have heard me play at the 1978 Degree Show. Anyway, I went to some practice sessions and played a gig with The Raincoats at the Cryptic One Club and then we spent a day in Spaceward recording some demos. These were not considered suitable for release. I remember (perhaps wrongly) that Gina told me that Geoff thought one of the tracks sounded too much like Them's 'Here Comes the Night', and I worried that this was probably a result of my contribution.

Ana Da Silva: I think essentially that was all Patrick could play. People would hear the tapes and say, 'It's good, but it sounds like "Here Comes the Night" ...'

After Palmolive got kicked out of The Slits and joined The Raincoats, we made a decision to go all-female. It was Palmolive who put the advert in Compendium Books in Camden – 'Wanted Female – Strength Not Skill'. Rock is very male in its outlook and we were often judged by the fact that we were women. So, it was important to us to try to be prominent so that we could be an inspiration to other women, to help them get the courage to go out and do things like be in bands themselves.

Shirley O'Loughlin: That was such an important moment when they decided to make the band all-female. Histories of music – well, of course they are always the writers' histories in the end. It is often the male experience. They are often written from the writer's record collection. For me, seeing Patti Smith or The Slits play was far more exciting than watching The Clash.

Gina Birch: Vicky Aspinall joined after seeing the ad. Vicky came to see us with her friend Caroline and Vicky thought we were terrible but her friend thought we were good and talked her into joining us. Vicky was a classically trained violinist and had been involved in feminist politics, which was a whole different world to us. We were more grounded in art, language and philosophy, but not politics, I suppose. So when Vicky came into the band this whole other agenda was forced upon us, the idea that politics couldn't be ignored. Once the feminist word got out the bag, we were asked about it all the time. It was good and bad. I'm quite proud of what we did. But at that time there was such a dreary aspect to feminism. Were you allowed to wear lipstick? What exactly *were* you allowed to do? The Raincoats were perceived as dreary and humourless, which was ridiculous, really. I thought we were vibrant, funny and fun people.

Geoff Travis: I loved them for their spirit and their sheer nerve, just the aliveness of it all. Ana's singing was a fabulous foil to Gina's bass playing. Ana had this great, emphatic delivery: Gina's bass was much smoother. They made a lovely, glorious noise together, especially when they had Palmolive in the group. Palmolive was one of the best drummers and had a style that was just unique. She wasn't trying to be Keith Moon. And I loved it that she played with such a big smile on her face.

There weren't many bands around at that time, either, who were prepared to write about the things The Raincoats wrote about – things like supermarkets.

Gina Birch: Mayo Thompson was going to produce the single 'Fairytale in the Supermarket' and came to see us rehearse. We talked about things. Mayo told us about drones and how we could adapt them to Vicky's violin playing, which we were nervous about fitting into what was essentially a rock framework. He explained to us how John Cale used the violin in unusual ways. The less Vicky played, and the longer the note became, the more we loved it. Mayo was a very good producer for us because he helped us get character out of that sound. Geoff was more a pair of ears, someone who would suddenly leap up and shout, 'That's it!'

Shirley O'Loughlin: That first single, which came out in May, did incredibly well and I think they sold about 25,000 copies in total. It made it to Number Ninety-nine in the charts!

Gina Birch: There weren't many all-girl groups and as a result I think we all got lumped in together. There was Delta 5, The Slits and us. Then there were the mixed groups like the Mekons and the Au Pairs. The way we were treated – there were areas that made me feel comfortable and other areas where it was completely uncomfortable. Journalists like Paul Morley or Ian Penman or Graham Lock were OK, others were not so good. Some journalists seemed to have a problem with the fact that we didn't dress up, or didn't dress up in the right way, or didn't rehearse in the right way.

Ana Da Silva: A lot of the journalists pitted the girl groups against each other. They would set up rivalries and then the bands would get annoyed and make comments about each other and so it would go. I don't think we felt any jealousy towards anyone, or in competition with anyone, but there wasn't any real sticking together either.

Geoff Travis: The single was reviewed by Paul Morley and got that all-important *NME* Single of the Week, which back then really actually meant something. After the single, I think they did a tour for us.

Ana Da Silva: We toured with Spizzenergi and Kleenex and it became clear that Palmolive was going to leave so we went and recorded the album with Mayo and Geoff before she did. We just reproduced what we did live. I found Mayo a little bit bossy – he did listen, but he could be bossy. Anyway, we recorded the album, mixed it, the lot, within three weeks.

Shirley O'Loughlin: I had started managing them and so the whole unit now was all-girl. Ana stopped working in the shop, as well. Pete Donne took over from her.

*

Pete Donne: By the start of summer 1978, I'd been up at the LSE for a year and was back for the holidays. A friend of mine managed Earth Records, which was a record shop owned by Dave Stopps who ran the Aylesbury Friars venue. This friend told me he was leaving and asked me if I wanted to take over. I hadn't particularly enjoyed my year at the LSE and so after a brief time considering the offer, I replaced him.

Pete Donne, third from left, back row, at an Earth Records get-together.

Earth Records was no more than a booth, really, a bit like a kiosk at a railway station. Two racks of records, an alleyway, two windows and an L-shaped bit where the live records were stored. It was a one-man operation. No loo. You locked up for five minutes if you got caught short. It was originally set up to sell tickets so that Dave didn't have to pay commission to middle-men on ticket sales. It was tiny and functional – probably a good model of what an independent record shop ought to be today. We sold mainly tickets and only really made money on records at Christmas.

The Friars venue produced these magnificent silkscreened posters and part of my job was to clean these bloody things and also to arrange what was called 'junior security'. Dave Stopps had a mate called Robin Pike, who was a chemistry teacher at the grammar school. Robin was also a music oracle and did a bit of work with Dave and came up with the idea of having schoolboy bouncers. They were cheap and enthusiastic. In fact, it was all a bit of a grammar school mafia. I remember just before I started, Friars were going to put Sham 69 on. Of course every Sham 69 gig turned into a riot. But this one didn't, and I don't know if it had anything to do with the schoolboy bouncers, or the fact that LWT filmed the show or the fact that Friars still had this laid-back hippie vibe from its earlier days, but I was impressed.

I was drawn straight away into contact with Rough Trade. My sister was already working there and I think I would have phoned them up to get an account with them. Dave recognised that he needed to tap into my enthusiasm and encouraged me to develop a relationship with Rough Trade. He'd also ask my advice on booking bands – a promoter would suggest a band and Dave would ask my advice. I once persuaded him to put on a Dennis Brown gig, which was wonderful.

Rough Trade used to Red Star the records to us on a Friday night. It was such a thrill going down the station and waiting for a box and then immediately opening it up and going through it. There would be five copies of *Inflammable Material*, five copies of 'Being Boiled', five copies of 'Damaged Goods', that kind of thing. The next day a little coterie of in-the-know punks would come into Earth Records and buy them up.

You'd buy the records from Rough Trade and then they would sell you a couple of extra things on top. What they pushed was invariably brilliant. I remember Richard Scott very enthusiastically selling me the first B52s single, which was only available on import, and also the Fred Locks album, *Black Star Liner*. Reggae was clearly very important to them – almost part of their mission statement. It was usually reggae that they were recommending.

Richard Scott: We used to sell to Pete Donne in Aylesbury and one day I just said to him: why didn't he come and work for us. I always encouraged good

people and the business was growing so rapidly we always needed people.
I think he came down around about May.

Pete Donne: One of my best friends in Aylesbury was Jake Arnott, who went
on to become a novelist. He used to hang out at Earth Records and we
became drinking buddies. He broke his leg messing around at a Generation
X concert and he was off sixth-form for about a month and never went
back, and his parents always blamed me. I was petrified of going to Rough
Trade and asked Jake to come down to London with me for moral support
and he did, hanging around while I went in for my interview, if you could
call it that. In fact, it was a bit of a shoe-in and after a few words with
Richard, I was just introduced to a couple of people and shown around.
I remember they had a *huge* telex machine in a room upstairs – it virtually
took up the whole room and on Friday afternoon orders were telexed to and
from the UK.

I knew nothing of Geoff Travis before I arrived but I quickly became
conscious of the fact that he was the most significant person there, although
a couple of other people might have had a challenge to that claim, particularly Richard and earlier Steve Montgomery.

When I started there was the first stirrings of a push to turn the
business into a real cooperative, but I seem to recall that quickly got put
on the back burner for some reason. There were meetings in the shop
after work and committees elected. It was all very democratic but I
noticed that if the process wasn't going Geoff's way he could get a bit
sulky and somehow or other whatever was being suggested would tend
not to get done.

Looking back now, some of the issues seem comical, but at the time
I thought the meetings were more significant than they probably were.
I remember big debates over whether or not we would stock The Slits'
album *Cut*, because of its cover. Ultimately, the record was sold in the shop.
There was another debate over whether the first Nurse With Wound record,
Chance Meeting on a Dissecting Table of a Sewing Machine and an Umbrella
would be stocked, for similar reasons. I think that wasn't stocked, but then
later we sold it in a brown bag. Eventually, nobody bothered bagging it up
and we just started selling it uncensored. All too often, the ultimate outcome
of the meetings was that things just went on. There was a problem also
with stocking records by Whitehouse.

Nurse With Wound's album, Chance Meeting on a Dissecting Table of a Sewing Machine and an Umbrella, *the cover image of which was a more transgressive variant of the 'primitive' cover of The Slits'* Cut.

Richard Scott: Meetings were very important. If we were a democratic operation then everybody ought to have a right to say what they felt about what Rough Trade did. It could lead to interminable discussions and then at the end just as consensus was reached someone would disagree and off we'd go again. But it was important to have the meetings.

Daniel Miller: I don't particularly like to use the term, but around this time a kind of political correctness started to creep into Rough Trade, which hadn't been there before. Early on, Rough Trade had very much an open-door policy when it came to taking things, but now records seemed to be being valued not on the quality of their music but on their perceived political content. When Whitehouse put out their record, which was around about the time of the move to Blenheim Crescent, there was a big issue with it. Rough Trade didn't want to handle it. People at Rough Trade were saying things about William Bennett and his record that were not true. I'd got to know William because he had been the guitarist in Essential Logic and they'd been on the tour and I knew that what was being said about him wasn't right. If they thought the record wasn't good, that was one thing, but it was wrong to reject it because it didn't fit in with somebody's idea of a political landscape.

This schism was further developed outside Rough Trade, in the press, where the music seemed to be used as a divide. If you were into Throbbing Gristle, who used controversial visual imagery, you couldn't possibly be into Scritti Politti, who didn't, and vice versa. It was tedious.

Vivien Goldman: Rough Trade's very existence was political – its way of doing things was a statement of inclusion at a time when things were still very stratified. The shop became a haven for *les marginals*. It was very much a small isolated spot where we could be free to be what we were and discuss views which, though idealistic, were not regarded as twisted but rather the norm. It really was our own little version of *Passport to Pimlico*.

Mayo Thompson: Politics was around Rough Trade back then. It drew in a lot of elements. There were people like Scritti Politti and the Young Communist League talking about the work of cultural historians Hindess and Hirst, about a post-productive model and inter-disciplinary and cross-cultural studies. I'd locked horns with Marxists before, back in my Art & Language days. That was one end of the spectrum. There were the anarchists – people like Crass. Then there was a whole politics coming in from the front line, from the reggae guys, the oppressed people who had been chopping down wood and carrying water for The Man since time immemorial and who had developed their own language. Then there were various university lefties, like Gang of Four. So, there were uptown Marxists, downtown Marxists, Rastas, anarchists, even some genuine Cambridge Commies hanging around, too, and Geoff who, of course, had studied at Cambridge under F. R. Leavis.

It was a real collision of conflicting ideas and all under the general rubric – is there progress? What could it be? Progress had a quantifiable shape to it – it consisted of doing things that had not been done before, or could not have been done before. It was realising that you could make records – records that nobody would dare dream of, because nobody thought anyone would listen to them – and then becoming aware that actually everybody *should* listen to them.

Jon Savage: The thing about the very early Rough Trade releases was that they weren't ideological in the way that later releases were. The Rough Trade aesthetic, such as it was, didn't really get going until later. It was the end of 1978 and into 1979 that it all started to get dry as dust, boring as dishwater. Somehow, dogmatic politics had crept into Rough Trade and started to strangle it. I remember just before I left London to go to live in Manchester I went to a triple bill to see prag VEC, Red Crayola and Cabaret Voltaire. Mayo Thompson was there and I had thought early on that Mayo was going to be fun but by then he wasn't, he was spouting all this dogmatic crap. In the end I felt, politics is serious, but *this* is pop ... Scritti Politti, prag VEC, The Raincoats, Red Crayola – I couldn't listen to the stuff in the end. I think the rigour of the politics squeezed everything else out.

Ideology and the mode of production got confused with the aesthetic, and it is always a problem when politics gets involved with the aesthetic. If in the end the politics is unattractive or doesn't work, it tends to cast doubt on something which might otherwise be perfectly good. I think a lot of the bands around or on Rough Trade at that time that seemed to carry the Rough Trade ideology just didn't work. The only band that made it work in some way was Scritti Politti and that was only after they'd gone to Virgin. It had all become very desiccated, bloodless really. It had all become head over heart.

*

Inimitable, legendary ...

Richard Scott: I first met Scott Piering in 1976 in a small club and bar called the Savoy on Grant Street in San Francisco. This was a club where I once saw Sylvester play two sets, one after the other – first as a man and then as a woman – and Scott was booking bands there. As I understood it, Scott had been on a university Ents Committee and that was how he'd started out, a bit like Harvey Goldsmith, but I never really knew anything about his history and he never talked about it. He booked Third World at the Savoy and that was their first ever gig in America. I'd been put in touch with Scott because he'd worked with Bob Marley. After Marley had been thrown off a Sly & the Family Stone tour, Scott had booked him into the

Matrix in LA in 1973 and got him a live broadcast on KSAN. It was a famous broadcast that broke Bob Marley & The Wailers in America. It was an extraordinary thing to have done, all the more so since it was on the West Coast.

Third World spent about a year touring and then I ended up back in London and at Rough Trade, and Scott went off and amongst other things started working for Island Records in New York, but that didn't work out too well. It wasn't surprising. Scott was always a loner and would go at a completely different speed and in a completely different way from everybody else. He seemed to run entirely on fags, alcohol, and other stuff that he used to keep him going. I never saw him eat. I once saw him with three fags on the go, all at the same time. He was so engaged in what he was doing he just kept lighting up without realising.

We kept in touch and started a long correspondence – long in terms of the length of the letters – and eventually I asked him if he wanted to come and join us. The way it worked at Rough Trade, anybody joining would basically be coming in to ease the load, rather than to do a particular job. That was how it worked and then usually people settled down into the job that suited them. Scott was managing The Cramps and I arranged for Geoff to meet him one time when Geoff was in New York. Scott had got Alex Chilton to produce demos for the first Cramps album and Geoff had been a big Alex Chilton fan and I think that turned Geoff positively towards Scott. I think the context in which they met was important.

Geoff Travis: I went to Philadelphia ostensibly to check out The Cramps but ended up on the night preferring The Ramones, who I went to see later in the evening at another gig. I'd loved the demos that Alex Chilton had done and I think to this day they are the best things The Cramps ever recorded, much better than anything that was eventually released. Richard had set up a meeting for me with Scott in Scott's office in New York, which was in the Flower District. The whole of his office was filled with flowers and was less like a workplace and more like a home, which it probably was. We got on very well and then he came over to work for us.

Scott was a great character, an absolute one-off who was a complete law unto himself. But he was always very passionate about what he was doing – many years later when he was working with Pulp, he had the word 'Pulp' shaved into his hair – that kind of level of passion and commitment you just can't get today.

He worked a phenomenal amount of Rough Trade bands – he did all The Smiths' records, for instance – and on and off was one of the longest serving at Rough Trade, counting when he went off to do his promo company, Appearing. But throughout all that time he was always a bit strange with me in a way I could never figure out. He always seemed wary of me and it really used to perplex me.

Richard Scott: I think when he moved over he may have come to stay with me but he quickly started to spend nearly all of his time in 202 Kensington Park Road and I am pretty sure he more or less started to live there. I think he used to drive Geoff up the wall. I mean, you couldn't tell Scott to do *anything* – he just carried on doing whatever he thought ought to be done. He moved very slowly and very steadily and very methodically. I remember early on him coming to me to ask how he could get hold of John Peel. He wanted to bombard Peel with records. I had to explain to Scott that that wasn't the way to approach Peel and that less probably was more. Ironically, of course, Scott became possibly the most successful person that worked at Rough Trade in terms of getting to the top of a particular pile, which he most certainly did. The Smiths, Pulp, KLF, Laurie Anderson, The Prodigy – Scott worked with lots of bands over a long period and they all loved him.

Scott had from a very early age a passion for messing around with gramophones, radios, video cameras, that kind of thing, so I think it was inevitable that he would start putting together his new-release tapes, which became legendary. Scott used to make compilation tapes of bands that we were releasing and distributing, and send them out to people as a sort of promotional tool. He did the first one in January 1980. It was ingenious, really. He would put on some of the most obscure things – the Stupid Babies, the Mandible Rumpus, Pankrti, as well more obvious bands like Joy Division or Josef K. They were wonderful things to behold. He had inners printed up eventually but at first he used to just hand write the things. He'd biro into the noise reduction box, 'No!' or 'Never!' and gave them titles like *Schitzoid Singles*.

Scott Piering handwritten tape insert, complete with commentary: Noise Reduction –
'Never!', ('The Great') Equalizer, and 'Ab-' Normal DB.

He left behind also a formidable body of work that he'd recorded live. From about 1979 up until about the late 1980s he sort of officially recorded a lot of gigs, about two hundred or so in total by about one hundred different bands. He taped twenty-seven different Fall shows. It's an incredible archive and one that really should see the light of day. I don't know how many live recordings exist of bands like Felt or the Fire Engines or Weekend out there in the big wide world, but they are in Scott's archive.

Jo Slee: Scott was an exotic animal in the zoo that was Rough Trade. He could be at once acutely perceptive, dry, acerbic, prickly, defensive and gut-wrenchingly funny. His high-pitched giggle reminded me of John, and his heart was pure gold.

His priceless legacy of taped music includes a ransom message for the Rough Trade vacuum cleaner, recorded on a cassette tape late one night and left for the daytime staff.

Richard Scott: After we moved to Blenheim Crescent, well he basically lived there. He had a sort of upright camp bed and he just camped at the back of the building. We used to get a lot of complaints from neighbours, which we assumed were to do with noise – Scott playing music loud or late at night – but it turned out that what the neighbours most objected to was the light. I really am unsure if he *ever* slept. If he did sleep, it was certainly in a sitting-upright position.

Geoff Travis: I think Scott living in Blenheim Crescent partly led to us moving out eventually, because when we left, although we needed somewhere bigger, we were sort of kicked out.

Richard Scott: Geoff and I came in one day and there was no Scott, just a tape on one of our desks with an instruction to play it. When we played it, it purported to be another ransom tape. Scott or somebody was shouting, 'Help, help, help! I am about to be liquidated!' I think it probably gave instructions on what we had to do next. I sort of knew immediately that it had to be Scott. His mind never stopped thinking up mad ideas. But he was like a child. I never, ever saw him get cross or irritated. The most put-out I've seen him was later after the so-called Night of the Long Knives – it wasn't that: it lasted a lot longer – at the end of 1982 when the company numbers were cut back and people got 'privatised'. Scott really blamed me for him being one of the casualties. But it was the best thing that could have happened to him: he set up Appearing, got all the Rough Trade work anyway, and was more successful than ever. It was exactly what he needed.

Jo Slee: He died from cancer in 2000 and at his funeral it seemed the whole of the music world had turned up – Rough Trade employees, now grey-haired, past and present, old friends, people from the mainstream music business. The crematorium chapel was packed and overflowing, and full of love and memories and sorrow. I sat on the floor in an aisle next to John Peel's right foot. Bill Drummond's no-holds-barred speech left out neither shortcoming nor gift. It was a day of reckoning. It felt like a slot machine was playing out a shower of gold coins.

*

Green Gartside: Towards the end of 1979 we put out two records quite quickly, the *2nd Peel Session* EP and the *4 A's* EP, both Rough Trade/St Pancras collaborations. We'd done our first Peel session after we had met John Peel at Broadcasting House, when he had played 'Skank Bloc Bologna' and asked to meet us. He invited us then to do a session, but I don't recall anything of it. Obviously, we were very happy with the second session, though, and were keen to have it released. I think now that it was quite poor. I don't think Rough Trade had licensed any BBC material before – in fact, I don't think it was at all common, generally – and I think Geoff was a bit sceptical of our being able to do it but in the end it was quite easy. It was the band that facilitated it in the end.

4 A's was important because that was the record that helped push me in the direction that Scritti would take afterwards. Geoff and Mayo were producing the record, but they didn't do a lot apart from offer support. At that time, we really didn't know how music was made, and tended to hear what we created as a whole, undifferentiated thing. Once you become professionally involved in music, you lose, it seems to me, that ability to hear things that way, and instead you start listening for things like the bassline, or the verse or the chorus. One of the extraordinary things about Geoff is that he has never lost that ability to hear music in that original way. I don't know if he doesn't hear music in a detailed way, or whether he is able to choose not to listen to it in that way, but it is extraordinary. It's almost prelapsarian, a bit like a great artist just before going to art school and having all that freshness knocked out of them.

On the other hand, Mayo had spent time as a professional musician and, when we played the songs, heard them in a different way. The big thing I didn't like at the time – which is of no consequence to anyone but me – was that I couldn't seem to get off the fence and write a proper pop song or decide that we should carry on as we had been going. When we played live, we improvised a lot, which I liked: there was a lot of noise, which I was as attracted to as a method of songwriting. I felt awful whenever

I veered towards writing a song that had chords that followed each other. Or at least that was how I thought I felt.

We had a quite pedestrian song on the EP called 'Confidence'. I played it to Mayo and he turned around and in mock playfulness started banally singing, '*I'm going to Louisiana, gonna buy myself a mule . . .* ' I was shocked. I was devastated. It summed up the struggle for me. I mean, I really liked Mayo. I liked his generosity, and his idiosyncratic way. We had toured with Red Crayola and he had been very protective of us. His reaction wasn't intended to be in any way offensive. But turning and effectively exposing the weaknesses of the conventionality of my song like that just threw me.

Up until I decided that we should go pop, we had very much defined ourselves by the point where we had come in, a point where non-musicianship was respected and valued. We told ourselves – though probably only consoled ourselves with it in private – that there was this tradition of the non-musician, often from an art school background, whose technical understanding or ability was very limited yet who could make some of the most exciting, fun and interesting music.

The first thing was a strategy of avoidance. It was incredibly important that you didn't write a proper song, that A didn't lead to E and B in chordal terms. It had to go somewhere else. The two main objectives were to keep the whole thing scratchy and collapsy – the instability on which the whole thing was built had to somehow be revealed.

I quickly tired of that. It was partly that in the end too many people were doing it, and partly that the more experimental things started to be edged out by something more formulaic. When records by Thomas Leer were replaced on the Rough Trade wall by records by groups like Echo & The Bunnymen, I realised that a formula had been decided upon, without one's involvement or consent: the formula said that the least interesting and the least demanding and the least challenging of what was around was going to sell in the largest numbers to young men in cars outside of one's immediate world. That was what indie was founded upon and what the Cartel was founded upon and I realised then that I didn't want to have anything to do with it.

So, on the one hand I was struggling towards writing pop songs and on the other I was increasingly appalled by the rise of indie, and it all sort of came to a head when we toured with Gang of Four.

I collapsed when we were in Brighton. It was a combination of things really – too much speed, alcohol and a bad diet. But I would say half of the problem was really a deep unhappiness. I thought what we were playing was rubbish. I thought I was rubbish. We were playing a lot of old stuff, improvised stuff. I certainly found it difficult to support Gang of Four – they were just so good. They could make an awesome noise.

I was immediately aware that the spindly music we were making that was trying so hard not to be predictable was not winning great numbers of friends in the audience. At some point, I decided that if I couldn't beat Andy Gill on stage, I would just beat him on the drink and drugs front. In fact, I didn't manage to do that either, because he was like some demented machine. So, for me – panic attacks, hospital: I thought I was dying and I thought it was just not worth it. Later, when I wrote 'The "Sweetest Girl"', I put in those lines, 'The sickest group in all the world/How could they do that to me?' That was me.

I somehow got back in touch with my estranged parents and my mother found me a cottage near them in Wales. Tom and Nial gave me an inscribed copy of Laclan's *Écrits* as a get-better/going-away present and off I went. I was very ill. I was looking for professional, psychological help, but I couldn't find any and in the end the only help I got was from music. I knew nothing back then of black, popular music. I don't think I even knew who Aretha Franklin was, unbelievably. John Peel didn't play black music. There was one black kid at my school. I had the reggae, which largely came via Rough Trade, and it was through Geoff that I started getting into things that he loved and would recommend, black R'n'B stuff I knew nothing about.

I carried on with my political reading, going further into Marxism and looking at current European thought, and I started thinking more and more about the music industry and pop music. Eventually, I wrote this thesis – the *Scrit Screed* – on why we should make pop music. It drew on lots of theory, stuff I'd picked up at art school, but the basic line was: must make pop.

I think of that period as . . . well, what it became was surrender. Surrender to something that I had always loved, the tooth-rotting sweetness of pop music. I gave it up to harmony and melody totally and wasn't fighting it any more. It was an act of submission. It seemed to me, as well, to be the only radical gesture left to make. There was no point in trying to be like Pere Ubu any more, banging some tin cans. All our gigs at the time had been supporting groups that were an anathema to me. It was finally time to get some history.

*

Richard H. Kirk: By the time *Mix-Up* came out, I came off the dole, which, up until then, I'd still been claiming. The dole office was starting to hassle me. We were selling quite a few records by that point as well. We paid ourselves £10 a week and became 'professional' musicians. I think we'd had to do that because we had received £4,000 in royalties from Rough Trade, which back then was a lot of money.

We'd put out 'Nag Nag Nag', a record which, over its lifetime, has gone on to sell 60,000 copies. Rough Trade asked us to rerecord 'Nag Nag Nag' with Adam Kidron at Berry Street to try to get a better sound. We'd done the original as per usual two-track up in Sheffield. When we rerecorded it, production was jointly credited to Geoff Travis, Mayo Thompson and Cabaret Voltaire. We set the equipment up and did it in one take, dubbing on the vocals after. They didn't add anything to the production, really, we were far too self-contained to allow that. One time Geoff had been up to Sheffield and helped record something and we'd given him a dummy fader: he thought he was adding something but he wasn't really. When we'd played at the Acklam Hall with prag VEC and Red Crayola, I remember Jon Savage had come up to me and said, 'On no account let Geoff mix the sound,' which is what Geoff had wanted to do.

Mayo Thompson: I think that Cabaret Voltaire's live sound could not be tamed. They made beastly music – music that included everything that people had tried to rule out, like white noise. Their sonic experimentation took strategies out of the art-world domain and placed it all in a pop context. When we mixed 'Nag Nag Nag' we basically blew the desk. What we were trying to achieve could not be achieved short of driving the machines mad.

Richard H. Kirk: Towards the end of the year, Scott Piering came to a gig of ours at the YMCA and recorded it. He sent us the tape and I think we came up with the idea of putting it out to look like a bootleg, with a white sleeve. It is a great document of our live sound at the time. We used to hang out with Scott when we were in London, and also with Peter Walmsley and Sue Johnson, and later Claude Bessy, who we would meet in LA before he came to work at Rough Trade. We used to drink in the Earl of Lonsdale pub just off Portobello Road. We'd hang out, waiting for Lemmy to go by.

*

Peter Walmsley: We decided to set up Rough Trade Inc. in San Francisco and in about the November or early December, Sue Johnson and I went out to get the thing going. Richard Scott had recommended Allan Sturdy, a soft-spoken white Jamaican, as somebody who might run it and he had found premises and set himself up in a house.

I don't know why we plumped for the West Coast – probably Allan Sturdy suggested it and perhaps we were mindful of Virgin and Chrysalis, both of whom had bombed out in New York. Vale was also there with his magazine *Search & Destroy*, which was one of the best punk magazines. I remember we talked endlessly about setting it up before we actually did it and at first Geoff didn't want me to go. Part of my job in production involved shouting at people who hadn't delivered parts when they'd promised they would, and you needed to be a bit aggressive to get the job done. I think Geoff probably thought I was a bit too aggressive to be going out and setting the operation up.

We went for a couple of months and ended up staying about a year, and when we left Steve Montgomery had arrived. We set up a structure of people, not too dissimilar from how the Cartel would be set up. There was a different ethos from the UK – the ethos was music-driven and there wasn't such a strong cooperative will. The problem we always had was we couldn't seem to get the right staff.

Richard Scott: By the end of 1979, after Sue Johnson and Peter Walmsley had gone off to set up Rough Trade Inc., I realised that we needed new premises in London since Kensington Park Road was completely overrun. As well as releasing more and more of our own records, other labels were starting to have big successes. Every single copy of *Inflammable Material* had passed through the door and we'd already had Joy Division's first album, *Unknown Pleasures*.

Factory had loaded up a van and sent 20,000 copies of *Unknown Pleasures* to us. By the time the van arrived at Kensington Park Road, the floor of it had basically collapsed with the weight, so they dumped 20,000 copies of the record on twelve makeshift pallets up and down the road. We blocked off the pavement. We had to box the entire lot up outside. If it had rained the whole course of post-punk history would have changed. We didn't have enough room in the shop to store them anyway. People had to come and collect the records in rotation.

I had realised for some time that we couldn't handle everything alone. We were trying to run everything from a cubby-hole. It suddenly occurred to me that rather than send records to thirty shops, or three hundred shops, why didn't I send a larger number to five shops and they could then distribute them. It was largely an act of necessity. The regional politics of the whole thing wasn't the primary reason why I was thinking this way, although it became very important to me once I realised what we were doing. Originally, I approached some people who didn't become part of the Cartel, people like Service in Altrincham, Manchester, who looked after UB40. Red Rhino came in first, though, and then Revolver and Probe; this was before the Cartel was formally set up. Fast was also very early.

In Distribution, we really never turned anybody away. We handled Industrial for Throbbing Gristle, Mute, Factory, Crass, which was run by John Loder. Not too long back, Crass sold their millionth record. Before he died, John came to see me and was very proud of that fact. I always loved what Crass stood for even if I didn't always like all of the music. When computers came in, John wouldn't allow any Microsoft product to be used in the business. Back in the day, we used to row with Crass all the time – they used insane, complex cataloguing numbers with millions of digits that couldn't easily be accounted: you certainly couldn't remember one if somebody was on the phone ordering a copy of the record, and they always asked for – and got – ridiculous margins with half per cents, and they sold their records at odd prices as well. A lot of people at Rough Trade didn't like dealing with them, but I did; I stuck with them.

Geoff Travis: We had completely outgrown the back of the shop and had moved into upstairs when the tenant had moved out. There was no room for the label. Distribution was completely overstuffed and there were a lot more people than we had ever imagined would be working there. It was important to us to find somewhere very close to where we were and for-tunately we did.

Richard Scott: We didn't move into Blenheim Crescent until late 1980 but we started the process at the end of 1979. It was a big, beautiful space. Looking back, the old Island model of everybody sitting around a big table and all being kept up to speed with what each was doing was doomed to go. Sales split off from the record company when we got to Blenheim

Crescent, for a start, although Geoff's office overlooked it.

The garden at the back of Blenheim Crescent had, I was told, been part of the racecourse that was the last surviving Central London racecourse before it went in the nineteenth century. I designed all of the Blenheim Crescent interior and built all of the shelving, as I had done at Kensington Park Road. The whole thing cost a lot of money – we had to get architects in, the place was soundproofed, we had an air-circulation system installed. It was a good place to work and we did a good job on our music in it, but there is no doubt that the cost of Blenheim Crescent and the money spent getting it ready contributed to the major financial crisis that wasn't too far around the corner.

CHAPTER SIX:

1980

'I'm proud to say that Geoff once said to me,
"You may not be our most successful artist or even
our best, but you're certainly our cheapest"'

Better Badges – Resuscitating an English legend –
Fanzine heyday – Sabbatical – Rough Trade bouncer –
Move to Blenheim Crescent

Tom Vague: I was living in Bournemouth and had started *Vague* in 1979. I'd been to a local Rough Trade gig where Red Crayola and Gang of Four played and had met and shown Mayo Thompson my fanzine, and he had suggested I take it into Rough Trade because they might distribute it for me. When I took it in to the shop, Rough Trade really liked it and encouraged me to carry on doing it so I started going in to 202 Kensington Park Road frequently.

There was a little circuit I used to do – Rough Trade first, then round to 286 Portobello Road, where Better Badges was, and then up to Talbot Road, where *Zigzag* was. I became a Better Badges salesman at gigs and really I knew them better than I knew Rough Trade. As well as the badges, they also printed up fanzines and would sell them back to the editor at cost price. It was a sort of fanzine co-op. Rough Trade would then sell the fanzines in the shop and distribute them.

Early Better Badges catalogue.

Pete Donne: The fanzines took up absolutely acres of space and by the start of the 1980s, which was I suppose their heyday in terms of numbers, you were forever filling out slips for someone bringing them in or trying to find slips for people who wanted paying for the fanzines you'd sold, which you could never seem to find a record of. At around 30p each, it was always capable of turning into a ball-ache unless you kept your eye on things, which we didn't. There was also a seemingly never-ending stream of people coming in asking how to make a fanzine, in which case we'd send them off to Better Badges to see Joly.

Joly MacFie: I bought a printing press from a printer who was going out of business and set it up in 286 Portobello Road because I wanted to learn printing and decided that the best way to experiment was to print a fanzine. I took over the printing of Tony Fletcher's *Jamming!* and tested the waters with an early issue of that. I printed fanzines up and the editors then took them round to Rough Trade to sell and distribute. I'd first come into contact with Rough Trade, though, right at their start.

I had been a roadie for the Pink Fairies in my late teens and when Twink left the band I went with him. We both briefly joined Hawkwind before moving up to Cambridge, where Twink made the band with Syd Barrett. I then did another stint as a roadie – I remember working with Suzi Quatro and also Billy Fury – before I moved back to London and started a booking agency called City Kids, where I took on Ace, Pink Fairies, Roger Ruskin Spear, Chilli Willi and Kokomo. This was 1973. I shared office space at 286 Portobello Road with *International Times*, who had just relaunched using money given them by John Lennon. Then I had a motorbike accident and broke my collarbone, and while I was recovering someone offered me an old badge-making machine.

I went back to my parents in Devon to recuperate and spent over a year insanely looking for missing parts for the badge machine, which eventually I located. My friends were all doing free festivals and in 1976 I went to a free festival at Stonehenge and set up there with the machine, doing a lot of drug badges like 'Pass It Along', which was one of the first.

I got busted for weed. As part of the settlement, I had to find proper work and I ended helping decorate Eric Idle's house in St John's Wood. I thought I'd go to the Roundhouse, which was virtually next door, and see who was going to be playing, since the hippie explosion had partly taken place there and I thought I could sell some badges. This was the week Patti Smith played. It was all interesting and in fact shortly after that, Martin Stone – who had been in Chilli Willi and who I knew – was playing with The 101ers in a pub in Fulham. Martin invited me down and we ended up back in the dressing room with the band. Joe Strummer was talking about punk and as the three of us walked to the bus stop at the end of the night Joe said he was thinking of quitting The 101ers and starting a punk band. I said that if he did I would make some punk badges, and in fact one of the earliest punk badges I made was a black and white Clash badge.

About a week or so later, The Ramones played the Roundhouse. A man called Des Kay had the concession there, where he sold joss sticks, tantric stuff and other hippie merchandise, and I persuaded him to let me set up beside him selling a Ramones badge I had made, along with the other crap of mine. Then I started doing a lot of punk badges: this was something

I was able to do because offset litho had just come on line and made it easier. By September 1976, John Curd, the Straight Music promoter who ran the Roundhouse, gave me the concession there entirely because he wanted it to be completely punk.

Quite quickly, one of my biggest successes was a Patti Smith badge. John Curd, who had booked Patti at that legendary Roundhouse show, asked her to come back to play the Hammersmith Odeon. He had given me the concession but approached me and said that he had been asked by Jane Friedman, Patti's manager, if it would be OK if a guy called Geoff Travis set up next to me and sold records on a trestle table. That was my first introduction to Geoff and I found him to be very affable. That was also the first time I paid a royalty on a badge and the cut of the sales on badges helped Jane Friedman pay her hotel bill.

Alan Travis: I did the stand with Geoff and I remember we sold about two hundred copies of *Punk* magazine in half an hour. Afterwards we went off to the ICA to see The Clash, where Shane MacGowan got his ear bitten off.

Joly MacFie: Penny Reel, the journalist, had got me to make badges in late spring 1976 for a Gregory Isaacs show at the Roxy in Harlesden and then I did the 1976 Notting Hill Carnival, which was one of my first major events. I produced a badge that read 'MAS IN THE GROVE' and stood under the Westway selling it. That line of policemen in that *Black Market Clash* record sleeve has me on the end selling badges in the original uncropped version of the photo. Afterwards, people asked me what the badge meant and I always said, 'Mash up in the Grove'.

Penny had some ideas about what badges I might do and together we cooked up a couple of designs: one that read 'FORWARD' and one that read, 'BUT WAIT'. This was based on a Jamaican joke about how slow change was within the country. We did another one that read 'I & I SURVIVE' after my friend Lepke, who later ran the reggae pirate radio station Dread Broadcast Corporation, got charged with burglary and needed money for legal bills.

I made badges for Bizarre and for Skydog Records in France, who were affiliated to them. They asked me to make badges for their releases; records like Iggy Pop's *Metallic KO*, the cover for which was designed by

Megan Green who later came to design for Better Badges. As a result of working with them, I got to set up at the second Mont-de-Marsan punk festival in spring 1977. I dropped the size of the badge from two and one-eighth of an inch to one and three-quarters of an inch – still massive compared to today's tiny badges – because I thought the smaller badge looked better. I made an absolute killing at the show and took about £700 or £800. I was selling the badges for three francs, which the French kids thought was ridiculously cheap. That was about 60p. Over here I got 20p per badge.

I used that money to help grow the business and started a distribution company. It also meant I could get a hire purchase deal to buy a process camera, a huge, incredibly expensive piece of equipment which just about fit in the premises and meant that now we were able to properly reduce down the size of artwork. It's hard now to imagine how difficult and complicated it was then to take a piece of normal-size art and reduce it down to the size of a small badge. The camera became a vital tool and solidified my relationship with other designers such as Jamie Reid, who would come in to use the camera to do stuff for the Sex Pistols. It became one of the ways I could support the bands in lieu of giving them actual money.

One of my earliest, most savvy customers was Rob Gretton, who had been down back in 1977 and ordered up some Slaughter & The Dogs badges. One of his first commercial acts when he took over Joy Division was to come in with a whole set of badges he wanted made for them. When it came to the first album, *Unknown Pleasures*, he sent down the wavy lines design and we made that up. They played the Acklam Hall, which was virtually next door to Better Badges, and Tony Wilson came to see me and we made up a special badge on the spot to be given out at the gig. It got to the point where I was selling so many Joy Division badges that I lost track and really couldn't pay them what they were owed. At the same time, because Factory had this fine-art approach, they couldn't decide whether or not the badges should be given a FAC number. In the end, we agreed that the badges were like fanzines, stuff coming up from outside rather than down from the middle, and as such a royalty was not important. We worked out another method of payment.

Jolyean MacFie, upstairs, 202 Kensington Park Road.

We were a proactive company – we never waited for people to ask us to make a badge: we were on the side of the fans rather than the bands, though usually a happy medium was reached. This tied in with the original slogan I had thought up: 'Image as virus, disease as cure.' As I moved from hippie, peace and love into punk I felt I needed a polemic to justify it. Punk rock might be sick, but the sickness was in fact the cure. Before Blondie first came here I had made up some Debbie Harry badges, which the band loved. Then they came back after having had success at a much higher level with their own merchandising stand and the manager warned me off selling Blondie badges on my stall. I had one Blondie badge and a whole table of other punk badges where a customer could choose whatever they liked. Their Blondie stall was merchandising; the Better Badges stall was Medium. They realised that this was a reversal of the usual rock 'n' roll power order. The kids now decided what badges they wore, what they wrote on the back of their leather jackets, whereas before the bands had control. Now the tail was wagging the dog. In the end, I worked out a system for remunerating the bands and it was this: every new band that came in with a design immediately got two hundred free badges and then we charged 5p per badge. The shops paid 10p. The public paid 20p.

One of the more bizarre jobs I did involved the Twelve Tribes of Israel, the Rasta organisation who were based in Stoke Newington. The connection came about through Lepke, who was Bob Marley's brother-in-law. As a result of his connections and the reggae badges I'd already done, I received a visit from the head of the Twelve Tribes of Israel, and was 'escorted' in a car to Chelsea, where Bob Marley was waiting in a hotel. The plan was to use Marley's money to fund some badges to help support the royalist cause in Ethiopia. They planned to flood the place with pro-royalist badges based on a design that a member of the royal family who came to see me would prepare. It was such a nightmare, this member of the royal household would change her mind every time we got to proof stage – the lion's head needed reversing, that kind of thing – and it was incredibly expensive so in the end I just said don't come back to me until you know exactly what you want and then I'll print them.

I went off to Europe selling badges on an Iggy Pop tour and on the day I arrived back I got a visitation from Bob Marley and John Holt. Marley started having this big argument with me about how I had disrespected the Ethiopian royal family. While he is doing this he is looking around the workshop and notices the 'FORWARD' and 'BUT WAIT' badges and starts accusing me of not respecting Rasta. Everything I said in defence he just dismissed as 'ras-clat, white-man talk'. He was pretty mad and stormed off to the other end of the workshop, where his eye caught the latest job we'd done. It was a backstage pass for Graham Parker's tour of Australia. It had a black, red, yellow and green background, reggae style, and printed on top were the words: 'I SHOT THE FERRET'. Marley was incandescent. We couldn't help but start laughing. He stormed off, although later Pepe did smooth things over and we did carry on making the Bob Marley badges we had already been making.

I bought three printing presses and had them installed in the basement of 286 Portobello Road. Tony Fletcher, who edited *Jamming!* fanzine, came in one day and said that he was having problems with his printer and I offered to have a go at printing the next issue for him. That was issue seven, which came out in April 1979. If you look closely at a copy of that particular issue of *Jamming!*, you can see where I had a few accidents – ink spilling over onto the pages here and there. I learnt to print through doing that issue of *Jamming!*

I think it cost or we charged 2p per double sheet of paper, so a ten-sheet fanzine, twenty pages, would cost 20p a copy for a run of five hundred. We then figured out that if we could put a page of ads in we could get the cost down to 15p. I did a similar deal with the fanzine editors as I did with the bands over badges and gave them a set number of free copies. We bundled up packs of different fanzines and would send them out gratis to those record shops who were ordering decent-sized amounts of badges. It was a little complementary thing.

I printed the earliest issues of *I-D* magazine – we probably did ten thousand runs of those. The later *Jamming!* issues got up to about five thousand. *Maximum Speed*, the mod fanzine, was another that we did a reasonably large print-run for, but generally the fanzines weren't anywhere near those numbers. Some of the other fanzines we did were *Kill Your Pet Puppy*, Tony D's fanzine after *Ripped & Torn*, *Panache*, *Poseur*, *Toxic Gravity*, and *Chainsaw*, Charlie Chainsaw's fanzine, which he used to type on a typewriter without a 'C' key, so every 'C' was biroed in after. We also did some work for Biff comics, guys I knew from *International Times* days, and we did Slim Smith's fanzines, *Dance Crazy* and *God Crazy*. Slim came to work for us as a designer.

Slim Smith: I'd known Joly from when he'd been up in Cambridge doing the band with Twink and Syd Barrett. I was working in a hippie café for a bit at the time. I went on to do some work for Better Badges – mainly the catalogues – and before that they had printed up my fanzines. When we did *God Crazy*, we used this collage on the front and some lettering which said 'Illustrations by the Benedictine Nuns of Cockfosters'. This lawyer came around representing the nuns and we ended up putting a sticker on the front to cover the words. I had absolutely no idea that the order could still exist – let alone go into the kind of bookshop where fanzines were sold.

When I went to work at Better Badges, it was great: the place would be full of punks furiously stapling fanzines together and Joly's cat crapping in all the boxes of badges. I think Joly had a room there where he slept, but he kept unusual hours. He'd often materialise at odd times of the day. After Better Badges, I went on and did quite a few designs for Rough Trade.

Joly MacFie: I used to go into Rough Trade at the end of the day and sit and talk to Richard Scott. I used to love doing that – the shop closed and me smoking a big spliff. I always used to let the fanzine editors sell their own fanzines into Rough Trade – I wanted them to have that experience – and I don't remember selling many badges into them, but Ana from The Raincoats recently said to me that they did have the badges in there when she worked there. I did some promotional booklets for The Raincoats and Young Marble Giants and some other Rough Trade acts and I used to go and sit with Scott Piering and come up with marketing ideas.

Later we moved out of Portobello Road over to Bethnal Green and not long after that, in 1983, I sold the business to the staff and moved to America.

*

Robert Wyatt: I was introduced to Geoff by Vivien Goldman, who I'd met at an art exhibition I'd gone to for which Brian Eno had done the music. Vivien knew that my relationship with Virgin Records had basically floundered and crashed, which made no difference to Virgin but a lot of difference to me. It meant I couldn't function. At the time, people regarded Virgin as a big break from the top but that was not the case in my experience – I found them quite predatory. There wasn't anything malevolent about Richard Branson; in fact, like many modern Conservatives, he had quite liberal social views. But he was a straight-down-the-line neo-Con capitalist, a Thatcherite before Thatcherism existed. I found the context in which I was working alien. They were very cross when I wanted to leave and I tried to be honourable about it. They were paying me a £40-a-week retainer, which I didn't really need to cancel but did when I said I couldn't fulfil the obligation being asked of me.

Richard was very good at dealing with his staff, and got a lot of loyalty out of them, but that sense of canny management or humane management didn't extend to the musicians or composers who were treated as stock to be bought and sold. This all came as a shock to me, initially, because I was one of their earliest signings and was treated in a matey way that suggested something different was going on here, something more user-friendly than the way I had been treated at CBS in the Soft Machine, when they would no more talk to us about our records than the farmer would tell the cows what the bull was up to.

My wife Alfie had taken over managing me, reluctantly and by default. She was forever trying to make sense of my affairs since I was broke all the time. I remember Nick Mason from Pink Floyd coming round and saying, we travel all over the world and everywhere I go I see Soft Machine records: you should be rich. Vivien brought Geoff to see us in Twickenham, where we were living, to talk about possibly making some records together. The trouble was that the Virgin lawyers had been in touch and told us that I was still contracted to them, at least for albums. We realised we wouldn't be able to take on the might of Virgin's lawyers so in the end we decided to make a bunch of singles.

Geoff Travis: I went to the house in Twickenham – a place filled with beautiful objects, paintings by Alfie and lots of other wonderful things. I'd seen the Soft Machine play at the Country Club, on Haverstock Hill, and it had been one of my favourite concerts. I thought the albums Robert had done for Virgin, *Rock Bottom* and *Ruth is Stranger Than Richard*, had been extraordinary, and I'd liked the Matching Mole material and even Robert's solo album without vocals, *End of an Ear*. So it was always in the back of my mind that it would be great to work with him. Robert is one of the greats of English music – he has an original voice, a musical vision unparalleled, and his work has a depth and humanity to it. It has an unusual strain but in spite of Robert having been in that world of complicated time signatures and Dadaism, which is still present in the work, there is real soul in the songs, a moving quality that embodies the most beautiful human spirit.

That first time we met, Alfie was quite militant in explaining that they weren't happy with Virgin and I felt that it was inevitable that there would be a separation.

Robert Wyatt: I was very politically engaged and I remember at the time not wanting to do anything that would involve colluding any more with the business world than I absolutely had to. So a spanner was in the works, so to speak, already. The records I recorded, the people I worked with, the fact that I sang songs not in English and recorded songs celebrating or at least acknowledging people who might have been regarded by some as our deadly enemy, was all done for a reason. And to his credit, Geoff supported my approach and in all our time together only refused to put out one thing I recorded – a version of 'The Internationale', which he didn't like at all. That he didn't like it and chose not to release it was absolutely fair. I thought the fact that he had to like stuff to put it out meant that he was participating aesthetically, which was so different from my dealings with the major labels.

Geoff Travis: I thought Robert's ideas for what he wanted to do great. I wasn't surprised by the songs Robert chose to record and to be honest I would have let him do anything he wanted to do, really. I trusted him implicitly. I loved the idea that he was connected to communities beyond the traditional lines of the English rock 'n' roll experience. It was very exciting, for instance, when Robert told me he was intending to record with Dishari, the group of Bengali musicians who recorded 'Trade Union' with him.

Robert Wyatt: When I was introduced to Geoff, I knew nothing of the local politics of the current state of rock musicians or of how they perceived what they were doing in relation to the Establishment. I had been away with the fairies, as periodically I am wont to be. I did go out a lot but only to hear reggae, or to Ronnie Scott's, or the Carnival. At home, the only radio programmes I listened to were Radio Moscow and a rather wonderful Radio London programme called *Black Londoners*. So this didn't prepare me in any way for what white rock musicians were doing at the time. I'd never been interested in rock music from an aesthetic point of view, anyway.

We did the records like journalism – we went in and banged them out. Although it wasn't guitar rock, it seemed to fit in with much of the music of the time, and of course Adam Kidron engineered, so that also added to it fitting in. There was no polish or finishing. The paradox is that I did seem to fit in with the methodology of the time.

My approach was different politically, though, in as much as I hadn't taken on the aesthetic idea of punk, which is that you express dissent through the use of dissonance. If you sang something loud and fast and shouted you would make the Establishment tremble in its boots. This didn't strike me as being very likely since my political education had taught me that not only could the Establishment handle it, but that they'd invented shouting. I saw punk more as a modern art movement. And it was non-academic, which I liked.

The thing that most touched me – I was quite shocked and moved by it – was how I was treated. Because of the barrage of hostility and contempt that some punk musicians had levelled at my generation, I just assumed that I would be *persona non grata*. I never put much ideological weight on trends in pop, and after ten years of long hair and long guitar solos, I'd expected a period of short hair and short guitar solos, when peace and love you would become hate and fuck you. But in fact I was welcomed and early on Scritti Politti invited me to one of their gigs, which was how I came to reacquaint myself with young England.

The gig I saw with Scritti Politti was magical, a wonderful blend of reggae and punk. The music had the same preoccupations as Two Tone, in some ways; both were genuine crossover attempts. This was a time when Rastas, young black Londoners, weren't trying, as their parents had, to be English, but were revisiting an imaginary rural Jamaica as a kind of conscious reassertion of independence. This had a big influence on punk. And Scritti's take on it was wonderful. For me, coming from a black music aesthetic, it seemed extremely authentic.

Green Gartside: I had written to Robert as a teenager and with no idea how to reach him had sent my letter via the John Peel show, hoping it would eventually get to Robert. When I did meet Robert he told me that he still had the letter. I went to visit him a few times in Twickenham and as well as inviting him to one of our shows took him out to see other gigs. We went to see The Clash at the Music Machine in Camden. Patti Smith was on the bill, and Tapper Zukie. I remember before going in to the show we all decided we needed another drink and ended up in a local Turkish restaurant. The owner was adamant that we could only be served drink if we were eating and Robert was equally adamant that we only wanted a drink. The whole thing gradually started to escalate until Robert suddenly shouted out, 'Look, we are the least racist people you have ever had in your restaurant, now just get us a fucking drink!' Which the manager promptly did. I thought, where the hell did that come from? Politically, as a Stalinist, he could be quite tanky.

Robert Wyatt: With the singles that we did, there was no attempt at proselytising, no attempt to forge a revolution, but my God when the records were collected together on the album *Nothing Can Stop Us*, people continually misinterpreted the title. I think they thought it was a statement about me – nothing can stop him: or that it was about the revolution – nothing can stop the revolution. It was from a book by Ludwell Denny, *America Conquers Britain*: 'We shall not make Britain's mistake. Too wise to try to govern the world, we shall merely own it. Nothing can stop us ...'

The first single was a reworking of 'Arauco', a song about the Araucano Indians reclaiming their lands in Chile. It was written by the great Chilean folk singer Violeta Parra. Violeta was important in Chile before the Socialist Party of Chile was elected, and a big inspiration to them. It's a beautiful piece of music. We released the record with my version of 'Caimanera' on the other side. 'Caimanera' is really a version of 'Guantanamera' – the song which is to Cuba what 'Waltzing Matilda' is to Australia – but with post-revolution words by Carlos Puebla. The words are about the insulting stain of the American airbase at Guantánamo, which of course very few people outside Cuba would have known about at the time the song was written. I managed to get the Caribbean trumpet player Harry Beckett to play a flugelhorn solo on 'Caimanera'. Whenever I make a record I try to make the music beautiful first, then after make it pregnant with resonances, even if I'm the only one who can see them.

We recorded the single, as we did the others, in a dungeon somewhere, and Adam Kidron, whose parents ran the wonderful left-wing publisher Pluto, engineered them. I was rusty at the time in terms of production technique, and I let Adam do more than I might have chosen in all honesty. In retrospect, I regret that there are no surviving original masters for me to rework. We got the job done quickly. I'm proud to say that Geoff once said to me, 'You may not be our most successful artist or even our best but you're certainly our cheapest,' and I've always thought that one of the greatest compliments I've ever received. I mean, rock people have a reputation for being Little Lord Fauntleroys in snakes' clothing and I've always been aware of that. Part of my disenfranchisement from rock wasn't just from the industry itself, but from that return to a kind of ersatz aristocracy, which didn't really fit in with my political aspirations at all.

Geoff Travis: Robert chose what to record and it was his decision to do a version of 'At Last I Am Free', the Chic number. We loved Chic at Rough Trade and we were all pleased when Robert's version, which is beautiful, got the thumbs-up from the Chic camp.

Robert Wyatt: 'Stalin Wasn't Stallin'' was a song written by Bill Johnson of the Golden Gate Jubilee Quartet. He sang like Elvis, like Elvis doing doo-wop, but was recording about ten years before Elvis's time. The song was Bill and the Golden Gate Jubilee Quartet's contribution to the US war effort and is about Russia asking the Yanks and British people to help them beat the racist devil Hitler. It seemed to me to be a reasonable war song, but blimey did I get some flak for it from the Trots, never mind the Tories. It was important to have Peter Blackman's poem about humanity, 'Stalingrad', on the record. The 'Stalingrad' side only has Peter's voice on and 'Stalin Wasn't Stallin'' features only mine. It's the first single I know of without any instruments on it.

Geoff Travis: I remember Greil Marcus being quite disturbed by 'Stalin Wasn't Stallin'' on the grounds that someone in the West could be singing the praises of a terrible, murdering, vicious dictator, but Robert was, of course, just singing about the fact that there was a moment in history when Stalin saved us and so I am sure you are allowed to mention that.

Robert Wyatt: At some point Geoff asked me to work with some of the other Rough Trade artists, which I was happy to do. I worked with The Raincoats and Swell Maps and Scritti Politti. I loved The Raincoats. They were a lot of fun and very witty. And the track I recorded with Epic Soundtracks, 'Jelly Babies', is probably my favourite of the least-asked-about collaborations: it was a lovely song with some nice work on it by Georgie Born, the cellist from Henry Cow. I used to like The Slits as well. They were a lovely bunch who got into an awful lot of trouble for rolling around naked in the mud. I didn't disapprove. There was a *Morning Star* fund-raiser at Crystal Palace, at which we both performed, and I remember them introducing one song with the words, 'Here's another tune for you fucking old Stalinists!' It was all very jolly, a wonderful mixture of old working men's choirs and new stuff.

Geoff Travis: The Rough Trade artists Robert worked with totally embraced Robert and he fitted into the family very well. I would try to encourage Robert to work more often with other people and he, in turn, would justify working alone on the grounds of standing up for disabled lib. We had an ongoing friendly debate about this. I thought that his line was nonsense and actually just an excuse for not having to deal with anybody else. I think he was always trying to save us money, as well.

I believe that records made alone can lack the inherent dynamic that records made with multiple musicians have. I can think of very few records that have benefited from being the work of one person that might not have been better through having the tension of the artist playing with others. I did appreciate Robert's view, and he is one of the few artists capable of building up a record perfectly well on his own.

The Rough Trade musicians all respected Robert: he is universally loved. I think, though, that he had an odd relationship with Green. They were both so intense about their politics and politically at odds with each other, I suspect. I mean, Green loved Robert and Robert loved Green.

Robert Wyatt: Politics came up but I was cautious about discussing it. I was well aware that ... Well, it was different for me. My party membership was kind of nostalgic from the start, entirely about the courage and aspirations and betrayals of the old anti-Fascist hardcore, which the young Communists were desperately trying to get rid of to renew their image. It would have been fairly easy for me to dissociate myself from what were seen as the dinosaurs of the party and take the opportunity to swim with the new elite. But I wasn't prepared to do that.

Green Gartside: Robert wouldn't stop talking about politics, really. I remember he used to go on and on about Rio Tinto Zinc. There were issues over our relative positions. I gave him a copy of Barry Hindess's and Paul Hirst's *Mode of Production and Social Formation*, an important book at the time, and he went a bit quiet for a while after that. The phone stopped ringing for a bit. But he was lovely and I felt very close to him.

Robert Wyatt: Eventually it became a fait accompli that I was a Rough Trade artist, and the singles were collected together on an album anyway, but the last single was done on behalf of some Bengali refugees, Dishari, who were wanted back in their country for trades union activities and were facing the death squad if deported. Part of winning the fight was to be able to say that the group were working here and part of the way to prove that was to show that they had made a record. Geoff happily colluded with this when 'Trade Union' came out, and thankfully some wonderful legal experts on the left eventually won their case and they were able to stay. The other side of the single was me covering Ivor Cutler's 'Grass' and I remember we tried to link the two songs through the cover, which attempted to join the idea of grass-roots union membership with Ivor's song 'Grass' and so the cover had a close-up of some grass growing. I'm not sure how many people made the connection . . .

'Trade Union'/'Grass', with its magnified grass concept cover.

*

Pete Donne: The collective ideal at Rough Trade didn't really extend beyond the workplace and people had different lifestyles. Richard was a family man and so he wouldn't be going out that much anyway. Geoff, on the other hand, was a huge consumer of live music and went out to see bands all the time – as he still does – but he'd go off on his own into a corner and watch the band alone. And then leave. Social interaction isn't his strong point. It's almost like some weird intellectual process takes over from any aesthetic enjoyment of the band which he might have.

Green Gartside: Geoff has always done that thing of going to the gig and then going off on his own to watch it in some corner. He is completely inscrutable.

Pete Donne: By 1980, my life was starting to revolve around the Rough Trade shop lifestyle, as opposed to revolving around any Rough Trade lifestyle. A bunch of us hung around the Grove and drank in the Warwick Castle, people like Keith Allen and his brother Kevin. Keith hung out a bit with my sister Sue and prag VEC and he had his own band at the time, The Atoms. He wanted to release a single and pestered Geoff, and in the end I think Geoff did an M&D deal for the single 'Max Bygraves Killed My Mother'. We all drank together and we started a cricket team – The Old Roughians. That lasted about ten years. Joe Strummer used to often come and watch us. We took it very seriously and I remember one time Grant McLennan from the Go-Betweens was banned for nearly killing someone with a fast ball.

I took an unintentional 'sabbatical' around this time. I went to Brighton with my girlfriend and we got a bit carried away and decided on the spot to go to France. So we grabbed our passports and caught a ferry over there. I was meant to be running the shop. I'd just dumped my car in London and Peter Walmsley had kindly agreed to drive it back to my mother's house. Almost as soon as we got to France, I started to get cold feet and pretty soon we were back. I suppose a little over two weeks went by before I plucked up the courage to go and face Geoff and beg for my job back. He said that he didn't think I was mature enough for it, and that was that. I went to everybody – Richard Scott, Jude Crighton, Peter Walmsley – and begged for work. Eventually I picked up a bit of work driving to and from pressing plants, collecting Rough Trade records stock, but by then Steve Jameson had replaced me in the shop. I hung in there, though, and it wasn't such a long time after that Steve Jameson started hanging out rather a bit too much with The Clash and tended not to show up and I was back. I suppose what I felt about the whole episode was that it showed me the irrelevance of the so-called cooperative spirit. I don't think anyone gave a flying fuck for what I felt. I could see that it was people like Geoff, Richard and Peter who were making the decisions, and eventually I don't think I was even consulted about certain things.

But it was so exciting that things like that didn't matter. Business went absolutely crazy and every week there would be something new in that was phenomenal. I remember 'Gangsters' by The Specials. We sold thousands and thousands of that single.

In fact, 202 Kensington Park Road was so busy that we had to employ a bouncer. The bouncer was a friend of Austin's called Shane and he was quite wiry and not at all what you'd think of in terms of a bouncer. He was massively into reggae and also massively into judo. There were so many people just hanging around the shop on a Saturday that it started to become a slightly uncomfortable place to be for the real customers. All the Ladbroke Grove skinheads would troop in and sit at the back, sniffing glue. They'd pop up from the floor occasionally to ask you to play an Adam & The Ants single.

Steve Jameson: Just before I started, someone got beaten up quite badly outside the shop by some of the Ladbroke skins. This is how we solved the problem. We decided to get on their good side. Their leader was known as Fat Freddie and when the Bad Manners album came out we put it in the window with a sign saying 'Album of the Week', and we drew on an arrow pointing to Buster Bloodvessel and wrote the words 'FAT FREDDIE' next to it. They loved that. That won them over. Saturdays in the shop was like being in a youth club.

Richard Scott: It was, of course, insanely busy and none more so than when a big record came out, like The Specials' single 'Gangsters'. We were responsible for setting The Specials on their way. Bernie Rhodes, who looked after The Specials, didn't want them to record because he didn't think Jerry Dammers could sing properly, so he never really tried to get them a deal. The band came and had a meeting with us upstairs at

202 Kensington Park Road and we told them that they should put a record
out themselves, which is what they did when they set up their Two Tone
label. Then they later went and did a deal with Chrysalis, who ended up
distributing them.

Pete Donne: Geoff always liked to work in the shop on a Saturday, and even
when they moved to Blenheim Crescent he carried on doing that. I think
he really loved hearing what people were talking about, hearing what people
were asking for. I think he found a lot out by *overhearing* people. He's never
lost that passion and he still comes in the shops a lot today. I think he still
comes in to overhear people . . .

Geoff always kept us informed. He'd come down and play us the latest
Rough Trade releases or the best M&D deal records. He'd play the acetates
on the shop stereo – that was always the acid test – and he'd sound you out
for your thoughts. A little later, when they were at Blenheim Crescent,
Geoff came in and played an acetate of 'The "Sweetest Girl"' by Scritti
Politti and asked me if I knew who it was. I thought, I have no idea who
this is but it sounds wonderful. I couldn't believe it when he said it was
Scritti Politti. Geoff said that it would go to Number One and I remember
going home that night and thinking, 'Rough Trade is going to have a
Number One hit record.' And they really should have done, that record was
so good.

*

Steve Jameson: I took over from Pete Donne after he had his little walkabout.
I'd grown up in Aldershot and came to London and started working for a
record import company called Charndale around the time of the first
Ramones LP. I had a friend who was a gofer for Lou Reed when he was
over and Lou Reed had given her a box of the *Foggy Notion* EP, which was
a sort of bootleg the band did themselves. She asked me if I knew where
she could sell them and I suggested she give them to me and I took them
into Rough Trade for her, which made me very popular there.

I quickly moved to working with Miles Copeland. I knew that Miles had
sacked a friend of mine who worked for him – for drug-dealing – so I went
to see Miles and said I am the man you need as a replacement. I was dealing
with stuff like Faulty Product, Step Forward, Deptford Fun City and doing
telephone sales. I went into Rough Trade all the time, because Miles fancied
doing his own distribution, but the trouble was that we couldn't really do

telephone sales and only had a few Cortinas or Alternative TV records to sell, so I used to take in our product for them to buy and I'd also buy some of their stuff which we would then try to sell on. Of course, Rough Trade were much more middle class and the college type than we were.

I became Miles's blue-eyed boy quite quickly. He knew that I loved US punk and I would always bring back from Rough Trade records by Television or Richard Hell and also 'Human Fly' by The Cramps on Bendix. One time when Miles was going to America, I asked him to get me some Cramps records for us to sell and when he got back he said he'd got the records but they turned out to be a box of records by The Mumps, which wasn't quite right. Then he went back again and returned and said to me, 'I didn't just get you the records, I got you the band.' He'd signed The Cramps.

Step Forward had put out stuff by The Fall and I think I was instrumental in getting them ultimately to go to Rough Trade. I got on really well with Mark E. Smith, apart from when we went to see The Cramps and Mark was calling them out as fakes from the side of the stage: he soon changed his opinion. I played on stage with The Fall around about the time of *Dragnet* and I was there when Geoff Travis and Mayo Thompson went to Wales to produce 'Fiery Jack', the best ever Fall single, which came out as a Step Forward record.

Geoff Travis: I'll always be dead proud of our period with The Fall. *Dragnet* and *Live at the Witch Trials* were two of our favourite records and we played them over and over in the shop. The way I came to produce 'Fiery Jack' was that I went up to Leeds to the Futurama Festival, the one that used to be held in an old aircraft hangar, and I plucked up my courage and went and introduced myself to Mark. I said that if he ever wanted to do anything with Rough Trade we'd be thrilled and he was really receptive and really open. In fact, he gave me a hug, which surprised me and which was really warm of him.

I got to know him a little bit and he asked me if Mayo and I wanted to produce a record with him, which was 'Fiery Jack'. We went off to Ridge Farm, Dave Ansen's studio in Wales, where we'd already recorded Young Marble Giants and The Pop Group, and made the record. I remember Mark did the vocals outside in the courtyard of the studio – he liked the echo it created.

The wonderful Mark E. Smith.

Steve Jameson: Around this time, I was taking a lot of amphetamine, working all day, then out to the Marquee or Music Machine or wherever, then on to somewhere else. I was homeless. I'd always end up at dawn walking back along the Bayswater Road to crash in the office, or, if I felt like it, I'd start packing up orders. I fell out with Miles and I was out.

I moved into a squat which Dexter Dalwood from The Cortinas and Barry Andrews from XTC were living in on Belsize Road. It was in the middle of a load of dodgy, druggy flats, full of Danish seamen on shore leave, drugs everywhere. I was glad they let me stay there but it was horrible. I went into Rough Trade looking for a particular record and I got talking to Geoff, who told me that Pete Donne had done some sort of runner and that they needed someone behind the counter, someone, he said to me, who could handle the skinheads who came in. Geoff started to tell me about it being a cooperative, which I thought sounded a bit soppy.

I not only went there but I persuaded Mark E. Smith to go there with The Fall. I had lots of conversations with him about it and his basic line/reservation was 'I'm not signing with that bunch of amateur college wankers', but I sold it to him a bit. I hitched up and stayed with him in Rochdale and we talked about it a bit more. Mark called them 'utopian dreamers' and told me to wait and see, and I'm afraid soon I had to admit he had been right. But when I came back from visiting him, The Fall signed to Rough Trade. Later it would feel like it was me and The Fall against Rough Trade, but that was later when things turned bad. What I loved about Mark was that he was just so resolutely himself.

Geoff Travis: We did 'How I Wrote "Elastic Man"', another great single, and then Mark wanted me to do 'Totally Wired', but came up to me and as an aside asked me if he could 'not have that Mayo Thompson come this time', and like a true friend I abandoned Mayo immediately. We recorded that at Cargo in Rochdale and I even mixed the record myself. I was chuffed with the drum sound we got, but then there was some politics and Mark's manager/partner Kay Carroll took my name off the credits. It made me laugh that during the 1980s, Rod Stewart would come on stage on his stadium tours to the sound of 'Totally Wired' playing over the PA.

I used to crash on the floor at Mark and Kay's place and I remember one time saying to him, 'The others, they don't say much do they?' They were all so terrified of him. It was a fantastic Fall line-up at that time and they were very receptive, and I think they weren't taking too many drugs, which always made it easier when dealing with The Fall. Always, the more speed involved, the less easy it was to communicate with them.

We put out *Totale's Turns*, the live album, in the summer of 1980, and towards the end of the year, we put out *Grotesque*. I not only produced *Grotesque*, I engineered it as well: me, a man who can hardly turn a stereo on. But then I think a gnat or a mosquito could produce a Fall record if it was lucky enough to be in the vicinity.

Steve Jameson: Not long after The Fall arrived, Rough Trade label and distribution shipped out to Blenheim Crescent and so the flat upstairs became available. I was going out with Sue Donne and we moved in. This had turned into the job of my dreams, I suddenly realised, and then of course as soon as I did things started falling apart.

Initially, I had all the weed I wanted and all the music I wanted, but after the move, drugs around the shop increased. Not too long after, The Clash put The Fall on a US tour with them and Rough Trade wanted to send Scott Piering. So I took some time off to go over there anyway. In the end I hung out with them longer than perhaps I should have done, since I was meant to be in the shop. It was starting to be an odd time for The Fall, as well. The Fall didn't get on with The Clash on tour and Karl Burns was falling out with Mark, and suddenly somehow I wasn't such good mates with him either. Shortly after, he would make some changes. I thought he'd sort of become the embodiment of everything he hated.

Anyway, I came back to the shop and suddenly it all seemed like a cage. I was starting to get worried about my amphetamine use. I'd wake up every morning and have a quarter gram of speed and open up the shop. Then I'd have a booster around three o'clock teatime. I had a guy who used to come down from Birmingham and bring in hash and weed and a guy who worked for The Fall used to bring speed in. I used to have to juggle payments to keep them both happy. Pete Walmsley came over from Blenheim Crescent one time and out the back was a big pile of amphetamines and next to them a huge pile of weed, and he looked at me and said, 'Well, you might as well change the name of the shop from Rough Trade to Drug Trade.'

I don't think anybody realised I was injecting speed until I asked some-body to go out and buy me a syringe. It all got a bit intense, especially when people knew that I lived in the flat above the shop. The shop bell would go at all times of the night and it wasn't people looking for music.

There had been a couple of pet rats, Scoot and Scout, one of which Sue Johnson had left behind – Scout. We had a couple of pet cats and the cats and the rat would drink milk from the same saucer.[15] One of the cats then had seven kittens and we gave them names like Sid, Nancy, Benny and one called Higgarty, which Mark E. Smith adopted and renamed for some reason Frau. The point is, my ideal life had started to go horribly wrong.

Geoff Travis: Mayo came back on board for the wonderful six-track *Slates*, which Adrian Sherwood also did some good work on. It was a phenomenal record. After that, I think my days as glorious producer were largely over.

There wasn't really a falling-out with Mark E. Smith, but after they went away to do *Hex Enduction Hour* and then came back for *Perverted By Language*, they'd sort of dwindled as kingpins, and I think they felt that. By then, of course, The Smiths had come on the scene and I remember Morrissey being in the office at the same time as Mark one day and Mark greeting him with a very caustic, 'Hello, Steven, how are you?' Nobody called Morrissey 'Steven', and I don't think he liked it very much. Mark was obviously pissed off that another Mancunian band had come and toppled him from his position. But we were also guilty because we didn't put in as much time and effort as we might have by the time it got to *Perverted By Language*, and in truth they deserved that. But by then it had stopped being fun and an awful lot of speed was being taken. I have to say that Mark always was and always has been lovely to me.

15. Scout had something of a pedigree, according to Richard Scott, and had appeared as a fully trained-up member of the Footsbarn Theatre, which may explain his impeccable attitude towards the cats, though not theirs towards him.

*

Dick O'Dell: Daniel Miller and I were the first to throw our lot in with Rough Trade and give them a whole label to play with, in his case Mute; in mine, Y Records. I'd taken across The Pop Group – we'd done 'We Are All Prostitutes' on Rough Trade the year before, in 1979 – and The Slits, who left Island to go to Rough Trade. I'd started releasing my own records as well, things like Pigbag.

When man first walked on the moon, I'd been working at a holiday camp and quit spectacularly by putting Jimi Hendrix's 'Purple Haze' full blast on the camp's PA system at 1.00 a.m. in the morning and walking out for ever. I worked for the Open Space theatre with Thelma Holt and later Ballet Rambert, before doing lighting on David Bowie's *Ziggy Stardust* tour and Pink Floyd's *Dark Side of the Moon* tour. I then quit lighting and did tour management and ended up tour-managing The Stranglers, which was a riot a night and left me locked up in the cells on more than one occasion. One of their support acts was The Pop Group, who were looking for management, and I just made the decision to offer to become their manager.

Gareth Sager: We'd supported Elvis Costello around Christmas 1977 at the time when Andrew Lauder was taking him from Stiff to Radar. I believe we blew Elvis off stage that night at the Nashville Rooms and consequently Andrew offered to do a record with us and pretty soon after we went to Ridge Farm to record Y.

A couple of problems emerged. We'd moved on essentially from the sound we were making when Andrew signed us and by the time we came to record Y we were more radical, deconstructing the tracks, pulling them apart and doing things like deciding not to have verses or choruses. Even before then, we'd done an eight-minute track on a John Peel session, which was quite an unheard of thing to do at the time. We felt that our original sound had created the mould which bands like Joy Division and Echo & The Bunnymen then took up and which we had quickly moved on from. Then, of course, while making Y we moved on again. So the record Andrew got, which I love and am very happy with, wasn't really the record Andrew paid for.

As well as all this, midway through making Y, a friend of ours – who ran an alternative bookshop, which stocked a lot of conspiracy theory books – told us that Warner Brothers were connected to the people that ran the car parks in America and were involved in giving money for arms deals. It all seemed dreadfully uncool to be associated with them. We suddenly thought we'd sided with the bad guys, with the enemy. We were a bunch of hypocrites. Vivien Goldman had started championing us in *Sounds* and so she put us in touch with Geoff, who we went to meet.

Dick O'Dell: I think both The Pop Group and The Slits were not suited to major labels. Lots of bands around this time were desperate to sign to an independent label, some without thinking of the consequences financially for them. I came to The Slits after The Pop Group, just at that time when they were recording *Cut*. Someone had phoned me up and said they were looking for management – they'd been through thirteen or so managers in two years – did I fancy it? Although I didn't contract it for them, I took them on at the time of *Cut*, and got flak immediately from every quarter over the record sleeve. A lot of people at Rough Trade did not want The Slits to be on the label over that cover. I tried to explain, I wasn't anti-feminist and after all it was Pennie Smith – a woman – who took the bloody photos.

Gareth Sager: Warners, I'm sure, were very happy to get rid of us. They probably felt we hadn't helped our cause with them by making what they saw as an extremely uncommercial record in Y. We all thought we'd made a marvellously commercial record at the time.

With 'We Are All Prostitutes', I think we got everything about The Pop Group exactly right. It was recorded at a completely different time from the album and was like a sort of explosion. We had a new bass player and there was a lot of good energy between us. It was the song that took us into our next phase, our more political one. With hindsight, I sometimes wish we hadn't gone quite so far down the political road. Back then, albums were made quickly and by the time we released the album on Rough Trade we'd barely had time to think about things. Also, we were very young by the standards of most of the bands at that time, nineteen or twenty when we made that Rough Trade album.

Dick O'Dell: 'We Are All Prostitutes' and *For How Much Longer Do We Tolerate Mass Murder?* – sellable titles, weren't they?

Gareth Sager: I think Rough Trade suggested the split single – The Slits doing 'In the Beginning There Was Rhythm' and us doing 'Where There's a Will'. We were sharing a drummer by then and a manager and of course we'd both used Dennis Bovell and I think it was treated as a sort of gimmick idea at the time.

Dick O'Dell: The one problem I felt with Rough Trade was that its collective approach meant that nothing could get done without a meeting. Consequently, if things started to get exciting, which later they did in the case of Pigbag, it was all hamstrung. I think that Geoff and Richard and one or two of the others quietly arranged a sort of putsch at that time to try to sort it out, but when they moved to Blenheim Crescent a lot more people suddenly appeared, all entitled to their say.

Gareth Sager: I think the politics was very much of its time and, don't forget, set against the background of Thatcherism. We'd been unemployed in Wales, all our mates were unemployed – some wanted to be because they were in groups. They were the ones who got trampled down when the yuppies arrived a few years later. And coming from Wales you felt that ugly arrogance that Thatcher had for anyone not from the south-east of England and also the brutality that that led to.

Dick O'Dell: The Pop Group inevitably didn't last. The tension between Mark Stewart, what you might call the political side of the band, and Gareth Sager, who was the musical side, just tore itself apart. It had probably reached a natural conclusion. It had worked very well for a couple of albums and some great singles but what had worked for the band dynamic at first eventually worked against it.

Gareth Sager: *We Are Time* was basically a bootleg album that we did ourselves with Rough Trade and they put it out at very little cost. I think we were about to be made bankrupt – it was a bankruptcy record. We did some gigs in America and came back and I realised I'd had enough. I was getting more into improvisational and avant-garde bands like Company, led by Derek Bailey, which seemed to me to be such a fantastic way of breaking up the traditional pop band formula. In fact, that was going in exactly the opposite direction of what was happening in the early 1980s when it turned out that being on the cover of *Smash Hits* was what it was deemed to be all about.

*

Geoff Travis: By the time we came to move, the record company had really established itself and, as well as *Inflammable Material*, we'd had a couple of other albums that had done exceptionally well. Young Marble Giants' *Colossal Youth* sold incredibly and, in addition to its intrinsic merits, I think that was because it went against the grain – it was quiet music at a period when there wasn't much of that around.

We got a consignment of compilation albums from Z Block Records in Cardiff called *Is the War Over?* and I played one and when I got to track nine, I think it was, I just stopped in my tracks, it was so good. I went straight into my A&R mode, tracked down the band and got them to come and see me. I think they thought I would ask them to do a single but I sent them off to Foel Studio to do the album. Stuart Moxham had pretty much got it mapped out and the whole thing was done in a couple of weeks.

I did the sound for them when they came down and played the Clarendon. They were wonderful but I think Alison Statton found performing live a bit terrifying.

James Blood Ulmer flyer, designed by Hil Scott.

Around this time I was in New York seeing Roger Trilling, who I'd got to know a bit. Roger knew a lot of jazz musicians and he introduced me to James Blood Ulmer and took me to see Blood play at a small club, the Tin

Palace, just off the Bowery, about two blocks from CBGBs. It was just one of those extraordinary nights and I loved his guitar-playing. I'd heard him playing on one of Ornette Coleman's records and anyone who got to play with Ornette Coleman had to be special.

What came about was a wonderful chance for us to make a record with somebody in a different musical world from us. Blood seemed chuffed to be working with a bunch of Londoners and Mayo and I and Roger worked on *Are You Glad to Be in America?*. It was a very popular record with other Rough Trade bands as well as the wider public. I thought it was nice that Rough Trade could get people to notice something, by virtue of it being on Rough Trade, which they might otherwise not countenance listening to.

*

Mike Hinc: I arrived in December 1980, just before the move. I had been working at the ICA as an assistant theatre director and they had wanted to broaden the programme and bring in some music. They had put rock bands on there before – The Clash had played in 1976. I started the ICA Rock Weeks, in conjunction with Capital Radio, and I suppose about half the acts I put on were Rough Trade acts.

I was aware of Rough Trade because my dad had a café in Portobello Road and I used to go in there to buy records. I vaguely knew Geoff and, in fact, had met him well before then when I was a student and working part-time at the Roundhouse and Geoff was standing in a guest-list line-up. My boss, John Curd of the ill-named but infamous and influential Straight Music, growled in my ear, 'That c— thinks he owns a record label – get rid of him now.' Of course, Geoff was far too nice and it was impossible to throw him out. He was so very non-rock 'n' roll that other bouncers came over to check him out. It was like strange news from another star or weird life from Planet Zog. I thought to myself, sea change in the zeitgeist . . .

We put some terrific acts on at the ICA – Siouxsie & The Banshees, Cabaret Voltaire, Orange Juice, The Raincoats, Josef K, The Fall ... It was through The Fall that I ended up working at Rough Trade. I'd been moonlighting from the ICA and putting on gigs at the Acklam Hall under the flyover at Portobello Road. I booked The Fall, and they broke the contract in that although they played, they'd played the 100 Club about a week before my gig. That split the audience and meant a bad night for everyone. At that time in London, the audience for a concert like this was about four hundred, at least half of which weren't going to go and see the band twice.

Mark E. Smith was furious about it and so I went to see Rough Trade because they had assured him that if he played both gigs, there would be enough audience for the two. I ended up working there and became the thirteenth employee. I went to work with Shirley O'Loughlin in Booking, who was doing a very good job, largely working with Rough Trade acts. I set out to broaden that.

Within a year, I think, we had a pretty good list of bands we were representing.

ROUGH TRADE
BOOKING
137, BLENHEIM CRESCENT, LONDON W.11.2EQ
TEL: 01-221-2761   01-229-5736
TELEX: 229579 -RGHTRD-

AGENCY REPRESENTATION

AZTEC CAMERA
THE BIRTHDAY PARTY
THE BLUE ORCHIDS
BLURT
CABARET VOLTAIRE
DISLOCATION DANCE
GENE LOVES JEZEBEL
KING TRIGGER
MAXIMUM JOY
MISTY
NICO
ORANGE JUICE
PALAIS SCHAUMBURG
PAUL HAIG's RHYTHM
OF LIFE
PERE UBU
PIGBAG
THE RAINCOATS
THE RED CRAYOLA
RIP RIG + PANIC
SCRITTI POLITTI
THIS HEAT
23 SKIDOO
THE VIRGIN PRUNES
ZOUNDS, WEEKEND

Rough Trade Booking had taken on a substantial roster of clients. Advert from early 1982, designed by Mike Hinc and based on a still from the 1959 film, Look Back in Anger *– 'rather appropriate given the events of the end of the year . . .'*

I'd worked with Josef K and Orange Juice before working at Rough Trade, when I'd put them on at the ICA, and then at Rough Trade I took on Aztec Camera. They left when they went to Warners and it just so happened that the same week I picked up The Smiths.

I liked working with Cabaret Voltaire – I thought they were one of the true postmodern bands of the 1980s. It seems to me that they virtually invented electronic dance music and I am sure had they carried on longer than they did their reputation would be colossal. What was good about them was that they always knew what they wanted – which was a minimum fee of about a grand, for which they would more or less play any venue. They weren't at all mercenary, they were just organised and I think, rather unusually for a band, they had lives outside music. I thought they were fantastic – and very nice people.

A couple of other bands that I always liked were Scritti Politti and This Heat. I never toured Scritti – I could have done and I always wanted to: the phone rang every day for them. This Heat were a fabulous band but also involved in possibly my worst moment as an agent. I put them on at King's College and Death in June supported. Doug Pearce, who played in Death in June, worked in Rough Trade. Death in June came out in brown shirts with lots of Fascistic regalia, and I suddenly realised I was in the middle of a nightmare. It was embarrassing. For some reason, a lot of people at Rough Trade believed Death in June were making a fashion statement . . .

Doug worked in the wholesale office, a room – known as the Bunker – painted entirely in matt black. It was all very Last Days of Hitler. I'm almost sure there was a picture of Adolf on the wall and nearly certain that late one night someone surreptitiously painted the place pink. Can't imagine who, but it was the only rational thing to do.

We were meant to help each other, and that is why I put Death in June on the This Heat bill. Back then, Rough Trade broke down barriers by mixing together bands that might not ordinarily be expected to be on the same bill: you might see a gig with, say, Cabaret Voltaire, Misty in Roots and Young Marble Giants. In these days of commodified music, that kind of thing doesn't happen any more.

Richard Scott: We finally moved in the early autumn of 1980 to Blenheim Crescent, leaving just the shop and its staff behind. For a long time we had outgrown 202 Kensington Park Road and initially we had tried to find a solution by taking over the synagogue, which was by then disused. Geoff's father checked it out but they weren't prepared to let us have it – I think they didn't want punk rock records stored in it.

I found Blenheim Crescent through a local agent. There had originally been a shoe company in there called ME Phillips. One of the biggest problems we had was ensuring that the air was taken out of the building without the noise getting out with it, hence the elaborate air-circulation system.

I have no recollection of the move, which I'm sure probably took place over a weekend. It was a momentous occasion but I don't recall whether or not we had a party, but then we had parties most nights at Rough Trade.

Zzzst!

PART TWO:

137 BLENHEIM CRESCENT

'FUTURISTIC RECORD LABEL'

'We stock all independent singles we think have merit, and we are happy to tell dealers the difference between a good record and a bad record. We are not afraid to act as arbiters of taste, because we have discovered that the two coincide, more than most people would think.'

Rough Trade Distribution, Dealer Information Sheet c.1980

By the time of its move to Blenheim Crescent in autumn 1980, Rough Trade had stopped being the sum of the worker parts and started being defined by the records it was releasing and distributing. The record company was entering a creatively rich period and had gone from releasing an eclectic and somewhat random raft of singles to releasing a cogent body of album work (much of which didn't lack in eclecticism). The Fall, Scritti Politti, Young Marble Giants, Pere Ubu, Aztec Camera, the Go-Betweens, the Blue Orchids and James Blood Ulmer – artists many consider to be amongst the 'classic' Rough Trade acts – all released signature works during the Blenheim Crescent period. Robert Wyatt entered the mainstream charts. Wire released *Document and Eyewitness*, a period live item, a curio, recounting a snapshot in their evolution, from which this book takes its name. Other outstanding Blenheim Crescent acts included the Virgin Prunes, the Red Crayola, Zounds and Weekend. Ivor Cutler, the idiosyncratic poet and humorist, also came to the label at this time.

It was also a luminous period for Rough Trade Distribution, which had increased the record labels it dealt with to over two hundred. Labels such as Mute and Factory had already had significant sales successes, which Distribution had wholly or partly serviced: even prior to the move to 137 Blenheim Crescent, *millions* of records had physically passed through the organisation. Some labels were set up to create empires: others, to facilitate the release of just one record. A Rough Trade Distribution document from the period lists labels posterity has seen fit to note more prominently, such as Crass, Mute, Industrial, Greensleeves, Fast Product, Factory and Rough Trade itself, as well some of the more short-lived and intriguing, whose glory is now largely lost in the moment – labels including Clever Metal, Deleted Fuck Off, Groucho Marxist, Lab Jab, Natty Congo, Smug and Subversive.

With its fabulous communal garden out back, Blenheim Crescent was opulent by Rough Trade standards, and much needed. Inevitably staff numbers increased, eventually to about twenty, although there was still too much to do, and, in truth, as was usually the case with Rough Trade, by the time of the move (which had taken a year to facilitate) they needed to move again.

Expansion brought with it problems. The heyday of independent record selling was between 1979 and 1982, the former, as has been seen, the point at which some purists, inspired by punk, felt that the original independent ethic had sold out and started to parody itself, the latter the moment when the market itself began to correct the overload and labels such as Rough Trade needed to become *pro-active* rather than reactive. Until the start of the 1980s, almost any independent single in a picture sleeve could aspire to sell a minimum of 3,000–4,000 copies and the better ones many times more than that – often, with minimum push required.

The change in the marketplace, the expansion that Rough Trade (and other independent record businesses) had undertaken, and, in the case of Rough Trade, some slack business practice – there was apparently no formal stock-control system or financial segregation between the different arms of the business – came to a head at the end of 1982 when thirteen people, at least on paper, were made redundant. Most simply became 'privatised'. Rough Trade Booking became All Trade Booking, the Promotions department changed from Rough Trade Promotions to a PR company run by Scott Piering (who would later call it Appearing), and the shop workers bought out and took over running the shop, having valued the stock themselves and borrowed the money from the bank, cunningly using the records as collateral for the loan to buy them. Rough Trade at this time endured colossal, near-fatal losses, which would almost certainly have sunk it but for the grace of a number of creditors, such as Daniel Miller, whose Mute debt (for records sold) was eventually paid off by debenture.

Nineteen eighty-two was also the year that the loose conglomerate of associated, regional distributive businesses, instigated by Richard Scott, was formalised. Named by Geoff Travis, with his tongue somewhat firmly in his cheek, the Cartel was the ultimate embodiment of a process of access and enablement that had begun back in 1977. The design flaw in the structure – the fact that records boxed up and sent out from London were then unpacked and boxed up again and sent out from Liverpool, Norwich, Bristol, Edinburgh and York – was also its most beautiful facet, meaning, as it did, that a large number of people who might otherwise have been denied access could legitimately work in the music business without having to move to London.

The Cartel had been mooted almost from the moment Richard Scott had realised that the selling of large numbers of records to other record shops could be coordinated in a way that was both commercially and radically penetrating. It was still largely unthinkable at the start of the 1980s that a serious component of the record industry could properly function outside the capital, except in a retail or manufacturing capacity. There was (and later remained) an almost complete disdain for the concept of independence within the industry, amplified by the political struggle to get an independent chart, and then to sustain and regulate it (with arguments continuing well into the late 1980s). The prejudice pervaded retail, promoted by the major record labels, until 'independent' as a concept virtually disappeared.

Now consigned to history, the Cartel epitomises the finest spirit of Rough Trade's communal unselfishness in action. Although its legacy is not, predictably, lauded in some quarters as highly as the legacy of some of the records Rough Trade released or bands they signed, it is the one area where – in human terms – Rough Trade really did make a difference.

New, significant faces appeared in Blenheim Crescent, some of them with past form. Bob Scotland, who had done a sterling job in production and been part of the St Pancras League of Young Communists and the Camden squatting scene, left to pursue an academic career and was replaced by Richard Boon, who had set up the New Hormones record label and eventually went on to edit *The Catalogue*. Simon Edwards joined, having left Inferno Records in Birmingham, where he had helped organise part of the first Rough Trade Tour. He became integral to Distribution. Scott Piering, who had appeared just prior to the move to Blenheim Crescent, came into his own, redefining 'indie' in a way that became acceptable to more monolithic, megalithic broadcasting institutions. His legacy survives long after his tragic death in 2000. Scott's genius cohort Claude Bessy, who had helped set up *Slash* magazine in LA in 1977, joined and – among other seemingly unfeasible achievements – managed to get the Virgin Prunes on the front cover of *Smash Hits*. Mayo Thompson, another import from the Kensington Park Road days, the leader of Red Crayola (later Red Krayola) and part of the Art & Language collective, an urbane, charming man of fierce intellect, became the in-house producer (and later label manager), producing or co-producing many important releases.

In spring 1983, The Smiths signed to Rough Trade. Their arrival helped stabilise a business vessel that was desperately trying to right itself. The outcome of the previous winter's 'Night of the Long Knives', as the financial crisis became known by some (it actually lasted a week), was that the business was left sound but struggling. It was hampered by the substantial debt to Mute being repaid to the tune of around £8,000 a month before being knocked even further for six by financial irregularities occurring at Rough Trade Germany, where 'somebody ran off with a lot of money'.[16]

Morrissey and Johnny Marr at Glastonbury 1983, shepherded by Scott Piering (left).

The Smiths were a phenomenon. Their attitude, their work rate and the sheer mesmerising quality, for many, of their recorded output, which came at times in a seemingly breathless sequence, deserved and demanded that Rough Trade equip itself for purpose. Armed with the potential of a very high-selling act indeed, Rough Trade hired the London Records strike force to help it sell their records and, in the process, ended up having sixteen hit singles in a row. The use of an outside agency, and a major label one at that, alarmed many in the ranks but Rough Trade had previously used such a tactic (although without success), and ideological complaints, such as they were, were largely taken up more vociferously by some of Rough Trade's fellow independent labels.

Blenheim Crescent was, arguably, the creative and ideological high point

16. Rough Trade Inc., the American arm of the business, was started in 1979 and Rough Trade GMBH, the German equivalent, was begun in 1981.

for first-era Rough Trade. The move to Collier Street in spring 1984 would open up commercial possibilities undreamt of in Blenheim Crescent, aided largely by the success of The Smiths, but it was in W11 that the staff numbers were probably at their most ideal (for the type of company that Rough Trade set out to be), and it was there that the workers' trust was conceived – the logical conclusion of the cooperative ideals that had informed early Rough Trade. Some of the finest records of the era emerged from the building. In spite of the financial woes, and rifts and fissures that were starting to open up between the record label and the distribution company, they really were halcyon days.

The first Smiths albums would be pressed up in Blenheim Crescent and released following the move to Collier Street. There were to be problems on the horizon with the alpha band: ironically, the band's success forced Rough Trade to take a more professional line and, in so doing, it faced fresh organisational woes.

'Fiercely independent and fiercely disorganised,' is how one wag summed up Rough Trade at this time. It was undeniably at its most fiercely beautiful, too.

CHAPTER SEVEN:
1981

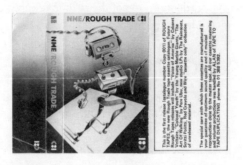

'And they've blown it all on plywood'

Toronto – *C81* – Rough Trade Inc. – Label deals – Scritti dilemma –
Masterbag

Jo Slee: After John and I had quit London and gone to Toronto in 1978,
I got three part-time jobs and John carried on doing the leather. John was
very serious about it and wanted to move to New York and I didn't. I just
loved being in Toronto, I felt so free and able to move around after the
nightmare of the pub and that area. John moved and started working for a
downtown New York fashion company run by Patricia Field. We went back
and forth, seeing each other for a bit, then John and I broke up. John was
diagnosed with cancer and he came back to England for treatment at the
end of 1980. Geoff moved out of his place at Vivien's and moved in with
Carolyn so that John could have a place to stay. Carolyn nursed him while
I wasn't around.

Meanwhile, I had started working again for Rough Trade, this time in
San Francisco, where I went to do 'press and promotion': things I really
had no idea about. Scott Piering came out on a flying visit to teach me how

to do it. We set up a card index with the names and contact details of the journalists, press and radio, and next to each he stuck a little coloured sticker – red for A-list, blue for B-list, et cetera. We worked fifteen-hour stretches then we'd go out and eat Hunan food and he'd tell me these outrageous stories about his past. Then we'd get up and start again. He was impatient of my ignorance of US promotions systems and passionate about his subject. Over the next week or so I began to find odd stickers stuck everywhere – on the car door, on top of the toilet cistern, in the fridge, on the tap on the sink ... He was pure gold.

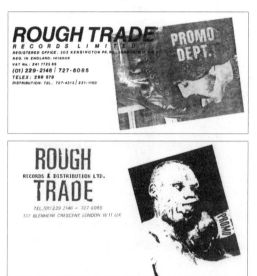

As the illustrations to these press releases show, Scott had a very fine understanding of the boot-licking, sucker-punched travails of the promo man.

I came back to England when John had his first operation and I came back when he had the second. I stayed with Carolyn and Geoff. John went into the Royal Marsden Hospital in 1981 and died two days before Christmas that year.

Geoff suggested at the start of 1982 that I might like to come and help again at Rough Trade in London: it was his way of seeing me through a difficult time. And I did go back. I used my return as an antidepressant.

When I first went into Blenheim Crescent it was in a total mess. They'd spent a fortune on it and the first thing I thought was, the profit on 100,000 sales of *Inflammable Material* and they've blown it all on plywood. There were suddenly a lot of people there I didn't know and who had no idea who I was. A lot of new faces popped up.

Chris Williams: I started hanging out at Rough Trade, 202 Kensington Park Road, and ended up working there after a phone rang and I just instinctively answered it and said, 'Hello, Rough Trade.' Scott Piering took me on, at first one day a week, then a few more days, until eventually I was full-time. Before I came in, Claude Bessy had joined. Together I like to think the three of us, Scott, Claude and I, ran one of the greatest promo teams ever. Scott in his American way took a lot of things seriously that Claude and I didn't necessarily worry about, and he thought about things quite deeply. Claude, on the other hand, being half-American and half-European, was more exuberant, all Gauloises and Gitanes. I was stuck somewhere between the two of them. We were quite hedonistic.

Claude Bessy and Scott Piering.

I'd never done PR work before – I had an awful lot to learn – but then the point is we were all pretty much making it up as we went along. We were reacting directly to the music we were given to work with, and it was a time when part of the job was finding out how you could promote it.

Claude – I adored him and he was brilliant. He'd written for *Slash* magazine in America, and was one of the two best music journalists ever, in my opinion, the other being Lester Bangs. He totally lived the life and he was naturally part of the scene. He spoke and thought in exactly the same way the bands did, which was I think why he got on so well with bands he worked with, like The Fall. Scott had more experience and took on the job of working television and radio. So eventually it settled down to Scott doing the TV/radio and Claude and I doing the music press and fanzines.

Mike Hinc: I'd met Claude at the time I was doing the ICA Rock Weeks. His engaging Franglais had been seriously seasoned by decades of red wine, Gitanes and Tennent's Extra lager. Mellifluous it was not, but passionate and persuasive he did in spades. What's more, he could write. His press releases impressed. He made the PC Raincoats sound almost interesting and postmodern minimalist dance doodlers Cabaret Voltaire ... very nearly exciting. Which, of course, they were.

He would champion music he loved and work amazingly hard for people he liked, no matter how quixotic the rest of the world found his taste. As far as Claude cared, the world was simply wrong, democracy was a flawed phenomena and reality was something to be bent into a more meaningful shape.

Chris Williams: I was at the *NME* one day, talking with Roy Carr, and I said wouldn't it be good if we could do a tape of all the new bands that we were working with and promote it through the *NME*. Back in North Wales, where I had grown up, I had got into taping, as lots of other people elsewhere had, by taping the John Peel show. Bow Wow Wow had released their *Your Cassette Pet* album on tape only, an awesome album which we all loved in the promo department. Around this time, Scott was doing his live taping of gigs and also the compilation tapes he was using for distribution and PR. This was a time when there was the big 'Home taping is killing the music industry' controversy – that was one industry slogan we were actively opposing.

I went back to Rough Trade and told Scott and he loved the idea. Then Scott went to a few other people and they all loved it as well so I rang up Roy and we agreed to do it together. It became *C81*, partly because of the year of its release and partly due to its length, which was deliberately set to come out at about eighty-one minutes, mimicking the 'C30, C60, C90' labelling of blank tapes.[17]

17. It was originally intended that the tape would contain a mix of 'popular bands like The Clash and Joy Division as well as great new bands like Orange Juice and Josef K', according to a letter Scott Piering sent to Kleenex, heaping lavish praise on the strengths of the *NME*. Unlike its later, oft-maligned offspring *C86*, *C81* was a mix of independent and major label acts. Like the later tape, it had a significant impact at the time (though curiously a less lasting one than *C86*). The Scritti Politti track, 'The "Sweetest Girl"', which opened the tape, was confidently described in Rough Trade's press release as 'simply and quietly a song without parallel or rival in recent British music'.

The tape was one of the *NME*'s biggest commercial successes and they sold about 35,000 copies. It was easily the best of those *NME*/Rough Trade tapes that were done.

*

Green Gartside: After I had spent the time in Wales I returned with a new idea of how I would go about making records. On the CD sleevenotes to *Early* I say some mad things about the earlier material being 'music with all the questions left in and assurances left out'. That kind of keeping-the-thing-teetering was what it had been all about. In the beginning nobody had any chops, nobody had any skills, nobody knew the names of the chords, nobody knew how to arrange a pop song. I had struggled with feelings of insecurity about not having any of that. That was what changed.

The manifesto I produced dragged the band along with me some of the way, but that didn't really last much beyond the making of the album before we fell apart.

After I wrote 'The "Sweetest Girl"', I went to Geoff initially and said that I didn't want to sing it. I had this idea that Gregory Isaacs could sing it and Kraftwerk could do the beats. I was so naïve and really had no idea how these things worked. We got a positive response from Gregory Isaacs's management – and nothing from Kraftwerk. I met Kraftwerk a little while later and they remembered getting the demo but said they hated reggae. Ultimately, I think it was all to my good fortune that it didn't happen.

I was sure that Geoff would like the new approach and I was certain that he would get it in a way that there would be a lot of people around him who didn't. At Rough Trade, there were some for whom punk was Year Zero and if, say, you'd played them a Chi-Lites record they wouldn't have known what it was.

Geoff Travis: In-house a lot of people felt betrayed by Green's approach, but I could understand what he was trying to do. He was pretty headstrong at the time – I don't think it needed much debate. I think it is amusing that Green woke up one morning and felt like the first white person on the planet to discover black music. He did a lot with that discovery, though.

Robert Wyatt: Green came to see me around the time I was recording 'Born Again Cretin', which was on the *NME* cassette. He seemed very intrigued by what I was able to do with the keyboards, about how I got from chord to chord, which was of course completely different from how you moved about chords on a guitar. He had this guitar-based song with a reggae beat which was rerecorded with my keyboards on it, with my *Rock Bottom*-type noise. I was touched that I could make a contribution.

Green Gartside: Robert came to the studio when we recorded 'The "Sweetest Girl"' and brought Alfie with him and Julie Christie, who seemed to be there for moral support. Alfie immediately got into the music and she said to Robert that it was 'music for kneading bread. I can really get into this when I am making bread,' she told him. Robert seemed to rather like that. I think she said it because it had that loping reggae rhythm and it sort of plodded.

A German film-maker at the time said a similar thing. Robert and I were asked to make some music for a Cinema Action film called *So That You Can Live*, about a striking family of Welsh miners – I think I used some tunes of Robert's and added some lyrics. I remember the film-maker at the end hearing 'The "Sweetest Girl"' and describing it as 'pachydermal'.

When I came to write 'The "Sweetest Girl"' I was listening to a lot of reggae, which is why of course it has such a strong reggae bassline. At that time, Culture – and in particular their album *Africa Stand Alone* – were everything to me, as were the records of Kraftwerk, which I was also listening to. I may have gone into that rehearsal room and consciously asked myself – Culture/Kraftwerk, what would that sound like? Or I might have just gone in there and discovered guitar chords and let free the sense of melody.

It was very Wyatt-esque. It owes a lot to Robert. People like Robert and

Syd Barrett had this huge influence on punk and after. I think undervalued also are contributions made by people like Chris Cutler, Henry Cow's drummer, who always went around the kit and avoided the kick and snare. Basically, 'The "Sweetest Girl"' let the melody in. So, the influences really were a bit of Robert, a bit of Culture, a bit of Kraftwerk.

'The "Sweetest Girl"' was the first track on the *C81* tape. There was a great opportunity for us to capitalise on that, arrange some tours, which I'm sure Geoff would have been all for, but I think my lack of stability prevented us from taking advantage. And the delay between the release of *C81* and the record coming out would have been down to my tinkering around with it. We did at least three different versions.

Geoff Travis: I was disappointed that 'The "Sweetest Girl"' didn't do better. It wasn't a problem that it was on the *NME* cassette. That should have worked in the underground way that a summer hit in the clubs can get picked up by radio. Pop music is for the masses and records become hits when they are on the Radio One playlist. Although 'The "Sweetest Girl"' deserved to be a hit, and should have been a hit – it was a masterpiece – I think in retrospect it was far too subtle to be Radio One fodder.

I don't think back then we were naïve about its potential; I don't think just because we liked it we thought it would be a hit. You only survive by having one foot in the real world.

I think that the problem at the time had more to do with the fact that the tried-and-tested method of turning great records into hits was a craft we were still learning.

Green Gartside: We recorded everything in Berry Street, the singles and the album *Songs to Remember*, and as usual Geoff just let me get on with it. I did occasionally go back and ask for more money and Geoff always gave it to me. I didn't particularly know my way around a recording studio at that point and it might take about eight hours before I'd realise that something wasn't quite right and we'd have to do it again. It was important: we were no longer fetishising the amateur, we were really trying to make something. It was always going to cost more money – we needed to record it in a proper studio, we needed a drum machine, there would be session musicians – and I was aware that Rough Trade hadn't spent that kind of money on records before, though the amounts involved have been greatly exaggerated in my opinion.

Geoff Travis: There seems to be a belief that Rough Trade was more col-lectivised and more focused and more pure and then the Scritti pop records came about and made Rough Trade more commercialised. The irony is, of course, that Scritti *left* to work in an environment that was more com-mercialised. Green was making more and more commercial music and wanted to be a success in the medium he'd chosen to work in and was concerned that Rough Trade didn't have the resources to propel him there. I happened to agree with him. I knew that our record company didn't have the money to make a £50,000 video, or hire expensive American producers. We just couldn't afford it.

I knew also that the culture of Rough Trade wasn't going to tolerate an all-out frontal assault on the charts in a glossy way. I saw nothing wrong in Green's ambition to want to achieve that. I knew we didn't have the resources to do justice to somebody making world-class pop music – it was the same situation with Aztec Camera not long afterwards, who left with my blessing. I never wanted us to be in a situation where we couldn't realise someone's creative idea.

Green Gartside: Rough Trade had just moved to Blenheim Crescent – I remember we were all amazed at how flash the new premises were. Geoff had this little glass booth where we'd go and have meetings. That was where Geoff would play me stuff, and it would always rock my world a bit. I think that like the rest of us he was tired for a while of somebody walking in from Manchester dressed in a mac and playing him another piece of guitar-driven music, and he encouraged me. I think Geoff has always been interested in having success: I don't think he sees a point in doing something just for the sake of it, even if he's never actively wanted to go and find or make a hit. He's never had a fear or dislike of commercial music.

Peter Walmsley: I'd returned from America and gone back to work doing licensing and very quickly had got deals abroad with Japan, France and Italy. I'd sort of done myself out of my production job but licensing kind of segued into it in that I would be sent masters from abroad to check for quality, so I was still involved in that side a bit. Many of the records we produced at home were ready-recorded or cheaply done because that was the nature of the beast. People didn't have flamboyant ideas about themselves or their records. I felt, however, that Scritti and in particular Green had this overweening sense of self-importance around the time of recording 'The "Sweetest Girl"' and the situation was made worse because they had originally come to Rough Trade almost sanctimonious in their belief in their political and egalitarian views, had recorded a DIY record fully supporting that ethic, and now became these monsters from the record industry wanting to make these perfect pop records which financially risked everything for Rough Trade. Certainly more money was spent on Scritti Politti than was probably sensible at the time. We had no magic formula, no guarantee any of it would work.

Taking the decision to do those records in the way they were done ran against the ethics Rough Trade held at that point in the strongest possible way. We shouldn't have got ourselves financially into the position where we were dependent on 'The "Sweetest Girl"' being a hit single. It was the most beautiful record but it had to be a hit to work, and it suddenly turned everything head over heels in terms of what we stood for because suddenly we were potentially dependent on making hit records. And that wasn't what Rough Trade Records was about and it wasn't what Geoff was about. We were a cooperative, all on equal salary, which was not a lot, and the big fear was that this could bankrupt us.

Geoff justified it with obvious difficulty – probably through the quality of the music, through the comparable ethics of Scritti and Rough Trade, and through the idea that it wasn't extravagant in that producing the perfect pop song represented some sort of value. It polarised views. We had endless meetings about it. In the end I went along with it, in spite of it being madness to do so.

I remember Richard Scott being upset about it. Once you spent that kind of money on a project you set down a marker and couldn't go back. If you could make it work – great, you broke the mould. But nobody really looked at the business at that point as a business of acquisition and someone like Richard Scott was a fundamentalist – he didn't believe we should have long-term contracts or acquire responsibilities in that way.

Green Gartside: I wasn't involved in discussions at Rough Trade where I heard dissenting voices about how and what we were doing; if they were taking place it was in my absence. I didn't sense that what we were doing was anomalous to what other Rough Trade bands were doing. I admit the album took much longer to make than anyone would have expected or particularly wanted. But at least a couple of the Scritti posse worked at

Rough Trade and any serious criticisms, anything striking, I certainly would have heard about because I heard about all the goings on at Rough Trade, usually at the squat at the end of the day. It was like a soap opera – alas, a soap opera whose plot I can no longer recall.

I had my theoretical and political reasons for doing what I did, and there were political shifts that went in tandem with the music-making and had an influence. When 'Skank Bloc Bologna' came out we had grown interested in ideas coming out of Euro Communism – *Red Bologna* had not long been published and we were all reading Gramsci – that started to acknowledge popular culture and its importance. It seems obvious now but back then there was this fairly new element to British thinking on the left that began to embrace popular culture and, by extension, popular song. This made me think again about pop music. That, broadly speaking, was one aspect of the argument that led Scritti to pop. Another argument was a kind of *via negativa* – being turned off by the way independent music was going and knowing what we *didn't* want to do, what we *didn't* like. Around that time – 1981–82 – in a slightly different way, the same conversations were taking place in Sheffield with Bob Last, the Human League and the Heaven 17 boys. We weren't alone.

Richard Scott: I loved Scritti Politti: I loved their music and I loved the fact that at first they were right at the centre of that whole DIY scene. Initially, I loved the political aspect of the band, the self-help approach, too. It was all so anti-star, so anti-ego. At that point they embodied for me everything that was correct about the approach to making music – an attitude that said, 'I like making music, I can produce something good, put it out, make my money back and that's the extent of my interest.' The idea of wanting to be on *Top of the Pops* is completely laughable.

But I think around about this time Geoff started to be drawn towards the magnet of the higher-selling side of things and he suddenly saw potency in Green. By our standards a lot of money was spent making *Songs to Remember* and frankly it was a poor album.

Blenheim Crescent was a magnificent building but it led to problems that I could not have foreseen. In Kensington Park Road we'd adopted the Island Records approach – a big table in the centre of the room around which all the work was done. It was impossible to not know what everybody else was up to. It encouraged us to be together in all senses. Blenheim Crescent wasn't like that.

Richard Boon: It was around about the time of Rough 20 – *Songs to Remember* – that change crept in. Geoff Travis and Richard Scott had separate offices in Blenheim Crescent and their doors would be shut. Geoff Travis on one side in his little office with 'GEOFF' above the door, Richard Scott on his side in his little office with 'RICHARD' above the door. The wholesale packing office was stuck in the middle. I think the relationship between Richard and Geoff started to deteriorate. I mean, they used to go out to gigs together. That was rent apart. Now they didn't seem to talk.

*

Steve Montgomery: Autumn 1980 I had flown out to LA to visit a friend and thought my Rough Trade time was over. I'd seen the flyer for Cabaret Voltaire playing at Sokel Hall and they had rung me up and we'd arranged to meet up. I was finally about to get my hands on some pay – severance pay – from Rough Trade and I was due to go up to San Francisco to collect it. Rough Trade Inc. had been set up in San Francisco, for reasons that remain to this day bizarre, given that the East Coast would have been a lot easier in terms of proximity to England.

Rough Trade Inc. had received my money from England, but somehow they had managed to spend it before I got there. They had managed to spend a lot of money. Richard Scott had been instrumental in setting up Rough Trade Inc. and he'd got Allan Sturdy, his former co-manager of Third World, to run it. Allan Sturdy had received a large sum of Rough Trade money and managed to spend it on unusual aspects of the business, with questionable benefit to Rough Trade.

Cabaret Voltaire asked me to go on up to San Francisco with them, which I did. I had very little money and I ended up sleeping at Peter Walmsley and Sue Johnson's place. Peter and Sue had been over for about a year, helping to set up Rough Trade Inc. I think it was the middle of the night when the phone call came from London – I had a dreadful migraine attack at the time, which now seems fitting – could I help investigate Rough Trade Inc. and help make good?

I had no option now but to jump back on board and, once Peter and Sue went back, sort out the mess. I had the grand pleasure of basically firing every lazy bastard involved with fleecing Rough Trade Inc. out of money. It was the only time in my life I have felt like a Fascist dictator and it gave me a very uncomfortable feeling. But it was either that or shut down the business.

There was a lot of sorting out to do. Geoff, for instance, had agreed to fund *RE/Search* magazine and they were taking us to the cleaners for a couple of thousand dollars a month, which was insane given the returns. We sold about five copies each month in the shop.[18]

But good things were achieved as well – we put out the US version of *Inflammable Material* and released one of the best Rough Trade albums ever, the compilation *Wanna Buy a Bridge?*, which was put together by Peter Walmsley asking the staff at Rough Trade London to draw up a list of what tracks should be on the record and then collating the results. It was the first Rough Trade US album.

The structure needed a lot of sorting out. When I arrived we were shipping American records over to England and they were reselling them back to shops in New York. Sometimes they'd agree to send records over to San Francisco for us to sell and I'd walk around the corner and find a competitor had already got them: Rough Trade in the UK had supplied them first. It was insane.

18. *RE/Search Publications* grew out of the punk magazine *Search & Destroy*, which V. Vale, a former employee of the City Lights bookstore in San Francisco, had set up in 1977 and which Geoff Travis had admired. The altogether more ambitious remit of *RE/Search* was to uncover 'the irrational shadow of official culture'. The first three 'shocking tabloid issues' were co-funded by Rough Trade and contained articles on punk prostitutes, Octavio Paz, Situationism, beat figure Diane di Prima, Kathy Acker, Surgical Penis Klinik, Throbbing Gristle, Fela Kuti and Nigerian rebel music. Plenty of Rough Trade acts were also given coverage, including Cabaret Voltaire, Young Marble Giants, The Slits and James Blood Ulmer. The plan was to co-launch a book imprint, Rough Trade Books, and publish a work by cut-up technique pioneer Brion Gysin (a co-collaboration with William Burroughs and with some input from Genesis P-Orridge). When the relationship with Rough Trade collapsed at the start of 1982, 4,000 copies of the magazine had been sold in total over the fourteen months of its lifetime and Rough Trade Inc. were selling five copies a month through the shop, yet had funded the venture to the tune of $10,000 (part of this money was used to repair the transmission on Vale's car, which had been lent to Rough Trade). According to correspondence from *RE/Search* to Rough Trade, Vale was a 'creative synthesizer' and Rough Trade 'a futuristic record label', albeit one that engaged in 'dictatorship politics'. It is a great shame that it ended so badly given the respective qualities of the two organisations. But in attempting to resolve the issue, Geoff Travis sent a stern instruction: 'RT is NOT your rich patron that is paid back in good will,' he told Vale. 'We are talking about the survival of RT Inc . . . . Please reply, not by phone.'

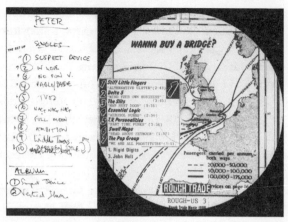

Peter Walmsley's handwritten list of tracks he thought should be included on the Rough Trade Inc. compilation, Wanna Buy a Bridge?

In my time there, we went on to do some good things – the business settled down and we released some of our own records as well, including those by Young Marble Giants and Joy Division, who entrusted us with their albums, to spectacularly good success when they became New Order and 'Blue Monday' came out, the US remix of which was a big hit.

*

Richard Scott: We never boarded up the windows at Carnival and we took no precautionary action around about the time of the 1981 riots.[19] We were accepted into the community and had nothing to fear from it.

Steve Jameson: The police came in and warned us that something was going down and that we ought to shut and board up. In fact, we knew before the

19. In his report published after the 1981 riots, Lord Scarman recognised that racial disadvantage and the problems of inner city decay had partly led to the riots occurring (this part of his findings was ignored by the Conservative government) in Brixton, London, Handsworth, Birmingham, St Pauls, Bristol and Chapel Town, Leeds. Two months after the April riots, riots broke out in Toxteth, Liverpool. CS gas was used for the first time on the mainland to quell the rioters. Margaret Thatcher poured scorn on claims of racism being a factor. Sometime between the Brixton riot and the Toxteth one, The Specials went to Number One with 'Ghost Town', a record often said to define the moment. It was a curious, unsettling period, not entirely dissimilar to 1977 when pockets of disaffected youth vented their displeasure in a year utterly consumed by royal events – in 1977, the Queen's Silver Jubilee, and in 1981, the ill-fated marriage of Prince Charles and Lady Diana Spencer.

police at Ladbroke Grove did, because people came in and tipped us off about what was happening. No one was going to throw a brick through our window.

After the Brixton riots, a lot of stuff came through the door, a bass guitar, a couple of £1,000 reel-to-reel tape machines – I had one of those; in fact, it set me up for when I left and started the demo studio. There were a couple of girls that used to come in with stuff. They were very good at roller-skating and used to roller-skate through jewellery shops, scooping up stuff.

Things went wrong for me at Rough Trade but I think Thatcherism put an end to many of the ideals they had and I think that is a big factor. I think Rough Trade never became Thatcherite, but let's say it bowed down a bit; it was forced to. I think they adapted to survive.

On the street, the whole punky reggae movement had been founded on weed and speed and all of a sudden you couldn't get any decent speed. All of a sudden there was a lot of heroin and cocaine out there, but it wasn't like the good old stuff, the stuff that didn't send you mad. Heroin, which used to be a dull, glistening white, was now brown and tarry: cocaine was gleaming white. The street was flooded with all this shit, I think deliberately.

I decided when I finished that I would set up a demo studio for artists to record in. I had this insane idea that what we would produce would be a cross between the sound of Lee Perry's Black Ark set-up and Phil Spector's studio. Grant Showbiz offered to help and so did Adrian Sherwood, but Rough Trade didn't help at all. After that I went on and co-formed World Domination Enterprises. Ironically, my leaving enabled Pete Donne to get back into the shop – Pete was the person I had replaced. According to some people, I was a burnt-out drug wreck, a mess, but I wasn't really. I was still pursuing my dream.

*

Chris Williams: When we moved to Blenheim Crescent, there used to be big meetings at the front of the building which everybody attended. I liked that. I believed in the Rough Trade ethos: I'd come in on the understanding that I was working for a collective and that we had a collective voice. I was quite disillusioned when I realised that wasn't the case. Geoff and the other bosses would actively resist decisions they didn't like and it created a lot of tension. Politics was most strong in Distribution, where there was a logistic chain that needed attending to. If you were driving a fork-lift truck all day, or just packing boxes, you were essentially doing a conventional job. There was a lot of the language of the left around at that time, not all of which I listened to. When bands like Scritti Politti used political language I thought that the politics was good, but you knew it was just never going to happen. I think that was one reason why it was such a shock when Scritti came back and presented 'The "Sweetest Girl"'. People were shocked when they heard it – pleasantly shocked.

Mike Hinc: We had a meeting in Blenheim Crescent about the Venue at Victoria, which was a concert hall Richard Branson opened and which had a capacity of 1,200. I wanted to put some of the bands we were handling on there and went to see them and got on very well. But when I got back to Rough Trade, there was a massive meeting about whether it was acceptable to put Rough Trade acts on at a Virgin venue – it was insane. I really didn't understand what venues the bands played, which should have been entirely their choice, had to do with the person making the vegetarian quiche or the man whose job it was to drive the van. It drove me nuts.

Chris Williams: I started to take on promo for the various labels we were distributing. At the start of the DIY thing it had been bands coming in with records that had no idea about promo that we would be helping. That then extended to labels when they started to develop. I looked after Factory Records and Postcard Records, two of the more significant labels. I'd met Tony Wilson at Eric's in Liverpool but didn't realise until I met him again in Rough Trade who he was. Postcard I just loved from the start, the way the singles came in the plastic bags with the postcards in. At that moment, the sound of Orange Juice and some of those other bands was amazing. Alan Horne (who ran Postcard) and Edwyn Collins (from Orange Juice) and I would go off around town giggling and laughing, we connected so well. It didn't seem like work.

I don't think Geoff Travis had any real relationship with them, apart from his love of the music and his obvious support of it. It's funny but none of the bands – like Orange Juice, Josef K or Aztec Camera – got anywhere near the level of creativity they reached with Postcard in their later label careers. Orange Juice scarpered off pretty quickly to Polydor, which I kind of helped facilitate by lending them some money to finish off their album. And then Alan Horne was just so irreverent – I mean scrapping the Orange Juice album because he wasn't happy with it on some refined, aesthetic level.

Geoff Travis: Alan Horne used to come in and play his Andy Warhol games. He was always a bit miffed with me because when he originally came down looking for a distribution deal and played me Orange Juice's 'Falling and Laughing' I listened to it and quite liked it but didn't say it was the best single I'd heard in my life and that really annoyed him. He went back to Scotland and Orange Juice made 'Blue Boy' and it got Single of the Week in *Melody Maker*. I read the review, listened to the record and loved it and said to myself that maybe I had been wrong about them. So I called up Alan and offered him a distribution deal. I think that not having embraced Alan's genius immediately counted as a big blow against me.

Richard Scott: That early Postcard stuff stood out a mile – it was just so good. And Geoff can take credit for bringing it in. But I think that was another early instance of our relationship starting to falter because I was adamant that Postcard was a regional label and should remain so and Geoff begged to differ. Alan Horne had ridiculous ambitions for the label, which would have been better served regionally rather than nationally, it seems to me.

Geoff Travis: A lot of nonsense has been written about the deal done with Postcard. Alan may have struck a hard bargain but essentially the deal was the same deal everybody else got. In fact, the deal Rough Trade did with Crass was probably the most generous deal it ever did – they came to us and explained why they believed in selling their records cheaply, and we supported them, so they got their distribution very advantageously.

The Postcard singles were brilliantly made and beautifully packaged. But rather like Fast Product, the fact they never made any albums doomed them to failure. They made a Josef K album and scrapped it. They made an Orange Juice album and scrapped it. We paid for the recording of the Orange Juice album, which Alan Horne went off with and sold to Polydor. That was going to be a joint Postcard/Rough Trade release. I'd set Orange Juice up with Adam Kidron and I remember going to the studio as they were making it.

When Alan sold the tapes to Polydor it didn't seem worth the effort of having a fight over. I just thought it was Alan Horne acting ridiculous. I moved on and we got the money back. I suspect that at the back of my mind was a suspicion that though the album was good, it wasn't that good, and certainly not worth arguing over.

*

Richard Scott: This Heat was, in my opinion, the best group Rough Trade ever released records by and they were undoubtedly the band of their generation, and seeing them perform live certainly supported that view. I used to go and watch them practise at Cold Storage, their rehearsal space, which was a disused meat fridge, complete with hinged doors on the outside.

Geoff Travis: This Heat was one of the best groups we have ever had on the label. I saw them play at the ICA once and it was phenomenal, one of the most extraordinary concerts of my life. The various members of the band had been around for a while, playing in different groups and, like Scritti Politti, there was a connection with Henry Cow, through Chris Cutler. I always thought they were fiercely intellectual in their own way and of course Chris Cutler had set up Rock in Opposition – a genuine attempt to oppose the mainstream record business culture, which was largely structured in a careerist way. It was all rooted in a real political movement – real people spending real time in their real lives talking about politics and participating – unlike punk, which was far more selfish. Cash from chaos, it seems to me, is a whole different thing from standing outside a factory on a Saturday morning handing out leaflets ...

David Cunningham had released the first This Heat album – the one with the beautiful blue and yellow sleeve – on his Piano label and we took over some of the distribution, then did a twelve-inch in collaboration with the band and then released the album *Deceit* as a full Rough Trade release.

Charles Hayward: Blackhill Enterprises had funded the first album, *This Heat*, and we hadn't got the best of deals. At one point, I remember Chris Cutler sitting in the kitchen and telling us to scrap the record and redo it, because that way the rights would be ours and not Blackhill's. Good advice, but by then we had more or less already made the thing. In a weird sort of way, anyway, I was so involved in the music side of what we were doing that I didn't have any interest in the business side of it. I was very naïve and tunnel-visioned.

The relationship with Rough Trade meant that we could do things like employ a mobile recording unit at our Cold Storage studio in Brixton. Previously, we kept coming up against situations where the recording company had a relationship with the recording studio so we were receiving money to spend on the company that was giving it to us in the first place. It all went around in a circle. We were constantly going to people and saying, 'Give us ten grand, we won't use it to make an album in a studio, we'll spend it on the studio, then we can make two albums.' They'd never get it.

Rough Trade gave us more freedom. We were not only able to choose what studio to finally record *Deceit* in but also to get a mobile into Cold Storage. Cold Storage had an incredible sound and the more time you spent working in it, the more you realised just what an amazing effect could be achieved by positioning equipment in a certain way.

Chris Cutler: I'd known people from This Heat for some time prior to the band being formed. Geoff Leigh, Henry Cow's old saxophone player, had worked with Charles Bullen and Charles Hayward when they had been in Dolphin Logic. There were all sorts of connections. In fact, Tim Hodgkinson (from Henry Cow) and I were partners in Cold Storage and the Art Bears used to rehearse there a bit. When Henry Cow broke up we gave This Heat our PA system. David Cunningham had space there as well.

Charles Hayward: Rough Trade was good for us because it connected us with punks and post-punks. We'd come out of a European, free-jazz environment and Rough Trade helped us connect with a younger audience. When we signed, we were already going to a lot of concerts put on by Rough Trade bands. I'd always been keen on The Raincoats and we got to know a couple of the other bands a bit, like the Television Personalities. I remember we had a good laugh with Spizzenergi one night. And CB and Gareth had been up to Carol Street where Scritti Politti were, although we found their approach to music a little bit too theoretical.

Geoff Travis: This Heat in full flow very much reminded me of Soft Machine at their height – there was an intensity to what they did, which was captivating. I went to Holland with them and Scritti Politti – there was a wonderful sense of togetherness – and I went to see them rehearsing *Deceit* in Cold Storage.

Charles Hayward: I'm unsure of just how aware Geoff was of our previous music but he would be aware that we were aware that the DIY thing had happened before, although it took punk to break it through to the mainstream. The organisation around This Heat reflected the way we wanted to present our music, so although I may have written most of the lyrics, it was all presented as a group. I think Geoff had a similar approach with Rough Trade – although it was his label, he presented himself as a part of the organisation. We liked that. That was good.

At that time, everything we did in This Heat seemed completely logical, completely natural, the next step. The opposition of ideas in the music, the deliberate contradictions, all felt totally natural. I used to shut myself off from everything but the music. It was either mass culture, and I was trying to synthesise everything, or it was what was right in front of my face. The spaces between those two places didn't exist.

Looking back, making the music didn't seem like a mad effort but we were making exceptional leaps all over the place. Charles and I were completely committed to music by the time we started This Heat – we were both twenty-five and had both been playing instruments for about fifteen years by then: I'd started piano at four and drums at nine or ten – and we gave it one hundred per cent. We started out best friends but very rapidly stopped being best mates and I'm glad we did, else we would have ended up making best-mates music.

Richard Scott: There were and would go on to be Rough Trade connections with This Heat. Phil Clarke, our van driver who sadly died, worked for them as well as working for us and ended up managing them at one point. And Doug Kierdorf, another Rough Trade employee and at one time van driver, also went to work for them and shared accommodation with Chris Cutler.

Doug Kierdorf: I'd house-sat for Henry Cow in a place they had in Clapham, which was a sort of semi-squat. They, of course, were always going off on the road and it was good to have somebody looking after the place while they were away. I ended up moving in and Phil Clarke lived there also. This was before I went to work with This Heat.

Chris Cutler: There were periods when the band spent its time living on a tour bus in Europe – in fact, we lived on the road most of the time and at one point ended up leaving our possessions in the Virgin Records warehouse. We tried not to squat, because squatting with a load of musical instruments was not a good idea.

In Lambeth, instead, what we did was go to the council, explain that we were people from the arts, show them a number of very nice buildings that they had lying empty, which were likely to get squatted and possibly vandalised and destroyed, and offer to take over one and look after it for a modest rent. Amazingly, Lambeth Council gave us a number of properties, one after the other, on that basis. They explained that we wouldn't be allowed to pay rent – that would give us rights – and it was agreed that we would have a short notice period in the event of them needing the property back. One time we moved into an orphanage that way, a school, some very nice places, sometimes places with up to thirty rooms which, beyond the six or seven of us who lived there permanently, we often filled up with visiting European musicians passing through. We even ran Recommended Distribution from one of the squats to begin with.

We had a good relationship with the man from the council but when Margaret Thatcher got in during May 1979, things got more difficult. The council realised the nightmare was never going to be over and they were forced to sell off a lot of buildings. But, one way or another, our arrangements continued up until the 1990s.

Charles Hayward: With our material, we thought we were taking the next step for music, but in fact it wasn't the next step, it was really way ahead. Later on what we did was called postmodernism but for me This Heat was about a sort of true anarchy, an anarchy that would really work. It wasn't necessarily an anarchy that was about not having a leader, it might occasionally have one person as the main man. It was an anarchy that was constantly reorganising itself, allowing itself to be a hierarchy at times, but always coming back to a flat, equal point of view. Different people would be the key. Similarly, different organisational systems would be employed from one music piece to another.

We could use maths, for instance – an almost Duchampian sense of number, as we did in 'Horizontal Hold' – and follow that with something like 'Not Waving', where all sense of bar and numbers is deliberately, completely ignored. The aesthetic of one would be the grid – hard squares; the aesthetic of the other, completely fluid shapes. One would be rehearsed and drilled, one would be anti-rehearsed and undrilled. That was how we were thinking.

Richard Scott: It was a truly fantastic experience to see This Heat play live –

Charles Hayward's drumming was extraordinary and there seemed to be a constant battle going on between him and the drum kit to keep the equipment together. All the time, what he was playing was amazing.

My most vivid recollection is seeing them play the YMCA with the *Trobriand Cricket* film projected onto a screen behind them. There was this wonderful music taking place in front of this amazing film about a group of islanders from Papua New Guinea who had been introduced to cricket by missionaries to channel male aggression and had completely rewritten the rules of the game to suit their culture – unlimited players, home team always wins, a six scored only when the ball is lost in the grass, that kind of thing.[20]

Charles Hayward: After This Heat finished, I became reassociated with Rough Trade when they gave us an M&D deal for the band Camberwell Now. This was a little while later. I remember one night working with Stuart Moxham from Young Marble Giants and Geoff came over to me and enthused about Stuart's songs. He said to me that a lot of people who had listened to This Heat's music had now paired off, bought flats, and they wanted music to reflect that.

A few years later I was in another group, Regular Music, and they had a deal with Rough Trade, although I'd had nothing to do with arranging it. I bumped into Geoff in the street – this was around about the time of Frankie Goes to Hollywood and Art of Noise – and he complimented me on the Regular Music album. He said, 'Things are changing again. Come back and see me in a year, eighteen months.'

I don't mean this as a criticism but I think by then he had maybe done what people tend to do, arrange themselves around the organisation to the extent that the organisation becomes more important than what the organisation set out to do. I don't know. But what Geoff did do was make some amazing things happen, for us and other people.

Jim Moir: I used to go and watch This Heat at Cold Storage around the time they were making *Deceit*. I'd moved to Brixton from Darlington. Before punk happened, I'd been a fan of Amon Düül and Henry Cow and Soft

---

20. Equipment is also blessed by a spiritual leader prior to the game, ritualistic dances are performed, balls are bowled underarm and the winner receives a feast. See *Trobriand Cricket* by Gary Kildea and Jerry Leach (1979), said to be a prime illustration of syncretism.

Machine, so I fell quite easily in with the This Heat crowd. I was quite brazen at that time about going up to people if I liked them – I'd just go and knock on their door. I did the same with Scritti Politti. Back then, you would often bump into a band after a gig at the bar.

Back in Darlington, I had played in a band called Trout and we changed our name every time we played – I remember some of the names: They Called it Rum and Bobbie and Jackie Charlton's Eerie Mansions . . . As soon as we all moved to London in 1979, I started going to the Rough Trade shop and I went to see Geoff Travis because our band, which had the collective title of the Fashionable Five, made a demo which we played him. It was pop tripe – one track was called 'Cakes and Pop', rubbish really. I realised as the tape was playing that it was awful. Geoff explained that it wasn't really what Rough Trade were looking for, but the look on his face said it all. It qualified everything.

I was living in Brixton and working in a factory at Croydon. I'd be up at six in the morning for work and virtually straight out to gigs when I got home. I was living on cod-roe fishcakes and Pro Plus. In fact, I started selling tapes I had made using the name International Cod through the back pages of the *NME*. I got fan letters from all over the world. Later, I remember playing Charles Hayward some stuff with a view to him joining me in a band, but it never happened.

*

Richard Boon: The appointment in 1981 of Simon Edwards was pivotal – he had a retail background and he knew that it wasn't just about bringing new music to a new audience but also bringing new music to retailers and making them sell it differently. If someone like me took records from my label in to him, straight away he would be thinking of how best to help promote them – 'You want a poster? Right, make sure the poster folds up square and fits into a twelve-inch mailer' – what seems obvious stuff now but was and still is actually brilliant. Simon had had experience of indie shops right from their start. He brought something crucial and special – he brought focus at a time when it really wasn't cleverly focused. I think when he came in to Rough Trade he asked questions that needed answering. Was the record label going to aim for the charts? Did Distribution want to build an alternative structure to rival that of EMI?

Richard Scott: I'd always liked Simon and it was one day while we were having a discussion about the cartels of Catalan that it occurred to me that he ought to come and work for us. Up until then, he'd been at Inferno and of course had helped organise the Birmingham leg of the Rough Trade Tour, so we knew how good he was.

Simon Edwards: I'd worked at the Inferno shop in Dale End in Birmingham and then left and gone travelling for a bit and I was planning on going back to college when I bumped into Rob Lloyd from The Prefects and he said Richard Scott had been asking after me. I went down to London to see Richard and we had a chat. I'd been interested in the Basque cooperatives and cartels that sprung up in the Franco-era Spain and I got talking to Richard and he told me about Rough Trade being a cooperative. It wasn't a cooperative in reality but it acted like one. It was one in spirit. And, of course, later it would become a workers' trust – in fact, one of the largest workers' trusts in England at its height.

I wouldn't say I had an interview with Richard, as such, but anyway he asked me if I wanted to go and work with them and I did. They'd moved to Blenheim Crescent not long before and that was where I went on my first day. I'll always remember it. It was a warm, sunny spring day and I bought myself a coffee in Ladbroke Grove and made my way to Rough Trade. The place appeared to be completely deserted. Nobody was in sight. And then this person came through from the back pushing a broom and introduced himself as Geoff Travis.

I started working doing wholesale – selling to shops, which I knew all about from being on the receiving end. Everybody was incredibly helpful and friendly at Rough Trade and beyond the company there was still that real sharing of information. But I realised that the place needed more discipline than it might have done in the past when it came to dealing with the marketplace. Up until the point I joined, just about any product they could get hold of would walk out of the door.

Up until as late as 1979, there hadn't actually been that many records available and what was available was often hard to get hold of. That changed. There was an enormous growth in the number of labels and what had once been an opening market by 1980 was starting to close up. People didn't really understand or know how to deal with the change. Whereas previously, a good review in the *NME* and a few plays on John Peel would result in a few thousand sales, that was not always the case now. Things weren't so obvious.

Richard Boon: There was this palpable shift from when all you needed to be was reactive – spot an interesting band, press up X thousand copies of their single and automatically sell them – to when you had to be proactive, when you had to think about marketing, about research, about selling, about being more *professional*.

Simon Edwards: There had been a time when Richard Boon might come down from New Hormones in Manchester with an Eric Random single and expect Rough Trade to take one thousand. Now the figure was more like two hundred. Now everybody needed to think about pre-selling. How did you get the thing from the point of production to the point of selling?

Not only were a lot of people making records in the UK, but there were more and more records coming in from abroad – from independent labels in America, France, Germany, Holland. It reached the point where you couldn't predict your sales accurately any more. Coincidentally, of course, labels that had had some independent success, like Rough Trade, were looking to build on that, but suddenly that was costing more money. Unpredictable sales, higher cost, and a realisation that you needed to get more competitive.

Geoff Travis would want to be more competitive – he would want his groups to be successful because that would make it easier for him to work longer with the artists that he had already got and help him get other artists. The last thing he would want would be issues over whether or not Rough Trade was capable of getting the best out of the records.

Patrick Moore: Richard Scott essentially poached me from Virgin central, where I was buying indie records for across the Virgin chain, to go and work at Rough Trade. I'd left college in London in 1979 and gone to work at Virgin Southampton, where I started buying independent records for them in quite an ambitious way. Then I got moved to the independent distribution centre, which was in West London, not far from the Nashville Rooms. When I was there I would often buy a complete run of an independent single or album and I was doing quite a lot of business with Rough Trade. In fact, we bought so much material from them that at one point they had to restrict what we were allowed to have, because there weren't enough records to go around.

I came in to work in Distribution and I was responsible for selling records to the shops that would eventually form the Cartel. I worked in that funny little booth that Richard had, which was opposite that funny little booth that Geoff worked in. I look back now and I think of Rough Trade as being like a free university: it was an education and it was genuinely utopian, or at least that was what you bought into. I'd become politicised at college and had joined the Anti-Nazi League and edited the ANL newsletter, so I was tied in already to what Rough Trade were doing. I loved the idea of everybody being paid the same wage, all having a say and eating the same food.[21] The problem was that in spite of my success at Virgin, the actual idea of having to pack boxes wasn't quite so appealing.

I was living in Beck Road in Hackney and the trek to and from Rough Trade was a long one. It was walk or catch a bus to Bethnal Green tube, then tube it all the way across to West London. At this time, I was a young kid staying up late and doing drugs, and the upshot of it all was that I often didn't turn up, and when I did turn up it could be as late as eleven in the morning. Richard Scott was long-suffering – he'd take me aside and tell me he had been young once and lecture me on the idea of alarm clocks. Or he'd congratulate me on a particularly late showing. I'd eat my Twix chocolate bar, smoke my first fag and drink my coffee thinking this is bollocks, but secretly I was really enjoying it.

By the spring of 1982, I was spending more time in production – I'd helped Bob Scotland design a couple of record sleeves and by now it was very obvious that I wasn't suited to the job I was meant to be doing. I'd been over to Brussels and met Michel Duval, who ran Disques du Crépuscule, and it seemed all my ambitions were artistic. I think Michel saw me as a potential power base in Rough Trade for his label, and for me Crépuscule was a sort of get-out clause.

Michel suggested that I set up an English arm of Crépuscule, which became Operation Twilight, and an agreement was set up whereby I would run the label and Rough Trade would partly fund it. Alan Horne, Richard Kirk, Richard Jobson and Bill Drummond were all directors and I set up an office in Rough Trade, which became a bit of a bone of contention. I'd met and begun managing the Pale Fountains, and Operation Twilight put out their record before they signed to Virgin. We did 23 Skidoo, Tuxedo Moon, Paul Haig; all the records did OK but when the Pale Fountains signed to Virgin, it sort of died out and I decided pretty much that I wanted to be a writer.

21. Far from the usual, clichéd image of Rough Trade being complete veggie 'brown ricers', Patrick Moore's diary for 1981 includes a record of Christmas lunch that year being turkey leg.

By then, Beck Road had become a sort of indie *Coronation Street*. Roddy Frame had come down to London – I think it was his first time in England – and was staying with us temporarily. Genesis P-Orridge lived down the other end of the street, as did 23 Skidoo, Jim Thirlwell from Foetus and some members of Microdisney. I always preferred east to west – that whole West London ethos in places had too much of the trustafarianism about it.

Part of the reason I thought I could get away with drifting in and out of Rough Trade was that it sort of operated like a club anyway – Tony Wilson would pop in, or Genesis P-Orridge, or Jah Wobble – so there were a lot of people coming and going. It was very fluid. It was a shame it didn't stop when the first wave of indie faded – it would have glowed in legend.

I think the presentation of the Rough Trade product was very amateur – it was too disparate and lacked an aesthetic in the way that, say, Factory or Fast Product had an aesthetic. I think it became too much of an umbrella and it could never seem to agree on anything.

Richard Scott: The idea of Rough Trade lacking an aesthetic was partly inevitable because we always invited the bands to design their own record sleeves. And they could come up with anything. We couldn't afford – and wouldn't have wanted – an in-house designer. It was all very practical.

Simon Edwards: I took on the job of liaising with those members who would go on to formally become the Cartel after Patrick Moore, who I think had been brought in with one eye on his paying attention to all this, moved over to running Operation Twilight. I think, by his own admission, Patrick hadn't become too engaged with it all.

The model of taking the business out to the regions was not a unique one, and one that would be familiar now to readers of Charlie Gillett's *The Sound of the City*, which was about people in America trying to find a way of getting distributed without having to go to the big city. Regional distribution in America was very different, though, from what the Cartel set out to do – which was nationwide distribution – and in America it was based to some extent on payola. There were some regions here that were stronger than others – the north-west was strong, labels like Factory were keen to promote Manchester – whereas an area like Norfolk suffered; Backs (the distributor there) always complained that it was hard for them to develop their markets, due to the lack of population.

*

Issue one of the ill-fated Masterbag, December 1981. *The editorial from issue four makes reference to political complaints about the title, which was viewed as potentially sexist. ('Masterbagging' refers to the method retail shops used to display record sleeves while keeping copies of the actual record behind the counter in a master bag.)*

Simon Edwards: We set up *Masterbag* at the end of 1981, which was a newssheet for independent wholesalers, to help the Cartel members. It listed all the new releases. Ian Cranna was the editor but there wasn't anyone with any business sense to look at the figures going into it, and down the line it lost a lot of money. The unused issues would pile up in the corridors, next to the unsold issues of *RE/Search*, which was a fantastic magazine we got in from America which we couldn't sell for love or money.

Masterbag would be only one of the problems contributing to the financial crisis by the autumn of 1982. The market had changed and caught everybody out. Costs were higher, demands greater. A lot of changes would occur all at the same time. Launching the Cartel was one thing, but it would take a few years of being rolled out for it to become an entity that could function and be competitive in the marketplace.

rough trade records,137 blenheim cres.,london w11.

nb⁺ shop & mail order still at 202 kensington park rd.,w11.

Gone but not gone ...

CHAPTER EIGHT:

1982

'When the Obscene Publications guys came in they
were rather jolly'

Falklands crisis – Obscene Publications squad – 'Shipbuilding' –
Formalisation of the Cartel – Scritti exit – Financial crisis –
Shop buy-out

Simon Edwards: The Falklands conflict – that was a strange war, and a strange time: we had people phoning up constantly wanting us to distribute their pro-war records. Some of the callers were quite posh. They'd explain their position and then get very abusive when we said that we were not really for the war, in fact we were actually very much against it.

We went out for the nurses that year as well. We all went out for a day in solidarity and left a message on the answer-machines saying that we were closed in support of them.[22] I'd known Rough Trade to be totally closed only once before: when I was working at Inferno I'd called up and the answer-machine had said that Rough Trade was shut because they were all at Austin the van driver's wedding.

22. The nurses held a rally in the autumn of 1982 and 5,000 marched to Central London in spite of the fact that their union was relatively benign and the Royal College of Nurses had a no-strike policy. Enough was enough.

Richard Scott: We'd had the Obscene Publications squad into Blenheim Crescent on a couple of occasions over various things and then we received a letter around the time of the Falklands War from the House of Commons, warning us off handling the Crass flexi, 'Sheep Farming in the Falklands', which used recordings of Parliament, and which we had been helping sell. The letter pointed out that the recordings were used 'in the course of a satire on the Falklands crisis' and that such use was forbidden in 'light entertainment'. I'd found when the Obscene Publications guys came in that they were rather jolly and not that interested: this letter was something quite different.

Geoff Travis: Clive Langer got in touch during the Falklands period and said that he and Elvis Costello had written a song, 'Shipbuilding', which they thought would be perfect for Robert Wyatt to sing. Robert heard it and responded straight away and it was done using some of Elvis's musicians, including Mark Bedders on bass and Steve Nieve on keyboards.

Robert Wyatt: I was never saddled with the idea that a small record label could possibly be the vanguard of a kind of mass revolution. It never occurred to me that Rough Trade could do anything but function in the system as it was. Hit records are fun and I've always been pro pop music, which, it strikes me, is just an industrialised version of folk music, which is the music of the people. So I never felt that conflict between commercial music and authentic music.

I realised when Clive Langer and Elvis Costello asked me to sing 'Shipbuilding' what could be done with it distribution-wise. Elvis wrote the words after Clive had written the tune. They thought it might suit me – did I fancy having a go at it? Elvis came around the house and did what people often do when they visit, enjoyed Alfie's memories of Chet Baker, which sealed our friendship. Then I went into the studio and sang it.

I knew it was good-quality stuff with wide appeal; I knew it wouldn't in any way be whimsical;[23] and I knew that they'd do a proper job with it. I had given up smoking, so it may be that I got a more effective vocal than usual. I always consider Elvis's own version to be the definitive version and had I heard his version before being asked to record 'Shipbuilding', well, it wouldn't have occurred to me that there might be any other.

23. Robert, however, could be. He beautifully introduced it on the *Old Grey Whistle* test thus: 'Here's another meaningless piece of pop nonsense ...'

Elvis's knowledge of music, as it turned out, was amazing. He knew more about big band music than I did, but then I wasn't to know that from hearing 'Watching the Detectives'.

Clive Langer had arranged 'Shipbuilding' not as a rock song but as an imaginary jazz ballad of the 1930s, which is why he had the inimitable Bedders on double bass, and I love the way Bedders's strings creak on the record like a ship's ropes, and of course he had the unique Steve Nieve on piano. I decided to put 'Memories of You' and 'Around Midnight' on the B-side because of the way Clive produced 'Shipbuilding'. Both were great, pre-rock 'n' roll popular songs written by great black American pianists. I was trying to recognise the breadth of black musicians' contribution. People said, I love it when you do standards – why don't you do some Cole Porter, whose music I love, but of course that wasn't relevant.

The only alien touch during 'Shipbuilding' was when I asked a very young musician who worked on the song if he was happy with his contribution and he said yes, it would look very good on his CV. That was a little chill draught of the incoming Thatcherite approach to art, which said everything was to do with career and not the beat sensibility, which has nothing to do with the Establishment and doesn't even want to fight it. It seemed to me that was a splinter in an otherwise fine piece of woodwork.

I knew that 'Shipbuilding' couldn't make a loss, but paradoxically it did. After we recorded it, Alfie and I were in Spain when we got a call from Geoff saying they were going to rerelease it and that they needed to make a video. Dave Robinson made a video which had little to do with the song at all. I remember him saying to me, 'We don't want any politics in it.' He made me seem very old and crippled and had me wheeling past a very old and crippled boat. The whole thing cost more than the record earned.

Several variant sleeves, all based on Stanley Spencer's paintings, were used on 'Shipbuilding'.

*

Jo Slee: I once borrowed Scott Piering's car. I found about fifteen coffee cups under the seat, used take-away food containers lying around and cigarette ash everywhere. The whole interior of the car had fag burns all over it. When I came back in January 1982 and went to work at Blenheim Crescent, I effectively chose my own job. There was the excitement of seeing some old faces and a whole lot of new people. So I went to work with Scott, Claude Bessy and Chris Williams in promo.

The promo department was like a council tip. Before I could even work there, I went in over the weekend and filled up fifteen rubbish bags. Empty beer cans, fag ends, pizza boxes, food decomposing after having been previously tossed aside six months ago, and general rubbish. It was truly disgusting. After I finished, Scott's nose was really put out. He wasn't just unimpressed with my cleaning, he was appalled. He was like – 'We are so busy, we don't even need to *think* about dealing with this.'

And the place was as chaotic as ever. There was the usual insane work rate. The press office was in a corridor. It was a thoroughfare and basically had no windows. I found us another space and set up work stations, sorted decorating, got storage units and organised it all as an office. I did that for a while and then Claude and Chris left, after some further redundancies in 1983, and I eventually started working also with Peter Walmsley in licensing, though I had to do it from the promo department since Peter's office was an even bigger tip than Scott's had been, plus it had a giant mahogany table, which took up all the space so you couldn't work in there anyway. Peter just perched in the corner at one of Richard Scott's ubiquitous plywood benches, a phone buried under piles of paper.

The point about Rough Trade was that if you wanted to do a job, you had to go and *make* it work. The democracy we enjoyed was a privilege, but it was also a responsibility and I think certain people just didn't want that responsibility, preferring to act like the recalcitrant rebels of the Lower Third. By not taking on the responsibility, it seemed to me people were missing out and by not pulling their weight they ended up putting extra responsibility on others. When I look back, I think we wasted so much time and effort fighting amongst ourselves.

Richard Scott: We could rarely cope with the volume of work or with the volume of records and pretty early on after the move to Blenheim Crescent it was clear that we still didn't have enough space. One of the ways we'd tried to alleviate that was by setting up the Cartel, which had been in existence as a loose group of affiliated companies for some time but which in the summer of 1982 we started to think about setting up into a more formal structure.

Way back, I think the first people we had approached were Service, a company in Altrinchham. Factory Records were obviously mad so I didn't think it would be a good idea to use them in that area. At the same time we approached Tony K at Red Rhino and they were the first of the proper Cartel members in. I liked dealing with Tony – he was always direct, always functional and of course, like all of them, he had a wonderful shop.[24]

Tony K: I'd been working in an office in the mid-1970s in York but music was always my passion and in 1976 I began planning to open a record shop, which I did in 1977. I opened it the same week I got married. Initially, I didn't stock any singles – I just wasn't interested – but as punk started to take hold I became a massive fan. The problem was I just couldn't seem to get hold of the records. I phoned John Peel up one day after he'd played a particular record and asked him for contact details for the record and he told me to go to Rough Trade. They have all that stuff, he said.

So I rang them up and went to see them. I became Rough Trade's first non-London account. I started ordering off them once a week, then twice a week.[25]

At some point, Richard suggested to me that I should wholesale on to some other shops and between us we hatched a plan to carve up the country – Scotland, the North, Midlands, South, East, West – into regional wholesale areas. Over a period, Richard Scott approached all of Rough Trade's best customers – Revolver in Bristol, Probe in Liverpool, Backs in Norwich – and sold them the idea. The only one without a shop was Fast Product, which Bob Last ran and which was a record label. I used to train up staff for the other members.

Lloyd Harris: Revolver came in just after Red Rhino – we were one of the earliest. Chris Parker owned the Revolver record shop and I had worked there in the mid-1970s. We had a very elitist view of ourselves and thought we were *the* place to go to in Bristol to buy anything of interest. We sold a

24. Red Rhino was the first member of the Cartel, and started wholesaling with 'setting-up' assistance from Rough Trade in June 1979. Probe would be the last original member, and launched its wholesaling venture in May 1981. In 1983, Red Rhino Midlands would be the last Cartel member to join, assuming its own identity as Nine Mile Distribution in 1984. The other three members were Backs, Fast Product (the only member without a shop) and Revolver.
25. Sales figures for some of the Cartel members tell the story of how the independent sector was growing at a furious pace. Red Rhino's wholesale turnover in the first year was £99,500. By year two that figure had increased to £302,700 and by year three to £387,400. Between June 1982 and October, the quarterly turnover had reached a staggering £117,100 for the three-monthly period. The first month of wholesale trading for Probe Records turned over £2,100 for the month (June 1981): by August 1982, prior to the formalisation of the Cartel, turnover had jumped for that month to £14,160.

lot of import West Coast US rock prior to punk, had a good jazz section, and a fantastic reputation for reggae, which we were buying directly from Jamaican importers. There was a big Jamaican community and they'd come in whenever they knew we had a delivery and we'd line up the records on the counter, and they'd line up behind it and we'd give each disc a fifteen-second spin and get the yes or no. We sold hundreds in one go. There were a lot of sound systems in Bristol and we supplied all of those.

I quit Revolver and went off to Brighton for a while and after I came back I started running a youth opportunities scheme at the local college, for disadvantaged kids. Then, in spring 1980, Richard Scott had approached Chris and asked him to come and talk about the possibility of coming on board as a wholesaler. Chris asked me if I fancied coming in with him and, after a lot of careful deliberation, I jumped in. I'd been out of the business so I didn't realise quite how the independent thing had exploded. I was really worried I might be making a mistake.

We drove down to see Richard Scott at Kensington Park Road and he sold us the idea. He talked about regionalism, about enablement, about giving people outside the capital the chance to be part of the thing. They were obviously completely stretched as well. There was a strong anti-majors feeling in the air at that time and I remember not really having a view before embracing the idea like an over-zealous convert. I seem to remember there were no chairs to sit in and we had to stand up for the meeting.

Bob Last: I had started Fast Product as a brand in 1976, but didn't know initially what I was going to do with it. We had a mission statement of brand values but weren't sure whether it would be music or some other medium that we worked in. I took time out from an architecture course and started roadying for The Rezillos, and that was when I decided that Fast Product would be involved in music and that was when and how I came into contact with bands from Sheffield and Leeds, because we were on the road. Our first contact with Rough Trade was notorious – my partner Hilary

Morrison and I put out a single by the Mekons, 'Never Been in a Riot', and Hilary was despatched to Rough Trade because we'd heard that they sold independent records. Back then it was an incredibly small scene and there weren't that many places where you could get the records. We'd heard that Rough Trade were a bit hippyish, maybe, and so we weren't sure because part of the Fast Product concept was that we liked the world of branding, marketing and capitalism, because it was oppositional; oppositional and interesting.

So Hilary went to London and duly played the Mekons' single to them and Geoff said something like this is too bad for us even to distribute. We, of course, were outraged, but then shortly after it got Single of the Week in *NME* and we were on our way. And of course Rough Trade, because they were such an important part of the distribution network, began taking the single. Soon after, I got to know Geoff and realised that there was common ground between us in that we had similar theoretical and strategic approaches. Early on I had an uneasy but entirely friendly relationship with Rough Trade.

I can't precisely remember when we got involved in the Cartel. The label was doing well and we had built up a little bit of infrastructure to support our distribution activity. We had a small warehouse and sales operation almost by default. Once we became involved in the Cartel, it was Richard Scott who took over dealing with us. Richard and I shared common aims in shaping up the idea of the Cartel. At the same time, I started to develop a strategy where we would deal with majors – we moved groups actively onto major labels so there was a gap between what Richard was aiming for and what we did.

Johnny Appel: We opened Backs in Norwich in 1979 and about eighteen months later Rough Trade approached us to come on board as a regional wholesaler. We'd done a lot of business with Rough Trade as a shop – when Laurie Anderson's 'O Superman' came out on import and John Peel played it, a lot of people came in the next day and asked for it, but I only had two copies. I phoned up Richard Scott and bought every copy they had – one hundred and seventy-five – and sold them all in three days.

I went with my brother and my other business partner to see Richard Scott at the Rough Trade shop. It was a bit cramped and my brother had to sit in a sink while we had the meeting. I remember thinking it could be something big for us potentially. Richard told us that they weren't coping and that they would hand over all their east England accounts and give us fifteen per cent discount and we would then sell the records on.

We had a toilet – a sort of kitchen area/toilet – at the back of the shop and so I had a little bit of space where I could run this thing and that is how we started out. The big problem back then – it was the same for everybody – was cash flow. It didn't seem to matter how good your trading figures were, money was always in short supply. With hindsight, it is obvious that Rough Trade had the same problems and didn't have the money to invest in a big warehouse and take on lots of staff, so instead they got us to do it for them.

But it was a fair deal and although the margins were low, the extra money we made in the first year enabled us to get the warehouse that we still operate from.

Early Backs ad featuring local bands The Higsons and the Farmer's Boys.

Geoff Davis: I'd started out at the age of fourteen as a runner on the Liverpool stock exchange and in 1964, at the age of twenty-one, I went on the hippie trail – before it was called that – and hitched to India, though I went the long way round, up and down Africa. While I was away, I got a taste for Indian and Arabian music and all kinds of what later went on to be called 'world music'. Between then and when I opened the first Probe record shop on Saturday, 16th January 1971, I had been through a lot of phases in my music appreciation: music I'd found on my travels, jazz, bluegrass, classical, blues, reggae, rock and what was popular at the time the shop opened, progressive. I wanted it all in the shop. In fact, I wanted it to be the perfect record shop. Me and the wife pooled our savings and had £300 which we used to open our shop, which was more of a kiosk actually. On the first day we took £47 – I'd have been happy with a tenner.

Richard Scott: When I first went to visit Probe, the shop was literally brimming over with extraordinary records: they were piled up everywhere and jammed into every available space. The depth of the stock was just phenomenal: they had fifty different Elvis albums in the boxes on top of the counter – that was before you even got to the Elvis section in the racks.

Geoff Davies: When I was getting the business going early on I would think nothing of going around the pubs in Liverpool selling records out of a carrier bag. I sourced records from wherever I could and above all I wanted the shop to reflect my taste. There was a company in London in the early 1970s called Continental Record Distributors and they supplied us with records from Turkey, India, the Middle East. Hot Wax, a reggae importer in Birmingham, sent somebody up regularly with new releases pressed the week before in Jamaica. I got a lot of American soul imports at that time – the mid-1970s – when American soul was in its heyday. A bit later but before punk, the French guys from Praed Street in London would drive up and drop off Skydog stuff, Stiff Records and Chiswick Records releases.

The rent on the shop was £8 per week and we were so successful that I had to talk the landlord into doubling the size of the place, which miraculously he did. An alleyway ran down one side and we persuaded him to knock down a wall, cover over the alleyway and thus give us more space. It still wasn't enough. A bit later I took a space in a giant emporium called Silly Billy's – I hated the name then and I hate it still. But that turned into more or less a black music outlet for us, so I was still no better off. Then, in 1976, Roger Eagle, who went on to set up Eric's club, convinced me to go in with him for premises just off Matthews Street in the centre of town. Roger's club, which was called something like The Revolution shortly before being renamed Eric's, was a couple of doors down. We took £994 in the new Probe on the first day.

I first came into contact with Rough Trade in 1978 when they started wholesaling and someone rang up offering me records. We went direct to labels, where we could. I used to drive down to Rough Trade in my estate car and load it up. I was still selling a fair amount of hippie paraphernalia, as I had always done, and I had a little circuit. Records from Rough Trade, over to a warehouse to pick up patchouli oil, joss sticks, tantric gear, stuff like that, and then on to Camden and Compendium Books, where I used to buy wholesale alternative literature – Timothy Leary books, stuff on spiritualism. We carried on with that after the alternative press ended – from when we had first opened until about 1973 we had stocked all the underground newspapers: *Oz*, *International Times*, *Friends*. Then I'd drive back home to Liverpool.

It was in May 1981 that Richard had asked me to take on the wholesale – I think I was pretty much the last one in of what would go on to be the original Cartel members. Nine Mile came in later but that grew out of Red Rhino. I was very reluctant to take the thing on and only did so because Richard convinced me that I would be able to handle the extra work. I'd got too much on already and I worried that I wasn't really a sensible enough businessman to be responsible for it. So I went in with trepidation and as it turned out I was probably right.

I covered a vast area and picked up ninety-three new accounts – shops who previously hadn't stocked independent music but who now took it on. But often I had difficulty getting money out of people, especially market traders. I could be owed £500 at a time and be out of pocket. I got done in Wigan, Wrexham, Blackburn . . .

'Fifty different Elvis albums . . . before you even got to the Elvis section.'

I used to call Richard Scott 'The Strategist'; he always seemed to me the businessman out of the two at the top at Rough Trade. Richard always had a plan, but on top of that he always had a strategy. I used to think Geoff Travis was the more hippyish one, the more laid-back one. Over a period I think I revised both of those impressions.

I attended the Cartel meetings, although of course it was really only an in-name organisation. Some of the people were posh and some weren't – I recall they wouldn't always understand my Scouse sense of humour. But I liked most of the people. It was obvious that what they all shared was the fact that they weren't businessmen. They would be good social events. I remember on one occasion when we had a meeting at Rough Trade, Geoff and I slipped out to watch *Black Narcissus* in a Michael Powell season at the Electric Cinema in Portobello Road. We were both nuts about Powell and Pressburger films.

Sadly, I think once the Cartel was named, it all started to feel too much like business in the straight world for me. I started to view Geoff differently and respect Richard Scott more. I remember standing up at one meeting when they were discussing targets or something and just silenced the room with one word: 'Music'. The more professional they tried to get, the more alienated I felt.

Bob Last: There wasn't any capital, most people just had turnover – at one point they wanted to borrow £250,000 – and ultimately the Cartel fell over, in my opinion, because it couldn't generate enough margin to grow.

Initially, I saw it as an interesting strategic intervention. But the point was it had to keep it possible to do more interesting things in the way that had been achievable in, say, 1977, 1978 and 1979. That was the only virtue in it for me – I wasn't interested per se in being a distributor.

The other part of my thinking was that at the time we were called 'independents' but in my view we should have been called 'dependants'. The real independents were the guys with a few million quid in the bank. We, because of our absence of capital, were dependants – dependent on the banks for our day-to-day existence. So the idea of the Cartel didn't isolate us from the pressures normal businesses suffer from and eventually I felt it wasn't creating enough of an ongoing creative window to be worth taking out a loan for a quarter of a million. I could see also that while Richard Scott might be thinking strategically and tactically, some of the others weren't looking beyond growing their local business.

When it came to formalisation, the danger for me was that any movement forward was likely to make us more like the people we set out to be different from. We couldn't be in denial of that. It was all very political, with people having different political interpretations about whether it was resisting capitalism or being an alternative to a form of capitalism or whatever. I suddenly woke up at one point and realised that for these people collectively the rationalisation was – well, because it's us, it must be better. I wasn't prepared to accept that; that alone wasn't enough.

So in 1982, I had fundamental issues rather than specific concerns about the Cartel. It was interesting enough not to drop it, though. I had a different perspective because by the time the idea of the Cartel was becoming grander, I had the Human League signed to Virgin, and other bands signed to majors, and some people involved in the Cartel thought I'd ceased to be committed and had gone over to the dark side. In fact, it gave me an alternative view and enabled me to be more brutal about judging whether what we were doing really was different. There was only some point to it if it was different, and one of the key things for me was that the difference had to be about sustainability. If it was going to be hand to mouth, it wasn't going to be different and wouldn't create a space where different things could happen.

I do remember some of the Cartel meetings but a lot of the discussions I had were with Richard and they tended to be back-channel discussions – I was a much more active participant in that dialogue than I was in the formal meetings. Those meetings – like all meetings where a large group of independent people are trying to cooperate – were not easy.

Tony K: We had some good meetings and some good nights out. I liked the name 'Cartel' because I felt it contradicted what people might have expected the organisation to do. At the meetings we'd sort problems out between us. Politics would sometimes creep in. Johnny from Backs got picked on occasionally – I think people felt he was too right wing, which he really wasn't at all.

Lloyd Harris: We discussed turf issues, tactics on selling, and even what kind of sandwiches we wanted, as I remember. Actually, I don't remember too many details about the meetings, but I do remember that they seemed to go on for ever. I think that what they showed in essence was that the vast majority of people involved weren't businessmen. But a weird thing happened and whether they liked it or not, they were forced to become businessmen. At that time a lot of records were selling in large quantities –

certain Mute releases, some Rough Trade ones, some Factory – and the releases became more demanding in terms of shifting units and in terms of the ambitions for chart success and high sales that the labels started to have.

I remember Scritti Politti's *Songs to Remember* being the first record where there was a genuine push on the charts from Rough Trade. That was a key moment. Another, of course, was when The Smiths took off. But records by Depeche Mode, New Order and others were also selling in vast amounts.

In the end, the dilemma became trying to hold on to the original access-for-all approach and the friendly way of conducting affairs that dispensed with contracts at the same time as professionally dealing with the business. At one of the meetings we had a discussion about the legitimacy of using the word 'units'. Some people felt uncomfortable with that. But quickly there was the big psychological shift from the access philosophy ideal to the acceptance of a process whereby we would become just like everybody else – if slightly strangely formed.

Johnny Appel: The meetings could be tedious affairs and you needed a jolly good reason to get away with not going to them. They were pointless as far as I was concerned. The minutes were pointless. They wanted them written up in a certain way, which I always did, though on one occasion I used a *Private Eye* cartoon with a load of lemmings jumping off a cliff as a header, which didn't go down well.

I think Rough Trade had an attitude about Backs – I think they felt we were too inspired by making money. The first Cartel meeting I was invited to was held in Scotland. It was a nightmare, just getting there. I walked in and didn't know anybody present – I didn't know anybody apart from Richard Scott, anyway. I sat down with a coffee and overheard somebody say, 'This time there's a new member – Backs from Norwich. But they're only in it for the money.' I found that incredible, quite surprising. Although what was said was incorrect, it did make me wonder what these people were in business for.

I went to one three-day Cartel meeting and the only resolution agreed upon was to ask the hotel not to cut the crusts off the sandwiches next time.

Richard Scott: Geoff came up with the name 'Cartel' at one of the meetings that was held in Bristol. I don't remember too much discussion about it and no one dissented, though I have always felt uncomfortable with the name. I realise it was intended to be ironic, but I thought the name sounded criminal. I was keen on us having T-shirts made up with CCCP on them – Central Cartel Company Personnel. It never happened. What interests me now about the Cartel is how we were able to give an opportunity to people outside London to be part of something and do something interesting and seeing how it affected them. Providing access structures for people to develop their creativity seemed to me to be a basic duty to provide. Of course, it was always going to be short-lived – the idea of a regional digital model, once we moved into the digital age, although interesting, was never going to happen. What was wonderful about those initial Cartel meetings and arrangements was that they were all done without contracts, all done by consensus.

A photograph taken at the time of the 1982 meeting in Bristol when the Cartel was christened. Left to right: Geoff Travis, Johnny Appel, Simon Edwards.

Simon Edwards: The development of the Cartel was something rolled out over a few years. For it to become really effective it had to pull together and become an entity that could function and be competitive in the marketplace, and that took a while to effect. Immediately there were the problems of dual distribution. Both Factory and Mute distributed their records through Rough Trade and other distributors and for the Cartel to be a force, we needed to get these labels with potentially commercial records to agree to sole distribution, which initially they didn't do. It needed, also, to make people aware of the need for pre-selling.

Lloyd Harris: The main benefits of formalisation were to do with public perception. We went from being a disparate group of half-arsed individuals doing some of the same things sometimes at the same time to something that presented the image and to some extent the reality of a national organisation. It was a moment, though, when we asked ourselves, are we ignoring our principles again? There was an awful lot of self-assessment that went on in those Cartel meetings at that time.

But when the big releases came along we now had an agreed strategy. We'd have a unified release date for records – previously it had been a case of flogging the stuff as fast as you could, once you got it. Now, everybody had to wait until physical stock was in place for all. Pre-ordering systems were introduced. We did proper pre-selling. We had sell-in material. And shops generally liked us. They saw we were organised and they knew we were on their side – we weren't part of some giant corporate structure.

Richard Scott: I'd asked that by the start of August, Cartel members send me thoughts on the viability and launch of the Cartel and we arranged for there to be a big meeting at Rough Trade on the 25th September.[26] This was where we would take some steps towards realising how it all might be organised, financed and launched for 1st January 1983. There was a lot of debate about it – I got into some wonderful theoretical discussions with Bob Last over it all[27] – and in the end some radical things happened, the

26. Geoff Davies at Probe summarised the industry as a whole as one in decline for various reasons: 'video, the depression, unemployment, the Falklands War, *The Day the Earth Stood Still*, *The Man in the White Suit*, etc . . . ', but felt that the independent sector was still growing. According to Red Rhino, 'fashion no longer dictated change', as it had, video sales were increasing, music was seen as less important, though again they saw the independent sector share as increasing. The increase in the sector was brought about through a more professional approach, an approach that, however, hadn't led to 'the loss of other endearing factors' (whatever they might have been). The importance of sole distribution was recognised by everybody, as were the strengths (though more often weaknesses) of competitors in the marketplace. There were formidable potential obstacles in the way of their aim, including major rivals such as Spartan and Pinnacle, Stage One, Graduate, Inferno, IDS and Jungle – all record distributors/labels/companies who had seen a potentially exploitable market open up through the growth of the independent sector.

27. In a couple of letters to Richard Scott, Bob Last urged caution in launching the Cartel along the full-on lines that Rough Trade proposed, and which was discussed at a Cartel meeting on 25 September, that would involve obtaining a quarter-of-a-million-pound loan and the setting up of regional promotions teams. The solution to how the venture might be realised was 'floating around in fairy land until such time as it has been established exactly what the Cartel is going to be or do'. In particular, there were concerns that Rough Trade handled the bulk of sales to those intermediary companies who supplied the large high street chains, such as Woolworths, Boots and Menzies (effectively direct competitors to the Cartel),

first being that I helped engineer a coup to oust Chris Parker at Revolver and get Lloyd Harris to take over.

Lloyd Harris: As everyone says, cash flow was always an issue. Just about every member of the Cartel had seen exponential growth yet nobody seemed to have enough working cash. Rough Trade had no money, but in order to take the business up to the next level, finance was required. Chris Parker wasn't prepared to do that, especially after a letter that Bob Last had circulated, throwing doubt on the viability of what was proposed, and so Richard helped me assume control. It worked for a while the way it was meant to work. In essence, I bought Chris out and went into partnership with two other people. We moved to a proper warehouse and took on staff. And eventually, just as Rough Trade did, we sold the shop off. It is clear now that we ignored one of the basic tenets of business, which is not to grow too fast without adequate funding. Our business model was a complete nonsense and at the end of every month we were always desperate for money to pay people.

Johnny Appel: Rough Trade itself was the cause of so many of our cash-flow problems. I was always concerned with how credit control was run. It all had to flow, and often didn't. Getting money out of shops could be difficult, but everyone had to pay Rough Trade within thirty days. Although I wouldn't go so far as to call it a boom time – I don't recall paying the taxman too much money during that period – there was the business around, particularly selling to shops who maybe hadn't dealt with independent records before. Some of them would ring up and order by the amount they wanted to spend. They'd say, can we have £100 worth this week and leave the selection to us.

I always felt that there was an impending threat hanging over us – what God (Rough Trade) had given us, God could take away. That was their attitude. It was rubbish, really. They said they would give us all the accounts

and that the only sensible way forward was for a new company to be created, hived off from Rough Trade, which handled these bulk sales and redistributed the profit to the regional members, which would include Rough Trade Distribution. Richard Scott seemed to concur in setting forward proposals for a contract of agreement: 'If the principles of devolution and socialism and collectivism are to prevail then those elements that see no further than survival or personal gain/glory or those elements that see the music industry as a convenient vehicle for individual vanity must be progressively excluded.'

in the area and they didn't – for ages they kept the Andy's account and Andy's were a decent-sized independent chain. They said they needed the revenue for their turnover, the same with the HMVs. Back then HMV was far more independently run than it would later be, and a good customer. We ended up getting HMV Norwich and had a terrific relationship with them. If they placed an order, we'd have the stock to them in twenty minutes. There was a moment when Richard Scott and Simon Edwards invited my main employee to London – they wanted to set him up in business, apparently, and then they would take over Backs. They wanted to close me down. I only found out about this about three years ago. That was when I found out about loyalty, too, because my employee had refused to go along with them.

Tony K: We saw ourselves as contributing to the community – by going on to work with bands that could get a manufacturing and distribution deal locally without having to go off to London. We helped bands like The Wedding Present, the Sisters of Mercy, Red Lorry Yellow Lorry, The Skeletal Family, Hula.

Each Cartel member did everything – and I think ultimately that was part of the downfall of the Cartel. There was duplication of costs and stock floating around all over the country. The people that made the most money out of the Cartel were Parceline and Securicor.

*

Green Gartside: *Songs to Remember* came out in 1982 and then we moved on. It was far too expensive a record for Rough Trade to have made at the time – or at least that's what I get told. But I don't recall any recrimination and in fact there were bigger issues and separations opening up at Rough Trade and personal politics emerging that had nothing to do with me.

Geoff basically got me out of it all by introducing me to Bob Last, who ran Fast and managed the Human League. The Scritti Politti that had commercial success was put together by Geoff Travis. It was Geoff who found David Gamson, the New York whiz-kid of the synths, and paid to have him brought over to London. It was Geoff who got Bob on board. And it was Geoff who paid for some of the work we did together.

Geoff Travis: I knew that a record like *Cupid & Psyche* was going to be expensive to make. I could imagine what Distribution would have said if I had gone in and asked for £150,000 to make Green's next record. Most of our records cost nothing to make. And even the Scritti singles prior to *Songs to Remember* weren't that expensive. I mean on 'The "Sweetest Girl"', Robert would have played for free, they used a drum machine. If I was ever going to spend the kind of money bandied around over Scritti, I would have to be making a record as good as 'Good Vibrations', so that was never going to happen.

Bob Last: My recollection is that it was Geoff rather than Green who approached me. Geoff knew that I liked to think strategically and at that point may have been changing his perception and thinking that intervention in the system was what Green was ready to engage in. I hadn't been fully aware of *Songs to Remember*. I was more familiar with the early Scritti and to my mind they were like refuseniks, and refuseniks did not interest me. I was aware that they'd read some of the same books I'd read, and in the case of Green he'd probably read them a lot more rigorously than I had, so they were sort of on the radar. But as I saw it they were refusing to play the game which said, let's work the system and see if we can get to the top. We might have to compromise slightly on the way, but we just might still be doing something interesting when we get to the top.

But Geoff played me a track Green had been working on with Nile Rodgers and it was fantastic – it blew me away. The fact that this was the area Green and Geoff had gone in told me they were ready to go on the journey.

It ruffled feathers, conceptually and theoretically. I enjoyed that. There was an element of 'Fuck you' in pushing Scritti in the direction of making the most glossy records anyone on the planet was making.

Refuseniks, in much the same mould as Scritti had been in, criticised them with a presumption that implied that they were the heroes and that other people made cowardly decisions. The culture Scritti came out of, which then didn't forgive them, was a deadening one, the opposite of what it imagined itself to be – smug and inward-looking. I felt that there had also been an issue of class. Glossy pop records really crossed class barriers. There were more working-class people listening to them and having their heads turned by them than there were people buying or being influenced by self-consciously revolutionary records.

Songs to Remember and 'Faithless', one of the singles from that album. Rough
Trade allegedly ran into trouble with Dunhill over the 'Faithless' sleeve.

*

Richard Boon: I can't help feeling it was partly some sort of tax dodge
when they set up the workers' trust. The idea of cultural collectivism was
something they couldn't really find a close precedent for, but they discovered
some paint company that had set up a similar operation. Work on the trust
was started before I arrived in the spring of 1983, and took a lot longer to
reach fruition. Part of this came out of a reluctance to embrace unionisation.
Richard Scott didn't want the staff unionised and I think he saw the trust
as a way around that. There had been – on and off – movements within the
staff ranks to unionise, but they'd all been resisted.

Richard Scott: I exerted constant pressure all the time to set up a trust for
the workers whereby they would own the company. I felt that the approach
chimed with and encapsulated everything that I thought were our politics
at the time. I have no idea why it took such a long time to come about – it
came into being in 1987 and was one of the things I was determined to
have in place before I left.[28]

Geoff Travis: The significant thing for me was that I was giving away

28. Rough Trade had originally been a partnership – after Ken Davison left, one between Geoff
Travis, Peter Travis and Richard Scott. That was dissolved in June 1979 and Rough Trade
Distribution Limited and Rough Trade Records Limited became incorporated. The owners
had three £1 shares. The initial aim of the trust was to hand over ninety-seven per cent of the
company to the workers but this was quickly revised down to seventy-six per cent, although
eventually they would end up owning all of it.

potential ownership of the company. I felt motivated by my Socialist principles and it seemed to me to be the right thing to do at the time. Certainly, I wasn't thinking of personal gain and there were quite a few raised eyebrows amongst my contemporaries, who asked if I really meant to do it. I've never regretted it. In retrospect, it was possibly bloody stupid, but on the other hand it gave the chance for an experiment to reach fruition. My father was probably apoplectic but as ever he was wise enough not to say anything and could see that I wanted to do it. It meant that wage differentials could be introduced, responsibility differentials. It was accepted that the structure would become more conventional and I don't recall that being contentious at the time.

Simon Edwards: Anyone who went to work at Rough Trade realised pretty quickly that it wasn't a cooperative, although it tried to act like one, and that in fact shares in the company were owned by three people – Geoff Travis, Peter Travis and Richard Scott: three shares probably written on the back of a cigarette packet. We all earned the same wage – £7,800 – although that changed as part of the process of bringing in the trust. The trust took an enormous length of time to get in place and it was constantly held up. It was sometimes said to be being held up by Geoff's dad, but it would become one of the largest workers' trusts in Britain at its time so it wouldn't have been possible to introduce it overnight. I'd always been a supporter of workers' trusts – one of the reasons why I have always been a supporter of John Lewis.

Jo Slee: Nick Mahoney was a left-wing management consultant who came to Rough Trade to give advice on setting up the trust and the idea of it was enthusiastically supported. I think we were all a bit naïve, actually, about what changes having the trust in place would actually make. By the time the papers were signed, the war of attrition within a malfunctioning management structure was so deeply entrenched, it was hard to see how employee power could be mobilised to change anything. And I learned fast that managers did not welcome 'interference' from trustees.

*

Richard Scott: Will Keen, the accountant, had arrived at the end of 1980. He just walked in off the street and told us that he had been working for Virgin but had had an enormous argument with them, which he never,

ever spoke about. Geoff asked him if he wanted a job, and we had a little conversation between ourselves, Geoff and I, and Geoff kept saying to me that Will wouldn't take the job because he'd be insulted by the salary. But Will did take the job and one of the first things he identified, and fairly quickly, was that we were broke.

We'd simply spent too much money and over a period it became clear – or rather Will pointed out to us – that the structures we had in place weren't working. Will was the first qualified accountant we'd had.

Geoff Travis: We always had our cash-flow problems and there must have been problems in the way we paid our bills.

Jo Slee: Will did the books and worked out that we were trading insolvently, and therefore illegally. I think we owed Daniel Miller at Mute about £750,000, which we had no way of paying. It was only through Daniel's good graces, really, that we were allowed to trade out of the debt rather than be forced into administration. When I came back from the US, I heard that there had been resistance to Will joining Rough Trade because he was a 'real' accountant. To me, he seemed like a lone voice of sanity: grounded, dedicated and unassailably fair-minded. He worked through the night sorting out the mess the finances were in at that point.

Richard Scott: Will Keen's notes to the six-monthly accounts leading up to November 30th showed colossal losses incurred in the six-month period. Rough Trade Distribution lost over £61,000 in the period and the record label lost £54,000. Within those figures, the Rough Trade shop lost nearly £30,000 in the period and *Masterbag* lost £43,000.

We had a meeting and decided that 'rationalisation' needed to happen. The shop went. The booking agency went. Scott Piering went. We closed down *Masterbag*. Reggae export went. In truth, I believe only one person got sacked – the others were what I like to call manoeuvred into a commercial position. The shop went to the people who were running it – Pete Donne, Nigel House and Judith Crichton – the agency became All Trade Booking, where once it had been Rough Trade Booking, and Scott started up Appearing. Austin Palmer and Steve Alexander, who were running Rough Lion, the reggae export department, also went. Scott was absolutely livid with me, but in the end for him and for virtually all of them, it was the best thing that could have happened.[29]

There was a series of meetings with each of the departments that lasted, I think, through the week and it was explained that we had to make these changes otherwise the whole thing would fold. Because of the way the company was run, we had to have everybody's support to do it.

Pete Donne: The period in the shop at 202 Kensington Park Road after everybody moved out was a strange one, really, a time of limbo when everybody knew something needed to happen but nobody quite knew what. We weren't given responsibility or authority and we weren't made accountable. Then, at the end of November, we were called in and told that the shop wasn't profitable and that it would be shut and we would be axed. We felt we hadn't been given an opportunity to prove ourselves.

We hadn't had much contact with Blenheim Crescent during that time, although Geoff continued to come in and work Saturdays: it fact, he still comes in the Rough Trade shops frequently now. I don't think he can stop himself.

I remember when we were called into our meeting, Richard was involved. I think Will was there and I think maybe Geoff was there. We all viewed Will as the outsider and saw him as the Devil. Richard would have spoken nicely in his typical way and I think would have said very little. It was difficult because Geoff had been and has been since such a sterling and fantastic supporter of the shop. I couldn't believe the losses. At the same time, I don't think we felt singled out in any way – it was pretty obvious that the company was in a lot of financial trouble.

We went away and the immediate feeling was one of having been betrayed, of having been held responsible unfairly, but almost immediately there was this feeling that we could take this over. We went to them and offered to buy the shop out. We did the deal with Richard and Rough Trade let us value the stock – I think that was a deliberate act on their part. We got a £7,000 bank loan using the records as collateral for the loan, which we were taking out to buy the records in the first place. We didn't tell the bank we didn't actually own the stock. By July 1983, we were set up in Talbot Road after having traded for a month outside the closed Kensington Park Road shop.

29. 'At least once a year there is a rumour of the imminent demise of Rough Trade and like the previous ones, this year's gossip is untrue,' began a press release sent out to steady the industry's nerve.

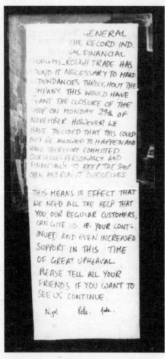

GENERAL

THE RECORD IND.
VAL FINANCIAL
ODUMS...ROUGH TRADE HAS
OUND IT NECESSARY TO MAKE
DUNDANCES THROUGHOUT THE
MPANY. THIS WOULD HAVE
ANT THE CLOSURE OF THE
HOP ON MONDAY 29th OF
NOVEMBER. HOWEVER WE
HAVE DECIDED THAT THIS COULD
NOT BE ALLOWED TO HAPPEN AND
HAVE THEREFORE COMMITTED
OURSELVES PERSONALLY AND
FINANCIALLY TO KEEP THE SHOP
OPEN AND RUN IT OURSELVES.

THIS MEANS IN EFFECT THAT
WE NEED ALL THE HELP THAT
YOU OUR REGULAR CUSTOMERS,
CAN GIVE US IE. YOUR CONT-
INUED AND EVEN INCREASED
SUPPORT IN THIS TIME
OF GREAT UPHEAVAL.
PLEASE TELL ALL YOUR
FRIENDS IF YOU WANT TO
SEE US CONTINUE.

Nigel   Pete.   fohn.

The shop and its staff were among the first casualties of the 1982 financial crisis.

Jo Slee: There were thirteen redundancies. I couldn't sleep during the period and was suffering from extreme anxiety. Will was taking these fantastic little blue anxiety-relief pills called Ativan, which were later taken off the market because they were so addictive. I asked him to give me some. They completely took away my anxiety. They were like Valium, only *much* stronger. I used to take half a pill at a time: I'd keep them ready for just before a meeting.

The crisis really was an opportunity for us to change the way we did things, to put in place new structures and bring in new people. It seems inconceivable but we never had record company meetings until I suggested that we should be holding them. I wanted people from other departments to come in and we could talk about how we would work the release. Geoff hated me making suggestions like this and said that things shouldn't be so regimented: any attempt to put a system in place looked to Geoff like a fence and he was allergic to fences. Of course, once we started having the

Geoff Travis, early 1970s, around about the time of going up to Cambridge

Jo Slee and John Kemp, Maple Sugar Festival, Northern Ontario, 1974

Steve Montgomery, photograph taken in the
Trafalgar, the 'Rough Trade Hotel', August 1977

Richard Scott at the time of joining Rough Trade,
June 1977

Carolyn Holder photographed around 1977

Peter Walmsley, photograph taken in the
Trafalgar squat pub, August 1977

Potted plants, a table and chairs, 'more
the feel of a Head shop ...' Interior,
202 Kensington Park Road, 1978

FRIARS MAXWELL HALL AYLESBURY

SAT. FEB 3 ROUGH TRADE

STIFF LITTLE FINGERS

+ROBERT RENTAL & THE NORMAL

+ESSENTIAL LOGIC

Tickets 170p from Earth Records Aylesbury.
Scorpion H. Wycombe — Hairport Amersham — Hi-Vi Buckingham.
FL Moore Luton, Dunstable & Bletchley — Old Town Records Hemel.
By post (with S.A.E.) from Earth Records, 72 Friars Square Aylesbury.
Or at door on night.   Life Membership 25p.   Minimum age for admission 16.

Flyer for the first Rough Trade Tour, 1979

The fruits of rapid growth –
Scott Piering japing in the
offices of Rough Trade Inc.,
Grant Street, San Francisco

A beautiful, early catalogue
of Rough Trade records
released in Japan on Japan
Records, which was run by the
formidable Noe Serizawa

'The "Sweetest Girl"' poster, design
influenced by the work of European
anarchists who dropped into Carol Street

Wendy Smith-designed and illustrated
Young Marble Giants songbook, printed
by Joly at Better Badges

Geoff Travis on an early visit up to see The Fall

Polaroids taken by the 'legendary' Scott Piering, *circa* 1979/80. All shots taken in or outside 202 Kensington Park Road

Ana da Silva

Vivien Goldman

Gina Birch

Genesis P Orridge & Chris Carter, Throbbing Gristle

Mayo Thompson

Young Marble Giants proudly displaying
their newly pressed *Collosal Youth* LP

James Blood Ulmer

Una Baines and Martin Bramah,
Blue Orchids

Charles Bullen and Gareth Williams,
This Heat

Mike Hinc

Steve Jameson and Sue Donne
larking around

Pete Donne

Edwyn Collins from Orange Juice, Chris Williams, and Alan Horne from Postcard Records

Robert Rental – 'a very sweet man'

The inimitable Fad Gadget (Frank Tovey) and Daniel Miller (The Normal)

Mark Beer, pointing to a poster

The impeccably tidy Promotions office

The poster reads:
'STATE CONTROL AND ROCK AND ROLL ARE RUN BY GREEDY MEN, IT'S ALL GOOD FOR BUSINESS WE'RE IN THE CHARTS AGAIN'

Wonderful promo photograph
of Morrissey taken by the late
Pat Bellis, Rough Trade employee

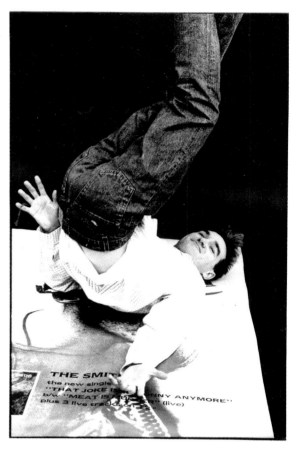

Johnny Marr promotional
card, photographed by
Andy Caitlin

Pantone 264C – used for the cover of 'Bigmouth Strikes Again' – sent to Rough Trade as a guide by Morrissey, who requested on the reverse that a book of Pantone colours be sent to him

The botched attempt to hype The Enemy Within's 'Strike' into the charts faltered, although the record raised a significant sum of money for the families of striking miners

IVOR CUTLER

Clockwise from top left: Sundays album cover; Ivor Cutler press booklet ('Born 100 yards from Glasgow Rangers football ground ... First gig 1957 at the Blue Angel in London – unmitigated failure' etc ...); Collier Street; advertisement from the *Independent* newspaper, 1987, which helped usher in a raft of middle management

ARE YOU?
OVERPAID & OVERDRESSED
DISILLUSIONED, DISCIPLINED,
DISENCHANTED, DETERMINED,
DISSATISFIED, DEMOCRATIC,
DISAFFECTED, DECISIVE,
DISENFRANCHISED, DYNAMIC,
DISTINCTIVE & DESPERATE

WE ARE!
ONE OF THE LARGEST (100+ STAFF)
EMPLOYEE OWNED & CONTROLLED
COMPANIES IN THE UK: IN THE
MUSIC & INFORMATION INDUSTRY;
INTERNATIONALLY SUCCESSFUL &
KEEN TO RECRUIT COMMERCIALLY
EXPERIENCED PEOPLE TO DEVELOP
OUR RADICAL EXPANSION PLANS.
SEND FULL DETAILS TO DEPT D,
ROUGH TRADE, 61 COLLIER ST,
L O N D O N   N 1   9 B E

Jeannette Lee
Step Into My Office, Baby

Jeannette Lee joined Rough Trade in 1987.
Uncommon people: Bernard Butler, Eddi Reader
and Jarvis Cocker all became management
clients not too long afterwards

Early promo shots:
The Strokes, 2001, and,
below, The Libertines
soundcheck at CBGBs

Faultless art within and without, portrait of Kauo Ohno from the front cover of Antony & the Johnsons' second album, *The Crying Light*

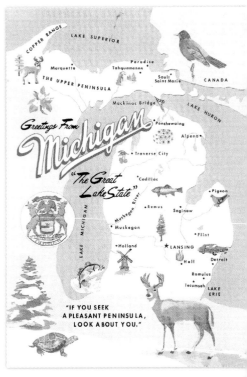

Promo card for Sufjan Stevens's *Michigan*, 'a geographical tone poem'

Green Gartside – *Early* and, as here, late

British Sea Power with friend

Rough Trade staff. All shots taken at Golborne Road

Janine Ellis

Jamie Woolgar and Ben Ayres

Ruth Patterson and Kelly Kiley

Jessica Park and Mog Yoshihara

Paul 'Shag' Jones

Patsy Winkelman

Joe Smith

Ned Hodges

Above: Jeannette Lee and Geoff Travis at the Rough Trade offices, photograph taken from the Rough Trade 2010 SXSW brochure. Below: the future

meetings and Geoff realised they weren't going to kill him, he became one of the strongest forces at them. That was part of what was great about Geoff – if you pinned him down and convinced him about an idea, he would enthusiastically support it. It was against his inclination but part of his good nature.

We put a stock-control system in as well. Rough Trade went for a long time without even having a stock-control system – crazy. We also began to have a weekly general meeting. I felt strongly that everybody should have a voice. Everybody should also have a responsibility and a right to come and say what they wanted to change. Unfortunately, I learned very quickly that a lot of people just wanted to moan in a corner. If the meetings weren't chaired properly, basically whoever was feeling most pissed off that day got forty-five minutes to tell everybody about it with a few minutes left at the end for everyone else to have a say.

Doug Kierdorf: I'd joined in 1981 as one of the van drivers. It was only after I joined that I realised that everybody got paid the same and that it was a cooperative and meant to be democratically run. It felt like a depository for people who were misfits. I was out on the road for most of the week when the meetings about the redundancies took place and I came back at the end of one day and went into my meeting, my department's meeting. The committee consisted of Geoff Travis, Will Keen and Peter Walmsley, and they presented us with the fact that we had to accept certain changes or Rough Trade would go under.

There was clearly a tension brought about by the fact that in spite of the anarchic, chaotic atmosphere, when push came to shove there were people who were owners and they could make some unpleasant decisions if they chose to. I was already in my thirties then, surrounded by a lot of kids who had a very starry-eyed view of Rough Trade. I could see the real position.

The committee said that people being axed were being chosen for reasons of efficiency and that it had nothing to do with individuals and their performances. This was a lie. The meetings really were a kind of ratification of what they'd already agreed anyway, but at some point we all then had to vote on the changes and, to my great shame and chagrin, we voted to cut the shop adrift and get rid of the others.

Richard wasn't there because it turned out that Geoff had suggested to Richard that he should leave. This was incredibly shocking to us all. Chris Wolfe read out a letter that Richard had written, which more or less said that he didn't want to talk about it and that he'd gone home for the day. We had to vote on whether or not to fire Richard and the staff voted not to fire him – at least not for the time being. It wasn't unanimous by any means; it was really quite close.

Pete Donne: There was some glee in some quarters, it has to be said, when Richard was also to be booted out. There was a sense amongst some that he had contributed to his own downfall by being part of the team that instigated the redundancies. It was a shock really, and quickly people realised that a political battle was about to be fought, which we, in the shop, were certainly glad not to be around to have to experience.

Geoff Travis: I don't believe I asked Richard Scott to leave, although as head of Distribution some of the responsibility for what had happened would naturally have fallen to him.

Peter Walmsley: I can't believe that Geoff would have expressly asked Richard to leave because, had that happened, it would have polarised the entire company. But I think Geoff went for Richard, rightly or wrongly, and it wounded Richard, and, probably, Richard thought it placed him in an untenable position.

It turned the whole company and there was a very poisonous atmosphere. The crisis in 1982 was just the usual mismanagement and not paying attention to cash flow – the typical Rough Trade problems. Richard had a responsibility as head of Distribution to be held accountable for some of the mess and he did fuck up. The problem became a part of the early real battle between the record company and Distribution for funding and for working out which was the tail and which was the dog. The record company had the best possibility of generating substantial success but it also carried the highest risk. The crisis was the first time the cooperative had had to deal with anything but growth, anything but a positive thing.

Simon Edwards: I can't remember the specifics, but I do remember Geoff coming up to me to talk about things and acknowledging that there was an issue over Richard's position. The crisis wasn't something that best summed up that period, though. In fact, I really think it was nobody's fault. The marketplace was changing and nobody seemed to have realised. Rough Trade had gone through this growth period and was now having to face the reality of having to fight and hold its corner of the marketplace. Unfortunately, a lot of things happened at once – the realisation of a phenomenal debt to Mute, the realisation that the market was changing, the shop making some horrendous losses, *Masterbag* making such a big loss. Rough Trade was lucky to survive at that time and it did so because a lot of people put a whole lot of energy into supporting it. At the same time, Daniel committed to stick with Rough Trade – he is a very special man.

Rough Trade survived because it was possible to adapt, and it did adapt. I think that Geoff would have turned to Richard for answers because Sales and Distribution, which Richard headed, were the places where those answers had to be found. At the same time, Richard had only the Cartel to rely on and of course that was still getting itself established.

Richard Scott: Geoff suggested to me at the meeting with him and Will that I might go. I got Scott Piering to drive me home to Clapham. I went to a gig that evening and there were a lot of Rough Trade people there and they all persuaded me to ignore the situation and go back to work, which is what I did. It must have been a fraught time for Scott – who himself was being let go – because he had to chair the meetings where the people leaving were being told.

Mike Hinc: I remember being called into a meeting and told that I was no longer required. We'd noticed in Booking that there seemed to be a big increase in accountancy staff and they'd always be in an office with the door shut, having a meeting, or they'd quickly grab a telex as it came through the machine, and rush off somewhere private. It was obvious a crisis was on the way and it was all rather sad.

The thing about Rough Trade up until that point was that the whole had always been greater than the sum of the parts. Booking was only a small part. This was true for every department. Afterwards, Rough Trade was *only* the sum of its parts – that *gestalt* disappeared and never came back.

The mood was completely confused. Scott was especially upset. I don't think Scott trusted anyone ever after that. Richard Scott almost lost his job. I remember him coming to me and my asking him what he was going to do and he told me he wasn't going to do anything, he was going to ignore it and go back into work. He said he wasn't going to recognise it. I thought – genius, and wished I'd had his balls.

When we split off I went to the bank and we discovered that Booking had never actually existed as a separate entity. Everything was lumped in together. The bank manager was appalled.

Simon Edwards: What the crisis ultimately led to was the realisation that we needed somebody to come in and take over the business, which would happen when Richard Powell was appointed. But the split between Richard and Geoff had the immediate effect of turning the whole company into two opposing camps. Distribution was on one side and the record company on the other.

CHAPTER NINE:

1983

'Just because we were southerners didn't mean we couldn't see the beauty of their uncovering of that particular layer of northern Englishness'

GrieveCom – The Smiths – New Hormones RIP – Fast Forward – Red Rhino Midlands – The New Professionalism – GLC – Planning to move

Richard Scott: Some time at the start of 1983, my problem had to go up before the GrieveCom[30], which was a soft committee charged with sorting

30. The Grievance Committee was one of a number of committees set up at Blenheim Crescent: there was also a Pastoral Committee, which met to discuss welfare matters, and a Building Committee, which looked after issues relating to the premises. GrieveCom set out

out grievances and which had a lot of softies on it, really, like Scott Piering, who I think chaired it. I was charged with the task of accounting for myself. In fact, the committee completely sidestepped the main issue by changing its remit to one of defining my role. In the end, I think the resolution was that I should just carry on, which is what I did.

Doug Kierdorf: I wrote to the committee at the time about the 'Richard situation'. In my letter I pointed out that Richard 'a little like Josef K (the Kafka character and not the Scottish pop group) ... is charged with and tried for a crime the nature of which no one will divulge'. It was the growth of the business that had caused problems, not Richard's skills. As I said, 'It would have taken someone with Napoleon's genius for organisation to manage the transition from homely little indie to overblown hit machine that Rough Trade has attempted in the last year and a half.'

Richard was a nice person: tolerant, calm and very thoughtful, and when panic was the common condition – 40,000 records coming in and 20,000 need to go out within the hour – he was in charge. He organised all their moves – Richard found Blenheim Crescent, Richard organised the move to Collier Street when it came.

I had my own run-in with the Grievance Committee. I objected to a record on the Come Organisation, which was a record label set up by William Bennett who would later start Whitehouse. I thought the Come Organisation were right-wing Fascists and I objected to distributing the record they put out, which was by Come, and refused to carry it on the van. I was hauled up by GrieveCom for that. I was called before them again when I refused to handle a record by the Last Resort – *Way of Life: Skinhead Anthems*, which I objected to.[31]

Jo Slee: By this time we had gone from no real meetings to having three a

findings with regard to 'Richard's Case'. It noted his 'conceptual insight and enthusiasm, his ability and confidence', acknowledged criticism of his managerial and administrative style – 'operating in a closed system, not disseminating information, being vague and tending to mystify things ... acting unilaterally', but laid any blame at the door of Rough Trade's phenomenal growth.

31. Although criticising Doug Kierdorf's 'unilateral' stance – i.e. disregard of GrieveCom – GrieveCom recognised that it would be equally reprehensible for Rough Trade members to have to handle material 'that goes against Rough Trade general policy'. The album, which celebrated Oi! and a particular aspect of skinhead culture, contained tracks open to interpretation, such as 'Rose of England', 'Lionheart' and 'We Rule OK'.

day around the building. Besides departmental meetings and the weekly staff free-for-all, we had several ancillary elected committees with varying degrees of power and effectiveness. The Pastoral Committee was supposed to be an embryonic HR outfit, but I'm not sure what it actually did – drug counselling might have been useful. Everyone had an opinion about equality and employees' rights. At one point it was suggested that people with children should receive £15 child allowance. One riposte was that people with children should be *fined* £15 – and no agreement was reached.

*

Richard Boon: New Hormones was starting to fall apart and lose money when Morrissey, who I'd known for a long time, came to me early in 1983 with a tape of 'Hand in Glove' and 'Handsome Devil' and asked me if I could help. I would have loved to have been able to release the record myself but instead I suggested that they take it to Rough Trade. Since they seemed to have some ambition towards releasing it on a label of their own – or at least that was how Joe Moss the manager presented it to me – I suggested they go and see Simon Edwards, who was dealing with quite a few of the M&D deals. As I understand it, they went down to see Simon, and Simon listened to the tape and then gave it to Geoff. And of course Geoff was immediately seduced with how brilliant the songs were.

Johnny Marr: I was working in a clothes shop in Manchester called X Clothes. I'd pretty much left school the year before, moved out of my parents' place, too, so it was a very liberating time for me. Clothes shops, as I understood it, were where you worked if you were a musician trying to get a band together. Through working at X Clothes I met Joe Moss (who would become The Smiths' manager) because he ran the shop next door, which was called Crazy Face. Angie, my girlfriend back then, who is now my wife, and I and Joe were trying to get a new band together.

As a kid I'd formed a few little bands and had been learning my craft – how to write songs and play guitar and all of that business. They weren't great bands but important bands, as formative bands are to me. As is often the case, finding a good front-man would always prove problematic. I knew Morrissey because of my friend Billy Duffy (who would go on to be in Southern Death Cult), who was one of a bunch of older guys I used to hang out with from Wythenshawe. Billy had been involved in a couple of bands formed out of the ashes of Slaughter & The Dogs, who had been *the* south Manchester punk band. Billy had been in the band that came after Slaughter, and Morrissey had sung in that version of the band for a very, very short period. Very brief. It stuck in my mind that here was somebody who took themselves as seriously as I took myself and would probably be as serious about music and having a decent, proper band as I was. That thought stuck in my mind, for a couple of years.

I put a band together in 1982 and tried out a bunch of people. It is always the way when you are trying to get a band together with strangers that you go for people who you think have the right vibe, the right look: but I was always coming up against people who just weren't as into the hard work as I was. They might have had the look. They might have been able to sing. But they didn't seem to have the passion or intensity that I had. After a while, I had the idea to go back to Wythenshawe and do some detective work and get Morrissey's address. I would just find out where he lived and go and knock on his door and make a proposition, as it were.

Around this time I was living in the apartment above Joe's house and we'd often sit around and listen to records. He told me about this *South Bank Show* on Leiber and Stoller where one of them wrote music and needed a lyricist and heard about this guy and just went around and knocked on his door. That's how I thought it would work out with me and Morrissey.

So I caught the bus and went and knocked on his door. I said to him something like, 'I'm forming a band and putting some musicians together. I write songs and I play guitar. I know Billy and I know that you are a singer. Are you interested in maybe writing some songs with me?' He let me in, which was a surprise – still is – and we sat in his room and, as has been told before, he invited me to put a record on.

I looked through his singles and found a Marvelettes record – I think it was 'Paper Boy'. I was impressed that he had a bunch of Marvelettes singles, all on their original labels. I was aware it was a test, but I was pretty snotty about music as well and instead of playing the A-side, I played the B. I think we both had the match of each other, really. In fact, we got on famously well, it was like sparks flying. We made an arrangement that he would call at noon the next day. But I remember leaving and thinking about those situations with front-men before and I wasn't exactly skipping down the street because I worried he might not call, he might not be into it as much as I was.

He called right on the dot and we were on and we arranged to meet the next day and from then on we started writing songs. In fact, on that first day when we were officially a partnership we had a conversation about many things and made a mental wish list, and on that list was that we should sign to Rough Trade Records.

We did our first demo at Decibel Studios in Ancoats at a place I had helped build as a trade-off for being allowed to rehearse there with one of my earlier bands. We recorded through the night – me, Morrissey and a drummer called Simon Wolstencroft, who I'd worked with before. I played guitar and bass and we did two songs, the first two songs we ever wrote together, which were 'The Hand That Rocks the Cradle' and 'Suffer Little Children'.

I hawked that demo a bit around Manchester – well, I played it to my mates, at least, and it would have found its way to New Order's manager Rob Gretton and, I assume, to Tony Wilson at Factory also. But I wouldn't have let The Smiths sign to Factory. The story has been told differently – that Factory turned us down – but the chance to do that was never in the offing, really. It was as important to me to *not* sign to Factory as it was to me to sign for *somebody*. I respected Factory and still do and had been asked by them to join Section 25 when I was about sixteen. A lot of my mates were in bands on Factory and a lot of people who came in the shop worked at Factory. So I was close enough to Factory. I didn't need the band I was forming to be on the label. I suppose the main reason was that signing to Factory was what people tried to do if they were in a band in Manchester, and I wanted us to stand out, or at least stand away from the pack and not do the obvious. Plus, Factory's aesthetic was so strong that if you signed to Factory you became a Factory band, which was a great compliment to Factory, but was a problem for me.

So hawking the tape around really amounted to playing it in X Clothes, full volume, on a Saturday afternoon. I didn't have the money to take it anywhere beyond Manchester, anyway. Those early versions of those songs were really slow and kind of heavy – even compared to the ones that were released – and they were hardly party time. Three-thirty in the afternoon, the shop would be heaving and I'd put on this really hissy, super-downy demo. Amazingly, I don't remember the shop clearing, though it was the time when we would also have played Clock DVA, Fad Gadget, Throbbing Gristle, stuff like that – not exactly the pumping house music you have in clothes shops today.

After that, a college friend of mine managed to blag a little time for us to do a demo in a sixteen-track studio in Chorlton, which EMI paid for. We recorded 'Handsome Devil', 'Miserable Lie' and 'What Difference Does it Make?'. That cost EMI about £120 and they turned us down.

We did a gig at the Ritz supporting Blue Rondo à la Turk and went on really early and did three original songs and a cover version of a song by the all-girl group The Cookies. We did that with the bass player from the studio we'd recorded the second demo in, but he wasn't right so I went to see Andy Rourke, who was a mate of mine from school, and played him the demo and then he was in. Then Mike Joyce joined on drums.

Then we played a very cool, very small gay club called Manhattan. This was the first time we played as a four-piece – in fact, we were a five-piece because Morrissey had this friend who danced on stage while we performed. The next gig, our third I think, was at the Hacienda supporting 52nd Street, but there were only about sixteen people there. It was at this show that we made a desk tape of the gig, just for us to listen to. Then we played a support for Richard Hell. The point is, we were playing these little gigs for free and didn't really play anywhere else before the first single came out.

Mike Hinc: Although the booking agency had split off from Rough Trade and become All Trade Booking, I think we were still in 137 Blenheim Crescent in the February when I received a demo tape of some Smiths tracks recorded through the desk at the Hacienda. Mike Pickering, the DJ there, had sent it to me because Joe Moss was looking for booking representation. So we got the tape first and we booked the Rock Garden show for them. I thought Joe was an excellent manager – a good man who was pushy in a polite way and wanted them to play every night of the week early on because he wanted them to grow up in a less public way than would be the case when they became big, which obviously they were going to be. And he was right.

Johnny Marr: We rehearsed in Joe Moss's warehouse in town, intensely, three or four times a week. Joe and I had a discussion about starting our own label if we had to – certainly the idea of making our own single was in the air. Joe paid for us to go into Strawberry Studios and record 'Hand in Glove', one of our new songs. It was a Dickensian, foggy Sunday night in Stockport, very appropriate, and I think the record captures that. We only had enough money to do one track so when we came to put the demo cassette together we used 'Hand in Glove' and added the version of 'Handsome Devil' that we'd recorded through the desk at the Hacienda. That was the tape I took down to Rough Trade.

I hustled together some train fare and went down to Blenheim Crescent, sleeping on my mate Matt Johnson's floor. Matt had his band The The. We didn't send the tape to anybody else. We'd made the decision on day two that this would be a good idea and as usual with The Smiths we went for it and it happened. We liked the Rough Trade aesthetic and 'independent' meant being brave, back then, not what it is today. Pretty much all bands want to be on a label because of other bands on that label and we liked the Monochrome Set.

I went in on a Friday. Rough Trade was this very shambolic, super-busy hive. The first thing that struck me was that there were records everywhere and lots and lots of people running around. Someone asked me if they could help me and when I said I wanted to see Geoff Travis I was kind of bustled out. Did I have an appointment? Would he know what it was concerning? Was he expecting me? I got the picture.

Simon Edwards: Johnny came in with Joe Moss and possibly Andy Rourke and when I asked them if I could help, they produced their demo tape. I listened to it and thought it was good. There was already a connection with Mike Hinc in Booking, and obviously they were able to say that they knew Richard Boon from Manchester, so I took it quite seriously. I gave it to Geoff and I have a feeling that he listened to it there and then.

Johnny Marr: I hung around for quite a long time, pretending to do stuff with records. I was hiding, really, maybe for as long as an hour or two. I could see Geoff in his office and lots of people would go in and out for meetings. Then he came out and I saw my opportunity.

Geoff Travis: I was heading to the kitchen to make a cup of tea when Johnny came up and stopped me. I think he was with Andy. He said he was from Manchester and that his group was called The Smiths. He handed me his cassette and said, 'This isn't like any other tape,' or something like that; would I listen to it? I remember thinking how prepossessing he looked, very stylish, a bit like a young Keith Richards. He wasn't a peacock but he had a look: anyone's interest would be piqued.

Johnny Marr: Geoff was very polite – he took the tape, promised to give it a listen and sent me on my way. Job done. Mission accomplished. I went back to Manchester for the weekend. And to Geoff's absolute credit he called Joe Moss first thing on Monday.

Geoff Travis: I took the tape home and listened to it over the weekend. I was really hooked, really intrigued by it. I loved the fact that I couldn't really place it – it didn't sound like The Byrds, it didn't sound like The Beatles or The Who, or anyone else. It sounded completely different. And although it fascinated me, I couldn't quite make out the lyric.

First thing on Monday I called the number on the tape, which was Joe Moss's, and told him it was the best thing I'd heard in ages. I suggested they come down to London the next day and that we'd cut the record there and then. I met them at the station, I think, and we made our way over to George Peckham's cutting room off Shaftesbury Avenue. That excited them – George had cut records for The Beatles and Apple Records and here he was about to cut theirs. It was a magical moment.

This was the first time I met Morrissey. He was very intense and quietly serious in his psychological scrutiny of me. He was unusual and immediately engaging.

They treated me with respect, as someone who might be important in their lives, but straight away I could see that they were a fierce gang. They had that thing that certain groups have: an insularity that manifested itself in a secret language, an exchange between them that said they knew what was going on in their world when other people didn't. But they were lovely.

Johnny Marr: We did the first single on the usual one-off, fifty/fifty deal that Rough Trade usually did. We had a piece of paper that said if any money was made it would be split between Rough Trade and the band, and said what the record would cost to make. We got some lawyer in Manchester who probably did house sales to have a look at it and he thought it looked all right and that was that. Really, we would have signed anything. All that concerned me was that after 'Hand in Glove' we got another record out. And then another. And another record after that.

Geoff Travis: We'd cut 'Hand in Glove' by the time they came down for the first London show at the Rock Garden in Covent Garden. It was just at the start of that very gentle ebbing and flowing of discord between Distribution and the record label, but a lot of people came out to see them. The show was transfixing, to me. What was fantastic was the transformation of Morrissey – when he walked on stage I had no idea that this interesting youth I had met was going to transform himself into this absolutely charismatic front-person, the likes of which I really hadn't seen before. At the show, a couple of Rough Trade people questioned how good they were, but I kept quiet: I knew they were fantastic.

Peter Walmsley: They were always pretty full of themselves and there was a flavour around The Smiths that we were competing. When Rough Trade people first came across them I don't think they saw them as the future of rock 'n' roll or anything like that. But Geoff was really enthused – and all power to him. I had difficulty at first selling them abroad – people would say they were too English-sounding. In Australia, I was told it was 'poncey, pouffy English music, might be all right in England mate, but it won't work here'. Sony signed them and they took off there, and I was able to call the shots – *we fucking decide what's good or not, you just licence it, OK?* The band worked everywhere.

Mike Hinc: By the time of the Rock Garden gig, we were completely separated from Rough Trade and I was dealing directly with Joe Moss. I remember that night Morrissey had his love beads on and I remember, like an idiot, telling him to get rid of them. There was a male dancer in the mix there somewhere, as well.

We went on to book them a lot in 1983. Geoff would break the rules for tour support in that although money was tight he would always find a few extra few quid for the tour if needed. We prioritised them: if there was a gig, they got first offer. For two years, Rough Trade Booking and now All Trade Booking had been developing this circuit of clubs around the country and the venues were getting larger so the timing couldn't have been more fortuitous. To be honest, I think from a booking point of view we were looking for another Echo & The Bunnymen, a guitar band that played live a lot that would help with our fiscal viability.

Johnny Marr: We were very single-minded. Things moved very quickly for The Smiths. But the atmosphere when we first started going to Rough Trade was interesting. You could tell at all times that the original principles and ethics were important. Geoff would always be talking about meetings. He'd tell us about things discussed at a meeting. He'd tell us about a meeting he was going to have. We'd come up with an idea or concept and he'd say, 'We'll find out what the meeting thinks on Friday.' This was all new to me. I was very young. But I found out very quickly what a collective was. Looking back now, I can see it was both a blessing and a curse. It really needed to move forward and I think Geoff, particularly, knew and wanted that.

We were the right band for them and they were the right label for us, but it was a time for the label of re-evaluation. Lots of things happened for the group – it was a steep trajectory and we got big quick. And the label had to move accordingly and change its ideals.

On one of the first visits Geoff took us to the 'art department', which was a little bit of space further along the workbench we were standing at. I saw a stack of paper labels for forty-fives – I think they were for a Weekend record and to me it was like looking at a stack of £50 notes. They asked us what colour we wanted our label to be. It was so DIY. And that carried on through to the way Morrissey designed the sleeves – he'd send the artwork through covered in masking tape, felt pen and crayons. Again, DIY.

Geoff Travis: Morrissey sort of took over driving the relationship with Rough Trade almost immediately and inevitably since Johnny focused so much on the music. There was a perceptible shift of dynamic tension, almost on day two. Morrissey, just like Johnny, was great to deal with: totally focused, he knew what he wanted and had a very clever aesthetic sense, deep and defined. There was a plan and it all made complete sense and it was our job to turn that plan into a reality. It was exciting watching Morrissey and Johnny's world unfold, step by step. I mean, it didn't take more than a couple of sleeves from Morrissey for us to work out that he wasn't going to be short of an idea – in fact, he probably had them all planned out meticulously. He'd set us challenges – like writing to George Best or Terence Stamp or Pat Phoenix or Shelagh Delaney to try to get permission to use their images on a sleeve: we'd have to explain to them, much as Johnny had to me, that The Smiths weren't just any other group. Being able to appreciate and understand and see the importance of the pathways Morrissey led us down was exciting. Just because we were southerners didn't mean we couldn't see the beauty of their uncovering of that particular layer of northern Englishness.

It was true, also, that their musical knowledge was phenomenal; their love and understating of it really can't be overstated. It was quite profound and looking back it was probably where Morrissey and Johnny met the most in their differences.

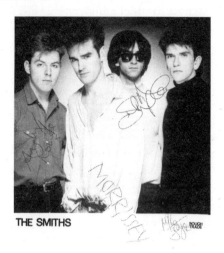

THE SMITHS

Early promotional shot of The Smiths.

Johnny Marr: When 'Hand in Glove' came out with its silver sleeve and blue label, for me it was like getting to the top of Mount Everest. It was a really big moment in my life. But, in fact, we got off to a bit of an inauspicious start. It was our first record and all our mates and aunts and uncles went out to buy it, only to find that it wasn't in the shops. You couldn't seem to get it in the North West. The reason we heard was that Probe, who were our part of the Cartel, had fallen behind with payments to Rough Trade and they weren't getting records sent up until they paid their bill.[32] Joe arranged to have a whole load of 'Hand in Glove' sent up and with our roadie he drove all around the North West handing them out to record shops on sale or return. They went to the Virgin in Manchester almost on a daily basis.

32. Probe was suffering a number of financial problems by 1983 and it was decided that Tony K from Red Rhino was best experienced to look into its circumstances. By far their biggest debt, both old and current, was to Rough Trade who, by October, would be owed £20,000. Tony K's findings compared Geoff Davis to ET ('everybody likes you and you are very soft') but noted Geoff's 'totally disorganised attitude to life, the universe and everything', while Geoff's staff, he claimed, suffered from a 'complete lack of ambition, interest, zest, time-keeping and concern for the well-being of the business'.

The band's success was swift and the period from 'Hand in Glove' to the first big chart hit, which was 'This Charming Man', was interesting. We were very young and at Rough Trade there were people who were young as well, I suppose, but who were adults, who helped us. Geoff had a lot of experience and it was important to us that Richard Boon was there, who had been Buzzcocks' manager and who we sort of knew, and Scott Piering, who was a really important person to the independent scene. Rough Trade was really lucky to have Scott Piering around.

John Peel had started playing 'Hand in Glove' and Scott had got John Walters, who was John Peel's producer, down to watch us play at the University of London and that was what led to the first Peel session. John Peel's relationship with his audience, and The Smiths' with his audience via the John Peel show, really can't be overstated. A network developed between John Peel and John Walters and Rough Trade via Scott. If we had a record coming out, a white label went to John Peel and he immediately played it. We had a similar relationship with the press, in particular the *NME*.

Richard Boon: Before New Hormones folded, I'd released a record by Dislocation Dance called 'Rosemary', which Peter Walmsley had included in a package of material sent out for licensing, and the band had subsequently got a deal in the Benelux. I'd sent a tape to Geoff and he had really liked it but it took him a few months to respond and say that maybe they would be right for Rough Trade. We all went down for a meeting and I asked him what had taken so long and he said that he was inundated with tapes. I said that maybe I could help him out.

Another couple of months went by and he asked me to come and talk to him. He was planning on going to America for about three months and wanted somebody to sit in his office and field calls for him and listen to tapes. I was actually interviewed. He invited me to his home and I met Carolyn Holder, who was off in a side room watching *Hill Street Blues*. Carolyn and I had a long conversation about *Hill Street Blues* being one of the greatest TV series of all time and then Geoff and I had a short chat about what covering for him would entail. Everyone got paid the same, he said, £7,800 per year; I would get pro rata for the rest of the year.

He never took his trip to America and I ended up assisting Mike Hinc in Booking. Then very quickly I became production manager after Bob Scotland left to pursue an academic career. It wasn't long after that I went with Geoff to watch The Smiths recording a Peel session, where they played 'This Charming Man' for the first time.

Geoff Travis: We knew that they were a great group and that they had great commercial potential. By the time we had released 'This Charming Man', the potential had become a reality. I'd been down to watch them record a John Peel session when they had played the song and straight away I knew that it had to be the next single and told them so. We'd had hit records before but we hadn't had a stream of them, as we would go on to have with The Smiths, and we hadn't had a group that was so dedicated to being successful. In their pursuit of success, they didn't change anything in how they went about their craft; it was just that they were intrinsically good enough to be successful. They worked very hard and made their mark in everything they did. And that made me realise very deeply that we had a big responsibility towards them.

Johnny Marr: When 'This Charming Man' came out it wasn't just that things went in the right direction but that the sun came out for the band and the label and the fans and for fans of indie music. We had these huge posters done and Morrissey thought up the idea of having some badges with 'CHARMING' and 'HANDSOME' printed on them. We were high on our success and so were the label, and it was a perfect union. I think we may have been the first Rough Trade band to go on *Top of the Pops*; no one could contain themselves, it was so joyous. One or two people's principles at Rough Trade changed a bit once we had that first hit.

Richard Boon: It made me laugh, really. They had a thing about not doing videos for a while, but Morrissey was more than happy to have these sixty-inch by forty-inch posters printed up which he could frame and then leave in his mother's house.

Jo Slee: I think the first time I met them was when they came in around the time they played 'This Charming Man' on *Top of the Pops*. Morrissey was wearing that green blazer he used to have and he was incredibly polite and soft spoken. He asked Pat Bellis, who was working in press, if he could have a look at some of the music papers and she told him quite sternly yes, but only if he gave them back. That *Top of the Pops* performance was a big deal for us – their first *Top of the Pops*, our first *Top of the Pops*. I remember

Morrissey sent me across the road to get some hairspray. At that time he wore beads and shirts from Evans Outsize, the ladies' clothing shop. Around then, we hired a minibus and drove up to see them play the newly opened Hacienda, but they'd just painted the place and it stank. It was really unpleasant and vile – and freezing.

Geoff Travis: I got in touch with Roger Ames who ran London Records and went to see him to propose that we use their sales force to sell 'This Charming Man'. I wanted us to have as much chance as anybody else of having a hit record. It didn't occur to me, of course, that Roger was probably thinking that London would do this for a couple of records and then steal the band. I just wanted the insurance of knowing that The Smiths had every opportunity now of being a big group.

Johnny Marr: Geoff took me aside and explained to me why they had decided to use London Records to sell the single and I appreciated him taking the trouble to explain it to me. My relationship with Geoff was all based on music and although later people have written that we didn't get on, that was all nonsense. I had and have great respect for him. When I'd finish a particular bit of music, it was him I was always excited about playing the track to, him I wanted to hear it and tell me that he liked it.

Richard Scott: The thing about taking on an outside sales force for The Smiths suggests we weren't in some way capable but of course we'd already had experience of handling high volumes of records sold by artists like Depeche Mode and New Order, both of whom sold just as many records as The Smiths would go on to sell. Although people are less aware of it, we had also used outside sales forces previously, too, though usually without any great success. There was a company called Aids, which was a sort of pressure sales company, but I don't remember them being that good.

Peter Walmsley: The use of the London Records strike force was really part of the ongoing spectrum of the old independent argument and I'm afraid I was on the side of the Devil because I was already licensing Rough Trade products to companies that had no part of the Rough Trade ethic. I was dealing with majors abroad. I was fed up anyway of the polarisation brought in by people such as Will Keen and, later, Richard Powell, who wanted the record label to put everything through Rough Trade Distribution to support Distribution. It was all so self-justifying, and frankly boring, and we got very little back apart from the begrudging use of our resources and skill. We got very little credit.

Of course, by selling records through London Records we were touching corruption really and I am sure that someone like Richard Scott would have wanted to achieve that end without going down that route. This came at a time, though, when there were constant, ongoing discussions about Rough Trade's reach and depth of reach in the marketplace. This was largely driven by bands who wanted hits and not just to be a Rough Trade band. They were pop stars in their dreams and in their dream worlds they wanted it proven.

Jo Slee: The point about the use of the London Records strike force was the band got big very quickly and Distribution wasn't set up to get the records into the right shops for them to chart. It was all about chart position. Geoff defended it quite rightly by saying it was the only sure-fire way we could show them success. He used money he received from Blanco to pay for the strike force – £20,000 on the understanding that when 'This Charming Man' had sold enough copies the money would be paid back. It wouldn't be the last time Blanco money was used to help out Rough Trade. In fact, we used to sometimes call it '*Banco* Y Negro'.

Richard Boon: Those issues over an independent record label using a major record label's strike force carried over for years. The question arose: how far was an independent label prepared to compromise its principles for the sake of success? At that point the Cartel hadn't built up a suitable network to do the same job – it didn't have people in cars going around record shops, teasing them with product. It was still very makeshift, still very ramshackle. Serious concerns ran through the little community of independent label owners at this time and people like Ted Carroll, who ran Chiswick Records, were, I know, very upset. Some people felt that this was crossing some mythical, ideological boundary.

This was coming on to a period when music magazines would run independent charts but feature in them boutique labels owned by major record companies. It was time when major record labels looked to the independents as A&R departments, and larger independents looked to smaller ones as their A&R departments. Labels like Fast Product and Postcard were talent-raided, but it wasn't just Orange Juice going to Polydor, it was Rough Trade coming in and saying, we'll take Aztec Camera, we'll take the Go-Betweens. In that hierarchy of approaches, major labels started to look at Geoff as well – they liked him, they liked what he was doing – and soon enough this led to Geoff setting up Blanco Y Negro with Mike Allway and Michel Duval, funded by Warners. That caused internal friction at Rough Trade because now he had a second revenue stream – if he liked something but couldn't get support in-house, he could say that he'd do it with his own money. That was the source of the money that enabled him to hire the London Records sales force in the first place.

But it was important that The Smiths as a commercial proposition worked for Rough Trade – they *had* to work. Somewhere along the line, Daniel Miller from Mute had called in his marker and there was an enormous debenture set up paying him back some crazy figure like £8,000 a month. Rough Trade Inc. still wasn't running the way it should have, and never would, and at Rough Trade Germany somebody had disappeared with a whole lot of money or something like that. We had a salary moratorium,[33] for God's sake, which was all meant to be hush-hush when we agreed to take a pay cut or a pay freeze for a while.

*

Robin Hurley: I had been at agricultural college in Yorkshire and I used to go into Red Rhino in York and buy a lot of records. I was one of their best customers. When I finished college, I didn't really know what I wanted to do. I started off in the agricultural industry but quickly realised that what I wanted to do was open a record shop. I had the idea that a record shop in the Midlands would work and I started looking at sites. The problem was that I had no credit references and when eventually I did find a shop that I thought was viable, the owner turned me down. Tony K suggested that it might be easier to get a warehouse and he suggested starting Red Rhino Midlands – there was clearly a market for supplying all those shops in those big cities, which presently were being supplied by the outer-reaching

---

33. In August, a policy group meeting suggested the spectre of pay differentials but began by suggesting that certain staff in certain circumstances should be paid *below* the current £7,800, such was the climate.

members of the Cartel. So that's what we did, and we set up in the spring of 1983.

Tony K: I put the stock in and Robin invested some money as capital and we got it going as a partnership. The Midlands was the one big area where there was lucrative business to be had but we had no presence there, whereas companies like Service and Graduate were going in and cleaning up.

Robin Hurley: I worked with Graham Samuels, who was a friend from college, and basically we just emulated what Tony did back up in Yorkshire. We got ourselves a van and three or four days a week that van would go to the major cities and pull up outside Virgin, HMV or the local indie shop and a buyer would come and look in the van and pull what stock they wanted. We were pretty green at first and some days the phone wouldn't ring, but gradually we acquired enough of a varied stock for any reluctant buyers to want to make up an order. We were getting stock of other Cartel members and so at first we were more of a wholesaler than a distributor, but gradually we started to pick up labels and distribute them to the other Cartel members and so we became a bona fide distributor. Within a year or two we started to look much like any other Cartel member and it was around 1985 that Tony and Gerri, his wife, and I decided to give Red Rhino Midlands its own identity and we changed the name to Nine Mile Distribution.

People didn't really know who we were at first in the Cartel but as we started attending meetings we were welcomed more and more into the fold. The meetings were informal, largely unstructured and, yes, some of the biggest decisions were about what we would have for lunch. It was important to keep the larger independent labels happy and so occasionally someone like Daniel Miller from Mute or Tony Wilson from Factory would be invited to a meeting. I vividly remember on one occasion Tony Wilson sitting cross-legged in the middle of the floor in a conference room espousing his latest manifesto while busily rolling up a joint. It felt rebellious. Yes, there were varying degrees – or often a complete lack – of business acumen but there was an awful lot of common sense. And that was what carried everybody through.

Richard Scott: It would be a long time before the Cartel became centralised in terms of selling. That really started to become a possibility once Richard

Powell joined, but in 1983 there was an ongoing discussion to try to further centralise some of the Cartel's functions. I wanted a structure in place that could coordinate activity and that could monitor activity without decentralising. In particular, Bob Last, I think, thought this was centralised selling in all but name.[34] I think part of the fear was that Rough Trade would dominate in a situation where it already had an unfair advantage, by sheer scale, over other Cartel members. We were always in a paternalistic position.

Richard Boon: That first summer I joined Rough Trade, there was a staff meeting at which it was decided that we really did need somebody to come in and help oversee the running of the place in a more professional way. Expectations started to become more realistic and whereas when the company had started it was advance on all fronts – we'll have a shop, we'll have a label, we'll have a distribution company, we'll have an agency, we'll have a publishing company, we'll even have a flat above the shop for bands to flop down in – now it was restructured, rationalised. There had been the redundancies and Geoff had learned that it was sometimes better to sell a band's publishing on because that funded them and kept them happy when Rough Trade hadn't the finances to do that. So, when the time came, The Smiths' publishing didn't go to Rough Trade Publishing, it went to Warners.

34. There were rumblings and ruminations on the old theme that, by naming itself, the Cartel had stepped one pace nearer the traditional model, the system it was said to oppose. 'Having decided to intervene in the system ... we have all had to make compromises,' claimed Bob Last, advocating that if any kind of centralisation was to take effect it could only work if it was ruthlessly applied, which was what Rough Trade ultimately went on to try to do. 'My own position is one of abhorrence of centralisation,' countered Richard Scott.

The workers' trust rumbled on and so did the setting up of a constitution[35] and *The Catalogue* started, which took over from *Masterbag* and which eventually I would be put in charge of. We still had no switchboard, so phones tended to be answered by anyone who happened to be passing if a person wasn't at their desk, and if it was Monday morning there was a chance that everybody would be at their departmental meeting and people in the know didn't even bother ringing up then, though meetings would come in even more soon after.

*

Geoff Travis: Pretty early into the relationship with The Smiths, Joe Moss stepped aside, which saddened me. Joe was enormously important for them and tends to get written out of histories of the band, for some reason. Joe was always very close to Johnny and it was my impression that Morrissey decided that Joe therefore couldn't be the manager of the band. I do feel that it was one of Morrissey's flaws that he thought everyone took sides. I was shocked when I heard that Joe was withdrawing. Morrissey sort of portrayed it to me that Joe was happy to take a step back, that he'd done his thing, got them to a certain point, but, now things were getting serious, felt out of his depth. I didn't see it like that. Joe always spoke sense, was always lovely to deal with and certainly wasn't being taken advantage of by anybody. I've always had my suspicions that Morrissey said to Joe that I'd said he wasn't up to it, though I may be wrong. Of course, I would never have said that and in fact my view of management is quite simple: the most important thing is having a relationship of trust with your artist – the rest you can learn. I think you can make a case for saying that nothing was quite right in The Smiths' camp after Joe left because they never found a manager that suited them. I think Morrissey could have been cleverer and kept Joe on board, even if he also had got somebody with more experience to give them advice as well, and in the long term maybe Johnny wouldn't have left.

Mike Hinc: It all started to get niggardly around the time that Joe Moss was edged out of the picture. Suddenly, instead of one person representing

---

35. As well as the various committees, under the terms of the constitution, there was a policy group of four culled from the three divisions – Distribution, label and accounts which would meet and be able to make grander decisions. Departments had a weekly meeting. The committees met as and when appropriate. Once the company moved to Collier Street, the company structure became fantastically more complex, as shall be seen.

The Smiths about sixty-nine people claimed to be looking after them. In the autumn of 1983, they did a tour and halfway through it Morrissey rang me up when they were playing UEA in Norwich and said could we get him back to London for a break. It had all got to him. He wanted to tour but there were so many people turning up and pestering him to be the manager of The Smiths.

Geoff Travis: For us, though, the merry dance with the band really began when we were courting them to sign a long-term contract and it seemed to take a long time from the release of 'Hand in Glove' to them actually signing the contract for the four albums. They were certainly courted by some majors during that period and I know for a fact that they had a meeting with Muff Winwood at CBS.

Johnny Marr: Because we got a lot of attention very quickly after 'Hand in Glove' came out, major record labels did start inviting us to meetings and this was before we signed the long-term contract with Rough Trade. We saw Warner Brothers and we saw CBS and what I remember about going to both – and major record labels are still the same now – is that there were *no* records anywhere, unlike Rough Trade where you couldn't move for records. The buildings were nicely air-conditioned and there were posters for the records on the wall, but there weren't any actual records. It was like being in a hospital.

Geoff Travis: The contract was eventually signed up in Joe Moss's warehouse in Manchester with me frantically making amendments by hand all over the document before Johnny and Morrissey signed it. The amazing thing about it is that in spite of all my scrawled changes it stood up well in court when it needed to. The contract was for one album with an option on our side for three more.

Tony English: The original agreement was a total mystery for many because it had lots of handwritten amendments on it, some of which were initialled and some of which weren't, so nobody really knew how many albums it was for.

Johnny Marr: We did what was to be the first album with Troy Tate producing but we wanted to redo it and I can't think why now because the last time I listened it sounded really good to me. It was more or less the songs that ended up on *The Smiths*, but we shelved it.

Geoff Travis: I suggested Troy Tate to the band as a producer – I'd really liked the sound he'd got on 'Love Is', the single he had done for us. I may have been a bit naïve and inexperienced in suggesting Troy because I think in truth he hadn't got enough of a track record, but anyway they went off to a studio near Wapping Wall and recorded it and we all knew as soon as we heard it that it hadn't come out as well as it might have. It sounded too flat. But it didn't create trauma; we just moved on and decided to redo it.

Johnny Marr: We had done a session with John Porter, producing for John Peel, and we had got on really great with him so we decided to go back in the studio with him and redo the album. It's possible that some of the problems first time around arose from the fact that we'd really moved on from the songs on the album by the time the record was done. We were very prolific, and we had kind of got ahead of ourselves.

We were touring when the record came out at the start of 1984 and lots of other stuff was going on at the time. The John Peel sessions were being repeated, there were big articles on us in the press and so perhaps the album coming out wasn't quite the landmark for me that the release of our first single was. It just became part of a whole bunch of amazing things that were happening around us at the time.

Mike Hinc: Around this time, The Smiths got a bit of a filthy reputation for cancelling things but often it was just because they had too much to do. They cancelled dates in Germany to do *Top of the Pops* with Sandie Shaw, which made absolute sense. They were, by now, able to pick and choose. When they'd started out I used to get letters from promoters who had booked them, saying they were the worst band they'd ever booked and that they would never book them again. It wasn't because of their music. It was because the band were demanding; they set their own levels of professionalism very high, and at a very early stage, and I think some tour promoters found that hard to deal with and confused professionalism with arrogance.

*

Richard Boon: When talk of pay differentials came up it always struck me that packing a few records into a box and sealing it up and putting it in the post room probably wasn't as stressful a job as the person's who has had to order up 250,000 copies of Rough 61[36] and find somewhere in Blenheim Crescent to stock them over Christmas. The boxes were piled up everywhere, in every available office and you really couldn't move for them.

Richard Scott: For some time we had been hopelessly short of space. Almost as soon as we moved into Blenheim Crescent we outgrew it. Then we outgrew the extra space we had taken in Philips' factory building next to it. Like the move to Blenheim Crescent, the move to Collier Street took a long time to facilitate and came about after we were approached by the GLC.

The GLC had done a cultural report which had identified Rough Trade, among others, as the kind of company that it should be supporting. I used to drink with the writers Dave Laing and Phil Hardy, both of whom worked for the GLC and both of whom drank in a pub called the Waterside Inn in York Way, Islington. I think the fact that we were in need of a building came up one time and later, through a man called Ken Walpole and through Geoff Mulgan, who went on to run Demos and work for Tony Blair and Gordon Brown, we were offered Collier Street. I went to see it and came back and said that it would need converting but essentially it was fine and we moved in spring 1984.[37]

---

36. *The Smiths* by The Smiths, pressing ordered up by the production manager, Richard Boon.
37. Cartel dignitaries were shown around the 20,000-square-foot premises in December 1983 and according to Cartel minutes 'a wonderful time was had by all'.

PART THREE:

COLLIER STREET AND AFTER

THE MODEL

Collier Street in King's Cross, North London, was Rough Trade's brave new world. In a year when the workers supported the miners in their struggle, just as they'd supported the nurses in their struggle two years earlier, a formal management structure was teased in with the appointment of Richard Powell, brought in to manage what was largely seen as unmanageable. In time, equal pay would disappear – partly in exchange for the workers' trust, and differentials of responsibility would be explicitly enshrined. A developing raft of middle-management would guide Rough Trade into its glorious future.

Promotional badge issued to support the 'Enemy Within' single in aid of the miners, 1984.

But before they were able to do that, company attention was distractingly turned towards The Smiths who, on 23 May 1985, by solicitor's letter, informed Rough Trade that they believed themselves to be out of contract or imminently out of contract with the label. They eventually signed a 'futures' deal with EMI on 25 July 1986. Rough Trade obtained an injunction on 20 December 1985 (served personally on Morrissey) and a twelve-month stalemate ensued from spring 1985 to spring 1986, with the matter finally settled on 18 April 1986. The magisterial *The Queen is Dead* was released shortly after. The Smiths then went on to record what some consider to be their best record, *Strangeways Here We Come*, before ultimately leaving the label and simultaneously disintegrating as a band.

By 1986, Rough Trade was ten years old. The terra firma upon which it rested had shifted, the company transposed from the gentrified paddock of West London to the more steely and urban, grim habitat of N1. Although its surroundings provided recognisable glimpses of sympathetic and similarly minded compatriots – Housmans, the long-established radical bookshop was just around the corner in Caledonian Road (as still it remains today), and Baker & Daughters, the local sandwich shop run by the three sprightly, elderly spinster Baker daughters distortedly mirrored the Wavy Line of Ron and Gloria – Collier Street itself was cold and reflected the new professionalism which Rough Trade purported to evince.

Staff numbers ballooned and the *consistency* of the staff altered – band-tinkerers who had formed the relatively unified core of the staff at Blenheim Crescent, and whose interests ran largely parallel to those of the company, were gradually replaced by a more divided workforce. Supposedly progressive, system-sympathetic managers ran up against an increasingly less engaged and militant shop floor, which felt distanced from Rough Trade's original ideals (albeit ideals which they'd largely inherited). On the cusp of the distribution company's collapse some five years later, dog shit would be sent through the post to its managing director and the warehouse turned into a virtual no-go bunker.

But in 1986, there was still enough life in independent music for Rough Trade Distribution to be growing at a significant pace. It began to embrace a far more varied range of labels, in all musical styles, where once pasty-faced, non-multicultural, indie had dominated, although indie was also doing well. The *NME* cassette *C86*, intended to document a scene long over by the time of its release, inadvertently ended up creating a genre that is still revered today. Established labels that Rough Trade handled, such as Mute and Factory, were joined at the top table by significant newcomers, like Alan McGee's Creation Records and David Balfe's Food.

A quibble at the time of the release of *Songs to Remember* by Scritti Politti that had grown into a quarrel around the time of the financial crisis of late 1982, had, by the end of 1986, firmly cemented into a rift between Distribution and the record label. Building a distribution company is a slow process: having a hit record is a sprint. Balancing the needs of both was something nobody seemed able to do and the two principal arms of the business became more confrontational. The introduction of dogmatic and fiercely policed business structures by the new management ran up against the realpolitik of Geoff Travis's historical status. There *was* a problem in working out which part of the company was the tail, and which the dog.

In its bid to become more professional, to become more like those it had set itself up to oppose, Rough Trade also became over-bureaucratised, internally weighed down by an endless meetings apparatus and the introduction of overly complex critical paths. The introduction of 'the Model', a logistical blueprint which killed off regionalism (and by extension the Cartel) and attempted to centralise distribution, was touted as hard (business-wise) externally and soft (radical philosophy) internally but ended up somewhat cross-wired, or so a number of staff felt. Personnel management in the hands of certain senior staff members was seen as a major failing.

The implementation of the workers' trust in 1987 was, in some respects, a last gasp for the cooperative ideals that had informed Rough Trade early on when essentially it had been a small number of workers and, before that, one man and his vision. The workers' trust ran contrary to such concepts as wage differentials and was messy to bring in. It took five years to launch. ACAS, through the Greater London Enterprise Board (which was part of the Greater London Council), came in and assessed Rough Trade's cooperative status. Their findings highlighted the difficulty of maintaining a functioning cooperative once staff numbers increased over twelve, and pointed out the obvious fact that Rough Trade was now, largely due to size, essentially a conventional business structure and one that needed managing in a conventional way. Where once a group of people gathered in a room and argued about the way forward, now there were boards, sub-boards, cross-pollinating trustees of an employee and non-employee nature. ACAS acknowledged the presence of 'middle-management'.

Internecine issues aside, by the time the 'second summer of love' in 1987 had translated into an explosion in the dance record market, Rough Trade was doing extremely well. It re-energised its American arm, diverting carefully structured UK funds to facilitate an expansion programme that was well thought out in business terms and, although criticised at the demise of the distribution company in 1991, might not have been as dramatically responsible for the collapse of the overall company as has sometimes been suggested. The record company also shook off any possible post-Smiths malaise and vigorously signed a whole raft of interesting new ventures such as The Sundays, who would break the Top Ten, A. R. Kane, and a number of acts from America, including Lucinda Williams, Galaxie 500 and Mazzy Star. By rights, they should have signed the Stone Roses, as well.

Jeannette Lee also joined the company and is currently its second longest-serving employee after Geoff Travis and now a co-owner of Rough Trade. Although her importance in the Rough Trade story would be hard to over-state, particularly in the company's present incarnation, the contribution she made to independent music prior to joining Rough Trade is often overlooked. At sixteen she went to work with Don Letts at Acme Attractions, the legendary King's Road clothing store, and had later joined Public Image Limited. Other significant new recruits at Collier Street include David White-head, recruited from Rough Trade's arch rival Pinnacle to oversee product management in Distribution, and George Kimpton-Howe, recruited also from Pinnacle to become managing director of Distribution.

Richard Scott left Rough Trade in 1988 and Jo Slee left in 1990: Richard, along with Steve Montgomery (who had left in 1984 after a stint at Rough Trade Inc.), had had a formidable influence on the ultimate shaping of Rough Trade and the nationwide independent network, and Jo Slee traced a link back all the way to the early 1970s and Geoff Travis's Cambridge days. But perhaps their departure had less impact than those of a significant strand of management who all left the distribution company in 1989.

The last days of Rough Trade Distribution (and by extension, Rough Trade itself) were like the last days of Pompeii. From the summer of 1990, it became apparent to a lot of people internally that something was dreadfully wrong and that something awful was likely to happen. There appeared a black hole of finance, slightly incredible given that in the previous four years Rough Trade's turnover had increased five-fold from around £8m in 1986 to approaching £40m in 1990. According to Daniel Miller, when Rough Trade collapsed it was during one of the strongest ever periods for inde-pendent music sales.

Rough Trade took on a new lease for premises in Seven Sisters Road in 1990, much larger and, inevitably, much needed, but failed to dispose of the old lease first and were effectively responsible for two premises. They purchased a bespoke computer system, costing in excess of £700,000, that to all intents and purposes failed to work and ultimately brought down the Cartel. And they were hit for bad debt in terms of credit control, which was woefully managed and had a spectacularly negative impact when Parkfield Video (a major video distributor) went bust, owing Distribution over £500,000. By the middle of 1990, America was eating up funds, not to develop but simply to sustain itself until a trading partner could be found.

Actions throughout the company were taken, as usual, with the best of possible intentions and sometimes the least possible expertise.

AND YOU GET AN IN-DEPTH PERSONAL SERVICE.

Part of an advertisement for KPMG Peat Marwick McLintock, the administrators.

The end, although mercifully quick for most, was a living nightmare for those who had to sort it out, not least Geoff Travis, who by the start of 1991 was pretty much alone in terms of senior management, terribly exposed and primarily – as figurehead of the company he had set up – held to blame. Rough Trade contacted the major labels it owed money to and a meeting was held on a freezing winter's day in January. A steering committee was set up to try to avert putting Rough Trade Distribution into bankruptcy and work out a plan for saving the business (not least, as it later turned out, because receivership or liquidation would have meant that The Smiths' back catalogue, a notable asset, would revert to the band and be lost). The principal label creditor was Rough Trade Records, which was owed over a million pounds. The major independent labels set up an escrow fund to collect money on behalf of all the labels and distribute it appropriately and in an apportioned manner.

In February, the Rough Trade trustees, aware of their general responsibilities, fearful of the legality of the escrow fund and mindful of the claims of other, non-label creditors, asked for and were allowed chartered accountants to be brought in as 'informal' administrators. Ultimately, when the administrators, label creditors and other creditors couldn't agree, it was decided to put the company into formal administration, which happened in May 1991. All of the holding company's assets, which included the record company, the global satellite companies and the ancillary parts of the UK operation, were thrown into the pot and the experiment, begun in 1976, was, for the time being at least and in its absolute form, over.

CHAPTER TEN:

1984–85

'At the end all he said was, *"Jesus Christ*! I don't think I could get anyone to buy this"'

Richard Powell – Buckminster Fuller and 'critical path' – Work ethic – Probe problems – Fast Forward – Miners' strike – South Africa – Smiths problems – Centralisation – Injunction

Richard Boon: Richard Powell arrived shortly before we moved to Collier Street and was appointed through a cricket team.[38] He played in a team called the White Swans, as did a couple of people from Rough Trade. We'd had the crisis at the end of 1982 and then the problems with Rough Trade Germany and the difficulty of having to pay Daniel Miller back and there was a general feeling – it amounted to an uprising, almost – of it all having the potential to go wrong again. So that was why people felt it to be so important that someone was appointed who could effectively oversee the business.

Peter Walmsley: There were big discussions about getting someone in to try to bring in shape and form to the unmanageable behemoth which we had created but didn't have the time or capacity to manage ourselves. A difficulty

38. A CV from the time intriguingly lists Richard Powell's personal interests as: 'DIY, golf, squash, and philosophy'.

was that although Geoff did ultimately decline ownership of the company he had created – and all credit to him for that – his status made it difficult for others to work around him. And he would, of course, quite rightly be passionate about fighting the record company's corner. Historical fact meant that to some extent people had to tiptoe around Geoff in kicking arse to get things done.

Richard Powell had a very fundamentalist view of the business, one from which he never shifted. If you packed boxes and shipped records out it was a guaranteed ten per cent; if you signed an artist to a record label, it could be shit or bust, roses or garbage. Geoff could argue that the record company might be able to do something good and turn the whole enterprise into a positive, but it was always speculative. Distribution, on the other hand, was always quantifiable. For someone with such a basic understanding of how a record label worked, Richard Powell grew an awful lot of power.

Richard Scott: Richard Powell had been working for the Greater London Enterprise Board and when he came to us he had been helping a telescope manufacturer who was being supported by the GLEB. Will and I interviewed him in the pub and I remember him drinking four pints of Guinness. Later, he told me he was a Stalinist.[39] He was certainly of broadly left-wing views and anyone who accused him of being Thatcherite, as people later did, was talking nonsense.

Richard Boon: The first thing he did when he came in was to find out what everybody thought and he spoke to each member of staff in turn, from the wonderful Jacko in the Returns department, who spent all day scratching records so they could go back to the supplier, all the way up to Geoff Travis. And out of all of that, he came up with a structure.

He introduced business management and tried to reduce some of the confrontational things going on – I mean, the trust was being set up at the same time that it became clear that wage differentials had to come in. In time, Richard Powell introduced pay differentials. That meant that people suddenly became more accountable. Differentials of pay brought

39. Interviews were always lackadaisical affairs at Rough Trade. People tended to appear by osmosis and on the few occasions when an interview was deemed appropriate, the interviewer would always be far too busy to spare the time interviewing. A member of the accounts department had admitted at their interview that they had embezzled funds from their previous company: they were still taken on.

PARTICULARS OF TERMS OF EMPLOYMENT
Given pursuant to the Employment Protection (Consolidation) Act 1978, s.1.

DATE.........26/6.......19.83

TO: (Name and address of employee)   RICHARD SCOTT

FROM: (Name and address of employer)   ROUGH TRADE DISTRIBUTION LIMITED
         137 BLENHEIM CRESCENT, LONDON W11

AMENDED: THIS 24/6/83 WITH EFFECT FROM....1/1/ 1983

Delete words in one or other set of square brackets. Insert date only if previous employment counts as continuous with this employment   [No] Employment with a previous employer counts as part of your period of continuous employment with us [which accordingly began on ....19.......]

The following particulars of the terms of your employment applied on ....
.... 19 ....:—

1. Job Title	
2. Remuneration *Details must include scale or rate, or method of calculation, and intervals at which remuneration paid*	£7,800 per annum and pro rata for part time employees. To be reviewed each year.Employees with children receive an extra £90 per calendar month,or pro rata for part time employees.Each employee is entitled to one Rough Trade record released free of charge.N.B. all these are before tax amounts. All other records,cassettes,videos,magazines etc. at cost price plus V.A.T.
3. Hours of Work *Details must include any terms or conditions relating to normal working hours*	42½ hours per week.Flat rate. Monday to Friday 10am-6.30pm. There is no set time for a lunch break or tea break ,although each employee is entitled to 1hour break per day to be taken at the discretion of each department. No overtime is paid to employees working more than the required 42½ hours.
4. Holidays and Holiday Pay *Details must include entitlement to public holidays and particulars for calculation of accrued holiday pay on termination of employment*	20Official working days per year or pro rata for part time employees,excluding statutory holidays. Commencing from Jan1st to Dec31st.Holidays not taken within any given year cannot be carried over into the next,neither will holiday pay be issued in retrospect of holidays not taken within said year. 1month notice should be given of intended holiday dates. In cases where through pressure of work or other special circumstances an employee is unable to take the full holiday entitlement the above rules can be waived at the discretion of their department in conjunction with the pastoral board.

oyez The Solicitors' Law Stationery Society plc, Oyez House, 237 Long Lane, London SE1 4PU   Form C.E.1B   ★ ★ ★ ★ ★

A Rough Trade employee contract. Equal pay at £7,800 per annum.

differentials of responsibility. He restructured the company as well. There was a record company board, and a Distribution board, and a main board, and watching over all of that a largely independent board of overseers.

It effectively brought in a career structure – you could go from working on the newly introduced switchboard, say, to running a department. People did. He also introduced a critical path, which was a Richard Scott suggestion taken from the ideas of Buckminster Fuller.[40] Everything internally had to be broken down into separate departments – wholesale, export, distribution, the label, international, *The Catalogue*, marketing, et cetera – and each department had to produce six-monthly performance forecasts, and, during the delivery of those forecasts, produce the next six-monthly targets, and so on . . .

40. Buckminster Fuller, 'the planet's friendly genius' and a man who coined the phrase 'Spaceship Earth', like Richard Scott, applied principles of architecture to solving everyday problems and invented, among other things, the geodesic dome. The epigram for his famous work *Critical Path* serves as a microcosm (or possibly macrocosm) for the labyrinthine way

Richard Scott: The Buckminster Fuller thing was a bit of a joke, really, and entirely of my making. It was largely the language of Buckminster Fuller that I played with and it wasn't in any way to do with how the management structure was meant to be set up.

Jo Slee: Richard Powell came in and was basically given the whole thing to run and when he first joined, everyone was more or less working towards the same goal. But it really was a poisoned chalice he was handed. The job he took on – well, none of us wanted it. We almost snatched his hand off when he agreed to do it. It was an impossible job – we really felt for him – and we didn't really care who did it so long as it didn't have to be one of us. The whole thing was pretty much unmanageable – you had a 'head of distribution', who didn't see the need for a stock-control system, and you had a record label that although trying to put structures in place still operated as an art rather than a science.

I was greatly in favour of organisation, of management structures, but Richard Powell's manner disaffected people. He could appear to be brusque and uncaring and didn't seem to want to engage people, which had been the whole ethos of Rough Trade in the beginning. I remember at one point we weren't allowed pencils because he worked out that we'd spent too much on stationery that month; no more photocopier paper for a while, that kind of thing. It was mad.

He wasn't Thatcherite – he used to spout a lot of left-wing stuff – but his methods were remarkably like those Margaret Thatcher used with the Cabinet, it seemed to me. That really didn't go down well.

Simon Edwards: Richard Powell brought in discipline – suddenly we had stock-control systems, financial planning, strategies in terms of what the business was aiming at, critical paths. Really, Geoff had been able to do what he liked up until that point and what Richard brought in was accountability. Looking at it from Will Keen's point of view – he was

---

Rough Trade operated at Collier Street: '*Conventional critical-path conceptioning is linear and self-under-informative. Only spherically expanding and contracting, spinning, polarly involuting and evolving orbital-system feedbacks are both comprehensively and incisively informative. Spherical-orbital critical-feedback circuits are pulsative, tidal, importing and exporting. Critical-path elements are not overlapping linear modules in a plane: they are systemically interspiraling complexes of omni-interrelevant regenerative feedback circuits.*'

carrying all that stress of the business and had been off ill with it – it was a very good thing. By creating the main board, both the record company and Distribution had to account for their actions. It cut both ways. On one occasion, we in Distribution advanced a label a very large sum of money and never recouped any of it. We were severely hauled over the coals for that and asked to explain ourselves.

Jo Slee: One unforeseen consequence of Richard Powell's arrival was that the rift between Geoff and Richard Scott presented Richard Powell with power beyond that of the appointment he filled. The more power he had, the more difficult Geoff found it, I believe. With the best will in the world, and although he did try, like a lot of creative directors, Geoff really didn't like it if he couldn't get his own way with money that he wanted to spend on an artist. That dynamic between business management and creative direction was always difficult.

But the idea that Geoff didn't get on with Richard Powell – I don't think many people got on with Richard Powell. Everybody wanted him to succeed, but I personally didn't appreciate him as productive, efficient or inclusive because primarily he came across as extremely patronising. He had an idea and a vision – and absolutely no personnel skills. The worst manifestation of that bloody-mindedness would come years later when his and Will's insane empire-building took them into America against all rational advice and experience and helped bring down the company. (Virgin tried, unsuccessfully, nine times to set up independent distribution in the US with Caroline Exports.) I remember Peter came back from a main board meeting one time and I asked him how the discussion about the US had gone. He said, 'The problem is, when you voice an objection, you're made to go and stand in the corner.'

Richard Boon: Richard Powell reined in spending. And by separating the company into distinct parts it was no longer so easy for money to flow unchecked around the company as it had been, say, at the time of Rough 20.[41] The record label and Distribution found themselves answerable to a board on which individually they represented only a tiny portion. Prior to Richard Powell, accountability was always the problem – something was always somebody else's responsibility. Suddenly, now there was a reporting

41. *Songs to Remember* by Scritti Politti.

system. This wasn't just accountability, this was personal accountability.

Richard Powell quickly highlighted the need with big clients for sole distribution. It took a long time to see that through but eventually 4AD came to Rough Trade and Factory went to Pinnacle. Daniel held out for a long time and really only threw his lot in with Rough Trade at the precise moment, although no one knew it, when it was all about to go wrong. Everybody benefited from sole distribution. It's jumping ahead, but shortly after some of this was resolved, 4AD had a Number One with M|A|R|R|S, distributed through Rough Trade, the same week Factory had a monster hit distributed through Pinnacle.

Rough Trade had some amazingly amateurish ways before Richard Powell joined. We had tried to become more professional in the past and it hadn't worked but by the time of Richard's arrival it needed to be professionalised. He encouraged staff to contribute: I remember bringing in a copy of a book I had on Communist China and the idea of democratic centralism and he was keen to feed the ideas into the debate.

His great mantra was – *professional on the outside, radical on the inside.* I'm not quite sure how well it worked ultimately . . .

Richard Scott: I think Geoff got on badly with Richard Powell, pretty much right from the start. Geoff was always at his best with a smaller team around him. I remember having a conversation with him once, back when we had conversations, and we agreed that Rough Trade had ceased to be fun after it grew over about twelve people. So Richard Powell coming in and looking at this larger structure and seeing that the structure had to be broken down into groups, and that the groups had to answer to each other and communicate with each other, would have been an anathema to Geoff.

Geoff Travis: I was happy to work with anyone, in any structure of any size, but so much bureaucracy crept in that it stopped being fun any more and it seemed to me that that hadn't been how rock 'n' roll was built. I was as committed as anyone to seeing the thing work but ultimately people spouting management gobbledygook started to take over and I lost some interest in keeping up with that.

*

Richard Boon: I think Morrissey had a genuine interest in the Rough Trade record label because much of the music he liked and championed was marginal – bands like the New York Dolls and The Stooges. I believe he liked the spirit of independence, but he wanted it professionally handled. It couldn't be run on an ad hoc basis any more because he had a script, and the script said he was going to be a star and everybody had to help him. The desperation at Rough Trade turned to exhilaration as everybody realised that if The Smiths could be made to work there would be financial security for the whole operation. By the time of the release of the first album in February 1984, The Smiths were on the verge of something very big, but we all knew at Rough Trade that for us it was make or break time, *underlined*.

Johnny Appel: We had a visitation at Backs before the release of The Smiths' album. Richard Scott and Scott Piering came to see us and seemed to be doing this grand tour with a white label of the record. We were told everybody had to be there. They refused to play the album on our stereo – they'd brought their own, the cheeky buggers. We got a complete commentary on the album, track by track. It was a real granny sucking eggs moment. It was obvious what could be done with The Smiths and that first album but somebody clearly wanted to make sure we were doing our job.

Geoff Travis: The halcyon years with The Smiths really were the halcyon years. Just before the release of the album we released the single, 'What Difference Does It Make?', which has that great turbine sound, and once again the band were back to *Top of the Pops*. Then just after the album came 'Heaven Knows I'm Miserable Now', which was our biggest hit in terms of singles with them and got to Number Ten in the charts. It is an absolute classic and just so unusual – apart from the lyrical imagery, which is just so funny, referencing Caligula and stuff you wouldn't normally expect in a rock song, it was also a marvellous lampoon of themselves. It was a mistaken, if somewhat commonly held view that The Smiths were miserable and I thought it was very clever that by the third single or so they were sending that view up.

Ultimately, they would go on to produce a stunning body of work – and over a relatively short period of time, too. There was never a dull moment working with them. Our relationship with Morrissey was, for years, excellent. He'd send the most brilliant, hilarious letters, there was always a good negotiation about what was going on and they did everything they said they were going to do – and the other thing is they delivered. Sixteen hit singles.

There was a change in mood at Rough Trade – we were becoming something we'd had no conception of. We were in the charts regularly, we had one of the best groups in the world – we knew they were special – and we were very proud of them and very protective of them.

Like The Beatles, they had a tremendous work ethic. If a hit single was needed next week, they'd just go off over the weekend and write one. Nothing got in the way of that.

Johnny Marr: There were some tabloid stories that emerged early on but they had no effect on us because in the day-to-day running of the band the only thing that mattered was the next song. The *Sun* newspaper accused us of all manner of things but it was nothing.[42] I was just happy to be in a great rock band. Things written and said about us were secondary and so far behind the issue of doing what we were doing musically. *They're the band that throw flowers* – great, but have you heard this song ...

Richard Boon: The Fall had been and gone off to make *Hex Enduction Hour* for Kamera and then come back for *Perverted By Language*, but in the interim The Smiths had arrived and I think Mark E. sensed that a new kid on the block had arrived.

Johnny Marr: A couple of bands who had been around Rough Trade a while, a couple of characters, had their noses put out of joint a bit, and I could understand that. I don't know whether it was jealousy or resentment. We'd come in like a whirlwind and to us it felt like the label became almost financially dependent on us. We did dictate to a degree the way the label was going to move. We were always aware of the imminent scare of financial difficulty, from whatever source. But no one ever looks at it from our point of view – bankrolling a label brought with it certain pressures and it was sometimes the case that we didn't get our royalties on time because the label was short. That was fine.

It was Morrissey who came up with the idea for *Hatful of Hollow*, the last thing we released in 1984. People went on to really like that album and I think it got done because we thought like fans. Collecting the B-sides and the John Peel sessions on one record was a great idea. I was quite surprised

---

42. 'The *Sun* controversy', as it was minuted, rolled on through the year and the album *The Smiths* was banned in certain major chains for a while. Rough Trade made a £400 contribution to the NSPCC over 'Suffer Little Children' and the band made a £400 payment to the mother of one of the Moors Murderers' victims.

when we put the idea forward and it was accepted because I had a traditional view of how you did things: singles, official album, singles, official album. It was breaking the mould of what a rock band did at the time and it was done in the spirit of those old Marble Arch and Decca compilations like *The World of David Bowie*. The label probably thought it was a weird idea but they were up for it and trusted us. We did two more similar albums – *The World Won't Listen* and *Louder Than Bombs*, which, for a long time, I thought was the record a person should buy if they were going to own just one Smiths album.

Geoff Travis: We were enthusiastic about releasing that record and, of course, it was so cheap to make. The radio sessions were so good that it just had to happen. A lot of people say it is their favourite album by The Smiths. All those compilations were wonderful – they were *Big Hits, High Tide* stuff, *Meaty Beaty* … They were almost like new albums and the fact they weren't called Greatest Hits albums was part of the fun. *Hatful of Hollow* had a price sticker mocking those on old budget albums, saying it was to be sold at thirty-six shillings eleven pence, or something like that.

*

Geoff Davis: At the end of 1983 I owed a lot of money to the various members of the Cartel and sometime in 1984 I went to Richard Scott and he offered to help sort it all out. I owed Rough Trade alone about £20,000 and I owed £5,000, £3,000, that kind of figure to other Cartel members. Richard offered to wipe my debt to Rough Trade and said that he would square it with the others if I handed over my accounts. So, essentially, Rough Trade took the Virgins and the HMVs and the bigger ones and the rest were divided up between Nine Mile and Red Rhino. I felt awful. I really felt as if I had failed at first, but afterwards it was just a fantastic relief. I stopped being a wholesaler and I stopped going to Cartel meetings.

I still acted as a distributor because I had the labels I was handling and I had set up Probe Plus, my own label, back in 1981. This was actually good news for my label because it meant that I could concentrate on it, something I'd largely neglected to do. In the end, my wife looked after the shop and I concentrated solely on the label and then when we split up a couple of years later I took the label and she took the shop. It just so happened that at that time, 1986, we had our biggest success with Half Man Half Biscuit who regularly topped the indie charts and sold like mad.

Richard Scott: Probe's problems all came to a head. Basically, they owed a lot of money. Tony K had been in and tried to assess the situation and he was the one who really sorted it all out: the outcome was that Geoff Davis left the Cartel. Bob Last at Fast left around the same time, about the middle of 1984. Sandy McLean took over and it went from being Fast Product to becoming Fast Forward.[43]

Sandy McLean: I'd been in retail since 1977 and had managed the two Bruce's record shops in Edinburgh. I'd been the guy behind the counter when Alan Horne tentatively walked in with a box of Postcard records and I had stored The Associates' 'Boys Keep Swinging' single on Double Hip behind the counter and fielded calls from David Bowie's publishing company who loved The Associates' version and wanted to meet them.

I knew Bob Last from when he used to come in and sell Fast Product to me and I ended up going to work for him in May 1982 when Simon who was working with him left and went back to university. I think they had all been at Leeds University or something. Simon head-hunted me for his own job and Bob and Hilary interviewed me. I turned them down twice but said yes on the third offer. From then on it was largely me at things like Cartel meetings because Bob was super-busy with bands like the Human League and preferred to hold back.

Everything went well until Bob decided to pull the plug on Fast Product around May 1984. Some time prior to that, Bob, who was an extremely astute businessman, had decided that rather than just distribute Cartel product we should operate like a One-Stop and offer major label records to independent stores as well as the indie stuff. Bob had contacts with Virgin and Island and Jive and others and so for a while we wholesaled major label stuff as well.

Bob Last: That was an experiment, which ultimately didn't work. We were doing it to see if we could bolster the business model and in terms of the independent shops we were dealing with, I didn't think they could survive

43. Rough Trade contemplated instructing its solicitor to retrieve £15,000 owed to them by Fast Product at this point.

by stocking only the things conventional record shops didn't have. The idea also reflected our ideology of audience-building in that we thought it would be great for someone to be drawn into an independent shop to buy a chart hit and become exposed to this other material. I was always thinking of ways of how to leverage other people into the market.

This wasn't, of course, Cartel strategy – I'm sure some would have argued that I was undermining the Cartel in doing this. In fact, it was done on a small scale and ultimately the margins weren't big enough. Either the margins weren't big enough or we would have to get even more serious about how we did it, and I was starting to go off the idea of distribution at this point.

Sandy McLean: We did a stock check – a quarterly one, not even a major one, and Bob decided that enough was enough. We were losing money. It was all great in theory but the figures never worked out. Just as later when Richard Powell centralised wholesale at the Cartel and gave too measly a margin to make it ever work, which was ultimately what brought down the Cartel, so our margins with the majors were unworkable.

After Bob had decided he was going to pull out, I posted our business figures down to Richard Scott and Tony K and they looked them over and decided that the business was viable. I met them in York and Tony offered to put me on the Red Rhino payroll and pay for an office in Edinburgh. We did the sales calling and then faxed over the orders to York, from where the records were despatched. It meant I was able to distribute records as well. In the morning we did the selling and in the afternoon worked on distribution from our offices at 21a Alma Street, an address found on the back of many records around that time.

There was no break in service to the shops either. As I recall, we kind of got going again over a weekend and since everybody called us Fast, and not Fast Product, I just changed the name to Fast Forward and nobody really noticed. I was still Sandy from Fast.

Bob Last: We put part of the business into administration so that Sandy and the people who had been working on it could keep it going as a concern – it purposefully went into receivership and out again – and they carried on. I cooperated to help them make it happen; after all, they had all worked very hard. I was only uncomfortable in as much as the seamless change brought about by partly retaining the name went against what we were still actively considering at the time, which was to reuse the Fast Product brand.

*

Jo Slee: Just after the miners' strike started, someone hung a painted bed sheet outside the first floor window at Collier Street which read: 'ROUGH TRADE SUPPORTS THE MINERS'. Like a lot of the political stances we supported, our action was well intentioned but I am not sure it helped sell any more copies of the 'Enemy Within' single, the record we released in support of the miners.

Simon Edwards: We did a jumble sale also where we got together a load of returns and took them and sold them off and gave the money to one of the miners' support groups.[44]

John Duguid: We got into the idea of doing a single for the miners initially as a joke. In the early days of the strike, there was a television headline on the news one night with the words 'No Ballot' and Marek and I joked about using the words in the same way that the words 'no sell-out' were used on the Malcolm X single 'No Sell-Out', which was out at that time. We would use Arthur Scargill's voice. We had a bit of fun talking about it one night but the next day we both separately realised that actually it was something worth pursuing.

Marek Kohn: I knew some people at Island Records and so initially we found our way there. The project seemed to progress very slowly and we were given a reggae producer to work with but the project didn't seem to be managed by anybody so it just drifted on. Eventually, they came up with a track to use but we didn't particularly like it.

John Duguid: What they came up with at Island Records was too dub-based, whereas I'd done a guide track to how I thought it would sound by cutting up bits of Test Department and adding some drum sounds from Public Image Limited. It was different and in fact very close to the record that

---

44. The record label also decided, in a meeting on 13 November 1984, to donate some records to the children of striking miners. It was agreed that records by Microdisney, The Smiths, Gregory Isaacs and Sandie Shaw would be appropriate.

actually got released. It felt like we were wasting time at Island and while we were working with them Dave Robinson from Stiff Records took over the management of the company. He heard it and said, '*No fucking way!*', or something like that. He may have said they'd do it but he wanted 'political balance'. It was absurd.

So I phoned up Geoff Travis to see whether he would be interested in releasing it and straight away he asked us to go in and see him. He was very receptive but when we went to see him he said he thought the backing track was rubbish and he put us in touch with Adrian Sherwood. Adrian was working with Keith le Blanc and they had a backing track that was almost note for note the same as the one I had in my mind. So it was put together very quickly after that – maybe in one or two nights – and then we got into the Rough Trade machine.

Marek Kohn: We couldn't really find the right image for the cover, so, like in *Spinal Tap* where no one in the band could agree on the cover, we went with a plain black sleeve, which obviously could be seen to represent coal. We did 'strike' badges and we had a sticker that adopted the classic 'Coal Not Dole' lettering.

John Duguid: Everything was meant to be done for free but there was a problem straight away because Rough Trade had the sticker designed and that had to be paid for, whereas we knew what we wanted – it was obvious – and I could have got that all designed for free at the union I worked for at the time. We were also bizarrely excluded from the credits on the record so it looked like the record was a Keith le Blanc single.

It was then decided that because I was working for a trades union and had various contacts in the miners' support groups, we could try to hype the record into the charts. Rough Trade would give us a list of all the chart return shops and we would tell all the people at the miners' support group to go in and buy the record in the first week and it would chart.

Marek Kohn: I remember I had a contact in Militant, the Trotskyist organisation, and I think we may have approached them but I seem to recall the contact I had didn't particularly like the record. Militant at the time were following a strategy of entryism, infiltrating the Labour Party and parasitising it, and were big in Liverpool but the members never claimed to be members – they always said they were merely selling the *Militant* newspaper.

John Duguid: The NUM made it clear that they wanted hands off. They felt they couldn't be associated with something that might be seen to be gimmicky. But they did covertly give their blessing and when I met Arthur Scargill he knew who I was and shook my hand warmly. There was an NUM official from Kent who loved the idea of hyping the record and I went to see him and played it to him. At the end all he said was, '*Jesus Christ!* I don't think I could get *anyone* to buy this.'

Richard Scott: At the height of the strike I did manage to get an appointment to see a very senior NUM official in London to talk about it, but when I turned up at their headquarters at nine o'clock one morning, the man was absolutely paralytic on the floor with colleagues trying to revive him. Basically – in an age before the internet and email – if the thing couldn't be coordinated almost immediately it wouldn't work. And it didn't.

John Duguid: I spent a long time marrying up miners groups' lists with the lists of record shops supplied by Richard, and tried to persuade people to go and buy the record and a lot of them did. The trouble was that a lot of the shops they were told to go to weren't supplied with the record. The record ended up getting to Number 152 in the chart and its catalogue number was RT152, so we sent out a communiqué – our final communiqué – saying it was all a conspiracy to suppress the record.

The conspiracy theory I now have about the hyping is that I don't think Rough Trade really gave a damn about the record. The big issue at the time for Rough Trade Distribution was that they had The Smiths on the label but couldn't get them to go with the distribution company because they didn't think Distribution was up to the job. I think the ulterior motive they had with our record was to show they could hype a record, especially an unlikely one, to persuade The Smiths to sign up with them.

Marek Kohn: Most of the money we raised we collected after the strike ended and so we gave it to Women Against Pit Closures, who were still active. I remember printing in my column in *The Face* that we raised in total something like £1,400 and I was very proud of it. It seemed a reasonable amount of money in the mid-1980s. It got a good reception, although I remember Penny Reel in the *NME* called it 'numb, clockwork funk' – I think my memory of that is quite accurate: some things just stick in the mind. A couple of weeks later, though, Richard Cook reviewed it again and made it Single of the Week.

It was our own video that we made that raised the bulk of the money. We had some scratch video pieces on it and the Duvet Brothers gave us their cut-up version of New Order's 'Blue Monday', which we didn't bother getting permission to use. It had the video for 'The Enemy Within' on it, footage of The Redskins and a Welsh NUM video narrated by Kim Howells, who went on to be a Labour minister.

There was some radio play for the record and there should have been some money from that but Richard Boon never got around to registering it for copyright because he didn't think it would get played, so we didn't get anything. Some time after, I bumped into Geoff in the street and gave him a bit of a hard time over it, but he had done his bit, the A&R-ing of it, perfectly well so wasn't in any way to blame.

Marek Kohn: They had all their internal politics because of the way the company was set up and although I was quick back then to take umbrage or identify shortcomings, probably unfairly, ultimately Rough Trade made it happen and they probably did it in the right way.

*

Richard Scott: Right in the middle of the miners' strike we had a big political hoo-ha at Rough Trade over South Africa. Jumbo Vanrennan had set up his Earthworks label, which we were to distribute, and wanted to release South African music on the label, which we would then sell. That would amount to trading with South Africa. People felt very strongly about it and quite rightly.

Richard Boon: There was a massive eruption amongst the staff over this and we had a big staff meeting, which I chaired. Jumbo and his partner came in to defend themselves. Rough Trade had a constitution and part of the constitution, apparently, said that Rough Trade supported the boycott of South African goods until South Africa was freed from the yoke of apartheid and Nelson Mandela was released. The problem wasn't the material, obviously, the problem was the handling of it.

The meeting dealt with general Rough Trade business first and when all that was done I opened the door and welcomed Jumbo and his partner in. At that moment, the entire room emptied – *everyone* got up and left. Jumbo went to Virgin and did a deal with them.[45]

Richard Scott: I was happy to subvert any regime and I thought that putting the right product in the right place could have a galvanising effect. We did talk about trading into South Africa at some point, and I can see how certain types of music, such as reggae, could be a force for good. We were never going to be selling Smiths albums or Aztec Camera albums in South Africa, so it wasn't really an issue in the case of a lot of our records. But quite rightly at Rough Trade, the feeling over Earthworks was that we should abide by the book.

Once, when we were in Blenheim Crescent, a man came in to see me and asked if we were interested in setting up routes whereby we could get stuff into South Africa as a revolutionary act. This man was training to be a lawyer and was the son of Samora Machel, the president of Mozambique. Some time later his father was killed when his plane crashed – allegedly the work of BOSS, the South African secret police – and I never heard

45. Some of the proposed releases had already gone into production when the matter blew up. In an irate statement of 10 May, Jumbo, himself a white South African, presented his case and argued that he 'hadn't lived twelve years in exile to be branded a fellow traveller of the thugs in Pretoria' and that the Rough Trade workers who had 'banned, boycotted – or should I say "blacked"' – his releases meant that the only losers in the boycott would be the black musicians. 'All reviews and specialist radio shows back up the music with hard political facts, and there is no way that this music can be of any support or succour to the fascists in Pretoria,' he argued, adding that an ANC member had said to him that 'music is going to play an important part in the future struggle'.

from him again. I always kept an eye out for Machel and noticed after his death that his widow married Nelson Mandela, thus becoming the only person in history to be the first lady of two different countries.

Throughout my time at Rough Trade I was always getting approached by wonderful and mad people who wanted help. I used to get a lot of requests from people living in countries behind the Iron Curtain who wanted records and couldn't pay for them. I must have received on and off thousands of Eastern European stamps. I always tried to send records back.[46]

*

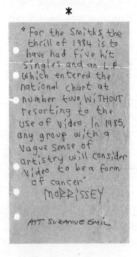

" For the Smiths, the thrill of 1984 is to have had five hit singles and an LP which entered the national chart at number two, WITHOUT resorting to the use of video. In 1985, any group with a vague sense of artistry will consider video to be a form of cancer"

MORRISSEY.

ATT SUZANNE GNIL

Johnny Marr: We released 'How Soon is Now?' at the start of 1985 and although Geoff was the man who rightly spotted that 'This Charming Man' was a single, he was less keen on 'How Soon is Now?'. It's all a balance, of course. I did three tracks over a weekend. One was 'William It Was Really Nothing'; then I wrote 'Please, Please, Please Let Me Get What I Want', both recorded on a new four-track porta-studio I'd acquired. Then, having done those two, quite short, harmonic, melodic songs, I felt like doing a long, modal, groovy song as the third track.

One of my favourite bands at the time was the Gun Club and I had this

---

46. One such letter arriving from Poland at the time read, 'Dear Mr Scott ... I have hearty request to make for you – I would like to exchange many attractive stamps from Socialist countries on the some of LPs my favourite group from your label: JOY DIVISION: *Closer*, *Unknown Pleasures*, *Still*; DEPECHE MODE: *Construction Time Again*. I am sorry to trouble you, but this is the only way for me these records to attain ... Yours ... Encl. 150 stamps'.

weird piece of lateral thinking – I remembered they'd done a Creedence Clearwater Revival song, 'Run Through the Jungle', and in my mind I was doing something similar, in a similar key and with a similar chord change. So it was me being vaguely Gun Club-ish. I got the three songs down on a cassette and sent it over to Morrissey for him to do the words. Then we went into the studio and recorded the tracks. When it came to 'How Soon is Now?', we put some red light bulbs in at the studio and got the atmosphere right, *maan*, and we created this monster through the night. I'm glad we did. It's obviously a great, great track and it was what I thought the band should be doing at that time. At that point I still felt that how far we could go was limitless; we certainly hadn't framed ourselves or backed ourselves into a corner. That song has become, incrementally, a very popular track of ours. Time has been kind to it and it has grown in stature as it has gone on.

Geoff Travis: I remember going to the studio around the time of 'How Soon is Now?' and liking it, but Johnny has previously said that I didn't like it, so one of our memories must be incorrect. I remember hearing it and thinking it was remarkable – that Bo Diddley riff was fantastic! You could say we were slow to realise it should be an A-side, but when we did, we knew it was something astonishing and flipped it and reissued it as a twelve-inch. I love the fact that Johnny has said they stayed up all night recording it, all casual like, when it is so obviously one of their finest things.

Johnny Marr: After 'How Soon Is Now?', we put out the second album. I am very proud of the fact that twenty years on people tell me that they became a vegetarian as a result of *Meat is Murder*. I think that is quite literally rock music changing someone's life – it's certainly changing the life of animals. It is one of the things I am most proud of. I think it was quirky to call the album *Meat is Murder* and it was ahead of its time, but again, we were on a label that let us do that kind of thing.

Jo Slee: *Meat is Murder* came out in February 1985 and there was a big UK tour and it was during a gig at Bristol that I turned up with copies of the new single, 'Shakespeare's Sister'. I was still in licensing but when a new single came out whoever was available would rush it to the band. There was a typo on the cover – this was back in the days when artwork was still pasted down on board and bits tended to drop off. They were absolutely furious about it. By the time of 'That Joke Isn't Funny Anymore', I'd moved into production because Morrissey spotted early on that I was a typo Nazi. And he liked that. But from that period, in early spring 1985, things were starting to bubble up and our relationship with them was starting to strain a little.

After the UK tour we had arranged a mini-tour of Europe, which included some TV appearances. There was some issue about whether they were even going to get on the plane, but they did and we eventually got to Rome, the first date, at about ten-thirty at night. We checked into the hotel and the rooms were the type of classic hotel rooms you get in Rome – all spidery and with Gestapo-style phones. No room service. The Smiths spent about thirty seconds in their rooms and then all descended on the lobby and announced they weren't staying there. I don't know who was the prima donna but it was probably Morrissey because clean, luxurious hotel rooms were dear to his heart, but by now there was quite a lot of the prima donna in all of them.

Peter Walmsley had done a fantastic licensing deal with Virgin Italy. They were interesting in that they weren't independent – we did most of our licensing deals with independent labels – but they weren't quite a major either. They had a terrific label manager who instantly found the band another hotel and we all trotted round there at about one in the morning.

The next night they were due to play in a gigantic circus tent just outside Rome to about three thousand people. Everybody in the audience lit cigarette lighters and held them up and I remember being alarmed at first, thinking, three thousand cigarette lighters held up to canvas – this could be the shortest gig in history. It was amazing. Afterwards, I asked Johnny what he thought and he was really negative about it. It seemed just like The Beatles, he said; they hadn't come to *listen* to the band, they were just thrilled to be there, as if that was a really terrible thing. I remember thinking then that he could have done with a smack.

Day three, we went to record the Italian equivalent of *Top of the Pops*. I was waiting on them hand and foot, which was kind of what you did. It was my job to keep them fed and watered, but it was thankless, and I found them increasingly irritable during this period. There was a problem with the lighting during rehearsal and I had a sense of foreboding. They had to stand around for about forty-five minutes getting restless while the problem was sorted. I went out for drinks and when I returned someone said that they had left the studio, they weren't going to do the show. This was like walking out of *Top of the Pops* on the spot – not good. The shit hit the fan and Virgin Italy dropped the Rough Trade label almost immediately. I was mortified and powerless.

Mike Hinc: I'd booked them on the European tour. Italy was difficult, not least because the promoter had lied, basically, and didn't provide what was promised to be provided. He didn't meet hospitality requirements for band or crew, which would have included hotels, and one gig was meant to be in a theatre and the theatre turned out to be a large tent. What was stupid about the whole situation was that the European tour was meant to be a warm-up for a large American tour that was starting just after. The American agent, Ian Copeland, got wind of the antics in Italy and the US tour was in jeopardy, so I flew up out to Spain, where they were going next to try to ameliorate the situation. It was very important. They were on the point of breaking in America, the biggest British band to go there since The Clash.

Jo Slee: The next morning I was flying home and they were flying to Spain to play a massive festival. I was in the hotel lobby, sitting next to Mike Joyce, when my anger poured out and I asked him if he had any idea how much effort had been put into arranging the tour. I said I felt that if I couldn't do the job properly, I might as well quit. He turned around and said, 'Well, if it's not you it will be someone else.' Coming from the drummer, that told me everything I needed to know.

They were pretty arrogant at that point. Too much too soon? I don't know. Mike and Andy seemed to just copy what Morrissey and Johnny did. Morrissey was insistent on their being treated well. And Johnny wanted all the trappings of stardom at that point, the Rolls-Royce picking him up at the door. Dealing with them was like going up the down escalator all the time and they seemed to take every excuse to sabotage what Rough Trade were doing. They seemed constantly to want to complain that we weren't doing a good job.

We had got a letter from Morrissey not long previously complaining that Rough Trade hadn't made the slightest effort to put on an end-of-tour party after the *Meat is Murder* tour. I thought, bugger that – I wrote to him and said that since nobody in The Smiths camp liked anyone at Rough Trade, what they seemed to be asking was that we put on a party for them but not bring ourselves. I didn't get a reply.

So after Italy, I came back to England and said that I didn't want to work in licensing any more and went over and started working in production. On day one, I walked in the office and Richard Boon got up and, being a prince amongst men, made me a cup of tea. Then we had a nice chat about cats.

Peter Walmsley: The Smiths arrived in Spain and I met them at the airport with their Spanish licensee who had done a tremendous job for them – they were in the charts in Spain and Portugal. Between the airport and central Madrid they managed to switch hotel.

Mike Hinc: When I got to Spain what The Smiths were now doing was trying to avoid Scott Piering, who had been managing them for a bit and who they now didn't want as a manager. So the first thing they wanted to do was change hotels, so that no one could contact them. As the booker, I *had* to do it for them.

Peter Walmsley: We had a huge press conference lined up and we hadn't got a clue where they were. They finally turned up, hating us, and we did the press conference and then went on to the venue. Once at the venue, Johnny and Andy wanted their supplies, so we had to go out and get them, and then of course we were all friends again. That kind of thing really stuck in the craw a bit. It was probably the tour from hell for them and, to be fair, they went on and played a fantastic show. On stage, they were great, superb deliverers.

Mike Hinc: Things, amazingly, got better. We went to a venue where there was a catwalk leading out into the audience, which Morrissey was supposed to walk down. No way. I got the promoter aside and explained that he wasn't a model. I explained to the promoter that The Smiths had had a bad experience in Italy and that this wasn't a good introduction to Europe for them. Could he help as much as possible and we promised to put on a good show.

The promoter suddenly stood up tall – he looked like something out of the Fabulous Furry Freak Brothers, with hair down to his arse – loudly clicked his heels together in military fashion and said, 'We understand you English because unlike the Italians we are both military nations.' After that, everything went smoothly on the Spanish tour. I was pleased, if a little nonplussed.

The next morning, Scott had found out which hotel we were in and was waiting in the foyer. It was all very difficult. He was my friend. Nobody in the band wanted to talk to him. Scott and I went off and did a museum tour together.

At this time, nothing was likely to be good enough for the band, in spite of everyone promising them the world. Everyone was waiting for something to happen and nobody knew what it would be. But it was a result of everything that happened to them that made them the band they were, and I think they knew what they were doing – getting themselves into a situation and then poking it to see if it moved.

*

Richard Boon: Richard Powell had introduced this concept of 'the Model'. The Model basically shifted business from the idea that we packed up records and sent them on to somebody who then unpacked them and sent them on to somebody else, to one where the stuff was sent out centrally.

Richard Scott: It seemed to me bleeding obvious that it saved money and was more efficient to send records, direct without the Cartel member in between – it was unarguable logic, as I said at the time. But I hadn't set up the Cartel for that reason – I'd set it up so that someone in Leamington Spa could work in the music business and be a part of what was going on. Of course, the business model changed and it was inevitable that the ideal would have to alter. The discussions started about centralisation but, as with everything to do with Rough Trade, it took a long time before anything was actually implemented.[47]

Simon Edwards: The Model was all about handling stock differently, perhaps a bit more professionally. Eventually, it all went through the Cartel but was

---

47. A number of potentially grandly conceived papers were prepared around this time – 'The Model', 'Further Thoughts on the Model', 'Thoughts on the Model and the Future' – and were presented outlining the way the Model would be introduced. A coordinated sell-in to major chains was one of the specific major aims, although keeping the Cartel's regional system was also an aim. Centralisation of as much 'pulling, packing, invoicing, receiving, and accounting as possible' was another. Reference was made to the Cartel being 'the gift of the feudal lord' who was able to 'giveth and take away'. Lack of communication between members was seen to be a fault in the present system and the financial difficulties Rough Trade endured in terms of the Mute debt, which, by the middle of 1985, was still being repaid £8,500 per month, was also an issue. The very real and emotive question of whether or not staff would be surrounded by boxes of records was left 'to each individual to think about', curiously. There was great resistance to the Model from Revolver, Nine Mile and Red Rhino following a Cartel meeting in June. The thoughts of Fast, Probe and Backs were not known at that point but would have been hostile. But Rough Trade had such enormous power, it would always win the day.

coordinated centrally by Tim Niblett, who had worked for Nine Mile, and the head reps who worked out of Collier Street. Orders were faxed in and records got sent out centrally.

Robin Hurley: Critical path was one of the cliché phrases bandied around Rough Trade at this time and it was the 'critical path' that would enable us to establish 'the Model'. In essence, there were six warehouses and the view from Rough Trade was that there should be one. It all became a lightning rod for the Cartel because to some degree it spelt the end of true independence. Shop orders were faxed down to London and the records were shipped out from there.

Nine Mile had a lot more belief in it being the right way to go than some others had. It was all about handling stock. Also by then there was a move to taking distribution stock from labels on consignment rather than firm sale, which it previously had been. The Cartel meetings got very fractious over the issue but the Model was eventually – if in some cases reluctantly – accepted. For some people it was the beginning of the end, instead of what it should have been – the start of a marvellous future.

Sandy McLean: The whole thing just got chopped down the middle – wholesale got taken away and the Cartel members got to keep distribution. There was a moment when we tried to join the game rather than making our own game and that was where it eventually all went wrong. I mean, Rough Trade was a brand, a *philosophy*, and if they'd concentrated on that and concentrated less on wanting to be the next Virgin or Island, who knows where it might have led. One of the other problems was that Mute always had so much stock stored at Collier Street, it was crazy. Hundreds of thousands of records there – free storage – and nobody had the guts to tell Daniel Miller to move it.

Johnny Appel: I could see the logic of centralisation – everyone singing from the same hymn sheet and all that – but what I couldn't accept was that we had invested in a business which they just took away. What the Lord giveth, he did indeed take away ... We got an extra discount for our troubles. It took years to properly come in but straight away centralisation led to a demotivation. That joy that every punter knows about in taking a record home and removing it from the bag and savouring it before putting it on the turntable was similar to that felt by the people selling it. Once the physical product was removed from the system, people stopped caring.

*

Geoff Travis: There was a big issue over 'That Joke Isn't Funny Anymore' because that was the first time when I had said to Morrissey that I didn't think a proposed song was good enough to be a single, and he just disagreed. This was our first musical disagreement. I felt it was a good album track but that it wasn't a worthy track in the tradition of those classic Smiths singles. It was Morrissey momentarily losing his artistic focus, rather than suffering any diminishment in his powers. I made my point and then agreed to release the record, because ultimately I had to back them. But I think my argument was justified: it charted unusually low.

Johnny Marr: I know Geoff occasionally had concerns that singles were coming a little bit too quickly and he did sometimes tell us that something might not be the hit we thought it was going to be. To his credit, though, he would never decline to release something. There was an issue over 'That Joke Isn't Funny Anymore' where not enough records were pressed or something, but to be honest I never really cared about how high the record went in the charts anyway. As long as I had a copy of the seven-inch and my mates did too, I was happy.

Jo Slee: I had gone over to production at the time of 'That Joke Isn't Funny Anymore' and working with Richard on those Smiths records was a real act of brinkmanship: he'd order too few and I would order too many. Between us we usually just about got it right. The problem was that with no firm sale policy you couldn't win. They'd ship ridiculous amounts to get a chart position and then a few weeks later get loads of them back. I'm sure there still exists, in a warehouse somewhere, pallet-loads of them. The Smiths usually went into the chart high and then dropped down quickly. It wasn't often that the singles hung around, although 'Panic', with its 'hang the DJ' chorus, I seem to remember, sold over 100,000 and stayed in the charts for about six weeks. I don't know why we did so many singles – probably because Morrissey is a completist and would have wanted to own everything on a single ...

I joined production at an odd time because not long after, Rough Trade's relationship with the band went seriously wrong and we were told that they were leaving us and signing somewhere else.

Geoff Travis: The first intimation of problems would have been the sense of the growing distance that developed between us. They never specifically said to me that they wanted to leave – that wouldn't be their way. Even when a problem first became apparent, I didn't take it too seriously because I knew that they were always surrounded by the utmost chaos and this was likely to be another example of it.[48]

The way I saw it was that they had made a legal move, by sending us a solicitor's letter, and that in turn called for the correct response. If I had felt that Rough Trade had let The Smiths down in any fundamental way, I'd have probably said, fine, goodbye and good luck. But I was convinced we had done a brilliant job for them – not always in the most ideal of circumstances in the sense that there was always an absence of management, which meant we were often their unpaid management by default.

It seems to me that a relationship between a record label and its artists is very strange and not at all a paradigm: in almost every case, the situation is different. Some people are close to the label and some people are very distant. The thought must have entered The Smiths' mind that they had led the label into unchartered waters and they were thrilled by that, but also they might have thought that they were now better than the label. Egged on by other people, courted, the grass looked greener elsewhere. That is so often the peculiar by-product of success. I think they were displacing internal problems.

Jo Slee: We all heard that they were shopping for a new deal. Once the letter arrived from the solicitors, the gloves were off. Geoff did really well in the way he handled the situation. It took a lot to make Geoff angry, but when he was angry you knew about it. And in this case he was very decisive.

By now Johnny hated Rough Trade, and the feeling was that Morrissey deferred to him. Morrissey demanded of us everything that needed to be done to support their success; he absolutely fought for all we needed to do, and he was right. But whereas Johnny, I think, in those days was susceptible

48. According to a copy of the deed of settlement signed on 18 April 1986, The Smiths had 'by way of letter from the Artists' solicitors' dated 16 May, contended that their original agreement from 1 June 1983 had terminated. The band wished to leave Rough Trade *before*, presumably, they even began work at Jacob's Farm on their masterpiece, *The Queen is Dead*. On 10 July 1985, Rough Trade issued proceedings and an injunction was granted on 20 December. Under the terms of the injunction, the master tapes of *The Queen is Dead* were to be delivered to Rough Trade's solicitors.

to flattery, Morrissey was different – he knew he was born a queen bee.

Johnny Marr: What Rough Trade and the band were trying to be was the biggest guitar rock/pop band on an indie label with no experience of having worked a big guitar pop band. So, you can't be too unkind to them. The main thing was that studio time was always at a minimum, and for me that was a bit of a problem. John Porter and I were always leaving the studio at 9 or 10 a.m., really under the gun, having to mix two or three songs, one of which was expected to be a big hit, following another big hit, in the night. Sometimes I felt we were trying to scale greatness while someone else was worried about . . . us getting out the studio the next day.

There was self-consciousness before going in to make *The Queen is Dead* because we were being called the sun and the moon and the stars by everybody and the saviours of rock music, and we *wanted* to be the saviours of rock music, so it was quite an ambition. I just remember when all of that was a realisation for me and for five or ten seconds I stood in my kitchen in Manchester and thought, *right, OK*. We had a few pretty good tunes hanging around – we had 'The Boy With the Thorn in His Side' and I had the riff to 'Bigmouth Strikes Again' worked out, and Morrissey had written 'There Is a Light . . .' and 'Frankly, Mr Shankly' and 'Cemetery Gates'. So right there we had five pretty good tunes to record. It wasn't an entirely blank canvas, but I knew we wanted to do something pretty classic.

When we finished the album I felt we had done the best we could and we had made a record that we really liked, which is always the criteria. There was obviously pressure on us, a sense that we were going to be judged, but that has to be put in perspective – we could only put ourselves through the hoops – no one ever needed to tell us to raise the bar, we were always capable of doing that on our own. It was good, it was good to go, we were pretty jubilant.

Jo Slee: It took a long time before anything seemed to progress. The injunction was not granted until just before Christmas and it was served personally on Morrissey. We had put a lot of work in. I was quite emotionally involved with them and I was sorry and sad at the prospect that we might lose them – it always felt that working with them was something worth doing. Then what happened was – deadlock for six months or so.

CHAPTER ELEVEN:

1986–87

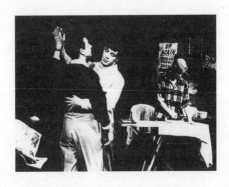

'Wear sunglasses indoors at all times — *tick* done
that'

Queen is Dead delay – Legal wrangle – Resolution – ACAS report – Equal
pay ended – Jeannette Lee – Workers' trust – Smiths leaving

Johnny Marr: The story of what happened is simple and sadly not as interesting as people think it is. We'd been together with Rough Trade for a long time, very tight. The band had had no manager so the two principal members of the group were dealing with the label and, like any relationship when you are very close and you are spending a lot of time together, things got blown out of proportion from both sides.

We had a couple of people around us who had given us bad and negative advice and had told us that we were out of contract. To be fair to us, and maybe to those people, what you tend to do when you have success is think you need to expand. Maybe that was also at the back of our minds. We'd put all these records out on Rough Trade; maybe now we could have a relationship with EMI which would be the same. We'd still put records out with integrity, we'd still do our own sleeves, blah, blah, blah, we wouldn't turn into a majors band, we would be exactly as we were.

I don't remember specific thoughts, I just remember the negativity towards Rough Trade which was basically the band throwing a fit and this lawyer shopping for a deal for us, which we didn't have the right to do, and then Rough Trade saying we owed them a couple more albums. We were in the middle of making *The Queen is Dead* when it all blew up and I don't know how Rough Trade found out about what we were doing but it caused a stand-off.

Simon Edwards: This had a direct impact on our financial planning, of course, on the critical path, which presumed we would have some sales stock. This was a big worry at the time because The Smiths accounted for a large amount of turnover.[49]

Geoff Travis: I didn't feel any sense of betrayal over what was happening. I was more concerned to get the relationship back on track. It was clear that *The Queen is Dead* was amazing, a major statement, and, like everyone, I just wanted it released.

Johnny Marr: We had, of course, never said that we were going to take *The Queen is Dead* to EMI, so serving an injunction on the album ... I don't know where they thought they were going to take that one. If you ask them, people at Rough Trade would talk about it in much more sombre tones; but it was a serious situation.

I remember we had a rare weekend break and I went back up to Manchester on the Friday. On the Saturday, I was sitting with my guitar technician, who used to live with us, and we were getting pretty laid-back and enjoying some refreshment. It got to about one o'clock in the morning when I just got myself so wound up I said to him, 'Right, come on, we'll go and get the master tapes, we'll go and liberate our soon-to-be-classic album from the clutches of the mad.'

49. An undated report from the time, 'THE EFFECTS ON ROUGH TRADE AND THE CARTEL OF ENDING OUR RELATIONSHIP WITH THE SMITHS', outlined the worry the wrangle would have on the future stability of the Cartel. The sales structure of the Cartel had been developed on the understanding that The Smiths would be a long-term project. Their departure would lead to redundancies, a loss in confidence with Rough Trade Distribution by other labels, and a potentially imposed retreat from those outlets such as Woolworths, W. H. Smith, and Boots, all of whom had become more open to Cartel product on the back of the success of The Smiths.

So, we got in the car and set out for Guildford in a blizzard of snow. It was already hazardous before we even got out of Manchester and it took us about seven hours to get to Surrey. We got there about nine o'clock in the morning. Luckily, the kitchen door of the studio was open so in I went, having said to my guitar technician to leave the engine running for a speedy getaway. I rummaged around trying to find the tape cupboard.

I think someone had seen us and phoned up the owner, who turned up, so I just came clean to him and told him that Rough Trade had injuncted the album, which I couldn't accept, and that I would just get the tapes and be out of his face. He told me he would have to speak to the label and I told him if he did that then I wouldn't work at the studio again. He stood his ground. I was lucky really that he turned up and not the cops. That was the end of my pirate adventure. I had to drive back up to Manchester for the next five or six hours. What felt like a good idea at one o'clock in the morning didn't come to anything. I'm glad it didn't really.

Jo Slee: The lawyers argued for four months while we got more and more desperate. We knew from the injunction that we had some right on our side, so it was a case of us grinding our teeth and standing by while lawyers made lots of money. I was talking to Morrissey at this time; in fact, I'd tell him where we were up to on our side, and he would tell me about where they were up to on theirs. A further frustration was that Geoff was very proprietary about it all and we were only allowed to find out legal information through him. It did feel sometimes as if Geoff deferred to the lawyers in the most aggravating way. On one occasion when Geoff was away on business, Peter Walmsley, who had trained as a lawyer and knew that lawyers worked for you and not the other way around, rang up our lawyers and gave them hell. When Geoff found out about this he accused Peter of being ungracious, but I knew that if Peter was on the case something would happen, because Peter tended not to take no for an answer. The opportunity arose when Geoff went to America.

Every time we were close to reaching agreement it seemed The Smiths' lawyer would raise further objections – a smokescreen. That seemed to be a tactic. So, at about 9 o'clock one night, while Geoff was in America, when we thought we were finally close to a resolution, Will, Peter and I were looking over yet more objections sent in at the eleventh hour. Will was always very good at demystifying the substance of the various disputes. We were desperate. I asked Will if the current niggles were material to the contract and he said he didn't think that they were; they were things that could be sorted out later. I said, 'Would I be justified in ringing Morrissey up and telling him this?'

Morrissey was, I imagine, pretty desperate himself at this point. When he finished a record he wanted it released the next day and we were approaching a very long time without a Smiths record out. If the dispute dragged on too much longer it would mean the release date for the album would get pushed near the Christmas period and might get lost in the glut of releases.

I phoned Morrissey and told him about the further objections and he said that he appreciated all we had done and that my calls had helped keep him sane in the bad times. I gave him all the reasons why The Smiths and Rough Trade would be the only losers if the thing dragged on. I was always completely, even compulsively, frank with him. We all went home and about eleven o'clock that night Morrissey rang back very angry and very determined: 'Please can someone, preferably Peter, bring the contract over tomorrow morning and we'll sign.'

Peter Walmsley: I went to see them with the contract and it was probably the first time Morrissey had properly acknowledged me. The whole thing had been a really silly argument. It was not only soul-destroying but it put the whole company at risk. It always amused me, though, that they were able to release singles while proclaiming to the world how awful we were.

The problem Geoff had over the matter was that to an extent his head had to be turned two ways. He didn't like confrontation, anyway. But he had to be a friend of the band without being seen to be their lackey. He was, after all, their voice to the record label, and at the same time he had a responsibility to the record label to act in the right way.

Jo Slee: The agreement was signed by Morrissey, Johnny and Peter Walmsley. We hit the ground running and had a single out, 'Bigmouth Strikes Again', and the album all within about eight weeks. I was happily able to go and take the tapes to the CBS cutting room where, several months earlier, I had prematurely placed an order for *The Queen is Dead* to be cut. The engineer, Tim Young, pointed to a mangy cup of coffee which had been made for me and had been sitting on the side for about three months. They certainly hadn't been holding their breath on the job. Tim said to me, 'I just put it in the microwave once a week in case you show up.'

Johnny Marr: The Smiths had a shark of a lawyer – I don't say that with pride because the shark bit us and ended up biting everybody, but it wasn't like we were steaming in there kicking Rough Trade around. It was just that we were told we were out of contract and we weren't, and the band ended up paying the price for it.

*

Johnny Marr: My role in the band was particularly difficult by 1986 because we had just got so big. I was writing the music and producing the music and performing the music and being a human being which, at twenty-three or whatever age I was, was plenty for me to be doing, on top of which I had to run the band internally in the way that I had done since I was eighteen or nineteen. But whereas when I had been eighteen or nineteen, it was a couple of days working for Joe to get some train fare to go to rehearsal, or to be able to give Andy some money for his bus fare, now everything was on a bigger scale. It was a major job just getting our gear from one place to another, having to book assistants for the tours, whilst all the time just wanting to make masterpieces.

I was drinking, but it wasn't some tragedy where I was left sprawling over my amplifiers like I was in some Jim Morrison biopic – it was nothing like that. But it was serious because I was doing the stuff and not taking care of myself. From being a kid I'd had a checklist – form a great rock 'n' roll band in Manchester – *tick*, done that; make a really great forty-five with a navy blue label like the Rolling Stones – *tick*, done that; wear sunglasses indoors at all times – *tick*, done that; crash a big car without a licence – *tick*, done that; make a classic album and drink loads of brandy – *tick*, *tick*, done, done.

I think what I was doing was being like a working-class rock star really. But never at the expense of the work because it is bullshit if the work isn't any good, it's just decadent crap. But if the work is good, which ours always was, then that is all it is about – the rest is just a story.

I wasn't in physically good shape because eating wasn't a big concern of mine and never had been – I was a stick when I joined the band. The thing about young men is that they are not very good at taking care of themselves and they are certainly not very good at taking care of each other, and at that time in 1986 I am a songwriter in what according to some people is the biggest or best rock band in the country or world and really that was enough of a job for me.

We didn't have a manager. Had we had an older or wiser overseer, that would have been really useful – on a business and on a personal level it would have solved so many problems. That lack of a calming, organising presence led to a lot of chaos and a lot of drama and a lot of neurosis and ultimately the band's demise, but it also led to some really good music and I would rather have had the music with the drama than some boring twenty-five-year career.

I did also feel worry about Andy's heroin situation. That was a worry for him and a worry for the band because of the dynamic of the band. I wasn't judgemental about it because I came from a council estate and I'd seen plenty of stuff before the band was even formed – we were shitkickers really, shitkickers with brains.

I certainly didn't want Andy to have to go but instinctively I knew things would get worse, that they weren't going to magically one day get better, and they did get worse, and we had to ask him to leave the band. That to me was cataclysmic, one of the worst things that ever happened in my world, but looking back now, we never played a gig without him, we never replaced him. That's how close we were, that's how tight. I think he was officially out of the band for twelve days, in spite of what some so-called pop historians have later claimed. It was twelve days that felt like twelve months, twelve days of torture for us and probably worse for him.

Ultimately, we had to have him back because we were a family. We were nice guys, too, because Craig Gannon who had joined to replace Andy – well, we didn't have the heart to say, 'False alarm, you were in The Smiths, now you're not, give us back your *Jim'll Fix It* medal,' so we said pick up a guitar and become the second guitar player. And luckily for us he was a very able guitar player and the band went through another kind of interesting, accidental chapter musically live because the shows we played were pretty great, super-intense as I've recently discovered.

Jo Slee: The period after the dispute was resolved was, I think, one of the happiest periods of all for us and our relationship with the band. I think Johnny was still determined to sign with someone else but at least he knew when he could do it now. We all started to pull in the

same direction. Problems were easily resolved. I remember just before
releasing 'Bigmouth Strikes Again', Morrissey was in favour of a different
A-side, and Geoff was in favour of still another, but they both deferred
to Johnny as musical director, as they should have done. And when *The
Queen is Dead* came out, we won a *Music Week* award for Best Independent
LP Campaign.

Morrissey gave me a special thank you on the sleeve of 'Panic'. I think
that was his way of acknowledging our work towards resolving the dispute.
We got on well with him. Richard Boon had made a couple of tiny errors
with the artwork but I just had to get it right and Morrissey liked that.
We'd get new artwork roughs in from Morrissey and then I took on the
Pinkerton's Detective Agency job of tracking down who was in the picture
or who had the rights. We had some initial refusals from people Morrissey
wanted to use on record sleeves – Harvey Keitel, as I recall. Gracious but
cautious. We wanted to use Colin Campbell, who was in the 1963 film, *The
Leather Boys* with Rita Tushingham, and we got an initial yes, but then
I think we got a no, probably over money. The producer Raymond Stross
owned the rights to the still and I rang him in LA, where he lived, and
I remember him saying, 'Have you *seen* Colin lately – does he still sulk?'
The theatre and film people treated you as if they'd known you for years. It
was all so wonderfully lovey. Their agents, however, were sometimes, by
contrast, abrasive and suspicious. Richard Boon and I, between us,
managed to forget to clear the use of a photo of the late Yootha Joyce with
the representatives of her estate, although we had obtained the requisite
TV clearance. Her agent accused us of everything from theft to exploiting
the deceased, and was barely mollified by our donation to a charity on her
behalf.

Albert Finney at first declined, but a couple of years later, to Morrissey's
delight, agreed. Sadly, the still was never used. Occasionally we ran into
difficulties of scale with big film companies. I once offered a representative
from Turner Films $300 for the use of a still of Rita Tushingham in *A Taste
of Honey*, and he said, '$300? What's that – lunch?'

*

Richard Scott: ACAS came in to do a study of Rough Trade's cooperative
structure with regard to employee relations in April 1986 and I think they
must have been suggested by the Greater London Enterprise Board, who
we had worked closely with. I remember some of us were interviewed and

all asked to fill in a questionnaire which asked all sorts of questions about how we felt at the time.[50]

Nineteen eighty-six was really the start of the whole middle-management thing being put properly in place and I think that was when equal pay was finally abolished. In fact, equal pay across the whole company ended in December 1983, according to a record I recently looked at. At that point, or at the start of 1984, somebody employed was being paid more. I knew nothing about this. I definitely thought that equal pay did need to end – I think that had run its course by this time and changes were needed.

Jo Slee: I had some real problems in that at a certain point I was £10,000 in debt and finding it really hard to live on £7,800. I thought about resigning and said that I needed more money. Geoff was really supportive about this and he had a meeting with Will, which I think was quite heated. Anyway, he came back and said that Rough Trade would be paying me £11,000 a year, which is what I'd worked out I needed to live on to pay the mortgage

50. The report noted that staff were motivated by the ideal of a cooperative, 'real or perceived', and were willing to put forward fresh ideas, work long hours and endure some dilapidated working conditions. A lack of personal organisation was evident, but not considered unusual. Due to the introduction of 'middle management' there was, however, now 'little contact between widely varying parts of the organisation'. It recognised the sacrosanct nature of the staff meeting, which had traditionally been the 'supreme body' in the eyes of most employees but pointed out the weakness that it could no longer carry its responsibilities in major decisions, which resided now with those who 'controlled the firm's capital and faced the firm's debitors and creditors'. Some of the staff were less concerned with equal pay and more concerned with the 'sense of failure from great ideals' brought about by no longer being able to run Rough Trade in a fully democratic way. But 'for a true cooperative to survive in its purest form it would have to be (a) very small and (b) free from competition ...' Such conditions 'would never pertain in the record industry, or in the alternative music industry where there will always be those willing to break into existing markets, or exploit new music opportunities'. It was noted also that cooperatives did tend to ultimately develop management structures, 'a road Rough Trade had started to go down', one that had led to the 'admission of failure syndrome' noted above. It concluded that staff goodwill was low in places, but not necessarily wholly due to the question of democracy: it was partly due to the stresses of living on an income that was below market rate. It also stated: 'The rise of middle management is resented, because it brings with it shades of authoritarianism.' The company was realigning its management methods, and pay differentials were about to come in. In some respects, this was written confirmation of the end of the cooperative ideal for Rough Trade. The workers' trust introduced the following year, in 1987, was important because it brought closure, an appropriate end to the experiment, but it was something of a pyrrhic victory in many ways.

and buy milk. I think it was pretty obvious to everyone that equal pay in our situation, in a company of that size in an increasingly competitive high-risk market, was ultimately unsustainable.[51]

*

Jeannette Lee: I used to hang out at Vivien Goldman's flat at 145a Ladbroke Grove and have a vivid recollection of being there one day while *Top of the Pops* was on TV and The Smiths were performing. I can't remember what the song was but it stopped me in my tracks. That was the first time that something had had that kind of effect on me in ages. That was some time, though, before I even thought about going to work at Rough Trade.

I'd liked music from a very early age – from about the age of eleven, I think. No one else in my family had the same interests. We had an old, plastic, portable record player that I used to take up to my bedroom. I'd sit in there obsessing over the records I was listening to. At first it was reggae. I started secondary modern around about the time of the skinheads – 1970 – and I remember reggae really capturing my imagination. School seemed to be going through a phase of loosening up – for instance, I don't think we really had a uniform as such – and I remember the boys wearing tonic suits, steel combs in their back pockets sharpened ready for action, steel-capped Doc Martens, crew cuts. Boys like these boys went on to be called racists, and undoubtedly some of them were, but I remember them obsessing over their reggae and at the house parties we would have, the boys would lead the dancing. We'd probably call it line dancing now, but that's what the skinheads would do – all dance in a line to something like 'Monkey Man'.

After reggae, I think the next thing I got into was Tamla Motown. When I look back now, of course, it was songs and productions I was hearing, great productions, and although I didn't necessarily recognise them I did, from a very early age, understand the structures of a song. I think of great radio when I think of Tamla Motown. I used to get ready for school listening to the radio back at a time, of course, when people

---

51. *Melody Maker* had run a scurrilous article in November 1986, 'Rough Deal', contending that Rough Trade's cooperative status was maintained purely so it could obtain financial assistance from Islington council. It pointed out a prevalent yob culture among staff, and claimed staff would be sacked in the run-up to Christmas due to the financial difficulties the company was in. In an irate telex, Richard Scott refuted the allegations, claiming Rough Trade were in the black and that Christmas, 'a capitalist concept', was of no concern to them.

listened to the radio more, and I'd be getting ready listening to Martha Reeves and The Vandellas or some other great artist blaring out full blast. Sunday was also a great radio day for me – nothing to do, the most depressing day of the week! The great thing about radio back then was you never knew what you were going to hear – today it is so much more compartmentalised.

As a teenager, the next phase I went through was glam but around the same time dancing suddenly became a big obsession for me. I'd be fourteen, fifteen. I have no idea where we got the money but my mates and I often went to clubs after school – I lived in Islington, so getting into the centre of town was no problem. It would be the Lyceum on a Monday night, Hammersmith Palais on a Thursday night, Whisky A Go-Go at the weekends. I guess it was cheap, I mean we certainly didn't drink alcohol or anything like that.

I have always been small and I looked younger than I was but we always seemed to get into the venues – the boys always had much more trouble than us and were often grilled about their ages. I think the Wag was really the only questionable one in that the other two venues were really discos for young people. There were other places as well – the big discos at the Mecca ballrooms were always great, and there was a venue in Waterloo called the Birds' Nest and one in West Hampstead, too, where they played almost exclusively black music. We'd go to these places – no drugs, no drink – and dance for about three hours virtually non-stop.

It was just at the tail end of my going-out-and-dancing-my-socks-off period that I met Don Letts, in 1975. I met him at the Lyceum. My boyfriend's sister and her friends all used to talk about this *bad guy* that she had been out with who you would not want to go near. So I knew him by repute first. One day I was at the Lyceum when Labelle played a showcase and during a break in the show I was sitting on the side of the stage waiting for the music to start when this crazy-looking guy came up to me and tried to muscle into my space. 'My feet are killing me,' he said, pulling off a pair of amazing winklepickers. He was incredibly striking – three earrings in each ear, masses of make-up and an outrageous see-through plastic mac. He was also rude, I thought, butting in like that, but as I started to walk off in a huff, he just kept trying to get a conversation going with me and to my amazement, it turned out he was the Don, the bad boy everybody was talking about.

Don Letts: I don't remember too much about Labelle, all I remember is Jeannette. She was very attractive and had a very individual style. Later, as I got to know her, I realised it was all wrapped up in shed-loads of attitude as well. She was always very forthright with her opinions, something you can only be if you've got taste, and she had that as well. I really found her fascinating, even at that early age. She was eager and open to information.

Jeannette Lee: I asked Don where he got his coat from and he told me that he sold them on the stall he was working on in the King's Road and that I should go and see him there. Acme Attractions was initially a stall but they were in the process of moving down into the basement of Antiquarius and becoming a shop. I went to the shop the following weekend and not only did he show me the coats but decided that I would be the perfect person to help him run Acme. So that's what I did – I dropped out of school, or at least didn't bother with college, and went to work with Don. It felt so like the right thing to do and it was the first time I had met anybody as obsessive about music as me.

Don Letts: Like many young, white, working-class kids, Jeannette was possibly looking for a new expression or spirit of rebellion and found herself enamoured of black music, and in particular reggae. I was coming from the other direction. I grew up with black music and took it for granted, and was coming towards the music my white mates were listening to at school –

like Captain Beefheart, Cream and The Nice. Unlike the working-class whites who had more or less deserted their white musical culture for black musical culture, I was juggling both. But Jeannette and I made our connection through reggae.

Jeannette Lee: Most people walking down the King's Road at that time were wearing jeans bought from Jean Machine, but people who wanted to know about us would find us out. We sold old stock from the 1950s and 1960s. But when that dried up we had to have our own made and we found a tailor that Malcolm McLaren and Vivienne Westwood used and they made us these amazing peg trousers and zoot suits. Everything was brightly coloured – pinks and baby blues. We had two-tone winklepickers. A pair of trousers cost eighteen pounds – the same as I earned a week for working at Acme.

I remember people like Rod Stewart, Elton John and Rudolf Nureyev coming in and Bob Marley used to come in all the time. Nureyev was very sweet and Rod Stewart was, well, quite ludicrous-looking, as I recall. People were curious but the fact that we were in a basement made it quite uncomfortable for them in the sense that we would see them appearing from their feet up to their heads and they couldn't really see us at all until they were at the bottom of the stairs. Spindly legs would come down the stairs, then a bit of cape and finally the person would materialise as Rod Stewart. I think some people thought it was meant to be an art gallery. But Don would be in his trademark shades and could look and be quite intimidating. Entering Acme was a bit like going down a catwalk. Reggae or, by 1976, punk would be blaring out from the speakers and, of course, we had a motorbike in the middle of the room.

I went from spending my time on a council estate to being right in the centre of a hotspot for freaks. Of course, I didn't see them as freaks; I looked up to them. Acme became a kind of meeting place for the more interesting and unusual people. The first wave of interesting people, I would say, were the Alternative Miss World crowd, people like Duggie Fields and Andrew Logan, and then of course with Too Fast To Live Too Young To Die just around the corner some of the more interesting people involved with punk rock started coming in.

Don Letts: People came in to Acme Attractions for one of three reasons – to hear the heavy dub reggae that was pounding out, to buy the clothes, or, to be honest, to see Jeannette and possibly try and chat her up. We were like good cop/bad cop. I'd be in my dark glasses, pretty standoffish, while Jeannette would be very approachable, very *naturally* approachable.

Jeannette Lee: I'd heard of this mythical person Malcolm – everyone seemed to have heard of Malcolm McLaren – but he was in New York when I started at Acme and it was Vivienne Westwood who I first met, that was probably in 1975. She'd been friends with Don earlier on but after a while I think she saw us as competition and stopped coming to the shop. I remember being awestruck, somewhat, at Vivienne. When I met her she was wearing a flesh-coloured body suit made entirely out of rubber. She was so uncompromising and everybody, at least in our world, was very impressed with her. I've said previously that Patti Smith was the first person to have a real influence on me, but thinking about it, in fact it was Vivienne Westwood.

Don Letts: There really wasn't any other woman like Jeannette, maybe Chrissie Hynde, who came in the shop a lot, came close. Vivienne Westwood really got her respect through being a lot older than those around her. Jeannette had that at sixteen.

It was Jeannette who jumped head first into the new scene. She was looking for that. I was reticent about it – not least because along comes this thing and it is stealing Jeannette's attentions from me. Before that, I was the man. I already had my rebellious soundtrack through reggae. Punk enabled the whites to get similarly tooled up.

Jeannette Lee: The Sex Pistols would come in a lot, but for some reason I think Don felt threatened by them. He could be unfriendly, particularly towards Sid, who I think he had a run-in with. Sid was just so goofy in those early days and quite soft: he came in with a magazine one day – *Honey* or *19* – and showed me a picture of Bryan Ferry and asked me how he could get his hair like Ferry's. He wanted me to go into great detail about how it could be achieved. He was utterly charming and I think pretty quickly the rift with Don went away and we were all great mates.

Jeannette and Sid at Acme

The Acme accountant was Andy Czezowski, a very straight man who one day came in and said that he and his wife were going to open a punk club and call it the Roxy. Andy asked Don to be the DJ on the grounds, I think, that he didn't know anybody else who could deejay.

I think I must have gone to the Roxy almost every night it was open and quite often we'd all end up back at Don's flat in Forest Hill afterwards. There would be a gang of us that included Don, Don's brother Desmond, Leo Williams, who was later in Big Audio Dynamite, Tony, or T, who was in Basement 5, a guy called JR, a guy called Jo and Dennis Morris, the photographer. They were all black – sometimes I think people tend to think of Don as the only black guy at the Roxy.

Don Letts: I'd never deejayed in my life. When I started at the Roxy there weren't that many punk records out and that's why I played so much dub reggae. In fact, when the punk records started coming out more, the punters asked me to not cut down on the reggae, which they preferred. I think Jon Savage once said that the reason the punks at the Roxy loved the reggae so much was because seventy-five per cent of the bands that played there were so terrible that the audience was grateful for this beautiful, spacious dub music they heard in between.

I told my black Rasta friends about the gig at the Roxy and asked them if they wanted to come and they all burst out laughing. They had a very tabloid view of punk. But when they did come down to the Roxy, they saw something different. They saw a lot of young, scantily clad women and an untapped herb market. Then they all wanted to come and work there. In the end, the Roxy was staffed by me and my five Rasta brethren. Desmond was on the door, Leo, JR and T were behind the bar, and Jo was the bouncer.

The thing about punks was that they were useless at making spliffs, so we used to pre-make them at home and sell them behind the bar.

Jeannette and I lived in Forest Hill and a lot of these guys used to come back there after the Roxy. There'd be punks, Rastas, anybody who didn't want the night at the Roxy to end and we'd sit at home and play music or watch bits of *The Punk Rock Movie*, which I'd started making. In fact, I wouldn't be a film-maker if it wasn't for Jeannette because I kept going on about wanting to make films and it was only when she told me to get off my ass and go out and buy a Super-8 camera that I did. She did a lot more to help make that film than is acknowledged. She was my muse and inspiration for all of that stuff.

Jeannette very quickly went from being a sixteen-year-old girl in the shop to someone who was moving on an equal footing with all of the key punk rock players. She struck up friendships and stood toe to toe with all those guys.

Jeannette Lee: After the Sex Pistols split up, John Lydon asked Don to go to Jamaica with him. I seem to remember I was to go as well but I didn't have a passport. Anyway, after they came back I became big friends with John, quite quickly. He started to trust me and I think it was because although I had strong opinions, I was very honest with him. I certainly wasn't afraid to tell him what I thought. One day he just said to me that he wanted me to come and work with him and be in his band. He talked about it being more like a limited company – everyone would have their role and it didn't have to be musical. I always remember him trying to talk me into it by saying, 'I know if anybody offered me a job that was going to take me to America, I'd take it.' Frankly, I didn't need much encouraging.

John had been manipulated by Malcolm McLaren in a way that was altogether uncomfortable for him in the Sex Pistols, and what he was looking for now was not exactly a manager, but somebody who he could trust and who might take on part of that role but without taking on the title. He wanted managerial benefits without any of the disadvantages. The way it was structured was that we were all equal partners and for a long time it really worked well.

I was very young and I had absolutely no fear. It did feel a little bit at times like we were getting away with murder, and I would only deal with the record company when I felt I should be available to them, and not at other times. Owning a record company, now I can see how frustrating for them it must have been.

Don Letts: By the time I went off to Jamaica, it was more or less over for Jeannette and me. That was a very messy separation and I think maybe she had reached a point where the Don Letts I'd been when she started out, who helped her see things, wasn't needed so much now that she was starting to see things through her own eyes. In any event, she's the only person who has ever seen me crying in the street . . .

Geoff Travis: Working with Public Image Ltd was where Jeannette learned her management skills and also her skills at being able to deal with record companies. PIL really set her in good stead for years to come because they really were a disparate group of strong characters, who experienced a lot of good times and a lot of bad times and probably everything that could happen to a band happened to them. To come out of working in that, you'd have to be a pretty remarkable individual.

Jeannette Lee: John went to live in New York for a while and I went as well, during the time that The Clash played their legendary seventeen nights there. I think I saw fourteen of those shows! Pretty soon after, I came back and my PIL time was over and I met Gareth Sager, who was playing in Rip Rig & Panic then, and we got together. I was pregnant in 1984 when I got a call from Roger Trilling, James Blood Ulmer's manager, who rang me out of the blue and said that Geoff would really like me to go and work with him. I was kind of flattered – but also appalled. Geoff didn't know me – what made him think I would want to go and work in a record company? Pleased as I was to be asked, it was a kind of thanks-but-no-thanks situation.

But that call always stayed in my mind and some time later, after I had been watching The Smiths at Vivienne's place, she had one of her legendary birthday parties where she gets together a large group of people, I ended up sitting next to Geoff and it was then that I realised that we had common interests, that we had very similar musical taste. We talked eventually about the possibility of my going and working at Rough Trade and he suggested I go and see him, which I did.

I went to see him at Collier Street and told him straight away that I had absolutely no office skills and no intention of acquiring any. He said fine. I think he just wanted somebody to work on projects with him. He treated *me* a little bit like one of his projects – decided he liked the idea, sorted me out and made it happen. I was very impressed really.

I wasn't comfortable with being Geoff's assistant because I've never liked the idea of having a boss but as it turned out he wasn't comfortable with the idea of me being his assistant, either, so whatever I started off as, it wasn't that. We shared a desk – him one side, me the other – and it quickly merged into a kind of partnership. I was surprised at how close our musical tastes were and, in fact, one of the first projects he asked me to work on was the Jesus & Mary Chain, who were signed to Blanco Y Negro. I absolutely loved them and the thing just got off to the best possible start.

Geoff Travis: Ever since 1976, when I had started the shop, I'd always worked with other people – I'd never said to anyone, this is my enterprise. It was the same with Jeannette. She always says that I A&R'd her but frankly when you come across someone like Jeannette, then you have to get serious about it; it's obvious.

Jeannette Lee: Collier Street was a lot different from when we used to go into the original shop to buy records. There seemed to be so many people at Collier Street. And there were meetings about everything, not that I had to go to many of them. At seventeen, when my mates and I used to go into 202 Kensington Park Road, all that collective stuff went straight over our heads. I see now that they were recognising original talent and trying to do something with it in an original way, but we just thought they were hippies. Too much long hair was what we thought at the time.

*

Geoff Travis: When the workers' trust was implemented in 1987, for me it was like the conclusion of an experiment that I had started in 1976 and I was happy to see it come in. Since Rough Trade had shareholders, it was necessary to ensure that everything was sorted properly. My father was one of them and I think he probably was a bit bemused by my wanting to take the company down a route that effectively, as he might have seen it, gave it away, but as ever, he supported me, or at least was wise enough not to say anything.

Richard Scott: In many respects, the workers' trust was the one thing I wanted to see put in place before I left Rough Trade, which, by the middle of 1987, I was seriously considering, although I didn't actually leave until 1988. We called it the Tim Niblett Trust in the end, named after Tim, who worked for Nine Mile and was tragically killed in a car crash. Setting up the trust meant that the company had to be reorganised again and overseeing everything there would be a board of independent trustees. The introduction of the trust sort of pleased me and made me cross because there were still some residual shareholdings – I was one of the shareholders – so it wasn't entirely owned by the workers.

Jo Slee: Unfortunately, the interminable war of attrition was still going on between Distribution and the record label at the time that the trust was set up. Distribution were having a bit of a heyday as well, selling a lot of dance records at that time, while we in the record company were doing steady business but of course, once The Smiths left, not as much as we might have been doing before. It seemed to me that Distribution were often spending huge sums of money, which they now had, in quite a reckless way – funding labels that would go bust two days after receiving a big Rough Trade cheque, that kind of thing. Geoff was also capable of splashing out large sums of money on bands, but then I think the market by then sort of demanded it – you could no longer pick bands up on, say, no-advance deals. It was very competitive. Inter-company relations were at their worst.

Distribution took a stand at Cannes for a big media festival and they had a giant poster produced with a picture of a baked beans tin and underneath it said: 'Rough Trade – The Best Thing To Happen In Cannes'. For some reason I got so outraged that I got out a Magic Marker pen and graffitied onto the poster next to the word 'Cannes' the words 'of worms'. The shit well and truly hit the fan. People were screaming that the poster had been specially made and cost £250. At the end of the day, I sent a message downstairs owning up and offering to pay for the poster, so long as I could keep the original. I never got a reply.

The ownership meetings took place over such a long time – back in 1982, a group of us were on the Ownership Committee and we used to take out the staff ten at a time to explain to them what it all meant. Of course, it was an important development – just making people aware of what it meant and seeing their responses was interesting. It meant that for the first time people would have to take ownership *and* responsibility. Some people had taken that ownership and responsibility from day one. For others, it was a bit of a change.

I remember the very day the trust came in. There was a lot of mistrust between the two main arms of the company – it felt like Will and Richard Powell were on one side and Geoff, Peter and I were on the other. I had the feeling that Will and Richard felt that they were winning some huge battle against Geoff on that day because, or so it seemed, they couldn't be as free to act as they wanted so long as Geoff was an owner. Peter Travis and Richard Scott were owners also. All three of them had to sign their shares over.

Peter Travis hadn't been involved in the company for years but it seemed he was still perceived as an obstacle. Some well-meaning freak in Distribution had found an old flea-ridden armchair and put it in reception for visitors to use. When Peter arrived he had to sit in it. Somehow it summed up how shabby the whole episode was, when it should have been a time of real celebration.

Then we had the formal signing down in the export department in the basement and I remember someone – probably me – insisting that we have some champagne. After all, it *was* a celebration and we had all worked hard to achieve it. But I'll never forget the forced smiles on the faces of Will and Richard Powell: the day sort of illustrated everything that was unworthy about Rough Trade at that point, everything that was unworthy about the endless arguments and struggles for power. That, ironically, was the point when I realised that Rough Trade would probably never be the place I had hoped it would be.

It was all a pyrrhic victory anyway, because in the end the point wasn't who owned it but how it was run. And I believe it had been run in quite a dangerous way and would go on to be run in quite a dangerous way for some time. The net effect of the trust was that trustees came in who were pretty ineffective. A little bit later, when it was close to bankruptcy, I was encouraged to stand as a trustee – we had appointed trustees and elected ones – but I just found that the people with the power didn't listen to anything and we just seemed to be on a helter-skelter journey to insolvency.

*

Johnny Marr: I don't think the band got over the problems with Rough Trade, but I felt that I did, personally. I started having three square meals a day, stopped drinking and taking drugs, and got on with the music. I know that we made a really great last record, and we had a pretty good time doing it too. And it was an unusual record, very much the record I wanted to make. It sounds very much like I was into things sounding at that time – it was fairly unadorned, and experimental in a couple of places, and not what was considered indie at the time.

Anyone who writes an article and says that in *Strangeways Here We Come* you can hear the disintegration or disenchantment of the band is just fooling themselves, because no one knew it was the end of the band except for me. And it had no effect on the way the music was produced – we made the record with the same intent we made all the others.

The recording sessions were inspiring and there was a much breezier atmosphere compared to that surrounding the recording of *The Queen is Dead*. That might be why there is a lot of acoustic guitar on there. We had a couple of little blow-ups that maybe wouldn't have happened earlier because I was starting to draw a line under some things, but it was the usual pioneering spirit, really – tricky, but pioneering.

Jo Slee: The Smiths split up pretty much after *Strangeways Here We Come* was recorded, as I remember – it was horrible, the end of an era. It was too soon. I think Johnny was getting 'incitements to disaffection' from various people and there were very real problems between them. I had the sense that Johnny was increasingly unhappy with Morrissey being afforded iconic status when Johnny had made such a supreme contribution to the whole thing and yet wasn't treated the same way. You sensed that people were whispering to him that he could do better on his own – and by now Morrissey, well it was quite uncertain whether or not he would turn up for things, and quite often certain that he wouldn't.

Geoff Travis: To be honest, I read about The Smiths splitting up just like everybody else did. That was how I heard about it.

Johnny Marr: I told the band that I wanted a break and that was construed as my leaving. I wanted to have a holiday and come back and re-evaluate our sound and how we approached things. I thought we'd boxed ourselves in musically and I didn't want to just carry on trotting out the old stuff, which was on the agenda. There was a lot of ego involved and a lot of paranoia. We definitely needed a break from each other. But there was nobody wise enough to make that a plausible and pleasing reality for everybody. The relationship Morrissey and I had – ultimately, it was the making of the band and the breaking of the band.

CHAPTER TWELVE:

1988–89

'Don't worry, Richard, nothing is lost to the universal mind'

Departure of Richard Scott – Turnover growth – Friction – Stone Roses – Cartel disintegration – Rough Trade Inc. – 'Gas' computer

Richard Scott: I left in the spring of 1988. Eleven years after I joined Rough Trade I was finally spat out the other end. I was exhausted – certainly physically exhausted – and could no longer keep up the pace. I'd stopped pulling and packing. The sheer workload of the period had taken its toll. The level of activity was so intense that only certain people who were drawn into it stuck. The wrong kind of person got spun off the wheel. It was hard work – hard, physical work. And it was always *very* loud.

In truth, the business had grown to a point where for me it lost the edge that had originally turned me on. There was no point in my trying to keep it steered in my direction because it had grown so much I could no longer do that.

Dave Whitehead: I had joined Rough Trade from their major competitor Pinnacle in 1986 to look after product management and left in 1989. In the period between, Rough Trade's turnover jumped from something like £8m a year to £24m. One of the biggest problems we had towards the end of that period was how to cope physically with stock in a building that was fine for running an £8m-a-year business but not for a £24m one. Logistically and operationally we were running out of space. We had pallets on the street, the warehouse overflowed. We were fined on a regular basis by the council. It was a labour-intensive, physical business.

Why had it grown so much? On the distribution side we had got heavily involved in the dance music scene, which was happening, and we actively went out looking for labels to take on to distribute. Simon Edwards and I A&R'd labels just the way a record label would A&R an artist. At the same time, big independent bands like The Smiths, Depeche Mode and New Order were selling more records than they'd ever sold before. UK independent music was doing well and we bought in a lot of American indie music as well.

Simon Edwards: There was no denying that Rough Trade conformed. It had to. The nature of survival then meant that you had to be out fighting the cause. You had to sell yourself. We went to exhibitions like MIDEM and touted for business, we looked around. We did everything on the back of the idea that Rough Trade was an indie/punk distribution company, but one that was also having major chart success.

Richard Boon: Some time around 1988–89 Geoff was invited, along with other A&R luminaries, to take part in an industry vote for the A&R man's A&R man, and he said he was going to nominate Daniel Miller for signing labels not artists. It was a joke, but the irony was Rough Trade was having a lot of success through handling labels – labels like Rhythm King, Big Life, KLF. M|A|R|R|S, Bomb the Bass, Coldcut, Yazz and KLF all had huge hits on labels going through Rough Trade. And when Daniel Miller took Mute to Rough Trade exclusively – indeed when sole distribution started to kick in properly – Rough Trade had even more success. And they diversified – it wasn't all dance records. They had labels like New Roots, Folk & World, DeMix.

Richard Scott: We'd had records in the charts in the past – it was fantastic when Stiff Little Fingers charted – but Rough Trade had grown into something where it was involved with records going into the charts regularly and I didn't like it. I had never liked the charts. When something appeared in the charts it instantly lost its appeal for me. *Uncharted*. That's much better, a word with dual meaning that signifies territory unmapped and unexplored. Uncharted territory is always more fascinating than that ruled by charts.

My problem was partly to do with my Calvinist background: we came originally from the Orkney Isles and my father had a view that any form of advertising is violence. For him, if something stood up, it stood up ... I think I inherited some of that outlook.

I had stopped having any real involvement in the day-to-day running of the business, as well, and there wasn't much to keep me at Rough Trade. The management had expanded.

Dave Whitehead: Once the business grew, it was obvious it needed managing and it needed managers. Richard Powell had come in and taken on the role of dealing with that managing, and the truth is that Geoff probably was happy for someone else to be dealing with all that and – great as he is as an A&R man – probably hadn't the skills for dealing with it himself. There can't have been any regret in him giving up control and there are no grounds for criticising the people who came in and managed the thing. Richard Powell took on the role of deciding where the money went – if the label got it, if the US company got it, if the Germany company or Dutch company got it. He could be brilliant strategically, at figuring how to go about business. He was very committed and very hard-working. But he was an old-school manager and one who worked on the principle that knowledge is power and I'm not going to share it. He had no time for explaining and he could be condescending.

There was a strained relationship between Distribution and the record label and I think it was strained largely because Richard Powell and Geoff Travis didn't get on. I think it was a question of personalities. Richard was good at figuring out the business but not so good at understanding the record label. He saw money as the foundation of the business: Geoff was looking for something different. Tony Wilson once said, 'Some people make money and some people make legends.' It was a bit like that.

But I think they weren't entirely dissimilar. They were both highly educated; Geoff had an excellent command of language and Richard had an excellent business command and they could both use their skills and advantages in a negative way.

Jeannette Lee: Almost from the moment I arrived, I noticed there was a friction between the record label and the distribution company but I chose not to get involved. I kept out of it. Geoff and I shared a desk and sat opposite each other. We rabbited on about music and discovered that we liked a lot of the same things. I came in specifically to work with Geoff and people tended to see me that way. I think some people saw me as a luxury item, or couldn't work out what I was doing. Peter Walmsley used to tease me that I didn't have a real job.

Peter Walmsley: The politics of the company were at their most divided and confrontational at this point. The rift between the two parts of the company got wider and the success that Distribution was having started to feel like a threat. It put poison in the system. We had genuine misgivings at the record label about whether or not Rough Trade Distribution wanted to deliver for Rough Trade Records in the way that they would for, say, Mute or 4AD.

What the company needed at this point was someone to come in, cleverer than we were, cleverer than Geoff was, and sort it out. We just didn't have anyone brave enough or strong enough or capable enough to deal with it. One of the problems was that Geoff, understandably, was always deferred to. He was such a figurehead that anyone coming in had to work with or around him.

It all became more of a business. We signed longer-term contracts after The Smiths, which was not something we'd had to do previously. In fact we'd steered clear of them because bands have a tendency to become artistically worse not better, usually. But we sold a lot of records and we were a good option for anyone. We had a lot to offer. We were successful and had a good reputation and, on the back of The Smiths' critical reception, we were seen to have good integrity, plus we had built up a complete worldwide network of support. We were competing.

Geoff Travis: The record company contributed a lot of revenue to the group turnover but this culture seemed to be engendered which said that the record company were dangerous mavericks, a bunch of miscreants. I felt that we were wrongly treated from the first day Richard Powell arrived. Of course, we needed somebody to come in and help, but help wasn't given in an open, we-are-all-working-on-this-together kind of way. It felt like Richard wanted to be in charge. I'd never seen myself as the head of the group, that's partly why I was willing to give it all up to the trust. Bringing someone in wasn't the wrong idea in itself, but I think it was the wrong individual ...

We just carried on doing what we had always done. We'd signed The Woodentops and Easterhouse not long before and we very nearly had a big success with The Woodentops. In their early days, The Woodentops were very exciting, they had some interesting songs and a very unusual sound in that it was so rhythmic: there was a contrast between the heaviness of the rhythm and the lightness of Rolo McGinty's vocals.

Easterhouse, I believe, could have been one of the great Manchester groups but they kind of self-destructed. Andy Perry had a very strong political agenda and that alienated a lot of people, although we did manage to get them a good American deal, as we did with The Woodentops. Back then, you could sign a band and sell them to an American label to fund the project. That happened in both those cases.

Peter Walmsley: Money from abroad would come in from licensing deals and I used to fight to have it ring-fenced for the record label. At the height of The Smiths' popularity, we were licensing the band in twenty-eight, thirty territories, and it was important to set some of that money aside as record company money, given the relationship we had with Distribution.

Jeannette Lee: When I came into the company I honestly thought that I'd be giving it a go for a couple of weeks to see how I got on. I didn't see it as potentially long-term. I worked mainly on Blanco bands and on bands signed to Blue Guitar, the label Geoff had through Chrysalis, groups like the Motorcycle Boy and The Mighty Lemon Drops.

Gradually, I started to get more involved and worked with more Rough Trade artists, like A. R. Kane, the group that developed out of Colourbox and M|A|R|R|S, who were an amazing band – one was a wonderful musician and one worked for a big advertising agency and would turn up driving incredibly flash motor cars and motorbikes. But they were very indie.

Geoff Travis: The song 'Baby Milk Snatcher' is one of the songs of the era, really. They were more of a project. They didn't play live much, but when they did it was always an event.

Jeannette Lee: It was with the arrival of The Sundays that I felt I had got something I could properly get my teeth into. It was then I realised this thing I was doing had developed into something proper. I worked very closely with them.

There was big competition to sign the band and we went to see them only to discover that everybody else in the world was already talking to them. In the end, 4AD turned into our big rivals and it was really in the balance. They were big Cocteau Twins fans and big fans of The Smiths. What tipped it was that Ivo Watts-Russell from 4AD apparently said to them, think which label you imagined yourself being on when you thought about being in a band and making records: which label did you dream you'd be on? The answer was Rough Trade.

They were great for the label. They had wonderful songs and their musicianship was excellent. They really were a fully formed band from the outset. The only problem was they took a long time to make decisions so it always took for ever to get things going. We put out a couple of singles before releasing the album *Reading, Writing and Arithmetic*, which went to Number Four in the charts.

After The Sundays, I felt I'd eased my way into the partnership with Geoff; this thing became all of a sudden integral to my life, and I'm still doing it twenty-three years later.

Geoff Travis: In 1988, we thought we'd also signed the Stone Roses, an experience that went on to become the worst disappointment of my career. We thought we had a deal and then it turned out that we hadn't, even although we paid for them to go into the studio to record 'Elephant Stone' and John Squire sent me down the original sleeve artwork for the Rough Trade single, which hangs on my office wall to this day.

Peter Walmsley: This was one of those occasions where Geoff's taste and mine coincided, which often it didn't. Basically we were double-dealt. We had wanted to sign the Stone Roses for ages. We went up to Manchester to see them live. It would and should have been a big signing at that time for us. In the end it was a real betrayal.

Geoff Travis: We'd received a phone call from Lindsay Reade, who was Tony Wilson's ex-wife, saying that she was co-managing this amazing band and that we should go up and see them because she thought we might be interested in signing them. Because it was Lindsay, obviously, we agreed to go and Peter, Jeannette and I went up to see the band play in the International II club owned by the band's other co-manager, Gareth.

Jeannette Lee: I'll always remember, Lindsay took us to her flat first and fed us salad. She had this tiny bedsit at the top of a house and we all trooped up to eat this salad. At the end, she said, 'Now who would like some chocolate?' We all said, 'OK,' and she came back with one tiny square of chocolate each and said, 'You can't have any more because you know it is fattening.'

Then we went off to the club and saw what we later agreed was one of the best live shows we had ever seen. They were amazing.

Geoff Travis: Next thing, the band came down from Manchester and I met them at Euston railway station and we went across the road to the pub for a drink. We sat for about two and a half hours just talking about music – about black music, about Love, about how important a danceable rhythm section is to the best rock 'n' roll – and then they went back to Manchester on the train and it was all going to happen between us.

We started paying for 'Elephant Stone' to be recorded and they suggested Peter Hook from New Order as a producer, which was fine. Peter Hook produced the record and sent it down and in truth it wasn't as good a job as it could have been and it needed remixing. I suggested they go to producer Robin Millar's studio to remix it, which they did. Had Peter Hook's production been better, I'm certain the deal would have gone ahead, but because it needed reworking, it created a fatal delay.

While they were in Robin's studio, as I understand it, some engineers who worked for Zomba heard this amazing thing and went and told their bosses about it. They ended up signing to Silvertone, which was part of the Zomba group.

This all went on over a long period of time. In fact, before signing to Silvertone, they came down to London to play Dingwalls and the place was mobbed out with record company people. They were astonishing to see perform again. It was a nightmare because originally it really was a north/south divide in terms of people knowing about them. When we saw them in Manchester, nobody in London really knew about them – and the place was packed out then, too.

There was some issue about our contract not going out, or not going out on time, and I'm not sure to this day whether somebody internally sabotaged the deal and the contract never got sent. It was a tragedy.

I'd recommended John Leckie to them as a producer while it was all going to happen and after we hadn't signed them I was talking to David Geffen and told him he should sign them for America, which he did. Even though we had been let down, even though we'd lost the deal, I just loved them so much and I thought they deserved every success, with or without us.

*

Richard Scott: My only regret on leaving Rough Trade was that the excitement of the politics of the early days had become dissipated and I felt that we had missed a big opportunity. We could have held our nerve and we could have seen the DIY thing all the way through, keeping the equal pay approach and all of that. We could have pushed the structure out – still expanded – but stuck to our ideals of developing the Cartel. Instead, it quickly reverted to a central unit approach.

Lloyd Harris: Things went wrong for me at Revolver just before they went wrong on a general level for Rough Trade and everyone involved. Sometime in 1989, I started to have doubts about wanting to carry on – I felt that the whole idea had lost its way. Revolver wasn't in a position to succeed as a business but at the same time, with all the changes to the Cartel and structure, we had lost the credibility of doing something we all believed in. I left on very bad terms, sold my share in the business over and got out. I didn't speak to anyone I'd been involved with until a Cartel reunion in spring 2009.

It was an extraordinary thing to have gone through. We felt – all of us – that we were part of something, something more important than the next business opportunity. I think that is why the whole experience had such a big emotional impact on so many people. It was meaningful and, like the cliché about the sixties, it was a time when we felt we were actually changing the world.

Johnny Appel: Other people knew it was all going wrong before we did. By the start of 1990, Revolver had got out completely. It had started to go wrong when God had, indeed, decided to taketh away. I could see the logic of centralised sales, but I couldn't accept that we had invested in a business only for them to come along and effectively say, 'Sod you.' They gave us a tiny cut on the margins in compensation. Collier Street and eventually Seven Sisters Road became overloaded. I heard that pallet-loads of stuff were disappearing out the back door.

Tony K: I started to fall out with Rough Trade around about 1988. Things weren't right. Earlier on we'd been threatened with things like The Smiths leaving because we weren't doing a good enough job and it all degenerated further. The relationship with the Cartel became untenable.

Nobody liked centralisation. I accepted that it was going to happen but it was all done very unpleasantly. I was met by a delegation from Distribution at a seaside guest house in Yorkshire, where I was told that I had to force the other Cartel members to go with centralisation or it would all be closed down and everyone would be put out of business. Rough Trade Distribution came up to see me, and they basically put a gun to my head.

The end result was that Red Rhino collapsed. It was one of my darkest days and I have never dwelt on it. It affected me very badly emotionally, mentally – it had been my life and I felt I had messed it up. Later I thought, well, we showed people that they could be in charge of their lives; that they could start their own cottage industries, and that was important.

Sandy McLean: There was a period when they were always trying to get rid of me. Somehow I always dodged the bullet until Simon Edwards told *Music Week* one Friday that I had gone bust because I couldn't pay a bill to the record pressing plant Mayking. The story was in the paper, the shit hit the fan, and I ended up winding down Fast Forward. I owed money to Mayking but we were still trading normally. It was an absolute disgrace.

Robin Hurley: Centralisation was for some people the beginning of the end when it should have been the start of a marvellous future. I could see the sense of it and had a lot more belief in it being the right way to go than most, long-term. I'd moved closer to Rough Trade because I became a kind of national sales manager in all but name and came down to London two days a week and went to see the chains.

Nine Mile was integrated into Rough Trade very early on because Richard Powell asked me to go to America and help reinvigorate Rough Trade Inc., which I did in July 1987. It was my political belief, rightly or wrongly, that Rough Trade had a terrific future. Looking back now I think there are probably a hundred things that could have been done differently but also I think there has been a lot of misplaced blame thrown around.

Richard Scott: In all my time at Rough Trade all I was doing on a day-to-day basis was responding to what had to be done that day. It was an extraordinary and strange mixture of people and ideas that worked very well. Only with hindsight did I begin to appreciate what we achieved. It was a privilege to have been involved.

Rifts and separations have been accentuated but in essence I think Geoff and I just had different ways of doing things. People say I drove the politics, which comes as a bit of a shock to me and is untrue: Geoff drove all that early on, he created it, and I was pulled into something which I then really enjoyed.

Geoff certainly had politics but his primary thing, it seems to me, was his obsession with the line between an audience and a band. He was always fantastically turned on by live performance and I think it drove him to constantly seek out new things, and probably still does. Morrissey fascinated him back then, and no doubt someone like Duffy did later, because there is a magic between Morrissey and the audience, between Duffy and the audience, and Geoff understands that magic intensely.

When I left some of us went out to a pub and Geoff came along to that and he was very pleasant about it all. Then I was gone. I picked up where I'd left on with the Last Museum and started working with new media. We got some grants and at one point Rough Trade helped with a loan.[52]

I kept in touch a little bit after but I wasn't that surprised that it all went wrong ultimately. I don't think anybody was to blame individually but clearly at the end the management structure just fell apart.

---

52. For some time prior to his leaving, Richard Scott had been working on a number of future technology projects. He had prepared a paper on a proposed 'Post-Vinyl Project', which looked beyond the centralisation of 'the Model' and saw that 'carrier development' was 'undermining the traditional basis of music and other information industries'. The Last Museum Catalogue was intended to be a mail order catalogue of '"information" in a variety of formats'. Items to be offered for sale included books such as Roland Barthes's *Camera Lucida*, William Gibson's *Neuromancer*, and HMSO's *Britain – An Official Handbook*, plus records from a variety of labels such as Rough Trade, Mute and EG, a video of a Buckminster Fuller lecture, a selection of DATs and CDVs, and an 'artefact – a De Graffe Video System'.

Original Last Museum booklet – A Part of a Room & A Part of a Book.

*

Dave Whitehead: I left at the end of 1989 because I felt that Rough Trade had all started to become so much more about the process than the actual doing of things – it was laborious, rigorous and demanding going through all those meetings. At first, it had all made a lot of sense; it had felt like the right way to establish control and balance. In the end, I just wanted to get on with the job.

Once the trust had been set up, board meetings were filled with all these trust people who had a role to make sure that things were done properly. They asked appropriate questions, but it was one more interference and slowed you down from doing your job.

When I left, it felt like Rough Trade was at a crossroads. It felt like a good time for the company. It felt like it could get bigger. But I didn't want to dedicate another few years of my life to it and left and started a label, which was always where my main interests had been.

I had no inkling at that time that the ship was in any way out of control, financially or otherwise. I loved Will Keen – he was as good a manager as could be found, an ethically minded guy who got vilified, it seemed to me, when Rough Trade went bankrupt, which was terrible because he ended up having a role which I don't even think he ever wanted.

Simon Edwards: Richard Powell had left for whatever reason – I still don't know to this day. It just came to me that I was in my early thirties, I'd devoted most of my twenties to this project and that it was time to move on. It was a completely natural decision. I decided to go off and work with Dave, but we very carefully handed over to other people. There was no set strategy to what we did and at the same time we didn't just creep off.

After we had gone, I assumed that Rough Trade would just bounce along as it always had done. I thought the balance of power was reasonably OK given that there is always friction between record labels and record distributors. That edge is a really important part of the creative process.

Jo Slee: By Christmas 1989, things were fairly grim generally. We wanted a Christmas party but were told that Rough Trade couldn't afford it. A bunch of enterprising souls pooled resources and hired a pub in Chapel Market for the night. It wasn't as if we were short of DJs or music. I was seriously reflecting on how much longer I could stay at Rough Trade: it was beginning to feel like a life sentence.

That night, with the help of a little ecstasy and a lot of TLC, I finally realised the simple fact that no one was listening to me any longer. I was free to move on.

In the end I was made redundant. I was offered £20,000 (my salary was £24,000), which I turned down. I said to my loyal production co-workers Kate and Andrew, 'I'm not sure what grounds I have to refuse £20,000.' Andrew's helpful response was: 'You could always threaten to stay.' Extraordinarily, £24,000 materialised and I went off to find out if indeed there was life after Rough Trade.

Simon Edwards: We were a bit shocked when, at the start of 1990, George Kimpton-Howe was appointed, coming from Rough Trade's competitor Pinnacle. I am not sure he had any more experience than the internal Rough Trade people had, who we just assumed would be promoted into the positions we had left.

I think that appointment was the start of managers from the supposedly real world – record companies like EMI – coming in without any understanding of the Rough Trade culture. It was a pretty swift collapse once that happened.

Richard Boon: I suspect a reasonable amount of money circulated around in support of the satellites – Rough Trade Inc., Rough Trade Germany and Rough Trade Benelux, which they'd recently set up. Money was certainly moving away from the mother ship. Label advances created problems as well. There was at least one dance label that got a six-figure advance and delivered no product.

Robin Hurley: At the time I went out to America, Rough Trade Germany had had a couple of good years and I think the management of Rough Trade saw the USA as the next frontier to try to master. I went initially in 1986 to meet people in San Francisco and talk with them.

When I came back in 1987, a number of things struck me. There was some goodwill and some dedicated people but it all seemed remote and difficult to monitor. I quickly realised that to develop a label it would be better in Los Angeles or New York: San Francisco felt like an outpost. We kept the wholesaling in San Francisco and had the label operation in New York. We had a presence on both coasts.

More staff joined as we started to take on more of Geoff's signings for release and we also established relationships with people like 4AD and licensed stuff off them. Geoff, I believe, had concerns about the changes and investments and time it would take to establish Rough Trade as a global brand and he was worried that this might affect his ability to hold on to some of the bands he was signing. By holding on to some bands for Rough Trade worldwide it would help develop the American business but I think there were two concerns – firstly, that it was traditional to license bands to US companies to recoup money to fund their projects, and secondly, that if we released material initially a band's sales might be affected compared to, say, if that band had been licensed to Sire, who were established as a label. As always, I think Geoff was supportive but concerned to make sure his artists weren't hurt in any way.

I was naïve in some of my approaches and possibly could have learnt more by going to work for one of our US competitors before setting up the label. I certainly had that Rough Trade belief that because it was us, we would succeed. We had our eyes open but quickly Rough Trade Inc. became a great drain on the UK operation. It sounds stupid but I underestimated the size of America – the sheer distances involved in shipping stock across the continent. Cash flow was always hard. We'd have a great month selling records but have no money coming in. Or, we'd have a great month and then three months down the line get a load of returns.

Large amounts of money had to be sent over to keep the business afloat – hundreds of thousands. We regularly asked for substantial amounts and I have no doubt that that played a big part in the UK company's rapid decline and insolvency. In the last year, Rough Trade Inc. was basically kept alive in the hope that someone would come in and invest in it. At one point Warners wanted to buy a fifty per cent stake and in our arrogance we wouldn't give up more than forty-nine per cent, and they pulled out.

Towards the end of 1989 and into 1990, I was also aware of financial issues looming for the UK company.

Peter Walmsley: There was a massive credit-control problem that was growing bigger all the time. Returns was a complete black hole that nobody bothered to adequately take care of and money owed wasn't collected properly. A bit later, in the middle of 1990, Parkfield Video went bust owing Distribution £500,000. Somebody was *very asleep* at their post in credit control ...

Geoff Travis: Parkfield may have hit Distribution out of the blue because surely any halfway decent accounts department would have noticed that? They took on the new warehouse in Seven Sisters Road without disposing of the lease on Collier Street. Really, you can't do that. I don't know what happened there or why we ended up in that situation but we were effectively paying rent for two premises. It was miserable from the moment we moved to that new office. That was the writing on the wall.[53]

Richard Boon: There was a party when the new building was opened and a PR company was hired to promote the event. Banners were put up and there were people from the PR company running around. Paul Smith from the record label Blast First was there and he saw all this activity and turned around to me and said, 'This looks ripe for a sell-off.' In fact, what happened

53. In 1987, GLEB wrote to Rough Trade explaining a change of policy that effectively meant Rough Trade might be best advised to vacate Collier Street, which of course they did. The relationship with GLEB was a very strong one and covered all manner of areas. For instance, in 1986, GLEB and Rough Trade were in discussion about establishing a specialised catalogue of Rough Trade product in public libraries, thus a decade later potentially fulfilling Ken Davison's desire to 'rent out culture'.

was the PR firm went bust and Rough Trade never had to pay the bill. Although some people say there is no such thing, it was a free launch.

Seven Sisters Road wasn't the only property either – as well as Collier Street, we had premises up in London Road near the Angel where *The Catalogue* and some of sales were. There was a lot that needed keeping an eye on.

I was up in London Road because I had inherited editorship of *The Catalogue* from Brenda Kelly. We had a Buddhist designer working on the layout and I remember on one occasion some copy that had been pasted down peeled off and got lost and we only noticed right at the point of press. I phoned the designer up and explained the problem and she said to me, 'Don't worry, Richard, nothing is lost to the universal mind.'

Geoff Travis: Richard Powell had approached me some time before a decision was made on the purchase of the computer and had said would I ask around other record companies and find out what kind of computer they used. I did a bit of asking around, a little bit of research and passed back what I found out to him. For some reason they then went out and bought something completely different from what anyone else was using. It cost a fortune, took months and months to get going and never worked properly.

Jeremy Boyce: I worked initially in telesales and when I came in from Virgin in 1984 I was quite shocked that they were still fulfilling orders by hand-writing invoices. Gradually, the first of what I call the 'gas' computers were brought in and put together Heath Robinson-style. I call them gas computers because they really were basic things – all the way through Rough Trade's life. The computer that caused all the trouble at the end really was a sort of horse-designed-by-committee thing. My job was to make sure it worked from a sales point of view and it was immediately obvious it couldn't do what it was supposed to do – and never would be able to. I couldn't understand why they had to go out and invite for tender a contract for a completely new system when there were obviously perfectly adequate models being used by our competitors, which could have been bought off the shelf.

Dave Whitehead: I do remember that the age-old Rough Trade problem of bad credit came into play when they bought the computer and they had to effectively spend cash to acquire it. It was a lot of money.

Richard Boon: It was going to cost around £700,000 in total. I remember when they first turned it on, it so overloaded the system it sucked power from everywhere and all the lights went dim. *It didn't work!*

Another major problem was that although the day-to-day economic management – called the critical path – was coherent, it went into far too much detail and in the end managing everything became very complex.

Jeremy Boyce: I became an elected member of the main board and so I saw some problems on the horizon earlier than others. I think the critical path, although a really good notion and a good idea, was the source of a lot of trouble. It worked but also had the adverse effect of sending everyone into prediction mania. It created a mania for predicting turnover. *What were your last figures? What are your figures now? What can you predict for turnover for the next six months? For the six months after that?*

The company had a lot of success in 1987 and 1988, and not just on the back of dance music: it was a time when bands like The Pixies and Sonic Youth really took off as well. Sonic Youth became the Rough Trade house band of preference – the joke was that the Rough Trade job application only asked three questions: *Do you wear black? Are you a vegetarian? Do you like Sonic Youth?* But all this success we came to regard as core business and so the predictions after that made the natural assumption that we were going to keep growing. Certainly in 1989, towards 1990, there were a number of delays with product we were essentially relying on, big albums. The problem was, we had created this monster and now it needed feeding. [54]

54. An extensive if infuriatingly undated (though it must date from 1990) paper prepared to help seek an investment of £1,000,000 described the background to Rough Trade's current plight. Profits had been good up until 1989 when there occurred 'significant changes and problems'. These were investment in the USA and in a new computer system, both overseen by a managing director who then left the company. 'The level of cash reserves and the continued high profits gave the remaining managers the confidence to continue the US investment … This confidence was misplaced. The costs during 1989 in the US and for the computer project were higher than projected, the record company fell into significant loss and whilst the distribution company continued to grow it was not as fast as predicted.' The record company was hampered by the increasing tendency of US record companies to sign UK acts direct, by the reckless spending of major labels, which was forcing prices up, and indeed it stopped purchasing bands around this time while a secure financial investment was sought. However, the general outlook for the label and Rough Trade was seen to be positive and even the US was expected to 'reach breakeven between 1991/2 and return profits thereafter'.

Geoff Travis: Ultimately, the business was mismanaged. We – the board – were incapable of managing a business that size. I assume, for instance, that on the board of a normal company someone would have questioned the taking on of a lease before disposing properly of the old one. Everyone was out of their depth and no one will admit it. It was a fantastic business – essentially really sound, and the synergy between the record label and Distribution as a structure was tremendous. We weren't *that* bad at business, really we weren't, but people got distracted: some people fell prey to petty, human power games instead of joining in together and trying to sort it out.

Peter Walmsley: At the end, lots of people were brought in on ridiculously high salaries and achieved nothing. They were a bunch of second-rate people. That was galling for someone like me who had started out being paid £35 a week in the back of the Kensington Park Road shop.

The business was hit by a tsunami – the fatal combination of a number of things going wrong at once – but of course you are not allowed to take a break at any point, you are not allowed to go to the bank and say, we've just been hit by a tidal wave, we've just smashed into a brick wall, can we have a six-month pause while we get our breath back?

At that point, nobody around was brave enough, strong enough or capable enough to deal with that. No one had the skill to make sense of the situation, no one had the sensibility of it, and no one had the heart to make it all work. Perhaps understandably, they'd lost the will, the power and the strength to deal with it.

It was a fine, fine business and it should have been able to work. It should have been saved. Instead, what happened next was just all about burying the corpse.

CHAPTER THIRTEEN:
1990–91

PULL BACK TO REVEAL HE
IS TALKING TO MUSIC
COMPANY DIRECTORS.

'Like some giant machine out of *Dr Who*'

Financial problems – George Kimpton-Howe – Move to Seven Sisters –
Collapse – Informal administration – High Court – Formal administration

Duncan Cameron: Shortly after I joined Mute Records as financial controller
in 1988, we ended our joint distribution deals with Spartan and Rough
Trade and went sole distribution with Rough Trade. This was a decision
reached on an operational basis. That was still the position towards the end
of 1990, by which time I became financial director. Mute did its own
physical exports and we had our licensing deals overseas. We also had some
associated labels like Rhythm King, Product Inc. and Blast First and they
were also being distributed by Rough Trade.

I knew Will Keen quite well; in fact, Daniel had asked me to have a chat
with him before he employed me. Daniel had told me that his relationship
with Rough Trade went back to the year dot and that he'd worked a little
bit out of their offices, so I knew the relationship was close. Indeed, after
I joined, Mute had one or two cash issues of its own that it had to resolve
and Rough Trade and Will Keen were helpful both in terms of advice and

cash advances, which, for a very short period, helped us out of a sticky situation.

Daniel had mentioned to me that there had been financial issues between Rough Trade and Mute in the past and at one point I think there had been a debenture to sort out a debt to us. Towards the second half of 1990, though, there was a more continuous delay in terms of Rough Trade being able to account properly in terms of the agreement. They were often coming up short. I did have concerns about this but it had happened before, the difference this time being that whereas previously it had been spasmodic, now the problems seemed to be getting a bit too regular. I remember having a conversation with Will about it and he was quite reassuring and I had faith in him, especially after he said that he would let me know if there was ever a likelihood that we were not going to get paid. That relaxed me a bit. The other thing that relaxed me slightly was the fact that we had managed to get some credit insurance on Rough Trade, not a massive sum, but a meaningful six-figure amount around the £250,000/£300,000 mark.

So, there was the combination of Will's assurances, the credit insurance, and the fact that there was a general feeling that it's Rough Trade, they might not account on time but they'll come through in the end. All of this meant that coming into the back half of 1990, I was concerned but not overly concerned at what might be happening there.

George Kimpton-Howe: Around the spring of 1990 I was head-hunted to go and become managing director of Rough Trade Distribution. I was recruited by Will Keen, through an agency. I met Will and I liked him very much. I thought he was a very, very credible man.

I'd been MD at Pinnacle and Rough Trade had been our absolute, main, direct competitor, and ever since I'd worked at Pinnacle from the mid-1980s the rumour mill always said that Rough Trade was about to go bust or had gone bust. Almost every month there was a rumour that it had gone pop. Until, that is, around 1988 when it became apparent that Rough Trade, just like Pinnacle, were having a fabulous year. I think the whole indie sector by that point was doing well. Lots of independent or independently distributed records were getting into the charts and selling in large quantities. So, when I went to see Will for my interview, two things were in play, so to speak – firstly, that I found him very credible and straightforward, and secondly that they'd had plenty of chart success recently and therefore must be in very good shape. I wasn't thinking, I bet you are all but bankrupt.

Will showed me figures for the last period of accounting, for 1988, and they were very strong – from memory, I want to say that there was something close to £5m in funds sitting in the account. To this day, I still don't know why I didn't say, 'Let's hold fire until you show me the next set of accounts.' Something clearly had happened between the fantastic accounts in 1988 and when I joined in spring 1990.

After a couple of months of being in there, I started to get the collywobbles. So far as I could tell, the company – the independent sector – had gone through arguably its best time ever, but something had had a very adverse effect on the finances of Rough Trade, and it wasn't the core Rough Trade business itself, and I started to sense that something was desperately wrong. I went to see Will one night and asked if I could have a candid conversation. What I said was, 'Is it me, Will, or is this company in dire straits?' He gave me a look and the look just said it all. That was his answer.

Will said to me that Mute were more or less keeping them afloat by not taking money due them on time, though, as he said, this was just digging a deeper and deeper hole. There were a number of things which had primarily taken their toll on that fund I'd seen in the audited figures, he explained to me, and America was one area where a large portion of it had gone.

It was around about July, then, around the time of the move to the new distribution warehouse in Finsbury Park, that my fears were starting to be confirmed. I was extremely unpopular, having come across from Pinnacle, 'the enemy', and to be honest I did myself no favours because I suddenly realised I had absolutely no faith in the business surviving.

Jeremy Boyce: It was a bit distressing to have lost Richard Powell, Dave Whitehead and Simon Edwards all in such a short space of time. There was a period shortly after when I thought I might be promoted into one of those management positions. But George Kimpton-Howe was brought in and, well, he was pretty much universally loathed and despised from day one.

I had to report to him and supposedly became one of his key right-hand men. It didn't work. George set about changing the culture of Rough Trade overnight from one where people's opinions counted to one where only one person's opinion mattered – George's. At Rough Trade there had been the terrible meetings structure but that structure at least meant that anyone could raise an issue or start a discussion that *might* go all the way to board level. Suddenly that approach was no longer relevant. A lot of people couldn't accept that.

It wasn't absolutely clear, either, from George's behaviour that there was no money, because he was going out left, right and centre spending it, buying up labels to try to buy in turnover. I couldn't understand how Will Keen had let the Rough Trade culture shift from one of growing and nurturing to one of just grabbing for cash. It was all too clear, though, why they felt they needed to panic-buy.

Also, we'd not long come out of the equal pay structure and set up the employees' trust and there was George with a big fat salary and a red BMW parked outside, paid for by the company.

George Kimpton-Howe: Just before the Finsbury Park move I was invited to a demonstration of the new computer where I was given the low-down on what this machine, which had so far cost £400,000, could do. I had a near coronary on being told how much it had cost, and that it was going to cost about the same again to get it up and running, but that was nothing to seeing the machine itself, which was like some giant machine out of *Dr Who*, with millions of wires and cables. It looked nothing like the computer we'd had at Pinnacle. It was being 'installed' by Rough Trade employees, guys talking a break from packing boxes, which made me a little bit nervous.

I asked whether, when fully installed, the computer would be able to track stock movement and everybody looked at me blankly. It couldn't do it. I asked what it could do and I was told that it could list every available item of stock. In other words, it was a £400,000 catalogue.

There was then a big meeting about how the computer would not only be implemented in the Rough Trade offices but also in the offices of the Cartel, which was going to add an extra installation cost of one million pounds. There were fifteen people in the meeting and I couldn't for a moment work out whether it was me, or that there really was a level of insanity about the place. I explained that we didn't appear to have a spare million pounds and I was told that if we didn't find it we wouldn't be able to continue working with the Cartel. I said that I didn't think we had the luxury of that kind of commercial choice and that while we should continue to be colleagues and friends of the Cartel, perhaps we needed to shut down our professional relationship with them. We couldn't afford to continue it. As soon as I said that, the internal animosity was even greater than it already had been. The next week there was a front-page headline in *Music Week* announcing I'd shut down the Cartel.

That was really the start of me becoming the face of the axe, but I was happy to take on that sort of dictatorship role because somebody really did need to do something. I would be having these huge confrontations with staff while people like Will and Geoff stood on the sidelines watching what they realised commercially was inevitable but making sure that ostensibly they had nothing to do with it. I'd fire the staff, they'd comfort them.

The way the business was run seemed very partisan to me – almost daft. Instead of being run as associated companies, the principal two parts of the company functioned as enemies. No one had control. Information seemed to come out slightly haphazard. It was a bombshell to me to be told that they'd taken on the new lease without disposing of the old one. I mean, they needed a new location – every time a new Yazz or Erasure album came out, the records would be spilling into the street – but I was staggered to be told that the functioning lease at Collier Street had something insane like another twenty years to run.

Every day I was going round in a cold sweat. There was *no* money. But people would still dream up these insane proposals at meetings. On one occasion at a meeting, I noticed innocently listed in the minutes for discussion, *Item 7–Purchase of our new vinyl pressing plant*. It had to be a joke. We had absolutely no money and even if we had, the last thing we could possibly want would be a vinyl pressing plant.

Jeremy Boyce: The pressures obviously got to George. He couldn't have failed to have been aware of the animosity. It affected him. On one occasion he came back from a meeting absolutely slaughtered. He was trashed – emotionally as well as by the alcohol. He was crying at his desk, moaning about dignity and how we all had loads of it and he had none and that he couldn't go on. We spent the rest of the day covering for him and cancelling meetings – we even covered for him with the other staff – and phoned up his wife to collect him since he clearly couldn't drive.

But you got nothing back for things like that.

George Kimpton-Howe: I'd been to the Ivor Novello Awards and returned a bit 'tired and emotional' to discover that a label I was chasing to sign had accepted a very large advance to stay at Pinnacle. It all got to me and I burst into tears. It was another of those punctuation points where I realised the business was going terribly wrong.

I did bring in what business I could but towards the end of 1990, we weren't sinking, we were plummeting. I started to look at job numbers and realised that in some areas we were overstaffed, not least in the warehouse, the most militant part of Rough Trade. I'd been warned off the warehouse very early on – told that it was a culture within a culture. On one occasion, I took someone from the record label Situation 2 around the warehouse, someone who wanted to move to Pinnacle and a more conventional business model away from the bowl of soup approach of Rough Trade. I wanted to show them the warehouse. We got stopped by one of the workers who flatly refused me entry on the grounds that 'only warehouse staff are allowed in the warehouse'. I suggested to this person that after my guest had left, we might have a chat, which is what we did.

Richard Boon: As a cultural anthropologist, looking back now to the end, I can see how the staff had changed at Rough Trade over the years. There were many committed people throughout. But it altered. In Blenheim Crescent a lot of the staff were in bands and really cared about what they were doing. In Collier Street, a load of goths moved in and the atmosphere changed. And by the time we got to Seven Sisters Road it was basically anarcho-crusties just doing it for the money.

George Kimpton-Howe: In all I lasted less than a year, not even twelve months to the day when I had quit a dream job at Pinnacle. They were smashing windows in the warehouse and sending me dog turds through the post; it was an absolute nightmare. Then Will resigned.

Will used to chair meetings in the most wonderfully non-confrontational way – the complete opposite to me – but he would also sit in his office at night, tapping away at the figures in private on a laptop. I think he was the first person I ever saw use a laptop. A very nice and very, very clever man, but towards the end, you just got the impression that the whole thing had become his guilty secret.

Jeremy Boyce: It never worked between me and George and one day I was called into a meeting in Will Keen's office and given three options – I could stay, change my attitude and be more like George, in which case everything would become lovely again, I could stay and not change my attitude, which would lead to a disciplinary offence and they'd sack me, or I could talk with them about how much I wanted to go away.

How did it make me feel? To say that to this day I still have particular feelings about George Kimpton-Howe is an understatement. It was the best job of my life and I lost it because of him. I felt completely let down, especially by Will, because I had always got on with him. Rough Trade even made me tell lies after I had quit and paid me off on the understanding that I told colleagues that I was suffering from stress and couldn't handle it any more.

ADVISING THEM NOT ONLY
ON THEIR BUSINESS PLANS

Geoff Travis: The end was an absolute bloody nightmare, the worst time of my life. It was quite literally like being in a war room. The phones wouldn't stop ringing and every time I answered one it was somebody we owed money to. We owed money to so many people. I have to say that I don't remember any personal abuse, or anyone from outside being particularly horrible to me, and most people were remarkably understanding of our problems. But it was the blackest period of my life.

I felt often during that period that I was being used. I became the focal point for everything, but having not run away, there really was no alternative but to stay and try to do what I could to help. Everyone in management around me had gone, disappeared as if they'd never existed. A lot of people in those positions left because they didn't want to deal with the coming disaster. As far as I am concerned, they ran away ... Will, to give him his credit, hung on as long as he could before virtually going under with a nervous breakdown. Will was genuinely trying to deal with the situation.

Jeannette Lee: I was involved and yet not involved. For me it was like standing in a river and watching everything rush by. I watched it rush by because I was so relatively new and didn't feel the effects the way that others did

who had been there longer. There was a hell of a lot of tension. On top of
the financial problems there was also the deterioration of the relations
between the label and Distribution. These two bad things were coming
together and all sorts of resentments seemed to come to a head. There was
a horrible, thick atmosphere – and through it all I was just trying to skip
over the top of it, trying to just keep doing my job. Geoff and I got through
it in different ways but ploughing on and refusing to stop looking for new
things to work on and trying to do the best with the things we had was one
way.

Duncan Cameron: Towards the end of 1990, I realised that January/
February would be tough for Rough Trade from a cash-flow point of view
and that that would be our risk period, because after Christmas the retail
trade just chucks back everything it hasn't sold by way of returns. Some
stores would owe Rough Trade money but effectively be paying it with
returns. So, I felt cash-flow problems might show themselves in that early
period of the new year. In fact, we got a Rough Trade cheque just before
Christmas but that still left them quite a bit owing because, of course, we
were selling a lot of records in that period.

Very early in 1991, I got a phone call from Will telling me he had
resigned. He said there was a problem in agreeing the direction that Rough
Trade should go in between him and others and that if he couldn't agree
or carry the day then he felt he ought to go. My impression was that he and
Geoff weren't of one mind as to what should be done next. Amazingly,
I still didn't know a lot about Rough Trade at that point: I found out an
awful lot over the next two weeks or so.

One Friday afternoon towards the middle of January, John Dyer, who
worked in marketing at Mute, walked into my office and said that we had
to go over to Rough Trade immediately. I looked out the window and looked
at my watch – late afternoon, mid-winter, dreadful snow. John said Daniel
wanted us over there and so I guessed it wasn't going to be good news.

When we got to Rough Trade, I found we weren't the only label there.
A number of the larger independents were there, also – Beggars Banquet,
Big Life, KLF. Geoff explained that Rough Trade couldn't pay us and his
line basically was that we were all friends and that we could sort this out
together. He had no details of what they could and couldn't pay but promised
to do everything to settle the debts.

Everybody went home for what was an interesting weekend with lots of bases being touched and the outcome was that we all felt we had to find a way through the problem that supported our businesses, our artists and our futures together. I came from a corporate background where the phones to lawyers would have been buzzing and it would have been every man for himself. I was very impressed at how well they all saw the big picture. Daniel had terrific vision.

BUT ALSO ROYALTY AUDITS, RAISING CAPITAL AND TOUR AUDITS, BUYOUTS...

So we all got together and formulated a plan that would continue to support Rough Trade, one that meant we would keep putting our sales through them so long as there was a sensible plan as to how the historic debt was met. The bigger independent labels agreed to sell the idea to the smaller independent labels.

The next meeting at Rough Trade was on 4th February, another dreadful day weather-wise. This was where a deal was hammered out, handwritten on a scrap of paper, and my recollection is that the deal – signed by the major labels – was that they would continue to put records through Rough Trade Distribution and that in return for support and for not taking any formal legal action to get their historic debt back, future monies coming in to Rough Trade from the retail trade would be segregated at receipt and label's share put into a separate trust account controlled by the labels. Roughly eighty per cent of receipts would go into that account and twenty per cent into the normal Rough Trade account to enable it to pay its overheads and other creditors.

In addition, I think the labels got a guarantee in respect of the historic debt from Rough Trade Limited – the holding company – that if the debt couldn't be paid through Rough Trade Distribution assets, then other parts of the company – the record company, the publishing company, Rough Trade Inc. and Rough Trade Germany – would be used to pay back the debt.

This was agreed and I went with Nigel Boult from Beggars Banquet and decamped in Rough Trade, where we became signatures on the account. We got summaries of what was owed to every label and apportioned the amount available and sent cheques out. The phones never stopped ringing from people owed money. The tragedy is that this had a very long tail and some of the smaller labels we wrote to and sent cheques to we never heard back from. Some letters with cheques in were returned.

Martin Mills: I was on the Labels' Committee and spent many long evenings over quite a period trying with others to help save Rough Trade. Geoff was clearly under a lot of pressure, and understandably not in great shape, but he very much felt that he needed to give everything for the cause, which meant putting the record label's assets into the pot. We recognised that he didn't really have to do that. There was no animosity, anyway, just an enormous sadness that Rough Trade was in the position it was in.

Duncan Cameron: Everything was done in an inter-label agreement, there was no formal or legal action taken. At this time, though, and I totally understand it, the trustees of Rough Trade, who weren't from the industry, started to get nervous about their responsibilities. They weren't involved in day-to-day management but they carried a lot of responsibility. They felt they lacked control and so they insisted on having a firm of accountants from KPMG Peat Marwick come in and help us run the commercial side of things at that point. KPMG sent in a team headed up by David Murrell and they decamped into the building as well. It was a strange situation and we had a very uneasy relationship with them.

David Murrell: In the early part of 1991, Rough Trade Distribution realised that they had insufficient money to pay out what they owed. Their overheads were too high and they were under-capitalised. We were asked to help. I took a small team into the distribution warehouse at Seven Sisters and we were there for about four to five months. The job really was to reach an informal administration – the aim was to keep Rough Trade *out* of formal administration and help restore it to health.

One absolutely key feature of Rough Trade Distribution was that they owned The Smiths' back catalogue, which was potentially worth up to a million pounds. It was a hugely significant sum of money. The rights in it would revert to Morrissey and Johnny Marr if the company went into liquidation or receivership. So, if any label put them into that position that asset would be gone from the business, which would have been worth significantly less. That, I believe, was uppermost in the minds of the labels.

Geoff Travis: When we started to have meetings with the administrators, another nightmare began. I found them a really despicable breed – city vultures that had no real understanding of the Rough Trade culture. They were hysterically excited by what they saw to be the glamour of the business. It was like one of the cartoons from a Hunter S. Thompson article, with reptilian, slithering characters. On the other hand, what was most remarkable was the way that all the labels and creditors would have meetings together and be really kind to Rough Trade.

Richard Boon: I remember someone from KPMG coming in and addressing the assembled staff and saying, 'From now on, I am your controller . . .' It was an awful moment, an awful time. They came from a completely different culture to that of Rough Trade.

Duncan Cameron: Had a smaller label rocked the boat then I believe the larger labels would have paid them off because the issue of The Smiths' back catalogue was a valid one. The fact that Rough Trade Distribution owned The Smiths' catalogue was convenient, really.

The labels quite rightly perceived that this was their world, the world in which this problem was unfolding and that they were best placed if some of Rough Trade's assets were to be realised or a buyer for Rough Trade Distribution found. That was the first aim. A negotiating committee was set up with the heads of all the labels and they basically worked their contacts to try to find buyers, to sort out the future. That was quite right. Whatever happened to Rough Trade affected their future.

KPMG were really brought in to try and bring the credit control up to date and to get some money in from the trade, but I think they saw themselves as the ones who might sort out the big picture as well. So there was a little bit of conflict there.

Credit control turned out to be a big problem and it was made worse, as I had anticipated earlier, by a lot of the trade instead of paying Rough Trade what was owed it in cash, sending in returns. In fact the problem was exacerbated because the retail trade realised that if Rough Trade went under they wouldn't be able to return records. So, some cash coming in and lots of records made the cash-flow situation worse at that point.

David Murrell: Geoff Travis was effectively suspended – not in a legal sense. He came to meetings and was kept in the picture. But he'd lost his management powers and that was the wishes of the labels because he couldn't pay them. In that sense, it was similar to a formal administration. But Geoff knew everything about the business and was enormously helpful to us.

Duncan Cameron: Geoff wanted to work through this and resolve it but he was a record company man and this was a logistical matter and I certainly never saw this as something which was his primary responsibility or interest.

David Murrell: By May/June we had collected a lot of money and made the labels an offer of 65p in the pound of what was owed. This was made in writing to all the labels. This was a full and final settlement offer and, like in Monopoly, it was the end-game for the player. This is all we've got, take it. The cupboard really was bare beyond that, and, of course, these labels were still being paid for their current record sales. We held a meeting and explained it all.

Certain lawyers at the meeting were not particularly constructive or helpful. People used to dealing and bargaining felt that if 65p was on offer then 75p must be in the pot. There were lots of suspicions that more was available and as a result of that the offer was rejected, to our absolute amazement.

Duncan Cameron: KPMG were on a pretty hefty fee, as I recall, about £10,000 or so a week to sort this out. They were running around trying to get money in and trying also independently to get some interest in Rough Trade Distribution, and the labels, who had a lot of the power, were collecting money through the escrow fund which worked to a degree and kept labels afloat. I always felt that some labels were more exposed to risk than others in supporting the arrangement. I was always confident that while Mute would take a hit on this, it wouldn't be threatened – we had overseas money coming in and credit insurance. I felt that Beggars would also be similarly cushioned and they had an alternative distribution through Warners. But labels like KLF, a band and a label who had just released *The*

White Room, and Rhythm King, who were just about to release their Betty Boo album and who may not have had much overseas business, were exposed to a big risk. Labels with less at stake than Mute proportionally took a bigger hit.

AND TAX PLANNING.

It all ground on and the weather didn't get any better so I couldn't get home and ended up staying in a bed and breakfast. Life moved on but there still didn't seem to be any interested buyers. There was lots of initial interest, then lots of waffle.

Aside from The Smiths' catalogue there always seemed to be problems with the assets, as well. Rough Trade Germany refused to remit money back, on legal advice, for instance. Then there began to be murmurings that the trust we had set up had dubious legal validity. KPMG checked it out, I believe, and encouraged people to keep putting records through Rough Trade Distribution. We'd put it together in a hurry but the legal advice about it that we got wasn't negative.

But non-label creditors got wind of it and we began to get letters from their legal advisers questioning why some money coming in wasn't being divided amongst *all* the creditors. At least one of the creditors formally challenged the validity of the trust and consequently we ended up going down a legal route to defend it.

There were a few meetings between KPMG and the labels where things just got frustrated and didn't seem to be going anywhere, and finally we arrived at the point where we decided to put Rough Trade into formal administration. KPMG were to be the administrators but David Murrell stepped aside. I think there had been a clash of worlds, cultures and personalities by this point.

There may have been as much as a million pounds in the trust account so we all went off to the High Court to say to the judge, you decide how valid the trust is. The labels got representation. The trust account was frozen. At the preliminary hearing I remember thinking it was going to be a nightmare because there were so many different classes of creditor.

The judge looked at everything and came back and said that the case could make legal history, but that it would be long and protracted and he advised us to sort it out ourselves. So Phil Wallace, the new person from KPMG who became the administrator, came up with a compromise. Although the labels didn't get all the money in the trust account, they got fifty per cent and the remaining fifty per cent went to the creditors, which included the labels. So the labels got two bites at the cherry.

David Murrel: The 65p in the pound that the labels had been offered ended up being 50p in the pound. That was after The Smiths catalogue had been sold. The company went into administration, which was a relatively new thing, and something not covered by The Smiths contract. If it had gone into liquidation or receivership, the rights reverted, but under administration they didn't. It was a great personal sadness to me that we ended up in the situation that we did. Rough Trade Distribution could have continued; instead everyone had to find alternative distribution at a time when there weren't that many distributors out there.

Johnny Marr: The whole thing went on to affect The Smiths really badly even although we'd been split up for years. We didn't get paid for a long time and I don't think the band members could have imagined the effect it would have – Andy Rourke and Mike Joyce blamed us for them not getting paid when Morrissey and I weren't getting paid either. We faced the prospect of our catalogue being sold off to some arbitrary company without us having any say as to how the records might come out or the band might be paid. All sorts of horror stories were being suggested to me. Then we heard that someone thought the fair thing would be for Morrissey and me to be given the chance to retrieve our back catalogue and find a buyer for it. We ended up mortgaging our houses, buying back our catalogue and selling it on to Warners, thinking they would take care of it.

I never heard anything from Rough Trade during that time, which I thought was disrespectful and inconsiderate really because your work, as people say, you regard as your family line. I thought it was pretty shitty at the time. But now I think someone like Geoff Travis was busy enough with his own affairs to have to worry about Johnny Marr's.

Geoff Travis: Of course I had to have been in touch with The Smiths because effectively I helped organise the deal between them and Warners. It was a three-way dialogue between the band, Warners and myself.

George Kimpton-Howe: Just before the whole thing went into formal administration, I left. The labels got together to set up RTM, the new distribution vehicle which was a kind of Rough Trade Distribution mark two, with the larger independent labels sticking together to get more power. I remember at that time Polydor wanted to take it over, but some of the more purist independents didn't like the idea. They then went to Steve Mason at Pinnacle to get help to set up RTM.

Once Pinnacle came on board, it was a formality as to whether I resigned or was asked to leave. We all sat round at a very sober meeting where it was put to me that I had to go. I was totally burnt out anyway. They honoured my service agreement and paid me off. I lived with a huge sense of personal regret – I'd chucked in a fantastic job at Pinnacle, lost an old friend who had really been good to me in the process, and gained in return the worst year of my life. It took me a long time to recover.

Richard Boon: I remember right at the end, George Kimpton-Howe was chasing somebody who was going to shove in a million quid. A million was always the figure – *Rough Trade needed a million, someone was going to put in a million* ... But it didn't happen. Just before he left, we all queued up to get redundancy cheques off George. I walked in the room and he asked me how long I'd been working there. Eight years. *Eight years* – he was touchingly sympathetic in a way.

I stayed in the building for about a month after and got paid for hours done. I saw through the last issue of *The Catalogue*, which the printers held up until they had part-payment of the full amount, which they knew they weren't going to get. It had a Spacemen 3 flexi on the front and inside a regular column where I picked a word and ran with it. That issue's word was 'WAR!' The first Iraq War had just started but when I opened a finished copy in the office and looked at the word 'WAR!' in large type, it had another resonance.

Duncan Cameron: RTM was effectively subcontracted out to Pinnacle and ran for about three years. None of the bigger labels involved wanted to be distributors, other than by default, so it was never going to last for long anyway. Looking back, I think those major independent labels escaped with a knock but nothing fatal. With our credit insurance and with the money we got back, the hit was something like £250,000 off an £800,000 debt. The hidden casualties were the smaller labels. I'm sure there were plenty of nascent labels who, because they never got paid promptly or fully for their earlier releases, never made it any further. I wouldn't go as far as to say that a whole generation of labels were killed off but there were ones who never recovered and who knows what might have become of them?

These record company people all came from pretty much the same place. They weren't businessmen: they were all fans of music. I think they all realised over a period of time that if they wanted to run a creative-led business in a commercial environment, sooner or later, particularly if they were to grow, they were going to have to get efficient management behind them to protect their view or philosophy.

Companies like Mute, Rough Trade and Beggars wouldn't have been what they were without being led by people like Daniel Miller, Geoff Travis and Martin Mills. The question was, how quickly did they realise that they needed an infrastructure to support their ideals? At varying times, they all did. In the depths of my Rough Trade frustration, I was in a meeting room with Daniel, Martin and others trying to dissect this dreadful problem. In frustration, I put my head in my hands and said, 'They haven't even got a cash flow! *Who* would start a company without a cash flow?' As I lifted my head up and looked around they were all beaming at me. They'd all done that, of course they had. It summed it all up. They weren't businessmen and they never pretended to be. Record companies aren't run by businessmen – they are run by visionaries.

Jo Slee: That black period for Geoff didn't end with Rough Trade Distribution going into administration: it ran on for years and I know he was very ill with it during this period. It is worth being reminded that the Rough Trade record label was the biggest creditor, owed the most amount of money of all, well over a million pounds.

Obviously, it was right that the asset went into the pot. Geoff had started this thing in 1976 and by 1991 he was the only one who cared about it and loved it enough to want to stay and try and sort it out. Everybody had vanished except him.

Peter Travis: I was supportive at the time of the collapse and I know Geoff feared it might mean personal ruin for him – that, after he had already seen the ruin of the company he had set up. His behaviour was exemplary. He has only ever sought to honestly promote artists without regard to personal gain. I have always been very proud of what he has achieved.

Carolyn Holder: Geoff had opened this little record shop and success had more or less been sudden and furious and I don't think anyone thought it would be that way and of course for a long time they either paid themselves no money or little money. I sometimes wonder whether that lack of money early on contributed to the lack of a financial structure which created the later problems.

It was a nightmare. Geoff was constantly looking for support, for a way to keep the company going. Right at the end some weirdo claimed he could save Rough Trade and promised to put £500,000 into the bank account and every day Geoff was assured it would be there. Nothing came of it.

At one point, a little later, Geoff was warned by the lawyers that it was conceivable that he might have to go to jail over the whole mess. We had two small children at the time. He lost it all – the label, the people he worked with, the back catalogue, the rights in the name, everything. And what he did was he got himself straight up and started again. He went straight back to work and straight back going out to gigs, and I have the most tremendous respect for him for doing that.

AFTER

CHAPTER FOURTEEN:

AN INTERLUDE

'As it turned out, there were far too many chiefs
at One Little Indian'

Post-collapse – Golborne Road – Blanco history – Management – One
Little Indian – Trade Two – V&A party

Rough Trade Distribution went into administration on 17 May 1991. For
some of the more vulnerable casualties of its collapse – such as the smaller
labels who lost everything – the nightmare was swift and brutal. For many
others, it was a protracted and drawn-out affair. It took the thirty secured
and unsecured major creditors the best part of two years before a creditors'
settlement could finally be agreed and the company liquidated. Geoff Travis,
as notional head of the whole Rough Trade organisation, was hauled across
the coals over matters by the Department of Trade and Industry as late as
1995: 'burying the corpse', as Peter Walmsley had it, took a lot longer than
might have been expected.

A pared-down, stripped-out Rough Trade Records was up and running straight after the collapse in 1991 – in fact, the record label as a cohesive entity barely skipped a beat – and the move to Golborne Road happened almost immediately. But it wasn't clear whether the label could release records, and, in so doing, whether it would be able to use the famous Rough Trade name.

Geoff Travis: We shifted down a gear in Seven Sisters Road, although we hadn't been releasing much since the year before when the problems had started. We were very unhappy in the building and one day just decided that we needed to get out. What was left of Rough Trade Distribution was being moved to an industrial estate in the middle of nowhere – the atmosphere was bad enough where we were. That whole period of the end went on for ever.

Carolyn Holder: For the first year and a half after the collapse, Geoff was on the brink of a nervous breakdown. He had papers served on him and was advised that he could end up in jail. It didn't come to that. He only ever had an interest in the music and thought that if someone wasn't paying enough attention to the business side, which many people weren't prior to the collapse, then that was their job and nothing to do with him. As he found out, of course, it was his responsibility.

Jeannette Lee: We didn't dwell on the problems. We carried on looking for new bands, even if we weren't entirely sure what label those bands might have their records released on. We didn't see what had happened as an end in any way. We never had a conversation where we said the thing was over and that we would move on to something else. For us, everything was always Rough Trade. The outside world might have broken things down differently. It was a technicality that the name had gone astray.

Geoff Travis: I'd never been possessive of Rough Trade, but I could see what we had lost. I didn't want it to stop, and I didn't want to get out. It all very nearly drove me insane. Truthfully, it had been a strain ever since the first person had walked into the company and started spouting nonsense. So, we carried on with our parallel jobs of working with Blanco and managing.

*

Blanco Y Negro had started in 1982 after Mike Alway – an A&R man, with sometimes compellingly eccentric taste, from Cherry Red Records – had approached Geoff with a view to working at Rough Trade, either for the label or for a custom-created label under a Rough Trade umbrella. Neither option was viable back at a time when Rough Trade was facing a major financial crisis. Instead, the two of them went to Rob Dickens at WEA – a young man in a hurry, who, at the age of thirty-two, found himself MD of the major label – and got him to fund a completely new label. Mike Alway brought in Michel Duval from Les Disques de Crépuscule (Belgium's equivalent of Factory Records), allegedly because he liked the label's record cover designs. Blanco got off to a promising start with releases by Everything But the Girl that sold over a million copies worldwide.

The setting up of a hybrid was a clever idea, but back at the turn of the still-politicised 1980s, the land between major labels and independents was seen as scorched earth. The music press dubbed the trio 'the gang of three' and at Rough Trade there was a degree of misplaced suspicion over the motives behind the label.

Geoff Travis: Nobody said anything to me directly, but it was obviously seen as a great act of treason in certain quarters at Rough Trade and I could feel a clear undercurrent of hostility towards the project. Some people, I think, felt it was politically wrong to be involved with Blanco and some people were worried that I might leave. It never occurred to me that anything I might choose to do would distract from Rough Trade or be done for any other reason than the ultimate benefit of Rough Trade.

Carolyn Holder: In 1982, Rough Trade was in deep financial trouble and Geoff got involved with Blanco solely to raise money to help Rough Trade at a very difficult time. He took so much flak from people for doing that and yet he hadn't and hasn't the slightest interest in the accumulation of wealth. He'll pour money into an artist but has no interest in money for himself.

Geoff Travis: I felt at first as if I was helping Mike out. He'd come to me seeing himself to be in an impossible situation with Cherry Red and was looking for a way forward. It was initially Mike's impetus. But after a couple of releases, Mike decided to leave, and Michel wasn't involved for long either, so I quickly found myself in charge of a record label which I hadn't intended to set up. It was difficult. I saw the way it was viewed by certain people at Rough Trade, yet always felt vindicated that on those occasions when an artist would be better suited to Rough Trade, that was the way they were steered. We signed The Sundays to Rough Trade when they might have been signed to Blanco, and earlier the Jesus & Mary Chain were a Blanco act when some people thought they were perfect for Rough Trade. At that time, the Jesus & Mary Chain, who wanted nothing more to do with indie labels, would only have signed to Rough Trade if they'd had *no* other option.

*

Eddi Reader released a number of albums through Blanco after her Fairground Attraction career came to an abrupt end.

Eddi Reader: After the first flush of success with Fairground Attraction, I had very quickly found myself to be in the company of strangers. Mark Nevin, who I had found and then joined forces with to form Fairground Attraction, had decided that I shouldn't write or contribute to songs for the band and it devastated me. We had had this enormous hit with 'Perfect', yet within a week of us falling out the record had been licensed behind my back for use in an advert, which was not something I would have approved of.

After the split, I was still personally contracted to RCA, so I went off and made the solo album *Mirmama*, which musically went back to my roots and some of the songs I'd heard in the folk clubs when I was growing up in Glasgow and Ayrshire. I was playing solo gigs and Geoff would often turn up to see them. Around the time of *Mirmama*, I think he was at virtually every gig I played. I was very nervous about my new material and Geoff said the one thing that proved there was a God and a lifeboat out there: he said he didn't really care for the Fairground Attraction material but that he loved *Mirmama*.

When I went to Geoff I was in a pretty bad situation personally. I had a broken marriage, one child and another on the way. I think Geoff still had ambitions towards Rough Trade as a label but said to me that I was going to need enough money to support myself and that he suggested taking my material to Blanco Y Negro. I remember him saying to me, 'I'll introduce you to Rob Dickens, he'll say the total opposite of what I say, but just don't listen to him.'

In fact, Rob Dickens fell in love with my sound and wanted to turn me into the new Cher. I didn't know how to fight that and I don't think Geoff did either, in a way. Rob would say things like, 'We can't just give her £35,000 to make a video; it is going to take much more to get her on the telly.' So I found myself in a strange place where I made the *Eddi Reader* album in a way that probably wasn't right for me. I think had I been a bit stronger, more bolshy perhaps and with a little more confidence and not just this skinny working-class girl with almost no education to speak of, I might have been able to fight it more.

Geoff Travis: Eddi struggled with being pushed in that commercial direction, even although she had the ability, if she so chose, to be really commercial, as she had been in Fairground Attraction. But I think in her soul, she was more like Edith Piaf, singing what she wanted to sing without feeling compromised. I remember someone at Warners telling her she had to wear glasses on the album cover to look like Buddy Holly. I don't think she felt free in that kind of setting.

Eddi Reader: I did a couple more albums with Blanco, but when the Rough Trade label got going again I moved over and made *Simple Soul*. It was all recorded at Roy Dodd's, my drummer's house, and more gentle than the stuff I'd been making on Blanco. The Faustian pact of working with a major was over.

*

Blanco Y Negro lasted an extraordinary twenty years and during that time funded Rough Trade, if not frequently, then at crucial moments. Money, which was by rights remuneration for Blanco services, regularly found its way into the Rough Trade coffers. Dinosaur Jr., Catatonia and the Dream Academy were all Blanco artists, as were, notably, Eddi Reader, The Veils and The Delays, all of whom moved across to Rough Trade when Blanco folded. Part of the label's success was due to the relationship of trust it had with Rob Dickens, who had no need to question its editorial judgement.

Following the Distribution debacle and the subsequent asset-stripping of the business, the relationship between Geoff Travis and Jeannette Lee and WEA altered. So long as Rough Trade Records had existed in its primary form, there was no question that that would be the main concern. But in

August 1991, Blanco was re-signed to WEA in a deal which had no connection with Rough Trade. Consequently, after a number of renewals on the
Blanco contract, when Rough Trade re-emerged in 2001 in a partnership
agreement with Sanctuary, it could only take artists as a 'second look' label.
That meant that all artists had to be shown first to Blanco, who could then
choose to release or pass on the material. The Blanco deal didn't end until
June 2002. Indeed, the Blanco arrangement may well have continued, but
for a disagreement over the artistic merits of a couple of bands Geoff Travis
and Jeannette Lee wanted to sign.

*

In the very early 1990s, in the effective absence of a record label, Rough
Trade began managing bands. They had tried to sign The Cranberries to
Blanco Y Negro but had failed, yet the relationship with the band had gone
well, and six months after signing to Island Records, the band approached
Rough Trade to be managed by them.

Geoff Travis: We were a little late in or something and they were almost
signed to Island Records anyway. They released *Uncertain* and went on
tour, but after six months weren't going anywhere. Dolores O'Riordan
called us up out of the blue and asked if we could help. We had loved those
early songs and so we swallowed our pride and said yes.

That ran for a while until Dolores got married and her husband decided
he could do a better job . . . Hardly any time after we took on The Cranberries
we suddenly found ourselves managing Pulp as well, after their PR John
Best came to see us and said could we help Pulp out as they were in a bit
of a mess.

Jarvis Cocker: Pulp hadn't had good experiences of independent labels when
we first came to Rough Trade. We'd been with Red Rhino, who had been
OK but didn't manage to sell any records and dropped us after our first,
unsuccessful album. We'd then gone to Fire Records, where we had a truly
horrendous experience. I'd got this downer about independent labels at the
time. We were in a complicated position. We wanted to sign to Island
Records, and they wanted to sign us, but we were still signed to Fire. Our
manager at the time told us just to lie and say we weren't signed to anyone.
We got rid of the manager but then found ourselves in a position where
nobody would touch us with a bargepole.

John Best suggested I go and talk to Geoff Travis. I went to see Geoff and played him some songs. I remember just staring at the floor while the tape played. Geoff pushed his head in and out like a tortoise pushing its head out of its shell. He was very quiet. I'm self-conscious. The whole thing was a bit of a painful occasion. I never like being a room with someone listening to my music: it is very uncomfortable. I knew also that whether Rough Trade took Pulp on or not would depend on what he thought of the songs he was listening to. He introduced me to Jeannette, probably so that he could ask her what he thought of me when I'd gone. They asked me what I wanted to do and I said that I wanted to make pop records. We had a real bee in our bonnet about wanting to be on *Top of the Pops* and have chart hits and things like that. This was, of course, in that period that led up to the dreaded Britpop. I can't remember whether they said they'd take us on there and then, but they came down to see Pulp play at Brighton and it sort of became official after that.

Geoff Travis: Jeannette and I went to see Pulp play at Sussex University and it was fantastic – we'd never seen anything so unusual. We hadn't really noticed them or bought their records, so we came to them completely unencumbered with any history and just agreed that they were the best pop group we'd seen in ages. Working together turned out to be the most creatively rewarding experience of that whole period between the old Rough Trade and the launch of the new.

Jarvis Cocker: Having Rough Trade as management hasn't been like having a manager in the traditional sense where someone makes you do things. It's been a much more personal relationship, one where they've always gone along with my hare-brained schemes, so long as they've agreed with them, because their initial approach is always to try to do what the artist wants. I speak to Jeannette nearly every day and we have a very direct relationship, one where I never feel the need to have to sell her anything, and one where when I talk to her she never makes me feel like I'm talking to the boss.

Jeannette Lee: I clicked with Jarvis from the start and part of the reason why our relationship has been so good and gone on so long is because he is one of the most interesting people I have ever met. He constantly has great ideas and he constantly keeps me on my toes. I find him challenging and interesting at the same time. I never know what he is going to come up with next, and I like that. He'll never come up with a bad idea, although he does sometimes come up with things that are difficult to put together, though always worth it. And just like Geoff, he's never scared to take a risk.

Jarvis Cocker: When Rough Trade took Pulp on it was a very exciting time. We had this idea that we could be a pop group when most other people just thought that was pretty impossible. We were slightly seen as a bit of a joke – no-hopers who'd been around too long. But Rough Trade went along with our idea, and then, of course, the dream started to come true. This was happening at a time when musically things were coming in from the margins and going into the mainstream. Britpop's legacy isn't that stunning, but the feeling of excitement that came out of the fact that indie was the thing that everybody now listened to felt almost like a revolutionary act back then.

Rough Trade got us to a place where we could do something. Not only could we make an album with the right producer, but we got to do it our way, for the first time. In the case of *His 'n' Hers*, even down to the nice airbrushed cover by Philip Castle who had done the famous Penguin book jacket on Anthony Burgess's *A Clockwork Orange*, something which wouldn't have happened without Rough Trade persuading Island it was a good approach. With Jeannette looking after us and Rough Trade behind us, Island treated us as a sort of fully formed thing, something they couldn't interfere in, which backfired on them when it came to *This is Hardcore*, but worked spectacularly well with *Different Class*.

The success was all driven by 'Common People'. We'd written the song and played it once at the 1994 Reading Festival, where it had got a big reaction. We'd played it again at a Peel session and it was then that I thought that the time was right. It sounds megalomaniacal, and it was. I was walking down the Portobello Road after visiting Rough Trade and it suddenly occurred to me that the mood in the country was right for what we wanted to do. I wanted the record to come out as soon as possible. So, I conveyed this news to Jeannette and instead of saying, as somebody else might have, calm down, she agreed. Even although we had no album ready, she persuaded Island to put us in the studio with the producer Chris Thomas and just record that song and one other, and got them to release it.

PULP. HIS 'N' HERS.

Clare Britt: I was working as marketing director at Island Records when Geoff and Jeannette came in with 'Common People', the record that really broke Pulp. They had such belief and passion in the fact that this was going to be a very big hit and we all in the end got right behind it. I worked Pulp myself, instead of farming them out to, say, one of my colleagues, because I had known about them from before. I had been to school in Sheffield, had gone to see them play when I was fifteen, and knew Jarvis's sister a bit from clubbing in Sheffield. They were fantastic to work with – eloquent and creative – but there was a little bit of trust required, too, because although Jarvis was confident about what he wanted to do, he was also pretty good at pushing boundaries ...

Patsy Winkelman: In the 1980s I had been helping run Vindaloo Records in Birmingham with artists like The Nightingales, Ted Chippington and We've Got a Fuzzbox and We're Gonna Use It, and then I'd moved on to working in major labels, which I didn't enjoy. Vindaloo had always had a good relationship with Rough Trade, who had distributed the label, and so not long before Pulp started happening I'd approached Geoff and he'd asked me to go and work at Rough Trade while Jeannette went on maternity leave. Of course, I ended up staying.

Even before 'Common People' became such a big hit, there was a feeling in the office that this was less like working a normal band and more like working a massive chart act. Much of that was driven by Scott Piering who came in to do PR. As well as having the word shaved into his head at the time, Scott just wouldn't let things rest until everyone understood how special Pulp were. Nothing changes in radio – and back then getting anything underground or left-field or different onto the airwaves was no less different than now, but Scott wouldn't stop plugging them and plugging them until eventually the song broke through. He was a hero, a total hero.

Jarvis Cocker: Rough Trade wholly believed in us, but in fact Island tried to hedge their bets by using a split-formats strategy. They planned to release the record on CD1 in week one, and on CD2 in the second. It was all to do with sustaining chart position, the marketing equivalent of Viagra. But we said no. It was our dream to get into the Top Ten and our belief that it was better to live one day as a lion than a lifetime as a lamb, and again Rough Trade backed us up. But it still took everybody by surprise when it got to Number Two in the charts.

*

Bernard Butler, the former Suede guitarist who went on to become a solo artist and then a producer, began to be managed by Rough Trade in the mid-1990s and, on and off, has been represented by them for almost as long as Jarvis Cocker has. Green Gartside reaffiliated Scritti Politti with Rough Trade later in that same decade when Green once again began to be managed by them. With the release of the Mercury Prize-shortlisted *White Bread Black Beer* in 2006, he reignited a recording relationship that has now entered its fourth decade. Butler, meanwhile, produced and partly co-wrote some of the songs on Duffy's album *Rockferry* (including the haunting title track), which, on its release in 2007, sold seven million copies worldwide.

Bernard Butler: I first saw the name 'Rough Trade' on the back of The Smiths' 'Hand in Glove' single, which I bought when I was thirteen. The Smiths were a big, big thing for me – and still are. They will always be my favourite group. I saw the name 'Geoff Travis' on the back of the sleeve for 'This Charming Man', where he was listed as being 'Executive Producer'.

In August 1984, I started playing guitar. I had a week off school because I had flu and I remember watching an *Old Grey Whistle Test* 'On the Road' with The Smiths playing at the Derby Assembly Rooms and thinking, that could be me ...

Ten years later, in 1994, while I was still in Suede, I was invited to play with Teenage Fanclub at the Forum in North London. It was a period during which I was getting more and more disillusioned. Suede was making the second album but I was working too much and writing too much and stuff that was far too diverse for the band. At the after-show party, I was approached by Geoff. He said, 'If you ever want to make a record, come and see me.' For someone who was a complete stranger, I felt he had come fabulously to the point.

I started going in and playing Geoff stuff, mainly instrumentals, and he was just listening, that's all. This was at the time *Dog Man Star* came out, the second Suede album. It was almost inevitable that I would end up being managed by him. There was a lot of shit going on in my life to do with the band and lawyers and I was personally a bit of a complete mess, and I think I gave him a bit of a handful. Looking back I feel bad, but he dealt with it, though occasionally would tell me to shut up and stop moaning, which made me sit up because nobody had ever said that to me before. I wanted to work on a creative and not conversational level – everything had to be about what you heard – and Geoff was so strictly to the point that he was the person most like what I wanted that I had ever met. If he liked something, he told you he liked it, and if he didn't like it, he told you also, and that was that. I desperately wanted to impress him: to this day I still crave his and Jeannette's approval.

I wrote a piece of music that eventually became 'Yes', which I later recorded with McAlmont & Butler. I played it to Geoff and he loved it. 'Come and see David McAlmont with me at the Jazz Café,' he said. He didn't say anything more, but the point was obvious. I went, and handed David a cassette of the song and the next day we recorded the track. That was the start of that.

A little later, Geoff and Jeannette took me out and asked me to do my own record, and so I started recording things and playing them to Geoff, who was positive, really encouraging. Then one day I played him something he didn't like and he suddenly said he thought the whole thing wasn't going to work. I was devastated. I was crushed. There was no big argument. Geoff said what he thought and so I went off and made some records with Creation.

I then started working again with David and bumped into Geoff and he was really praising of my work and asked me if I wanted to produce a band for him. So I did that. Around about this time, there was a change in my life because I started looking in a much less awkward way for what I wanted out of my life and at how I might get that. And Geoff helped me there, though not in an overt way. And he offered to manage me again, though he said he couldn't do it until Jeannette, who was away, came back and I'd met up with her. Things had changed. First time around, Jeannette had been more of a mate – I'd go past her desk and chat and joke with her and with Patsy: the real world – before going into the serious, dark cauldron of Geoff's office. Had I known her better, I might never have left. I went for a coffee with Jeannette and eventually they agreed to take me back on. I started doing more production for them, working with people like The Libertines and The Veils.

*

The feeding frenzy that ensued once Rough Trade had become holed in 1991 led to unsavoury behaviour on a scale unprecedented even in an industry as ruthless as the music business. The Rough Trade record label's back catalogue was ripped apart and consumed and Rough Trade Publishing, the other notable asset left standing from the original structure, was sold off arbitrarily despite assurances to the contrary that Peter Walmsley and Cathi Gibson, who had diligently built up the somewhat internally disrespected business, would be allowed to make an offer.

Peter Walmsley: We were just lied to. The irony is that they'd had to come to us to value the business, to verify it, to get the contracts. Then they just sold it to somebody else in spite of our being willing to make a matching offer as good as anybody's. For me personally, the way I was forced to accept the terms of my leaving Rough Trade, where I was screwed out of money in an act of gross chicanery, was something I can't dwell on. The devious, soft-spoken, so-called well-meaning philanderers and crooks and under-the-table dealers just had me spitting, and in the end I wouldn't even have paid £20 for the business.

Cathi Gibson: We had a very good list, which had been built up with very little money and very little enthusiasm internally for the publishing arm. We had bands like the Violent Femmes, Lydia Lunch, the Jazz Butcher. At the end, when Distribution collapsed, we didn't really know who we were dealing with. People were leaving all the time and, since they had to have a quorum of directors, every five minutes there would be someone new pop up. Unfortunately, when Peter and I offered to buy the publishing it alerted these faceless people to the fact that they had this asset and suddenly they were shopping it all over London. I had people ringing me up saying, if you leave Rough Trade Publishing do you want to come and work for me?

It wasn't just Peter and I who suffered. The musicians did as well. Lee Ranaldo from Sonic Youth phoned up and said he couldn't believe that his songs were being flogged off to somebody he had never heard of without being asked or told about it. We represented Henry Rollins, an important artist, and his record label phoned up alarmed and asked me to go in to the warehouse and rescue all the records and CDs that were stored, which I did.

The Rough Trade name, of course, had been impounded, but we just decided we deserved the right to keep using it. We approached Geoff and Geoff said he didn't have a problem with that. We started up again as Rough Trade Publishing.

*

They didn't need to worry about continuing using the name. In spirit, Rough Trade has always belonged to everyone, and when Peter Walmsley and Cathi Gibson simply continued to call themselves 'Rough Trade', no one dared question their right. Just like the shop before them, Rough Trade could have a number of manifestations.

Ownership of the name of the record label was treated as an altogether more serious matter, however, and Geoff Travis and Jeannette Lee could only look on as the famous name was put to market. Brian Bonner of Mayking Records acquired the rights to use the name but after only a handful of records were released Geoff Travis and Jeannette Lee were employed to run 'Rough Trade'. They thought they would be working with Derek Birkett, who ran One Little Indian (which was also part of the group), but ended up having a closer relationship with Brian Bonner.

Geoff Travis: We went there in 1992 and stayed for about three years. Things like Tom Verlaine's *Warm and Cool*, Robert Wyatt's *Dondestan* and Ultramarine's *Every Man and Woman Is a Star* came out but had already been finished before we went there. We did some new things, like Shrimpboat and Spring Heel Jack. I seem to remember we argued with them a lot, especially after it became obvious that it wasn't going to work out. They never seemed to trust us.

Jeannette Lee: Everything – every decision – was over-analysed. And Brian could tend to be a little crass at times – there was lots of shouting, things flying all over the place, not exactly the Rough Trade way. There were far too many chiefs, as it turned out, at One Little Indian. It was a demoralising set up, as well. We worked in a horrible room with no windows. To be honest, I found it all a bit humiliating . . .

Geoff Travis: By 1996, things had run their course and I was convinced that it was the end for Rough Trade. Or at least I couldn't see a way of moving it forward. But we decided to have another go with Island Records. We had a relationship with the MD, Mark Moreau, and had worked with him on Pulp and so we set up Trade Two, but then Mark left and we were back to the usual struggle. We signed My Bloody Valentine to Island during that period.

The problem was that we couldn't bring them anything that was an instant success, nothing that could establish the label. We had Tiger and Spring Heel Jack, who were of course wonderful. But I think we knew that around seventy per cent of what we would want to do wouldn't fit into a major label structure. Had we thought otherwise, we would have just done Rough Trade with Warners.

Jeannette Lee: Trade Two is barely worth a mention. Personally, I think it was a mistake. It was one of those situations where everyone would have *liked* it to work but it just wasn't going to happen.

*

By the end of the 1990s, in spite of everybody's best efforts, Rough Trade seemed to have run out of steam. In 1999, however, Geoff Travis and Jeannette Lee were able to buy back the rights to the Rough Trade name. Although Blanco Y Negro remained their primary focus, at the start of the new millennium a few Rough Trade releases trickled out; singles by Terris, Birthday, Cadallaca, Ooberman, and Hope Sandoval and the Warm Inventions, and albums by Eileen Rose, Jeb Loy Nichols, David Kitt and Spring Heel Jack. Then, at the start of 2001, the Rough Trade shop held a twenty-fifth anniversary party at the Victoria and Albert Museum.

Geoff Travis: It was a great night at the V&A. The shop asked us to deejay, which was a wonderful gesture, and so many people came up to me during the course of the night that it was just very apparent how much love there still was for Rough Trade. It remained precious to so many people, as I was constantly reminded, and it really set off a train of thought, which said that Rough Trade shouldn't be consigned to the past, or left on a back burner. It made both Jeannette and I realise that we had something special and that we should really make it work.

Jeannette Lee: Rough Trade had started going wrong almost as soon as I'd joined in 1987, but of course I was enthused and optimistic about the job I was doing and at the time I didn't feel the negativity that some others felt. Consequently, in 2001, my spirits in regard to Rough Trade probably didn't need lifting as much as those of Geoff, who'd gone through hell at the time of the collapse and after. That party really lifted his spirits and he came away from it revitalised.

*

By spring of 2001, they had acquired their name back and received plenty of encouragement and motivation to properly relaunch Rough Trade. A serendipitous meeting with an old friend would give them the means to actually do it.

PART FOUR:

66 GOLBORNE ROAD

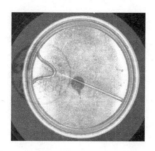

ROUGH TRADE *REDUX*

'... *keep the fire burning, be passionate to the end* ...'

Jeannette Lee, Keynote Speech, Music Industry Uncovered, South West Sound, 2007

Rough Trade formally relaunced and joined forces with Sanctuary Records on 8 June 2001. The first shared fruits of the agreement came in the form of The Strokes' debut album, *Is This It*, which notched up UK sales in excess of 700,000. In bringing the band to the fore, Rough Trade did more than just reinvent itself – it singlehandedly reinvigorated indie guitar rock. A door was opened through which there rushed an awful lot of talent, not least The Libertines, Rough Trade's second significant signing, who joined the fold at the end of 2001. The Libertines, with their combustive genius, would set Rough Trade challenges in all sorts of ways.

The success of The Strokes and The Libertines enabled the Rough Trade label to pick up where it had left off all those years before, pursuing its time-honoured, culturally all-roving task of finding new talent (this time around, without having to worry about the financial backing – or so they thought). It embraced some friends from the recent – and not so recent – past, such as Jarvis Cocker, Eddi Reader, The Veils and The Delays. And it brought to the stable some new talent, such as the Moldy Peaches and maverick singer-songwriter/comic artist genius Jeffrey Lewis – both of whom had grown out of the New York anti-folk movement – plus Mormon slowcore heroes Low, the iconoclastic and individual British Sea Power, and the peerless Belle & Sebastian. It found time also to revisit the legacy of sonic polymath Arthur Russell ('unfinished business') and reissued a buried Rough Trade classic from the past: Virginia Astley's pastoral masterpiece, *From Gardens Where We Feel Secure*.

For the first few years, Rough Trade's arrangement with its trading partner worked formidably well. Sanctuary had been set up by two former managers of Iron Maiden and knew better than to interfere in what they must have perceived to be a golden goose for them. When Geoff Travis and Jeannette Lee ended Blanco Y Negro in 2002, things looked even better to Sanctuary, who now had first call on talent spotted, and the Sanctuary/Rough Trade contract was renegotiated in 2004, effectively rewarding Rough Trade for success and guaranteeing further and greater investment from Sanctuary in the future. The very oppositeness of the two parties seemed to be what made the relationship work.

2005 turned out to be arguably both the best year Rough Trade had ever had and a year when the seeds of future problems, unknown to them, would be sown. Merck Mecuriadis, who ran Sanctuary US and also managed Lou Reed, alerted Rough Trade to a formidable and languishing talent. Antony Hegarty had been plucked from New York obscurity and asked to sing 'Candy Says' on a Lou Reed tour. After the tour, though, the journey back to obscurity seemed just as swift, and in spite of having made an astonishing album, there seemed to be no takers for Antony's indescribable genius. When Geoff and Jeannette flew to New York to offer him a record deal, the bemused singer was somewhat sceptical of what might turn out to be yet another empty promise.

The haunting, deeply mesmeric *I Am a Bird Now* went on to win the 2005 Mercury Prize and in that same year, Rough Trade released Sufjan Stevens's wildly praised and highly successful *Illinois* and Arcade Fire's equally admired, bestselling album, *Funeral*.

Rough Trade were back at the Mercury awards the following year when Scritti Politti's *White Bread Black Beer* narrowly missed out on the prize. Belle & Sebastian released an important album that year in *The Life Pursuit* and there were significant releases by Jenny Lewis, Cerys Matthews and the Hidden Cameras. Rough Trade had signed up Duffy to their management and they were working with her on the songs that would ultimately end up on the album *Rockferry*, which would go on to sell an astonishing seven million copies worldwide. Everything was going well.

Then the money stopped flowing. The bills stopped being paid. It became apparent that Sanctuary was having difficulties.

Sanctuary was forced to refinance in 2006, and later was sold to Universal pretty much for a song. This wasn't a process that happened overnight. Rough Trade had to survive a long, grim period of uncertainty before extricating itself from the original agreement and becoming a trading partner with Beggars Banquet in July 2007. In joining Beggars, Rough Trade completed the journey back to true independence (Sanctuary had been partly financed by the major record label, Universal). With its shared ethos and more or less symmetrical history, Beggars not only comes from the same culture and speaks the same language as Rough Trade but can also communicate with it as equals.

In 2009, Geoff Travis was asked to become an ambassador for the Rough Trade group of shops, reassigning him responsibilities he had first undertaken back in February 1976. There is a temptation for some to look back to that former Rough Trade and make comparisons with the present one. But the temptation is pointless and must be avoided. Although the world is an almost indescribably changed place, the same qualities are enshrined in both Rough Trades and in terms of artistic output the contemporary Rough Trade more than gives the old one a run for its money. At the same time that Geoff Travis took up his new ambassadorial role, the *NME* published the results of its Album of the Decade poll. It wasn't particularly surprising that The Strokes' *Is This It* was the winner, or that this was hotly followed by The Libertines' *Up the Bracket*. Controversy dogged the result, though,with many outraged that Arcade Fire's *Funeral*, which had been voted fourth, hadn't topped the poll. There really was only one winner – Rough Trade: it had released all three of the albums in question.

CHAPTER FIFTEEN:

2000–05

'The call would come in: Peter was in jail and
needed bailing out'

End of Blanco – Dai Davies – Sanctuary Records – Arrival of The Strokes –
The Libertines – Renegotiation – Problems

Geoff Travis: Dai Davies, an old friend of ours – who was the former manager of The Stranglers and now managed Levitation – had been in touch. He said he was working for Sanctuary Records and had a proposition to put to us.

We weren't fully aware of Sanctuary, which had been set up by the two managers of Iron Maiden, Andy Taylor and Rod Smallwood. Dai came in to Rough Trade and said that Sanctuary were trying to have a contemporary record label but hadn't had much luck in getting one going. Dai had suggested to them that he approach us on their behalf to get us to run the label. Sanctuary had been mainly a label with a big reissue catalogue and a management company. It had access to rehearsal studios, it had an American operation, it had offices, a canteen, et cetera. This is how Dai sold it to us. What it didn't have was a contemporary label.

We'd always liked Dai and we thought that if he was on the board that would give us some protection and so we went to see Sanctuary for the first time at their rehearsal studios in Sinclair Road. Again, we liked Andy, who we met then – he was very amusing and avuncular, with his cigar and feet upon his desk in a very non-offensive way. We knew nothing about Iron Maiden, very little about Sanctuary, but the very oppositeness of it all seemed as if it might complement Rough Trade, might be a curiously perfect fit, and for a long time it did and was.

As serendipity would have it, the Sanctuary deal all fell into place immediately after the V&A party and just before we signed The Strokes.

Dai Davies: I'd merged my company into Sanctuary back in the early 1990s and ended up as chief executive of Sanctuary Music Productions. Once Sanctuary floated on the stock exchange, money became available to be invested in other companies. I'd known Geoff since way back, when I'd been putting on bands at the Nashville Rooms and Rough Trade was just a shop. The idea of bringing Rough Trade on board had been identified as a good one early on, though there was some resistance at Sanctuary – not from Rod or Andy – because of the way the deal would have to be done. Whereas ordinarily we would buy a company outright, this was more of a partnership arrangement. They'd only recently acquired the rights to the name back.

Joe Cokell: The board at Sanctuary took the view that we needed a contemporary label and very early on it was agreed that Rough Trade would be the ideal partner to have. It was my job as the CEO of the recorded music division to steer Rough Trade into the Sanctuary business and work out with Geoff and Jeannette which services Sanctuary could provide. The plan was to bolt them onto an existing structure but give them autonomy and freedom to go out and find the artists. When they had done that we would then all get together to work out how to build the business.

It was obvious with Geoff and Jeannette's track record of finding and developing artists at the cutting edge of a lot of new music that we shouldn't second-guess them on an A&R front, and we didn't. My role, really, was just to sit down with them and work out a business plan each time they signed an act.

Dai Davies: The original deal was one of a sliding scale of ownership so that the more profit Rough Trade made on Sanctuary's investment, the more ownership they would have. I think there was a belief that perhaps in the past, Rough Trade hadn't been very good at marshalling its resources and it was hoped that the sliding scale of ownership would make them focus more closely on the business.

Of course the deal Geoff and Jeannette had with Warners for Blanco was still in place and for some people I think this was a complication. My view was that the two arrangements could work in tandem, with some of the more commercially viable acts possibly being taken up by the major label but with Rough Trade generally putting out acts with potential sales of between 5,000 and 50,000. I never expected that one of the first albums they would give us would go on to sell 700,000 copies. When the deal was finally done and dusted The Strokes were starting to happen, so we did expect them to do well, but not that well.

Geoff Travis: Frank Riley, Patti Smith's manager, said to me one day that I ought to know a guy called Matt Hickey, who was the main booker at the Mercury Lounge in New York. Frank suggested that Matt was very much a person with his finger on the pulse of what was happening. So I got to know Matt a bit, and liked him, and I asked him to always let me know if he came across something which I might like. One evening I was working late when Matt called and said he had something he thought I might like. He played me 'The Modern Age' over the phone and as soon as I heard the opening chords I just thought it was fantastic and I think at that moment said I would release it. He then very quickly sent me the demos which became the *Modern Age* EP. At the same time, Ryan Gentles, another booker at the Mercury and a friend of The Strokes, became their manager.

As soon as it arrived, I played the tape to Jeannette and she just agreed it was amazing and we made a plan to release it and we made a plan to try to sign the band.

Jeannette Lee: Hearing The Strokes for the first time gave me the same sort of feeling I'd had when I first heard the Sex Pistols or The Clash. I never thought music would be able to do that to me again, but listening to The Strokes I felt like I had when I'd been seventeen and listening to music.

Strangely, we'd only just got computers at Rough Trade and after we heard the tape, we tried finding the band on the internet. They had a website and we were shocked because not only did they sound great but they looked amazing, too. We decided to go and see them.

Geoff Travis: Under the terms of the Blanco deal, what we had to do was go and play the tape to Warners. By now Rob Dickens had gone and I had to play it to his replacement, John Reid. Rob would have immediately told me to go straight out and sign them, but John Reid said he wanted to send his East Coast A&R man to see them. I'd never been second-guessed on my A&R calls before and what it said to me was that Warner Brothers didn't believe in my judgement.

I let it pass and Jeannette and I flew to New York and met up with the Warners A&R person and went in his limousine to a tiny bar in New Jersey where The Strokes were playing.

Jeannette Lee: Hardly anyone was there to see the band. This was a suburban bar with blue-collar workers who were in there for the beer, not the music. Geoff and I did our usual thing of splitting up at the gig and we watched the band. They were phenomenal. After the show ended, we didn't say much to each other, we didn't need to, though we couldn't have got a word in edgeways anyway on the drive back since the A&R man didn't stop talking.

Geoff Travis: We'd had a chat with the band after and had a bit of a laugh and then the A&R guy had us driven back to New York City. He talked about himself almost the entire time we were in the car and only mentioned The Strokes to say, 'America is full of bands like that.'

Jeannette Lee: The next night The Strokes played the Mercury Lounge and that was more their environment. Their friends were all there and once again they were fantastic, so good that I think from that moment on there was always the fear that someone else would come along – probably with more money – and snap them up.

Geoff Travis: We asked The Strokes to come over to England and play around the time we put out the EP. I think by then they were still slightly bemused at these two strange English people who were incredibly enthusiastic about their music. We set up the tour, put the EP out – and the press went ballistic.

Clare Britt: Geoff emailed me at the start of 2001. I'd not long become a mother and I was looking forward to spending some time with my baby. I wasn't working for Island any more. Geoff asked me to call them, and

when I did he said that they'd got 'this little band' that he thought could be massive. Did I want to work it for them, do for this band what we'd done together for Pulp? Of course I said no because I'd just had the baby and was looking forward to a rest, but when I went to see Geoff and Jeannette, they were persistent – and brilliantly accommodating about it all. I could work from home, bring the baby in if I needed to come to meetings. So that's what I did: I ran the campaign from home. In fact, it was a very small team that ran the Strokes campaign: Geoff, Jeannette, myself, Kelly Kiley, who was very involved with making it happen, and Glen Johnson, who worked in production and made the records. Rough Trade at that time was a small outfit. Patsy Winkelman was there, Colin Wallace in International, James Endeacott doing A&R, Geoff and Jeannette, and that was about it as I recall.

Geoff Travis: The first gig The Strokes played was at the Wedgewood Rooms in Portsmouth and it was absolutely jam-packed. Completely sold out. Incredible. The Strokes walked into the show expecting there to be about four people and instead the gig was a sensation. From then on, every time they played it was wonderful. They played the Barfly in Camden and the singer Julian Casablancas was really nervous – I think he just became aware of the enormity of what was happening to them. James Endeacott, our A&R man, was outside trying to calm him down and of course the delay in the show starting merely heightened the tension and once again the band played another amazing show.

They got an offer to play an American tour and, even though we weren't their record company, we gave them some support money, which they paid back, I believe as a sign of faith to say we want to work with you. Of course, by now the whole world was mad for them and everybody wanted to sign them. Every label in America with the exception of Warner Brothers wanted to sign them. I sent the demo tape directly to the head of Warners A&R in America – I'd never done that in my life before – and I never heard a word back. The Strokes were incredibly supportive and went as far as to say they would sign to Blanco for all territories except America, but Warners – our Blanco bosses – said they didn't do split-territory deals, which was untrue. That was effectively the end of our relationship with Warners, although it formally ended in 2002, twenty years after it had begun. I made the decision to sign the band to Rough Trade. Warner Brothers have accused me of stealing the band from them even though I did everything by the book. Afterwards, John Reid flew to New York to try to make his peace with the band, but I'm sure the more he talked to them, the less likely they were to sign with him.

Virtually at the same time, we'd tried to sign the White Stripes and had run up against a similar problem. We weren't the only people after them but we were in there in a good position. The White Stripes' lawyer told me that the band were potentially interested in making a deal with Blanco but that Jack White had a lot of conditions and that as he wasn't an ordinary artist, latitude was required. The Warner lawyers just proved too inflexible.

So we had wanted to sign the two best bands on the planet at that time and in both cases it hadn't been possible through Blanco. I saw this as a fundamental breakdown in trust and in the relationship. It was a sad end to what had been twenty largely good years.

But the experience energised us in a way because now we knew it was just going to be Rough Trade, and that was psychologically uplifting.

As a result of The Strokes we picked up a couple of other good artists from America as well. Ryan was managing Adam Green and we went to see him play at the Sidewalk Café and signed the Moldy Peaches and through Adam we signed Jeffrey Lewis, who Adam put me on to and who I tracked down to the University of Texas.

Jeffrey Lewis: I had been making my own tapes, which I considered to be 'albums', and selling them at my shows. I'd fold little black and white comics into the tape case. The blank tape cost me less than a dollar, the photocopying was about ten cents. I'd get about $3 for them at the shows, a decent profit on the handful I sold at each show. That was my music business. Comic books were what I had done my whole life, really, but I had found it difficult to make any money out of them, and they took so long to make, whereas a tape I could record in a day. I did very elaborate flyers for my early shows and I think in a way I was doing the show to advertise the flyer, rather than the other way around.

By 2000 the scene in New York was centring on the open-mic nights at the Sidewalk Café, where I played. It was there that I met Adam Green and Kimya Dawson who, as the Moldy Peaches, got signed to Rough Trade. The success of The Strokes had suddenly drawn a whole lot of attention to New York. Kimya and Adam had taken some of my songs and put them on a CD and given them to Geoff Travis, who I was supposed to bump into at the music festival South by Southwest in Austin. I was at college in Austin. I don't think I did get to see him but in the end he got in touch and said he would put my stuff out and gave me an advance of $1,000, a great chunk of money to me back then. I am sure had I seen him in person I'd have bungled it, so it was better it worked out that way. *The Last Time I Did Acid I Went Insane* came out in September 2001 and I went to England to do a few shows, including one at the Rough Trade shop in Covent Garden and one in Camden, which is where I met Ben Ayres, who asked me to tour with Cornershop.

Ben Ayres: It was through Jeffrey Lewis that I started working at Rough Trade. Towards the end of 2001, I was tiring of new music and had been listening to a lot of old reggae. I was feeling very jaded about new music, which is odd for me, and didn't think I was ever going to find anything I would like again. Then I heard Jeffrey Lewis's *Acid* CD and it was as if it was what I had been waiting for – it seemed so full of possibility. Jeffrey came over and I met him and he eventually did some gigs with Cornershop.

By summer 2002, Cornershop had kind of ground to a halt. We had had a few problems with our label and we were suffering from mental exhaustion as much as anything. Colin Wallace was a friend of mine who worked in International at Rough Trade and I'd called him up and he advised me to go and see Geoff. I went in to see Geoff and got on well with him and he said he would think of something I might do. Geoff played me some old records, and some new things he was excited about like the Hidden Cameras, which I loved, but I couldn't see the meeting leading to anything. Then he called me about a week later and said did I want to do in-house press.

*

Joe Cokell: Barely six months into the agreement with Rough Trade, there were broad smiles on faces all around because The Strokes really were a major success. We had planned on getting the business up and running properly within fifteen months or so but straight away, virtually, we were off to a flying start. And then, immediately after, there was another great spot by Rough Trade when they picked up The Libertines.

Geoff Travis: The Libertines had been knocking around London for years, trying to get a deal. David Balfe once told me that they used to camp outside the Food Records offices in the hope of getting him interested in them. They came to us through Banny Pootschi, a lawyer at Warner Brothers, who was managing Carl and Peter. She bumped into James Endeacott one night after a gig and bribed him with Coca-Cola and crisps to come and see The Libertines play at the Rhythm Factory, as it later came to be called. James reported back that they were really good and we went to see them in rehearsals after that. We had a demo tape, which we loved, and we just thought they were a great band. We drew up a contract with Banny and we were going to sign them on Christmas Eve in 2001. They were due to be at the office at seven o'clock and seven o'clock came and went and there was no sign of them. It started to get late and we just assumed that they'd changed their minds, when finally they arrived. They'd got off at the wrong tube stop and become hopelessly lost. They were in a terrible sweat because they thought we'd have gone home. There was no question but that we would wait for them. They were without doubt the most thrilling band at that time.

Jeannette Lee: They were an incredibly fascinating, incredibly funny double act. They were very cheeky and you had to be on your toes all the time. They really had something special going on between them and they were exciting because you just didn't know what they were going to say or do next. Peter was very literate, super-bright and ultimately became fascinating for a lot of people because he embodied that deadly cocktail common to rock 'n' roll – genius mixed up with self-destruction.

Geoff Travis: It became apparent very early on that the speed at which Peter lived his life was abnormal compared to the speed at which other people lived their lives. It was a continuous show, as well, with Carl and Peter as the court jesters. It was non-stop and I suppose the intensity of it eventually was bound to take its toll. They were forever competing with each other – even if it was only in the telling of jokes – competing with each other and complementing each other. It was a fine line between the two and while it worked it was wonderful and exhilarating to be around and witness.

Patsy Winkelman: Peter was absolutely charming and could charm the birds out of the trees, and he knew it. They were very funny, and also difficult – perhaps more difficult than most – but then artists are very rarely straight-forward. Someone as creative and fantastic and as chaotic and disorganised as Peter Doherty wouldn't find another label capable of releasing those Libertines albums. Rough Trade has to take credit for being able to see through the process of getting all the necessary people involved to turn the chaos into *Up the Bracket*, which was a truly wonderful, classic English record.

Bernard Butler: Some time in 2001, Geoff came over to see me to hear some new material – he never does that: it's always me tearing across North London to Rough Trade – and, in the course of our meeting, said that he had signed a band that he wanted me to produce. The band was The Libertines. Geoff played me a couple of songs and it was great stuff – terrific and full of character. After we listened to the tracks, Geoff told me that he thought the band was the best band he had heard in years and that he thought they could be as big as The Kinks or The Clash or The Smiths. He asked me what I thought should be done with them.

At that time, the sound took in their two voices – they sometimes sang a verse each – but the whole sounded as one, and I told Geoff that I thought they needed to find two distinct personalities. That was my entry point for a voyage that was crazy and lasted about a year.

We went into RAK studios to do 'What a Waster', and I spent a lot of time with them. It was very exciting. They'd play these mad, stupid shows in pubs and half your energy would be spent chasing around trying to find out where the place was. After 'What a Waster', I was supposed to do the second single and the album. I did all the pre-production on the album, spent a week chopping up songs, helping them with structure and arrange-ments, and then the day before we were due to start properly on the album, I had problems with my back and when I went to the doctor he said I was suffering from nervous exhaustion. Since the studio was booked, and the material sorted out, Mick Jones was asked to go in and do it. I was very upset. I felt I'd set it up and then someone had just walked in and taken over. They ended up doing the album effectively 'live'. I'd always said to them that we shouldn't do it live in the studio until they sounded like a brilliant live band. Even during 'What a Waster' they'd always wanted to do everything live, and really they were just starting out and not playing great.

Geoff Travis: There were people around The Libertines from the publishing company and management who were less keen on using Bernard and they sort of ganged up on us in the end when they heard the results of 'What a Waster'. We loved what Bernard had done and thought it was incredible and the whole matter of Bernard moving aside deeply annoyed us.

Jeannette Lee: There was definitely a work-ethic issue involved, as well. Bernard would have insisted that everybody work really hard on the project. When he gets his teeth into something, he doesn't stop until he gets it right. His methods were probably too regimented and disciplined for Peter. We told them to stick with Bernard because we knew ultimately that the results would be good.

Peter was constantly taking drugs and of course Bernard would have had no time for that. But the truth of the matter is that those records wouldn't have got made if they'd have been finished the way they'd been started. They only got made at all because of the relaxed atmosphere. Mick had Bill Price, who had worked on The Clash album *London Calling*, working with him and together they made it work. Certainly, by the time we got to the second album – and it was touch and go whether we even had a record, most of the time – it was only going to happen because Peter felt comfortable around Mick.

Geoff Travis: Mick Jones deserves a lot of credit for sticking it out, really. A lot of people seem to think that the recording sessions were a lawless jamboree, but Mick working with Bill, who is one of the best engineers in the world, meant that we were going to get something. We weren't just sanctioning anarchy. Bill was our insurance against that.

Clare Britt: I was still working The Strokes when Geoff called me up and said, 'Guess what? I've got another little band I want you to work.' I felt that The Strokes had worked for me because that was all I did at that time, so I was once again wary of taking on the job. But then it felt like we were on a wave and so I took it on and started going into the office more and ended up working there. James Endeacott deserves a lot of credit for The Libertines – they were really his baby.

Bernard Butler: I was asked back by them to produce The Libertines' single 'Don't Look Back Into the Sun', in 2003. That was an amazing break for me – being asked back.

So off we went to make the record and on the first day Peter didn't show up. I remember Jeannette calling at the studio and telling me to go home and forget about it. But I stuck it out and the next day went back and got on with it. It was pretty much a living nightmare. We spent two weeks in the studio and Peter was there for about three hours in total. The band were great. I got on well with all of them, including Peter. By now, Peter wasn't getting on with Carl, mainly I think because Peter was into crack and wanted Carl to go down the same road and be as crazy as him and Carl didn't want to do that. Carl seemed to have a problem physically dealing with Peter and somehow I ended up getting caught in the middle. I caught a lot of flak.

It is hard to find words for it, because to say it was shocking makes me sound like a *Daily Mail* reader. Occasionally, Peter would go on at me. He'd burst into tears, get aggressive. He would be really cold. I had so many feelings about it all. I felt sorry for him at the same time as just wanting to kick him. My view was that he could have a crack pipe up his arse as long as he was making good records.

We did seven or eight takes of 'Don't Look Back Into the Sun' and in all he sang about four lines, most of it gibberish, some of it lyrics made up about me. I ended up comping the vocals syllable by syllable. I didn't see him after he had done the vocals until the last day when the record was mixed and he came down and I asked him if he wanted to hear his record.

I did about a week on the second album. Same routine as before – he'd turn up and then go off, this time with his new band Babyshambles. He kept asking me why Gary and John, the bass player and drummer in The Libertines, were at the studio and said that he had sacked them. I tried to explain to him – *they're in the band, they're over there.*

When we had mixed 'Don't Look Back Into the Sun' I could see the megalomania, the monster coming out of him. But I always wanted to work with him, because at its best the music was wonderful. Peter was a phenomenal songwriter who, it seemed to me, just gave up trying.

Jeannette understood that whole approach and she was absolutely crucial to the whole Libertines moment. There was the lunacy and the madness but also the rawness and the energy and she understood all of that. Both Geoff and Jeannette did a lot for Peter and in the end he just wasn't very nice to either of them.

Jeannette Lee: Early on it was pure joy to be around but as things started to deteriorate and Peter started to get into a bad way it was very, very sad.

Geoff Travis: For quite a long time the work really wasn't affected and then we began to hear stories of Peter not showing up for things and acting strange. Peter had a good heart and he has a lovable side but there was also another side, an irresponsible one. His irresponsibility became more and more apparent as time went on and although his cheeky grin and epitome of a charming man meant that he could generally get away with anything (and he knew it), in the end it blunted some of the charm for me.

We did a lot to try to save Peter from himself but ultimately when someone is taking as many drugs as he was back then, only they can save themselves. We met his father and his sister, who were appreciative and could see that we cared, and at one point we even suspended his contract but nothing worked. And the tabloid frenzy around him was horrendous – we'd get phone calls out of the blue saying he'd been arrested, saying he was in court: it was one disaster after another. You were always trying to work out what had happened, what was going to happen next.

Ben Ayres: On more than one occasion, the call would come in: Peter was in jail and needed bailing out. Colin Wallace would go to court with money to pay off the bail. The lengths Geoff, Jeannette and Colin went to beggars belief.

Jeannette Lee: It was a very difficult period. In the past, I have seen and occasionally even worked with serious drug users so I had some understanding of what was going on. I imagine for Geoff it was just appalling to see. We tried very hard to deal with it. The first time, we called a meeting at the local pub and sat there – Peter, his manager, Carl, James, myself and Geoff – and I began saying to him that we needed to talk to him because we thought he was developing a serious drug problem. He sat there and didn't take it too badly but said he didn't agree with us and that he was fine. We didn't really get very far that time.

What was unusual about Peter's drug use was the way he never tried to hide it. That made him fascinating to an awful lot of people. Most people who take drugs take them behind closed doors but Peter's view was, if I'm doing it, I'm doing it, I don't need to hide it ... This was a new thing to me, this being so public about it. And it carried over in all sorts of ways. He would, for instance, put absolutely anything he wanted to on the internet, so I might have what I thought to be a private, confidential conversation with him only to have somebody call me up and tell me that Peter had posted all the details online. I think we all fell foul of that a few times.

It was important that we helped him, and it was important, aside from reasons of his health, because we really believed in The Libertines, we truly believed that Peter was one of the great artists. Ultimately, I believe The Libertines may have been underrated as a result of Peter's behavioural problems.

I kept thinking that the problem couldn't get any worse, but it did; it got a whole lot worse. Our next tactic was to try to suspend him. We wrote him a letter saying that we weren't going to give him any more money or put any more records out until he took care of his health. We just didn't know what to do. It sounds silly and pompous now, but back then we were desperate.

On another occasion, I got a friend of mine, who had had drug problems and had come through them and was now acting as a sort of counsellor, to come in and talk to Peter. Again, we went off to the pub and my friend had a big talk with him about how near he was to death and how bad it was. I think the fact Peter was talking to someone who had been an addict made him sit up and listen more and eventually throughout the course of the meeting he agreed that he would go into rehab. So we said, OK, we'll go right now. This really shocked him: it wasn't what he was expecting. We grabbed Geoff and off we drove to a rehab clinic in Kent. It took about three hours to get there because of traffic and even longer to get back. Just before we got back to London we got a call from the clinic saying he was about to check himself out. My friend spent a further hour on the phone trying to talk him around. Peter stayed a week in the clinic, so some progress – however temporary – was made, I suppose.

In the end they switched management a few times and unfortunately the new managers often seemed in as bad a way as Peter was – basically, if you are that into drugs you just can't have a normal manager, or at least it is very hard to find someone who is capable of dealing with it.

*

Joe Cokell: The success of Rough Trade was so swift that a renegotiation of the contract with Sanctuary took place earlier than might have been expected. There was a clause in the original contract that said that once a certain financial threshold had been reached, Geoff and Jeanette could renegotiate the terms. This happened in 2004. At that point, of course, Blanco no longer existed as a label and the success of bands like The Strokes and The Libertines had been so great that Rough Trade were in a very strong position and able to negotiate a deal that was probably better for them. But everybody at this point was happy.

Geoff Travis: The new deal was done direct with Joe Cokell, who was fantastic to be dealing with. There was no big issue – trading partners are there to help us get on with the job that we have to do, which is find good music. Around about the time of the renegotiation, Joe was wise enough to always leave us to get on with things without interference, within the constraints of budgets which we'd already worked out. Sanctuary were financially stable during this time and we were all about to have another wave of great artists and albums.

By this point, we had put out some fine material by The Veils, the Hidden Cameras and Low, and we'd put out a couple of Jarvis recordings as Relaxed Muscle. The Jarvis period with Island had come to an end and there had been changes at that company. Relaxed Muscle was Jarvis expressing himself and having a bit of fun and we decided to support him on it. In 2003 we had also signed up British Sea Power, a band with an original vision whose preoccupations can be wonderfully non-rock 'n' roll.

Martin Noble: We were called British Air Power but had changed our name to British Sea Power, I think for no other reason than we thought the acronym 'BSP' was better than 'BAP'. We were all in Brighton and ran a club called Club Sea Power, where we put on shows and booked support bands that were a bit more unusual. One support was a fashion show through the ages, organised by a couple of girls who called themselves the

Patrick Mooreheads, which began with somebody coming on just covered in wode. Another time we got the folk singers the Copper Family to play. The Copper Family had lived in Rottingdean for over two hundred years and sang songs handed down through that time. The fee for performing was a keg of Harveys beer.

We released our first single, 'Fear of Drowning' on our own Golden Chariot label. It had a design partly modelled on the book jacket for Eric Williams's POW account, *The Wooden Horse*. We sent the single to Chris Stone, who ran a PR company and who had, I think, worked for Rough Trade. She suggested we send it to Geoff Travis and we did and he came down to see us play not so long after. He came to see us but didn't introduce himself at that time. On that night, I remember Yann, our singer, had jumped off the stage and landed sprawled out at Geoff's feet. His head was literally on Geoff's shoes. We released the single 'Carrion' on Rough Trade and then put out the first album, *Decline of British Sea Power*, which we'd largely written by the time we'd signed, so, having signed, things moved quite quickly.

From the Club Sea Power days we had started to love the idea of not playing ordinary gigs. We were always ambitious of where we wanted to play, even when there wouldn't be that many people turn up to see us. We played the Grasmere Village Hall and had to put 50p pieces in the meter for the electric, we played Fort Perch Rock, a small fort just outside Liverpool, and we played Carnglaze Caverns in Cornwall, a magical show where it snowed and where the acoustics in the cave were incredible. Diarmuid Gavin, the 'rock 'n' roll gardener', asked us to play at the Chelsea Flower Show and Candida Lycett Green, who is John Betjeman's daughter and a fan of ours, asked us to play at a Betjeman centenary event.

Interests like the fell-walking and the bird-watching are really part of our experiences of where we grew up. Some of the band came from the Lake District – Yann and Hamilton grew up in a village outside Grasmere, which has only a post office; actually, I don't think it has the post office any more – and our interests are reflective of where we were and what we did when we were growing up. Bands coming from London – like The Libertines or The Clash – are inevitably likely to be that bit harder, that bit more guitary, that bit faster and more reflective of where they come from.

When it came to renewing the contract, it wasn't as if we needed to look around for other options: who else but Rough Trade would give us the freedom to do what we've been able to do? Another important thing for us was that Rough Trade have tended to sign a lot of women artists, either solo or in groups, and there are a lot of women working there as well. We like that.

Patsy Winkelman: There have been and are some very powerful women at Rough Trade and the success that Jeannette achieved has been an inspiration to us all. Long before the rest of the industry figured out that women could do a million things at once, be decisive and finish what they had started, Rough Trade took a lead. I'm an old feminist and anarchist and still allowed to think that way, and that says a lot, I think, about how Rough Trade operates. Everyone here is equal.

Geoff Travis: We won the *Music Week* Label of the Year Award in 2005. We had at least three extraordinary records out that year in Sufjan Stevens's *Illinois*, Antony & The Johnsons' *I Am a Bird Now* and Arcade Fire's *Funeral*.

We had signed up the Hidden Cameras, who were Canadian, and they played a show on the same bill as Arcade Fire, who were also Canadian. An A&R person who did some work for us in America had seen the show and urged us to check them out. By the time we got to sign them, we were about five minutes ahead of the rest of the world – five centimetres – just there before people like David Bowie and David Byrne started saying how much they liked the band.

Funeral did really well here but took off incrementally. It was a classic case of a great record getting its due over time. Radio One didn't want to support the band, which irked me, but a turning point occurred when the *NME*, who hadn't particularly been convinced either, reviewed them at Reading Festival and became converted.

A publicist in New York recommended Sufjan Stevens to us and Jeannette and I went to New York to see him play. He performed *Michigan* and it was a wonderful experience, the whole band dressed up in their parody outfits. Sufjan has been remarkably loyal to us, all the more so considering that he has his own label and could quite easily put the records out himself in our territory if he wanted to. Every major in the world has courted him and been turned down by him.

In 2005, we also won the Mercury Prize with Antony & The Johnsons' *I Am a Bird Now*, an astonishing album. Merck Mecuriadis was the president of Sanctuary in the US but also managed Lou Reed, and Lou had asked Antony to sing 'Candy Says' on a tour Lou was doing. This plucked Antony out of his New York obscurity, but having done his album he then found there were no takers for it. On Merck's recommendation we went to New York and saw Antony.

Jeannette Lee: We visited him in a rehearsal room and he was very gentle, intelligent, endearing and obviously very smart. He was possibly suspicious, also, that we might not be for real since he'd been turned down by so many people. He told us all about the people who had claimed to like his songs and then vanished.

Clare Britt: The night of the Mercury Prize was fantastic. Our table won several thousand pounds that night because such was our belief in Antony that we all bet a substantial amount on him winning the prize, in spite of him being a complete outsider according to the odds. It was the end of a journey that had started when Geoff had called me in to his office one time. That had been a typical Geoff moment. As is his wont, he'd called me into his office and said I want you to hear something. This is a classic Geoff tactic. No preamble. No talk of signing the artist. No clues. Nothing. I was overwhelmed when I heard Antony's music for the first time in that office. I couldn't tell if the artist was male or female, white or black, a new artist or an old one. It was strange and absolutely wonderful. During 2005, it really was a privilege to be working at Rough Trade. One after another there seemed to be a succession of acts – all of them amazing, all of them different – to deal with and it was hard to see how that was ever likely to change, given the optimism.

Geoff Travis: We had relaunched and it seemed as if in a short time we had got ourselves into a position where things were going well. In fact, 2005 turned out to be probably the most successful year we had had up until that point. What we didn't realise, however, was that our trading partner company Sanctuary was not having such a good time. Suddenly rumours were going around that Sanctuary was a house of cards waiting to come down. We were, in the course of our business, going in and seeing them and they were constantly assuring us that these rumours weren't true. It turned out to be a classic case of no smoke without fire but for a long time we knew nothing of the problems they were going through until those problems were practically right in front of our faces, which pretty soon they were.

CHAPTER SIXTEEN:

2006—

'A suck-it-and-see deal: bang in a quarter of a
million pounds or thereabouts and give it a spin'

Sanctuary Collapse – Return of Scritti – Beggars Banquet – Duffy –
Tomorrow calling

Tony English: From Sanctuary Records' point of view, the original agreement with Rough Trade had been a suck-it-and-see deal: bang in a quarter of a million pounds or thereabouts and give it a spin. It was a foot-in-the-door move, done for the moment when the arrangement Geoff and Jeannette had with Warners ended and they could properly come to the table. Sanctuary probably felt they had little to lose and it was good for Geoff and Jeannette because it got them to the next stage of their relaunch. More or less the first act they signed, of course, turned out to be absolutely huge, and suddenly Sanctuary thought they'd come across a gold mine. Quite quickly any contractual provisions about funding were forgotten and they started to sign off almost anything Geoff and Jeannette asked for.

Then, by 2004, the relationship deepened and a big, formal share-holders' agreement was drawn up. Sanctuary were happy to put more money in and I would say at one point it led to Rough Trade having almost as many artists as a major label. But suddenly, around about the start of 2006, Sanctuary got into financial difficulties and along with every other part of the Sanctuary business, Rough Trade was very nearly dragged under.

Geoff Travis: To begin with we were called in more to talk in greater detail about the projects we were trying to acquire. That had never been the case. We were slow to realise that money was disappearing and that, in fact, there wasn't any money. When I realised, that was another black day in my Rough Trade life.

Jeannette Lee: One day we got a phone call saying there was no more money. Don't spend any more money, we were told, and don't pay any bills. We had not long taken on Duffy for development and were talking to Sanctuary about the possibly of bringing out records by 'this artist' – we didn't name her – on a separate label. As it happened, events overtook that possibility.

Patsy Winkelman: One part of my job at Rough Trade was looking after certain aspects of the money side. I think I noticed before it was common knowledge that a big problem was developing with Sanctuary. People some-times say that Rough Trade has never been business savvy but that's not true. In the 1980s, Rough Trade had to battle against not only its own failings but also some very real attempts on the part of the majors to destroy it. And in this case, we were quick to spot the problems and act on them. Sanctuary kept us in the dark about it all and bills were either unpaid or paid very late. In the end, Tony English had to get involved.

Joe Cokell: The problems for Sanctuary all derived from financial issues. There was under-performance generally across the Sanctuary Group, and particular problems in America, where Sanctuary's aggressive strategy of attacking the market created a lot of mess. The upshot was that as a result of problems in 2005, the company had to be refinanced in 2006 and this affected Rough Trade in the same way it affected every other part of the Sanctuary company. There were cash-flow problems; it was harder for Rough Trade to sign artists and compete. It was forced to pick its shots far more carefully. Previously, when a big artist came to market – like Belle &

Sebastian – Rough Trade could compete, whereas now they were being forced to rein themselves in.

Tony English: In any kind of shareholder's agreement of the kind that was in place, there are theoretical things attached like business plans that need to be updated – but these weren't drawn up as the partnership went along. The financial set-up at Sanctuary was very loose – they had accounts but not proper budgets. At first, after the renegotiation, money was just sent over to Rough Trade when required, but in the end, because systems weren't properly in place, when there was no money to be sent over, Geoff and Jeannette had to dip into their own pockets for large amounts of money just to keep the Rough Trade company afloat.

Clare Britt: It was like being back in a major for me. More meetings had to be attended to get things done, more red tape needed to be cut through. We were hardly renegades but from being treated as this small, beautifully focused thing we were suddenly treated as if we were an extension of a major label. It all started to become a battle. There were some light moments. At one point, Geoff and Jeannette were asked by Sanctuary to do formal annual reviews of the staff. We were a family. This had never happened before. I went in for my review and it was somewhere between funny and uncomfortable. They had a piece of paper on a clipboard, which they'd periodically fiddle with. It was so not them. 'We think you are doing great; how is it for you?' they asked me. I just burst out with 'I love my job!' The one chance to sound off about things and all I could say was that I loved it. I went back downstairs and my assistant told me she had said the same thing.

Tony English: The lawyers came in, formal board meetings were held, there were threats flying about, and the end result was the relationship between Rough Trade and Sanctuary turned pretty bad. Sanctuary didn't have the money to hand over to Rough Trade at this point, and I suppose made the best of their situation by arguing that they had no obligation to hand over any money. The result was that records couldn't be released properly, studios couldn't be paid and the business was grinding to a halt.

Sanctuary realised that they hadn't done a good job because of their lack of funding – they'd gone from feast to famine – and ultimately it is hard to say anyone is at fault in such circumstances, but it became apparent that it was in the interest of both sides to part company. Thus began the long, protracted agony of moving out of Sanctuary and finding a new trading partner. And it was during that period that Rough Trade was particularly vulnerable.

Geoff Travis: One of the unfortunate consequences of Sanctuary's troubles was that they started treating Rough Trade less as a partner and more like we were one of their companies. But we carried on as best we could. In that awful period we released a number of great things. We released Jarvis's first solo album, Belle & Sebastian's *The Life Pursuit* and put out the first Scritti Politti release in nearly thirty years on Rough Trade. We were back at the Mercury Prize again that year because *White Bread Black Beer* was shortlisted.

Green Gartside: Back in 1999, within weeks of *Anomie & Bonhomie* coming out, I got back together with Geoff. I had a very ineffectual manager at the time and after I had fired him I was talking to Robert Sandall at Virgin and telling him about the fact that I no longer was managed. I'm pretty sure Robert mentioned it to Geoff and Geoff then called me up. 'You have made a wonderful album but nobody is going to hear it,' he told me, prophetically. 'I think you are on the wrong label and I would like you to come back to me.' I didn't hesitate for a moment to take him up on his offer.

Geoff started funding me pretty much straight away to work on a new album. I went to New York and did some work with Mad Skillz, the rapper. Geoff was enormously proactive about helping. I then rented a cottage in Walberswick and started working on what eventually became *White Bread Black Beer*. I had a home studio put in, again with Geoff's help, and after a very long time the record was finally completed and released in 2006. Geoff would come by to listen to stuff and say, take all the time you need, which is probably not the best thing to say to me ...

Just before that, in 2004, *Early* had been issued: the compilation of the old Scritti material that had been previously released on Rough Trade and St Pancras in the late 1970s and early 1980s.

I was in New York and very surprised when Geoff phoned to tell me that the record was shortlisted for the Mercury Prize. It picked up some flattering reviews and it was all very exciting doing things like being sent off by the *New Yorker* to have my photograph taken by David Bailey for a piece they were running about me.

Geoff asked me at this time if I fancied playing live again – I hadn't performed live since stepping off stage and finishing up in hospital on the

Gang of Four tour in 1979. Geoff suggested I play a low-key venue, like a pub, and if I liked it then all well and good, and if I didn't like it, nothing was lost. I spent most of my days squirrelled away in my studio and after work I would drop around the corner to the local. That was where all the people I knew were, and that's where I decided to recruit my band. I decided that the only way playing live would be bearable would be if I was in the company of those people whose company I enjoyed. Alisha worked behind the bar and I knew her taste in music was good so she became the bassist, even though she'd never played a bass guitar in her life. Dickie was some-body squatting on the same street at the pub – he became the guitarist. An eighteen-year-old came in and played the drums. They all came around my house and listened to the album and we took it from there. Geoff, in his usual generous way, bought all the equipment.

Jarvis Cocker: The last Pulp album had been *We Love Life* and was really me tidying up after having trashed the house. There seemed to have been a point to Pulp in the early years – whether it was a hare-brained scheme inside my head didn't matter, so long as I believed in it. But I started to get disillusioned. I'd done the Relaxed Muscle stuff as a sort of off-the-cuff project. Every so often I would threaten to pack it all in and Jeannette would tell me to carry on, tell me that I still had something to say. I realised, though, after the Relaxed Muscle material came out that I couldn't walk around with a skeleton suit and make-up on for the rest of my life.

I moved to France, kind of toying with the idea of either retiring or doing things from a safe distance. I thought maybe I could write some songs for other people, inflict the material on them, let them have the pain. But I kept sending songs to Jeannette. 'Is there any reason for the world to hear this?' I would ask. After a couple of years, it was felt that there were enough good songs and the *Jarvis* album came out, an album that simply could not have happened without Jeannette.

We did the record in Sheffield and finished it off in France. I was pleased that we could release it on Rough Trade – the rigmarole of signing to a major had no appeal for me whatsoever. I felt good when the record came out – it was the record that sounded how I wanted it to sound. It was a big deal to me that it wasn't a Pulp album because Pulp had represented a lot of things but *Jarvis* was me. It was finally me. It was my Mike Yarwood moment.

Jeannette Lee: We gave Jarvis the option. We were managing him so there was an obligation to explore possibilities that might end up being of the best benefit to him. But as it happened, I think Jarvis had had enough of major labels then and has always been a great supporter and admirer of Rough Trade. And he got to make the record his way, probably for the first time.

Belle & Sebastian were an act we had admired from the moment we had heard the first record, *Tigermilk*. We probably got that album the same day as everybody else in the music business got it, and we fell in love with them and wanted to sign them and when we realised that they were signed to Jeepster we sent messages saying we would love to manage them, but it seems our messages all went astray. For a long time, we desperately wanted to work with them. Occasionally a band comes along who, for whatever reason, you are not able to work with and it seems ridiculously unfair that you can't work with them. That was how we felt about Belle & Sebastian.

Geoff Travis: We temporarily gave up on them but then not long after they had released the album *Fold Your Hands Child, You Walk Like a Peasant* we ran into Francis MacDonald, the drummer with Teenage Fanclub, at South by Southwest in Austin, and he dropped the bombshell that he thought Belle & Sebastian were out of contract. Within about ten minutes we were on the phone to their manager in Glasgow, trying to get to them before anyone else did. The worry wasn't so much that someone back home might get in before us, rather that there might be other people in Austin who had bumped into Francis and been told the news.

I got back from South by Southwest and caught the plane up to Glasgow the next day and met Stuart. Then we did a deal.

Stuart Murdoch: As soon as we first heard the rumour that Rough Trade wanted us to sign with them, there was no question that that was what we wanted to do. It turned out to be the best bit of business we ever did, and I say that because up until that point we hadn't really paid much attention to business.

We'd officially formed on 1 January 1996. I'd been at Stow College in Glasgow where my head of class, Alan Rankine (who had been in The Associates), asked me to make a record of some of my songs for the course I was on. Previously, the college had only released singles, but I was convinced I could make an album for the budget we had and in the time we had. Alan was dubious it could be done at first, and then claimed the credit for it afterwards.

When we started out we did little with any degree of conscious thought –

we were a bunch of kids trying to make pretty records most of the time. If we had any side projects, then those side projects were our lives, if that doesn't sound pretentious. I was aware that songwriting and record-making were delicate things and I was worried about concentrating on them too much because I thought the stories might dry up. So for quite a long time – for four or five years – we all kept our day jobs and stayed around Glasgow. I kept my job on as a sort of janitor looking after bookings at the church hall where we used to rehearse.

I was very aware of Rough Trade's pedigree and history. I had probably worked my way backwards from the bands that were big when I was growing up, like The Smiths and the Go-Betweens and The Woodentops, to the earlier post-punk Rough Trade material, things by Swell Maps and Young Marble Giants. I had worked in a record shop and somebody once came in and sold us a whole load of late 1970s and early 1980s fanzines, and I went through those and started collecting all the records listed in the charts in the fanzines. I could see immediately that Rough Trade was always the broadest, most catholic, the most substantial of all of those early labels. After we signed, I felt like Dougal in that episode of *Father Ted* when someone tells him he's going to be on television and he stares vacantly into the distance and says, 'Am I going to be on television?' It was like that for me – am I going to be on Rough Trade?

Around 2002, everything changed. That was when we moved from Jeepster, who had previously put out our records, to Rough Trade. I realised that the band had to become more focused, had to become more professional, more committed, and that was a demand that all members of the band had to take up. That was when some band members left. Geoff and Jeannette came up to see us rehearse and there was this terrific feeling of sort of coming home. We had an instant rapport with them. I have always found Geoff interesting – the man with the history – and to be honest I think I have a lot in common with him in that my only desire is to make or be a catalyst for good pop records.

Clare Britt: When *Dear Catastrophe Waitress* came out we sold over 100,000 copies, which is incredible looked at from today. The band had been perceived as being very indie, and between the benefits of that, them altering their sound slightly, and what we did, we nudged them up a long way. That was a wonderful project to work on. Today, of course, it is much harder to get the physical sales – sharing music other ways is so much easier. Most albums are either a runaway success or stall somewhere around 20,000 sales. In 2009, the BPI figures showed something like only six new acts who sold over 100,000 in that year.

Stuart Murdoch: Rough Trade released the *God Help the Girl* album in 2009. I'd had this notion that I could start writing songs for female singers, and then I thought I should write a screenplay to sort of encapsulate them in. I think I took for granted the fact that Rough Trade would want to release it, but in fact when I told Geoff about it he was very supportive and put up the money to enable me to release it. I took a break from Belle & Sebastian, finished off the songs, recruited the singers, and wrote the screenplay.

*

Martin Mills: Geoff and Jeannette had been to see me back in 2000 when they were getting the Rough Trade label re-going again. At that time it didn't quite seem the right fit for Beggars Banquet and we certainly didn't have the spare capacity for it back then. Problems of an overlap seemed much more of an issue then as well, so ultimately I wished them well but in essence said, no thanks.

Then, in 2006, it became very clear that the Sanctuary ship was heading for the rocks, and that Rough Trade was going to need a new trading partner. I had changed my mind and now thought that maybe we could get involved, so I called up Geoff and Jeannette arranged to have a lunch with them.

Jeannette Lee: Martin had changed his mind and no longer felt that the labels would be competing. He decided to get involved and there began an

enormously drawn-out process of making it happen with both Martin and
Tony English, the lawyer, having to put in an incredible amount of work.

Martin Mills: When we came to look into it, one of the problems was that
Sanctuary, at least in financial terms, seemed to be a construction of smoke
and mirrors. Rough Trade was clearly having a successful time in terms of
the top-line sales, but it was very difficult to see what was happening on the
bottom line. The Strokes, The Libertines, Arcade Fire, Belle & Sebastian
and others had all done well for them, but it was difficult to gauge the
effect.

We made a quick decision internally that we would like to become
involved but it took about six months to actually put it all into effect. We
operate in the same world as Rough Trade, a world that Sanctuary never
really inhabited, and we communicate with each other in a way that we all
understand. Beggars would never try to impose in any way on Rough
Trade – forever, Geoff Travis's name is going to be synonymous with Rough
Trade in a way that neither mine nor that of Beggars could ever be.

Joe Cokell: Within the Sanctuary group, Rough Trade had its own board,
upon which I sat. I'd been involved in bringing Rough Trade in and I had
to be involved at the end when negotiations with Beggars began. It was
very, very painful for me – I felt that Geoff, Jeannette and I understood
each other well. But Sanctuary was really heading in one direction only.
Martin Mills and Beggars Banquet were the perfect partners for them and
that has subsequently proved to be the case. It was sad, but ultimately
Sanctuary played an important part in putting Rough Trade back on the
map and that should never be forgotten.

*

Geoff Travis: The point is worth making that Beggars Banquet evolved out
of a record shop and then started an independent record label: the parallel
evolution of both Rough Trade and Beggars has been significant. Martin
Mills financed 4AD and Situation 2 and, like Rough Trade, therefore was
involved in an interesting and complicated structure which supported other
labels and shared their vision. Martin has a very different and deeply
ingrained sensibility in understanding the independent way, and understanding musicians and supporting A&R people, that Sanctuary could never
have had. Sanctuary were wonderful to deal with for a long time but

essentially saw Rough Trade, I am sure, as something they might make money out of.

Rough Trade has to and continues to punch its weight within the Beggars group, but our way of doing business in a fair-minded way is echoed by the way Beggars deal with their artists and see things. So the transition from Sanctuary to Beggars has really been a lot more comfortable than either side could have imagined. We share a fundamental philosophy. Martin made it clear that regardless of the successes the bottom line ultimately is to start from the point of having a business that is breaking even, and that is a radical business philosophy in anyone's language. It is the complete opposite of what the City would think and shouldn't be underestimated. It has given us the ability to take chances and back things that at first appear non-commercial but have the capacity for growth – something which in normal circumstances, in the absence of being self-sufficient, we would be prevented from doing.

*

Bernard Butler: It was in late 2004, I think, that I got a call from Jeannette saying that they'd met this Welsh girl called Duffy with an amazing voice. They weren't sure what to do with her, or even if anything could be done with her, but there was something special that they liked about her. Jeannette said that she was coming in to Rough Trade the next day, did I want to come and meet her? Typically, nothing more needed to be said and I went along the next day.

Jeannette Lee: Richard Parfitt from the 60Ft Dolls contacted me to say that he was writing some songs with Owen Powell from Catatonia. Owen had been a judge on a Welsh talent show called 'The Wawffactor'. Duffy had been one of the contestants. Owen had encouraged Richard to travel to North Wales to hear Duffy sing. At this point, Owen and Richard had written a song called 'Enough Love' and, impressed with Duffy's voice, they made a demo of the song with her and did two other songs and sent them to me at Rough Trade. I called back pretty quickly to say that I thought she had a great voice and that they should keep working with her. We gave Richard small amounts of money to make demos over the next few months. After a while, then, Aimee and Owen didn't see eye to eye and so three became two.

Richard spent a lot of time during this period giving Duffy guidance. She often slept on his couch in Cardiff. After about six months had gone by I asked to meet her. Richard brought her to London and we met in a pub off Portobello Road, myself, Geoff, Duffy and Richard. Before the meeting, Richard had coached Duffy not to mention 'The Wawffactor' or the record she'd made in Welsh, *Aimee Duffy*. He also introduced her as 'Duffy'. He told us to think Lulu or Cilla (Black). It was a curious meeting – we certainly hadn't met anyone like her before. I would describe her at that time as a flibbertigibbet; she talked and talked and was very funny. I was charmed by her.

Up until this point, Duffy had been singing Richard's or Richard's and Owen's songs. She contacted me after a while to say that she wanted to write her own material and asked me to find other writers for her to collaborate with. She said she wanted to 'move on'. I introduced her to Jimmy Hogarth. Duffy and Richard attended the first session with Jimmy together but afterwards Richard didn't attend as I don't think he was that interested in the production side. Richard eventually went back to university and is now a lecturer at Bath Spa University. Later, we used a few of the early songs on the *Rockferry* deluxe edition of the album and as 'b' sides.

At around the same time as introducing her to Jimmy Hogarth, I put Duffy in touch with Bernard Butler, a meeting that had a huge impact on the sound of the record.

Bernard Butler: Duffy was very outgoing – big grin, very happy. She was like a fizz-bomb – that was the word that went through my mind when I met her. She was nervous. But we got on and agreed to try to do something together. The next day we went to my drummer's studio room in Kensal Road and started work. There were drums in there and a laptop. I had a guitar and a piano. Friday afternoon. Duffy gassed and gassed and I was trying to stop her so we could get on with the work.

I'd recently been in The Tears with Brett Anderson and had come up with a big riff on piano with Mako my drummer, which got higher and higher as the chords progressed. It was a shift of two chords that went up a fifth and went back down again, like a blues movement, and that was it. We never used it in The Tears. On that Friday with Duffy this was going around my head. The Duffy demo Jeannette had played me was very sweet but didn't move melodically. I thought I'd try the riff on her.

I did the guitar, piano and a click track for the vocal and asked her to sing along. To my complete surprise she just started singing straight away, when most people might have gone into another room to rehearse or asked to come back the next day. I put a big reverb on her voice. We talked about journeys, about how this riff was a journey, you went all the way to the top and came back down again, and she started singing about trains and journeys. She did a first verse, and I recorded it – just the once. She asked me about the chorus, and I said there wasn't one and that we moved on now, up a fifth. She did it, and she was fucking great. She then asked me what we did next and I said we keep moving up, which she was really nervous about – someone had told her not to sing high. What we ended up with was 'Rockferry'. I took the tape home and was really buzzing with it. I phoned Jeannette and said that I thought we'd either made something that was really brilliant or really terrible but that I thought it was great.

Over the weekend I put some drums on it and a string part and made a terrible mix of it and on the Monday called Jeannette again and said I was bringing it across. Jeannette and Geoff were leaving to go somewhere when I arrived. They took the tape to play in the car. As I was making my way back, they phoned me to say they thought it was absolutely fantastic. Over the next two years, I kept thinking we'll go up to Abbey Road studios and record the track properly, but when the album came out that track was more or less as it was done that Friday – there are *some* real strings on it, but it is still a drum machine, and the vocal take was done in one and you can still hear the click track at the start of it. What was amazing – and this could happen in no other record company – was how quickly things had moved. In four days we'd gone from meeting to finished track.

Jeannette Lee: From that moment on, the project had a direction and possibilities opened up. This was now 2005. There was a huge talent there: the job was to work out what to do with it. She came to me around that time and asked me to be her manager. I want you to be my manager, she said to me, because at the moment I am telling people that you are and I know I haven't the right to say that and I feel like when you say someone is your boyfriend but they aren't really.

Bernard Butler: Duffy started coming around my place to work together. She was still living in Wales so she would book into a B&B and I'd pick her up at Finsbury Park tube. We'd sit in my front room and go through my record collection, listening to songs. At that time, all these terrible TV programmes like *Pop Idol* and *X Factor* had started to distort music. People who were technically quite good singers were put onto this conveyor belt where all the heart and soul was stripped out of them and they were surrounded with really shockingly bad music. With Duffy, I thought we could take someone who might end up in a similar position and do something different. Duffy was the blank canvas – the person who didn't have the complete Rough Trade back catalogue and hadn't heard 'Venus in Furs' when she had been twelve – and was up for anything. And I realised quite quickly that when Duffy sang from the heart – when she sang about Duffy – it was completely pure. On the tracks I worked on with her, I tried to make sure there was no clichés, no rock poetry. For instance, 'Distant Dreamer' is a really obvious song – about a girl from North Wales moving to London – but it is quite charged emotionally. I had a go at 'Mercy', a tune I thought was great, but on the couple of times I tried to do something with it, it turned out a bit too dirty and noisy and lost something – probably its Number Oneness!

Jeannette Lee: It took about a year for us to accumulate enough songs to be able to put together the album. They were invariably exceptional but just occasionally an absolute gem would come in like 'Warwick Avenue', and it started to become clear what kind of shape the album would take. I've talked about being a kid and sitting playing the same records over and over again while getting ready to go out – that was how I wanted this record to be, the kind of record where when it was finished you just wanted to play it again. I think ultimately that's how the record did end up sounding.

The next thing was working out what was best and right for Duffy. I could see Duffy was never really an independent record label girl – she wanted to be mainstream – and although Rough Trade could quite easily accommodate mainstream, the Rough Trade world just didn't seem right for her. Around about the time of making this decision we also were going through a tricky transitional period of moving from Sanctuary to Beggars Banquet.

We were bombarded with interest – it was like the whole world came to our door because by the time we'd worked on the record to get it complete, the rumour mill was in overdrive. In a sense, Duffy and I had put the album together in my office and we'd excluded everybody until it was finished. I didn't want some A&R *man* telling me what needed to be done and that was why we presented the thing as a finished product. I was nervous about signing her to Universal, which isn't just a major record label but probably the most powerful major record label in the country, but to my absolute delight the whole thing was a fantastic experience and Universal were supportive but respectful, too, and never interfered unnecessarily.

Tony English: Artists sign to independent record labels in the knowledge that they are likely to get a lot more latitude than they would signed to a major, where the process is more formulaic. An artist who signs to a major is pretty much in a box from the beginning. The getting together of Universal and Rough Trade management over Duffy was fascinating. You wonder whether Duffy's career could have developed in the way it did without Jeannette's continual input.

Jeannette Lee: The success of Duffy enabled me to stand equal to Geoff on my own merits in a way that people could see for themselves. Geoff and I have always been equal partners but some people haven't always recognised it as being that way. To have to measure up to his reputation anyway, and be a woman, and be a *small* woman . . .

Towards the end of the *Rockferry* cycle, which had started in 2004 and ended in 2009, I began to realise that if I wanted to stay at Rough Trade something would have to give. I had never intended to remove myself from the frontline of the record label, so after much soul searching I decided to re-focus all my attention back on to Rough Trade and give up managing Duffy. I saw no way that I could do both well going forward.

Geoff Travis: It was inevitable that Jeannette was going to be busy with Duffy – I'd ask her if she wanted to come with me and see a new band at some small pub and she would say things like, 'Sorry, I can't, I've got to go off to Monte Carlo.' In truth, she balanced both working the label and managing Duffy. It would certainly be impossible for Rough Trade to function without Jeannette.

Rough Trade is a team and Jeannette and I work together as equal partners and as part of that team. Jeannette is so crucial to the whole Rough Trade dynamic and is part of what makes it work. So often in the music world, teams of two are teams of two men and I think Jeannette sometimes comes up against a clichéd view of what is the norm in the industry. The fact is she has great A&R vision, doesn't shy away from giving an honest view of things and is involved in all the strategic planning for the company, which, combined with her musical history and sensibility, makes her invaluable. It is not just a case of our being equals in every sense, it is the fact that she has been part of an extraordinary working relationship that hasn't just survived over all these years but has positively flourished.

In that period, which coincided with the first period of Beggars, we put out some excellent albums by some bands who had been around a while with us, bands like The Veils, The Decemberists and Super Furry Animals. We released Arthur Russell's wonderful *Love is Overtaking Me*, a piece of unfinished business really in that we had been working with him first time around before his untimely death.

Martin Mills: I think the decade between 2010 and 2020 will prove to be Rough Trade's most successful ever. Geoff and Jeannette are more ambitious for Rough Trade than ever before and I know that Geoff wants to achieve more in the American market where perhaps they haven't always had as much success as they should have had in the past. I believe they are in the best possible position now to increase their international reach and still be secure.

Geoff Travis: We have actively sought to sign the very best American acts to help support the American label and that is why we signed Warpaint, the Morning Benders and the Strange Boys. The Strange Boys are one of the most exciting rock 'n' roll bands in years. We saw them play at the 2009 South by Southwest convention and ended up watching them about five times. Thoughts of watching anybody else just flew out of the window. They'd released their album *The Strange Boys and Girls Club* on In The Red, a very good label in Los Angeles. We licensed that record for Australia and Japan and then *Be Brave* for the world outside America. But we loved them so much that they did a future deal and they have now become a worldwide Rough Trade act. We included In The Red in the deal because that seemed only fair and the band were pleased with that, since other people who were trying to sign them were suggesting that they just ditch their old label.

Somebody else that we think is just incredible is Dylan LeBlanc, a twenty-year-old from Shreveport, Louisiana. Dylan had grown up knocking around with the Muscle Shoals Band, but knew nothing of their legend, and came to us through a producer friend who described his music as a cross between Ray LaMontagne and Neil Young, which piqued my interest. When I listened to Dylan's songs I realised that the description wasn't completely wrong and that he really was something. So in January 2010, Jeannette and I flew out to Nashville and signed him up for the world.

Another person with an amazing talent is Joe Worricker, a young English singer with an amazing voice, currently working with Green Gartside. We signed up Joe and he said to us that he was very pleased but that we really

ought to be signing up this girl he'd met with an amazing voice called Rox. Rox is the genuine article – a gifted singer with an amazing amount of soul and when we heard her, we fell in love with her immediately.

*

Bernard Butler: The thing about the music business it seems to me is that you have your moment and then you don't hang around. Geoff and Jeannette are wonderful people with a great track record but that view of the moment is one I think they share. I have tried talking to Geoff about The Smiths and he won't really talk to me about them. He would much rather go on and on about some stupid band he's heard and loved from Ontario that nobody else has heard about yet. There aren't that many people in the record business like that – most people want to go on for ever about things they've been attached to. The resounding thing I think I've learnt from them is that it's not about the record you made on Friday, it's about the one you're going to make on Monday.

Eddi Reader: I say thank God that there are people out there like Rough Trade because without them the mavericks who don't fit into the showbiz frame – the ones that have the ability to fit into it but don't want to – end up getting lost. It can be a terrible business. I had some horrendous experiences early on which I wouldn't wish on anyone – one of my former managers is in jail for swindling pensioners and an accountant involved is still on the run ... Geoff has been wonderful – I have never, ever, ever had a conversation with him where he has said the words, 'It is not possible.'

Don Letts: If music is a religion then Rough Trade has always been my church. The whole thing hasn't been so much of a job for Geoff as a life – it is certainly how he relates to the planet. And Jeannette is this incredible person, a Tinkerbell kid from a council estate who has made it all the way yet still won't rest on her laurels. The music industry needs more people like them – when Rough Trade first started putting music out we were glad to pay for it.

Patsy Winkelman: Music isn't so powerful any more, so you can't tag politics onto music and make a big movement in a way that you could even as late as the 1980s. There isn't that rallying flag. It seems to me that everything has become so postmodern and broken down and no one bothers to revolt any more: accumulating consumer goods has become the same as winning the revolution. If you are a kid growing up, you don't revolt against what your parents are watching on TV, you just go into your room and watch what you want on your TV. The revolutions are happening, the riots are going on, but they're taking place in Iran, in Greece, in the Mediterranean.

   We play our part now by recognising the genius and releasing records that nobody else can quite see. So many wonderful artists from The Libertines to Antony & The Johnsons wouldn't really have got a start anywhere other than on Rough Trade, and the level of enthusiasm we all had for them is the same now for artists like Rox, the Strange Boys and Dylan LeBlanc.

Carolyn Holder: People love Geoff now more than they have ever loved him. The world has become such an utterly different place from how it was in 1976, but Geoff has become nicer, too. I was talking recently to somebody about the possibility of Geoff ever retiring and telling them that it was an impossible scenario. He comes from a very long-lived family on his mother's side and when the time comes to die, he'll die at a gig.

Green Gartside: People often ask me about the differences between Rough Trade all that time ago and Rough Trade now, and I always tell them that what is more striking is what has remained the same. The generosity and the enthusiasm, the total commitment to music and musicians, the fabulous musical detours they can take you on and their enthusiasm for it, is every bit as insatiable as it was back in 1976.

EPILOGUE:

The Last Cartel Meeting, 25/04/09

Richard Scott organised a 'final Cartel meeting' (although there may be others to come), which took place at the Plough pub in Museum Street in Central London. The get-together could as easily have taken place in Bristol, in Norwich, in Edinburgh, in Leamington Spa or in Liverpool. Nothing to the untutored eye signalled out the fifty or so people present as having made a direct, colossal, unselfish and often overlooked contribution to our social history. They came to remember, and, most importantly, to not forget. The reminiscence was unguarded, the nostalgia unapologetic and deserved: something different from pride was at work – an overhanging sense of chivalry, perhaps. A long time ago they had done something (often for self-consciously altruistic reasons) that made your life different, if not better. And although you may have forgotten or be too young to forget and they may not always choose to remember, their achievement lingers.

It was a dissipated and appropriately low-key evening. In a corner, a group discussed a forthcoming Bob Dylan concert with all the enthusiasm of their former seventeen-year-old selves. Only they were explaining how Bob wasn't so nimble any more and neither were they: there was a joke about Zimmer frames mixed in amongst powder-keg reminisces of every Bob Dylan concert you might have wished to have seen, which, of course, between them they *had* seen. In another corner, people were talking about absences and, more sadly, gaps. There was a palpable sense of belonging, and a sense of belonging to something that continues.

The past is such a foreign place and the future is unwritten. Like the centre of the wagon wheel that once adorned 202 Kensington Park Road, Rough Trade remains the axis of something that spreads outwards, that continues to spread outwards. What remains, as Green Gartside says, is more important than what is absent. Rough Trade, as it always has been, is for you, for me, for everybody.

CAST (AS THEY APPEAR TO BE NOW)

Geoff Travis remains a Rough Trade employee; Jackie Rafferty is an academic; Alan Travis is the Home Affairs Editor at the *Guardian* newspaper; Vivien Goldman is a journalist, lecturer and author of a number of highly regarded books; Jo Slee is an artist and healer, working near Bath in eco-sustainability and integrated health; Jon Savage is an eminent cultural commentator and writer – his last book was *Teenage, The Creation of Youth, 1875–1945*; Carolyn Holder is married to Geoff Travis – they have two children; Peter Travis is a retired loss adjustor; Steve Montgomery lives in New York and is an interior decorator; Pete Flanagan runs Soho Music; Savage Pencil is a journalist and artist and also an archivist for *Wire* magazine; Sandy Robertson remains a journalist; Richard Boon is a librarian in Hackney; Peter Walmsley lives in Berlin and remains part of Rough Trade Publishing; Richard Scott lives in Hastings and is working on a number of projects, including the Allen Road Project, a panoramic tableau of 174 photographs taken of one side of Allen Road, Hackney, on the same day in 1972; Robert Christgau remains 'the Dean of American rock critics'; Daniel Miller runs Mute Records; Richard H. Kirk remains a musician; Green Gartside is a current Rough Trade artist; Mayo Thompson still plays and tours with Red Krayola and lives in LA; Simon Edwards remains in the music business and co-runs Real Time; Gina Birch remains a musician and active member of The Raincoats; Ana da Silva remains a musician and active member of The Raincoats; Patrick Keiller is an academic and film-maker and made the classic films *London* and *Robinson in Space* for the BFI; Shirley O'Loughlin remains involved with The Raincoats and has recently reissued the band's work on CD; Pete Donne is a co-owner of the Rough Trade Shops Group and spends most of his time at Rough Trade East, the UK's first independent 'megastore'; Tom Vague is an archivist for the Borough of Notting Hill Gate & Kensington; Joly MacFie lives in New York and continues to produce badges and DVDs; Slim Smith is still a designer; Robert Wyatt remains a musician, currently contracted to Domino; Steve Jameson is a

DJ; Dick O'Dell is 'a manager and adviser of musical artists'; Gareth Sager remains a musician; Mike Hinc is a distinguished artist and now lives in France; Chris Williams is involved in a number of web-related projects; Charles Hayward remains a musician; Chris Cutler still runs Recommended Records; Doug Kierdorf is a leading world academic, specialising in medieval Spanish; Jim Moir is better known as Vic Reeves, the comedy writer, performer and artist; Patrick Moore reverted to his real name of Philip Hoare after leaving Rough Trade, and became an author – his last book, *Leviathan*, won the prestigious Samuel Johnson Prize for 2009; after a long struggle with illness, Tony K, who was determined to contribute to this book, sadly died in spring 2008; Lloyd Harris no longer works in the music business; Bob Last makes film music and still covets the Fast brand, which he may reuse at some point; Johnny Appel continues to run the highly successful Backs Records; Geoff Davis runs Probe Plus Records and continues to release work by, among others, Half Man Half Biscuit; Johnny Marr remains a musician; Robin Hurley works for Warner Brothers in LA; Sandy McLean runs the chain of Avalanche Records shops in Scotland; Tony English remains a music business lawyer; John Duguid continues to work in the public sector; Marek Kohn is a successful author whose recent works include *Trust: Self-Interest and the Common Good*; Jeannette Lee remains a Rough Trade employee; Don Letts left Acme Attractions to become a member of Big Audio Dynamite as well as a Grammy Award-winning film-maker and author; David Whitehead co-runs an artist management company in New York, Maine Road, where his clients include David Bowie and David Byrne; Jeremy Boyce left Rough Trade and developed a passion for indoor kite-flying and became, along with other members of the British team, winner of the 1995 Synchronised Kite Flying World Cup; Duncan Cameron now works at Mute Song; George Kimpton-Howe is a music licensor and author; David Murrell continues to work within the music industry; Martin Mills still runs Beggars Banquet, which includes Rough Trade Records as part of the group; Eddi Reader remains a musician; Jarvis Cocker remains a musician; Clare Britt runs a PR company; Patsy Winkelman is a Rough Trade employee; Bernard Butler remains a musician and producer; Cathi Gibson co-runs Rough Trade Publishing; Dai Davies has retired; Joe Cokell now works for Cooking Vinyl; Jeffrey Lewis remains a musician and artist; Ben Ayres is a Rough Trade employee and remains a musician with Cornershop; Martin Noble remains a musician; Stuart Murdoch remains a musician.

THOSE WHO SERVED
(AND CONTINUE TO SERVE)

Geoff Travis
Ken Davison
Jo Slee
Steve Montgomery
Richard Scott
Sally Griswald
Ross Crighton
Judith Crighton
Edwin Pouncey
Daniel Miller
Sue Donne
Sue Johnson
Peter Walmsley
Anne Clarke
Bruce Dickson
Steve Alexander
Barbara Gogan
Sue Gogan
Jane Gogan
Steve Alexander
Shirley O'Loughlin
Sally Murray
Austin Palmer
Andy Dade
Gill Sheehan
Sue Scott
Steve Jameson
Chris Wolfe
Caroline Scott
Mayo Thompson
Scott Piering

Will Keen
Bob Scotland
Ana Da Silva
Pete Donne
Nigel House
Simon Edwards
Doug Pearce
Allan Sturdy
Nikki Sudden
Epic Soundtracks
Chris Williams
Bethan Peters
Phil Clarke
Simon Edwards
Claude Bessy
Mike Hinc
Nick Jones
Paul 'Pablo' Carter
Jocelyn Cook
Caroline Leifer
Jamie McKelvie
Bernadette Maguire
Binna Walde
Debby Sazer
Gareth Ryan
Martha Defoe
Mark Southow
Patrick Moore
Tony Wakeford
Leo Solomon
Chris Maguire

Pete 'Pinko' Fowler
Nick Jackson
Neil Hamilton
Nick Clift
Pat Bellis
Christine Sellars
Dave Watchorn
Doug Kierdorf
Joan Gay
Cilmar De Silva
Christine Moynihan
Joseph 'Zep' Gerson
David Birch
David McReynolds
Jane Simon
Brenda Kelly
Dierdre Ann Thorne
Nick Hobbs
Graeme Pellow
Steve Connell
Albie Halls
Cathy Carrington
Peter Hogan
Nina Chatham
Stephen Kennedy
Simon Harper
Dave Harper
Alison Wilson
Hil' Scott
Chas Bardsley
Bella Gough

Richard Powell
Zina Manda
Richard Boon
Mark Ellerby
Nicholas Hamlyn
Molly
Richard Williams
Cathy Brice
Max Liddle
Philip Arkush
Julie Earl
Jackie Hall
Sara Hunt
Nilesh Patel
John Tozer
Francine Palmer
Harry Russell
Colin Simmons
Ian Tomlinson
Jonty Alderly
Andrew Boak
Howard Clark
Russell Clayton
Laura Gentle
Andy Goodman
Steve Goodman
Mark Harris
Geoff Muncey
Ashley Robinson
Juliet Sale
Andrew Smedley
Anthony Sykes
Andy 'Spike' Hyde
Dave Lee
Angela Swart
Dave Whitehead
Richard Balfour
Sallie Fellowes
Alison Wilson
Jay Barbour

Lauren Bromley
Karen Brown
Chris Stone
Dawn Clelland
Abby Hains
Nicholas Jackson
Mac
Wendy Marchington
Vernon Mead
Steve Sawle
Bill Schaessens
Kay Turner
Jon Warr
Jeremy Boyce
Mike Holdsworth
Peter Keeley
Mark Stratford
Sandy McLean
Cameron Fraser
Chris Barrett
Paul Ireson
Simon Holland
Nigel 'Skip' Morris
Mandy Newey
Harry Harrison
Peter Theelke
Sean Mayo
John Shaw
Janet Faulkner
Alan Hale
David Williams
Andy Blackwood
Robin Hurley
Graham Samuels
Rod Thomson
Linda Kelly
Hazel Mucklow
Jeannette Lee
George Kimpton-Howe
John Best

Martin Aston
Andy Childs
James Endeacott
Patsy Winkelman
Clare Britt
Simon Esplan
Ben Ayres
Kelly Kiley
Colin Wallace
Pru Harris
Ruth Patterson
Yvette Lacey
Jessica Park
Ryan McCann
Roxy Walton
Dan Symons
Zoe Davis
Gary Walker
John Moore
Kasra Mowlavi
Jamie Burgess
Gabriella Traub
Melanie Johnson
Kaori
Theo Carter Webber
Glen Johnson
Gill Monaghan
Olly Parker
Sam Willis
Paul Jones
Janine Ellis
Ned Hodge
Shaun Delaney
Joe Smith
Valerie Janin
Rosie Ware
Jamie Woolgar
Mog Yoshihara

BIBLIOGRAPHY /
SUGGESTED READING / NOTES

Included here, in among the inevitable survey books, are a number of what might be called 'influencing' books, books whose names came up often during interviews as having a big effect on the interviewee at the time they were talking about – an example might be J. G. Ballard's *High Rise*, published in paperback when the Rough Trade shop first opened in 1976, when W10/W11 was the subject of urban regeneration. Two other regularly referenced books were Germaine Greer's *The Female Eunuch*, the Paladin paperback edition that has the 'torso' cover design by psychedelic poster artist Michael McInerney (who had designed the poster for the 14 Hour Technicolour Dream); this design is still used nearly forty years after it was first created; and *Children of Albion: Poetry of the Underground in Britain*, the groundbreaking poetry anthology published in 1969 and compiled by Michael Horowitz, with contributions from Pete Brown, Alexander Trocchi, Michael X and Roy Fisher.

Aitken, Jonathan, *The Young Meteors*, Secker & Warburg, London, 1967

Artrocker, Tom and Cox, Paul (eds), *Artrocker Rough Trade 25th Anniversary Edition*, London, 2001

Bailey, Ron, *The Squatters*, Penguin, London, 1973

Ballard, J. G., *High Rise*, Jonathan Cape, London, 1975

Beckett, Andy, *When the Lights Went Out: Britain in the Seventies*, Faber & Faber, 2009

Booker, Christopher, *The Neophiliacs: The Revolution in English Life in the Fifties and Sixties*, Collins, London, 1969

Booker, Christopher, *The Seventies*, Viking, London, 1980

Bracewell, Michael, *England is Mine: Pop Life in Albion from Wilde to Goldie*, HarperCollins, London, 1997

Brand, Stewart, *The Media Lab: Inventing the Future at MIT*, Penguin, London, 1989

Burroughs, William S., *Junkie*, NEL, London, 1966

Burroughs, William S., *The Wild Boys*, Calder & Boyars, London, 1972

Cavanagh, David, *The Creation Records Story: My Magpie Eyes are Hungry for the Prize*, Virgin, London, 2000

Cohen, Stanley, *Folk Devils and Moral Panics*, MacGibbon & Kee, London, 1972

Dylan, Bob, *Tarantula*, MacGibbon & Kee, London, 1972

Farren, Mick, *Give the Anarchist a Cigarette*, Jonathan Cape, London, 2001

Fountain, Nigel, *Underground: The London Alternative Press 1966–74*, Comedia/Routledge, London, 1988

Frame, Pete; Tobler, John; Childs, Andy; McNight, Connor; Needs, Kris, (eds.), *Zigzag #1–134*, London, Kendall, Paul; (April 1969–February 1983)

Friends/Frendz #1–35 (November 1969–September 1972)

Gandalf's Garden #1–6, London, May 1968–Winter 1969

Geering, Ken (ed.), *It's World That Makes the Love Go Round: Modern Poetry Selections from 'Breakthru' International Poetry Magazine*, Corgi, London, 1968

Gimarc, George, *Punk Diary, 1970–79*, Jonathan Cape, London, 1995

Gimarc, George, *Post-Punk Diary, 1980–82*, St Martin's Press, New York, 1997

Gray, Christopher (trans. & edits), *Leaving the 20th Century: The Incomplete Works of the Situationist International*, Free Fall Publications, London, 1974

Green, Jonathon, *Days in the Life: Voices from the English Underground 1961–1971*, William Heinemann, 1988

Green, Jonathon, *All Dressed Up: The Sixties and the Counterculture*, Jonathan Cape, London, 1998

Greer, Germaine, *The Female Eunuch*, MacGibbon & Kee, London, 1969

Harris, John, *The Last Party: Britpop, Blair and the Demise of English Rock*, 4th Estate, London, 2004

Haslam, Dave, *Not Abba: The Real Story of the 1970s*, HarperPerennial, London, 2005

Haynes, Jim, *Thanks for Coming!*, Faber & Faber, London, 1984

Haynes, Jim; Hopkins, John; Mairowitz, David; McGrath, Tom; Miles, Barry; Stansill, Pete (et al) (eds.), *International Times (IT) #1–164*, London October 1966–October 1973

Hebdidge, Dick, *Subculture: The Meaning of Style*, Methuen, London, 1979

Horowitz, Michael (ed.), *Children of Albion: Poetry of the Underground in Britain*, Penguin, Harmondsworth, 1969

Ink #1–29, London, May 1971–February 1972

Melly, George, *Revolt Into Style: the Pop Arts in Britain*, Allen Lane & the Penguin Press, Harmondsworth, 1970

Miles, Barry, *In the Sixties*, Jonathan Cape, London, 2002

Miles, Barry, *London Calling: A Countercultural History of London Since 1945*, Atlantic Books, London, 2010

Moorcock, Michael, *Mother London*, Secker & Warburg, London, 1988

Music Week, *Celebrating 25 Years of Rough Trade*, Music Week, London 2001

Nelson, Elizabeth, *The British Counter-Culture 1966–73: A Study of the Underground Press*, Macmillan, London, 1989

Neville, Richard; Dennis, Felix; Anderson, Jim (eds.), *Oz Magazine #1–48*, London, January 1967–November 1973

Neville, Richard, *Play Power*, Jonathan Cape, London, 1970

Nuttall, Jeff, *Bomb Culture*, MacGibbon & Kee, London, 1968

Ogg, Alex, *Independence Days*, Cherry Red Books, London, 2009

Oldham, Andrew Loog, *Stoned*, Secker & Warburg, London, 2000

Palmer, Tony, *The Trials of Oz*, Blond & Briggs, London, 1971

Reynolds, Simon, *Rip It Up and Start Again: Postpunk 1978–1984*, Faber & Faber, London, 2005

Roche, Pete (ed. and introduces), *Love, Love, Love: The New Love Poetry*, Corgi Books, London, 1967

Savage, Jon, *England's Dreaming: Sex Pistols and Punk Rock*, Faber & Faber, London, 1991

Savage, Jon, *Time Travel: From the Sex Pistols to Nirvana – Pop, Media and Sexuality 1977–96*, Chatto & Windus, London, 1996

Sinclair, Iain, *Lud Heat*, Albion Village Press, London, 1975

Sinclair, Iain, *Suicide Bridge*, Albion Village Press, London, 1979

Sinclair, Iain, *White Chapel, Scarlet Tracings*, Gold Mark, Uppingham, 1987

Smith, Mark E., *Renegade: The Lives and Tales of Mark E. Smith*, Viking, London, 2008

Solanas, Valerie, *S.C.U.M. Manifesto*, New York, 1968

Souness, Howard, *Seventies: The Sights, Sounds and Ideas of a Brilliant Decade*, Simon & Schuster, London, 2006

Squatters' Handbook, The, Islington Squatters, London, 1975

Stansill, Peter and Mairowitz, David Zane (eds.), *BAMN! By Any Means Necessary: Outlaw Manifestos & Ephemera 1965–1970*, Penguin, Harmondsworth, 1971

Vale, V. (ed.), *RE/Search #1–3*, 'Shocking Tabloid' issues, RE/Search Publications, San Francisco, 1980–81

Vale, V. (ed.), *RE/Search #4/5*, William Burroughs/Throbbing Gristle/Brion Gysin, RE/Search Publications, San Francisco, 1982

Vale, V. (ed.), *RE/Search #6/7, Industrial Culture Handbook*, RE/Search Publications, San Francisco, 1983

Vale, V. (ed.), *RE/Search #8/9*, J. G. Ballard, RE/Search Publications, San Francisco, 1984

Whitehouse, Chris (ed.), *Squatting in Central London: A Survey*, Royal Borough of Richmond & Twickenham, Middlesex, September 1973

Young, Rob, *Rough Trade (Labels Unlimited series)*, Black Dog Publishing, London, 2006

Music papers across the period give a good reflection of the times, but more than anything, I found, the fanzines of the late 1970s and early 1980s seem to be more of a reflection of the essential essence of Rough Trade – something to do with haphazardness. For those wishing to pursue this further, the *NME* was particularly assiduous in running fanzine round-up columns during the fanzine heyday, including in the following issues: 10/02/79; 07/07/79; 22/09/79; 29/09/79; 30/08/80; 29/11/80; 13/12/80; 02/01/82; 28/01/84; 28/04/84; 01/09/84; 26/01/85; 29/06/85; 06/07/85; 24/08/85; 31/08/85.

Many Rough Trade artists, in the course of interviews with the major music papers, have found time to comment on Rough Trade – most extremely positively, some in famously adverse fashion. Of the stand-alone pieces on Rough Trade itself across the media, the following stand out: *Melody Maker* 10/03/79: 'Post-punk Tensions – and Resolutions' by Simon Frith; *Melody Maker* 01/03/80: 'The Humane Sell' by Ian Birch; *NME* 10/02/79: 'Beat, Activity & Conservation' by Ian Penman; *Music Week* 13/12/80: 'Coping with Growth at Rough Trade' (unattributed); *Rolling Stone* 24/07/80: 'Wake Up! It's Fab, It's Passionate, It's Wild, It's Intelligent! It's the Hot New Sound of England Today!' by Greil Marcus; *San Francisco Express* 15/05/81: 'The Rough Trade Collective: Young, Idealistic, Stubbornly Independent and Responsible for Some of the Most Outrageous Music Ever Put on Vinyl' (unattributed); there were almost weekly bulletins on the fate of Rough Trade in *Music Week* from the start of 1991 until its collapse in May, the most significant of which was a large spread, 'Rough Trade: Death by Committee', 01/06/91; *Q Magazine* 08/91: 'Rough Trade Records: Life After Debt?' by Phil Sutcliffe; *Record Collector* June 91: 'Rough Trade Records' by Johnny Rogan; *The Times* 20/07/91: 'Like Punk Never Happened' by Philip Bassett; *Independent on Sunday* 10/09/06: 'Rough & Ready' by Fiona Sturgess.

The two best sources for counter-culture/underground ephemera from Beats to post-punk and beyond are:

www.beatbooks.com

www.sohomusic.com

The best and most indispensable sites for Rough Trade and the records they release are:

www.roughtraderecords.com

www.roughtrade.com

Amplifications, outtakes and ephemera on the project, which will gradually be added to, can be found at:

www.neiltaylorassociates.co.uk

NOTES

BEFORE. *PART ONE*: The photograph of the original Rough Trade logo is from Richard Scott who, to this day, still possesses the original cut-out sign. Jo Slee provided the photograph of Ken Davison with her at Niagra Falls. To the best of my knowledge, this is the first photograph of Ken to appear, and long overdue. The Grosvenor Road postcard comes from the excellent online squatting archive (www.wusu.org). Jim Flanagan sourced the images of the pre-punk fanzines and Soho Music may well be able to supply copies of some of them for those wishing to purchase: their website is mentioned above. The prototype logo stamp and the *Frendz* spread detailing The Electric Gypsy Roadshow were supplied by Richard Scott. *CHAPTER ONE*: Carolyn Holder lent me a number of family photographs, including the one of Geoff with the Hillman Imp. I tried and failed to contact Barney Platt-Mills: the cover image for *Bronco Bullfrog* is taken from a DVD release. The wonderful picture of John Kemp reading, and of Jo Slee with a typewriter, came from Jo. Andrew Sclanders, helpful as ever, located the *Squatters Handbook* and pointed out to me the rough symmetry of some of the information contained in it. *CHAPTER TWO*: The picture of Rough Trade at the head of the chapter (featuring the 'Bootleg Man' entering the store) was provided by Richard Scott. Jo Slee provided the image of Steve Montgomery deejaying and the only known image of the original 'Rough Trade shed': those with superior eyesight will just be able to make out the original 'swirly' sign. The picture of the Ramones in-store event is courtesy of the Rough Trade Shops and was taken by Gerald Ruffin. The image of Mark Perry in the Rough Trade doorway is from an issue of *Temporary Hoarding*, 'ripped off from *Punk* magazine'. The images of the punk fanzines were provided either by their authors and/or Richard Scott and Andrew Sclanders. *CHAPTER THREE*: The chapter heading is from a postcard featuring a photograph taken by Steve Montgomery who was, and remains to this day, an excellent photographer. Carolyn Holder provided the early Rough Trade Mail order catalogue. The photograph of 'the Scottish plague' taken in the Trafalgar Pub comes from Jo Slee's private collection. The photograph of Richard Scott, Allan Sturdy and Third World comes from Richard Scott's private collection. The customer mail order list is taken from Richard Scott's diary for 1977. *CHAPTER FOUR*: The annotated Rock'n'Roll Zoo column by the brilliant Savage Pencil is Jo Slee's, given to her by Carolyn Holder whose observations pepper the image. The I & I Survive badge which Carolyn gave to Steve Montgomery after the robbery is the very same badge in the text, photographed and supplied by Steve Montgomery. (Various badges dotted throughout the book are derived from Richard Scott's overflowing 'badge bowl' currently on display in his kitchen.) I thank the designers of the various Rough Trade catalogues. The photograph of Cabaret Voltaire outside the shop is a Scott Piering Polaroid. The original handwritten contract is supplied courtesy of Richard Scott. *CHAPTER FIVE*: There were various examples of Rough Trade stationery: the walkie talkie image at the start of this chapter is one of them. The photograph of Pete Donne outside Earth Records is from the excellent Friars Aylesbury site (www.aylesburyfriars.co.uk). The Polaroid of Scott Piering is one of his own; the Schitzoid Singles tape inlay and the tape inlays here and elsewhere were the work of Scott, as was the 'Killer Plugger From Hell' flyer used. The photograph of the communal garden at Blenheim Crescent was supplied by Richard Scott. *CHAPTER SIX*: The exquisite Japan Records flyer belongs to Richard Scott. Slim Smith, at short notice, not only contributed to the book, but helped with some images, including the one of the Better Badges catalogue. The photo of Joly at the shop is a Scott Piering Polaroid, as is the one of the smiling Mark E Smith. The wonderful James Blood Ulmer flyer was designed by Hil' Scott and supplied by Richard Scott. *PART TWO*: The Dixie jazz band image is from Rough Trade notepaper and the photograph of The Smiths was taken by Paul Slattery. *CHAPTER SEVEN*: Scott designed the promo sheets. Richard Scott provided the photograph of Scott and Claude Bessy, one of the warmest and most apposite images in the book. Claude's early death deprived the world of a formidable talent. Peter Walmsley's handwritten suggestions for what might be the track listing of *Wanna Buy A Bridge?*, a record he had dreamed up, are from Richard Scott's archive, where approximately another half dozen or so suggestions by other members of staff reside. The postcard at the end of the chapter was printed up at the time of the label move to Blenheim Crescent. *CHAPTER EIGHT*: The Cartel member advertisements are taken from various issues of *Masterbag*. The photograph of Geoff, Johnny Appel and Simon Edwards on the Clifton suspension bridge at the time the Cartel was named comes from Richard Scott. The photograph of the note put on the Rough Trade shop door outlining woes is from the Rough Trade Shops archive. *CHAPTER NINE*: The genius of Biff is harnessed and taken from an issue of *Masterbag* where the illustrators allowed Rough Trade to doctor one of their magnificent pieces of art. *PART THREE*: Richard Boon's makeshift Christmas card to Jo Slee from 1987 is hewn from a warehouse docket and has the feel, it seems to me, of something from a World War Two POW film. *CHAPTER TEN*: The Enemy Within image is taken from a Rough Trade promotional photo. The handwritten Morrissey Post-It note is from Jo Slee's archive. *CHAPTER ELEVEN*: The Alan Bates image with ironing board was intended to be used for the cover of a single by The Smiths but wasn't. The photograph of Jeannette Lee is from Jeannette's personal collection. *CHAPTER TWELVE*: The photograph of Richard Scott with one of his children is from Richard's personal collection. *CHAPTER THIRTEEN*: All the images in this chapter are taken from an advertisement in *Music Week*. The image at the end of the BEFORE section repeats Ken Davison's original logo – God Bless, Ken. **AFTER**. Jeffrey Lewis was commissioned to provide the wonderful image that heads this section. *CHAPTER FOURTEEN*: The header is taken from a Pulp tour programme. The Beggars Banquet advertisement celebrating 25 years of Rough Trade is taken from a *Music Week* special supplement commemorating the occasion of Rough Trade's silver jubilee. *PART FOUR*: The Rough Trade Records logo is taken from a clothing line. The Strokes photo is courtesy of Rough Trade Records. Jeffrey Lewis' magnificent *History of Rough Trade* was completed in 2003. *CHAPTER SIXTEEN*: The press photo of Belle & Sebastian was provided by Rough Trade. *COLOUR PLATE SECTION*: Carolyn Holder provided the photographs of herself and of Geoff Travis with car and Geoff visiting The Fall. Jo Slee provided the photographs from the pub, the shot of her with John, the wonderful Japan Records Rough Trade catalogue, the images of The Smiths, the handwritten Morrissey postcard and the Ivor Cutler booklet. Richard Scott provided the image of himself, the shot of the interior of the shop, the seventeen Polaroids taken by Scott Piering of staff and the Polaroid of Scott, all eighteen of which belonged to Scott Piering. The marvellous Friars Aylesbury organisation (see above) provided the image of the flyer for the first Rough Trade tour. The shot of the interior of Collier Street was taken by Chris Ward. Photographs of the contemporary Rough Trade artists and some of their wares were provided by Rough Trade. Jeannette Lee's 'Step Into My Office, Baby' paperweight was temporarily stolen from her office, scanned and returned without her knowing. The photograph of Jeannette was provided by her from her own collection. The photographs of some of the present Rough Trade staff were taken by Ben Ayres who unfailingly provided support/images/encouragement when called upon, often at short notice and always with good grace. Jo Slee, Richard

Scott, and Carolyn Holder provided a similar and some cases even greater degree of support in my quest for appropriate visual images. I am grateful also to the support and help Jon Savage gave me at various times.

It is hoped that at some point in the future a Rough Trade archive can be established. The sixteen or so large boxes of material in Richard Scott's possession should be collated and added to. In allowing me access to these and other items, Richard Scott's contribution to this project goes beyond all call of duty and has set me on the road to ensuring that the material is adequately preserved for posterity. Jo Slee provided a similar service to me with her also not inconsiderable cache of materials. Scott Piering's recorded archive should also reach a wider public. If anyone has any material they wish to donate or dispose of please contact me.

This story should end where it came in.   Record shops are the entry point for most people who find themselves caught up in the magic of music and its world, tribal meeting spots where vital information is culled and exchanged, sounding posts in every sense.   At various stages I have been encouraged and inspired by the Rough Trade group of shops (and others) whose legacy it has not been possible to fully explore in this work. It is fitting, though, that the book should be published on the third anniversary of the opening of Rough Trade East.

ACKNOWLEDGEMENTS

All interviews were conducted fresh for the book and I thank everybody for their time. In many cases, those I interviewed allowed me to see them repeatedly, not least Geoff Travis, Richard Scott, Steve Montgomery, Jo Slee, Jeannette Lee, Green Gartside and Richard Boon. The book had a strange genesis and I would like to say an especial thank you to Tom and Paul Artrocker, whose excellent twenty-fifth anniversary *Artrocker* edition was meant to be the launching point for a book which morphed into this one. Ian Preece commissioned the project with some passion and Stephen Fall did a fine job on the text. Helen Ewing had the unenviable task of steering the book through production and did a sterling job. Thanks are also due to: Karen Walter, Andrew Sclanders, Rob Young, Jim Flanagan, Barney Hoskyns, Peter Carbert, Chuck Warner, David Taylor, Paul Williams, Ben Cardew, Chris Wilson, Daniel Scott, Todd Austin, Pete 'Pinko' Fowler, Sebastian Hunter, Faye Brewster, Mike Barnes, Kirsten McKenzie, Maurice Suckling, Travis Elborough, Jim Pennington, Sue Gogan, David Taylor, John Williamson, Janice Chaplin, Richard King, David Hesmondhalgh, Harriet Wood, Gavin Friday, Robert Scotland, Colin Newman (with apologies to all three), Emilíana Torrini, Jane Skinner, Joe Moss, Kirk Lake, Karen Morgan, Peter Radcliffe, Will Godfrey, Rob Lloyd, Vale, Charlie Higson, Alex Ogg, Bob Stanley, Richard Scott, all the staff at Rough Trade Records and Rough Trade Shops, anyone else I have forgotten (in which case your name will appear in the mass-market paperback edition) and last, but not least, Alison Taylor.

BACKWORD

It's sometime in 1980, I'm in a band called . . . .and The Native Hipsters. I get the call from Rough Trade: 'We need another 25 copies of "There Goes Concorde Again" as soon as possible.' No need to ask twice, I have received the clarion call and before you can say 'squat' I'm out of Clapham in my rapidly falling apart Renault and heading for Kensington Park Road. The journey takes an hour or so. After a quick row with a drunken Rasta I leave my car, pick up my little box of goodies and cross the road to Rough Trade. The shop is busy, but the shop is so small that 'busy' is a relative term: it's relatively busy for a large phone-box. There are some Japanese tourists in there, all of whom swivel in my direction simply because I have dyed blonde hair. I approach the counter. That's what you do in all shops, isn't it? Approach the counter, tell the shop assistant what you want, pay for it and leave. Not the most intimidating of tasks, really, is it? Well, at Rough Trade you weigh the necessity. If you can avoid approaching the counter you will. Approaching the counter at Rough Trade is like approaching an unexploded bomb with a fly swatter. On one occasion I approached the counter at Rough Trade, panicked, forgot what I was there for, forgot my own name and asked for 'Politics' by The Thompson Twins. I was halfway home before I realised what I'd done, before I came out of shock. I have never played that record to this day.

But I'm not buying today; I'm delivering, I'll get some respect at the counter. A thumb is jerked (respectfully?) over the shoulder and I move through to the back of the shop – all is chaos – to what appears to be a shed. And here is Geoff . . . Phew! A friendly face at last. He takes the singles from me and hands me a small wad of cash. That's it, business done, cash on the nail, no accounting period, no returns, just good old fashioned folding green.

I arrive back at Clapham as the phone is ringing: 'Hi, Rough Trade here, we need another 200 copies of "Concorde" – today please.' I climb back into the Renault and repeat the whole process. That's just the way it is at Rough Trade: disorganised, teetering on the edge of total collapse, incredibly exciting and very, very intimidating.

Sometime during this period Geoff proposed that we enter into a P&D deal (production and distribution: the record would remain on our label but Rough Trade would take care of making and distributing the record. A benefit of such a deal would be that I didn't have to spend half my life buzzing up and down the Bayswater Road). We, the band, assembled in the flat above the shop along with Geoff, Richard Scott and, maybe, Scott Piering (the memory fades). We all agreed that the deal sounded like a good idea and we never heard from them again. That's just the way it was.

Of course 'There Goes Concorde Again' wasn't the end of my record releasing days – far from it. Shortly after 'Concorde' had successfully annoyed most of the world with its seemingly endless repetition of 'Oooh, look, there goes Concorde again' I hooked up with a young northerner with more names than pairs of trousers – to me he was Rod, to others Jim, many called him Chin, later he'd settle on Vic Reeves. We both worked at Our Price Records (but we didn't go around shouting about it) in the Charing Cross Road and were very much outsiders with very little interest in the chart progress of the latest Bee Gees album. Rod (that's what I called him then so that's what I'll call him now) discovered that I'd been involved with 'Concorde', which he loved (he was an odd bugger even then) and proposed that we get together and make some music. I use the term 'music' loosely. I recall blowing bubbles through a straw as Rod intoned a poem about 'Old Man Moss'. Now, that may sound straightforward enough, but it took hours, simply because Rod kept cracking me up (he was a funny bugger even then). Eventually we had a 'cassette album' (all the rage for about two weeks back in the day), we even formed our own cassette album label – Boy Smells – and took out an ad in *Zig-Zag*. By this time Rough Trade had moved to Blenheim Terrace. The impression remained one of chaos, but now it was large-scale chaos. Now that Geoff was busy with the label he was no longer the arbiter of taste as far as distribution was concerned, he was off in his little office. So we had to play our tape to a young lady in a green boiler suit who pronounced it: 'a bit self-indulgent'. We were appalled, self-indulgent? A bloke blowing bubbles while another bloke read a poem? That's not self-indulgent, that's the future of Pop that is. Despite a few doubts about our ability to take on Wham! the lady in the boiler-suit ordered a dozen or so and that was that. Imagine our amazement when a few weeks later we came across our cassette album in a Virgin store. It may have looked like chaos at Blenheim Crescent but product still managed to get out of there and into the shops, even Boy Smells tapes – nobody can have been more surprised than Rod and me.

Eighteen years later and I'm still at it, still in bands, still releasing records, still skint. It's 1998, dark days for music, one of the periodic slumps that music goes through. My band, Fraff, decide to refer back to punk and post-punk, to be a bit arty in a Television/Voidoids kind of a way. Some get it, some don't, confused by songs

(songs!?) that last a maximum of three minutes and don't feature a guest bassoonist. We are castigated in print as 'Artrock' but decide to 'spin' the insult to our advantage by admitting that we are indeed Artrock and to prove the case we decide to create a fanzine called *Artrocker* that celebrates ... Artrock. We are only two issues in when, in time-honoured fashion, we wander into the Rough Trade shop in Talbot Road where we peddle our wares. They not only take some copies but go on to sell them. Everybody is happy. Then, in late 2000, Paul returns from a visit to the shop with a request from them: would we be prepared to produce a special issue of Artrocker celebrating the 25th anniversary of the opening of the original shop? A CD compilation is also to be produced that will feature, amongst other gems. ... Yes, you've guessed it, 'There Goes Concorde Again'. We jump at the chance of creating the first official history of Rough Trade and are rightly proud of it. When it comes out it is a damn fine work of art(rock), running to nearly 60 pages and complete with a free cassette of era-defining Rough Trade tracks. It sells out pretty fast, including at the V&A museum where we are invited for the 25th anniversary party and where we watch Geoff Travis and Richard Scott make some sort of peace, defying predictions of bloodshed.

And some bright spark says: 'Hey, this should be a book!' And we say: 'You're right!' A deal is negotiated with Orion, Paul and I set up in the old Too Pure Records office at Highbury Corner, plug in the PCs, twiddle our thumbs and wait for the advance to turn up. And it is in this period, between signing the book deal and receiving the advance, that things go terribly wrong. Or is that right? You see, the time we'd spent working on the fanzine version of the Rough Trade history had inspired us, had made us look back at those halcyon days in the late seventies, had made us wish that it could be like that again: DIY, devil may care, enabling great new music. In no time at all we're running a weekly club and releasing records and, thanks once more to Geoff's golden ears the musical tide was changing, that thing we'd been missing, the thing that would change it all and make rock'n'roll exciting again was in Geoff's hand, a demo by a band called The Strokes from New York.

So how about the book? I have to admit that it went on to the back boiler: we were too busy living the Rough Trade story to have time to write it, the scene exploded (all scenes 'explode' it seems) and we were carried along on a tide we'd helped create.

Years passed, literally. *Artrocker* became a 'proper', monthly magazine (over 100 issues and still going strong), you can get it in Smith's and everything! Paul and I just kept pretending that we would get time for the book. But we didn't – today was enough to deal with, yesterday could wait.

But publishers can't. In the end our agent (because he is a kindly chap) decided to help us out by writing the book for us – though we did give him lots of advice and help. And the net result, dear reader, is the tome you hold in your hands ...

Tom Fawcett (with Paul Cox).